岸本斉史

Uh... Oh! Right! I wanted to let you all know that with this volume begins Part Two, so I look forward to your patronage. To those who have not yet read Part One, please read from volume 1. Then again, feel free to read it from the middle as well... (laughs).

—*Masashi Kishimoto, 2005*

Author/artist Masashi Kishimoto was born in 1974 in rural Okayama Prefecture, Japan. After spending time in art college, he won the Hop Step Award for new manga artists with his manga **Karakuri** (Mechanism). Kishimoto decided to base his next story on traditional Japanese culture. His first version of **Naruto**, drawn in 1997, was a one-shot story about fox spirits; his final version, which debuted in **Weekly Shonen Jump** in 1999, quickly became the most popular ninja manga in Japan.

NARUTO VOL. 28
SHONEN JUMP Manga Edition

This graphic novel contains material that was originally published in English in **SHONEN JUMP** #61–62. Artwork in the magazine may have been slightly altered from that presented here.

STORY AND ART BY MASASHI KISHIMOTO

Translation/Mari Morimoto
English Adaptation/Deric A. Hughes & Benjamin Raab
Touch-up Art & Lettering/Mark McMurray & Inori Fukuda Trant
Design/Sean Lee
Editor/Joel Enos

Printed in the U.S.A.

Published by VIZ Media, LLC
P.O. Box 77010
San Francisco, CA 94107

10 9 8 7 6 5 4 3
First printing, March 2008
Third printing, January 2011

www.viz.com

PARENTAL ADVISORY
NARUTO is rated T for Teen and is recommended for ages 13 and up. This volume contains realistic and fantasy violence.
ratings.viz.com

THE WORLD'S MOST POPULAR MANGA
www.shonenjump.com

SHONEN JUMP MANGA EDITION

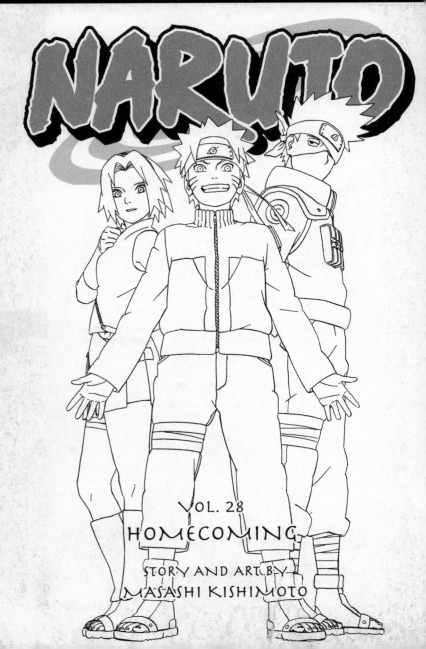

NARUTO

VOL. 28
HOMECOMING
STORY AND ART BY
MASASHI KISHIMOTO

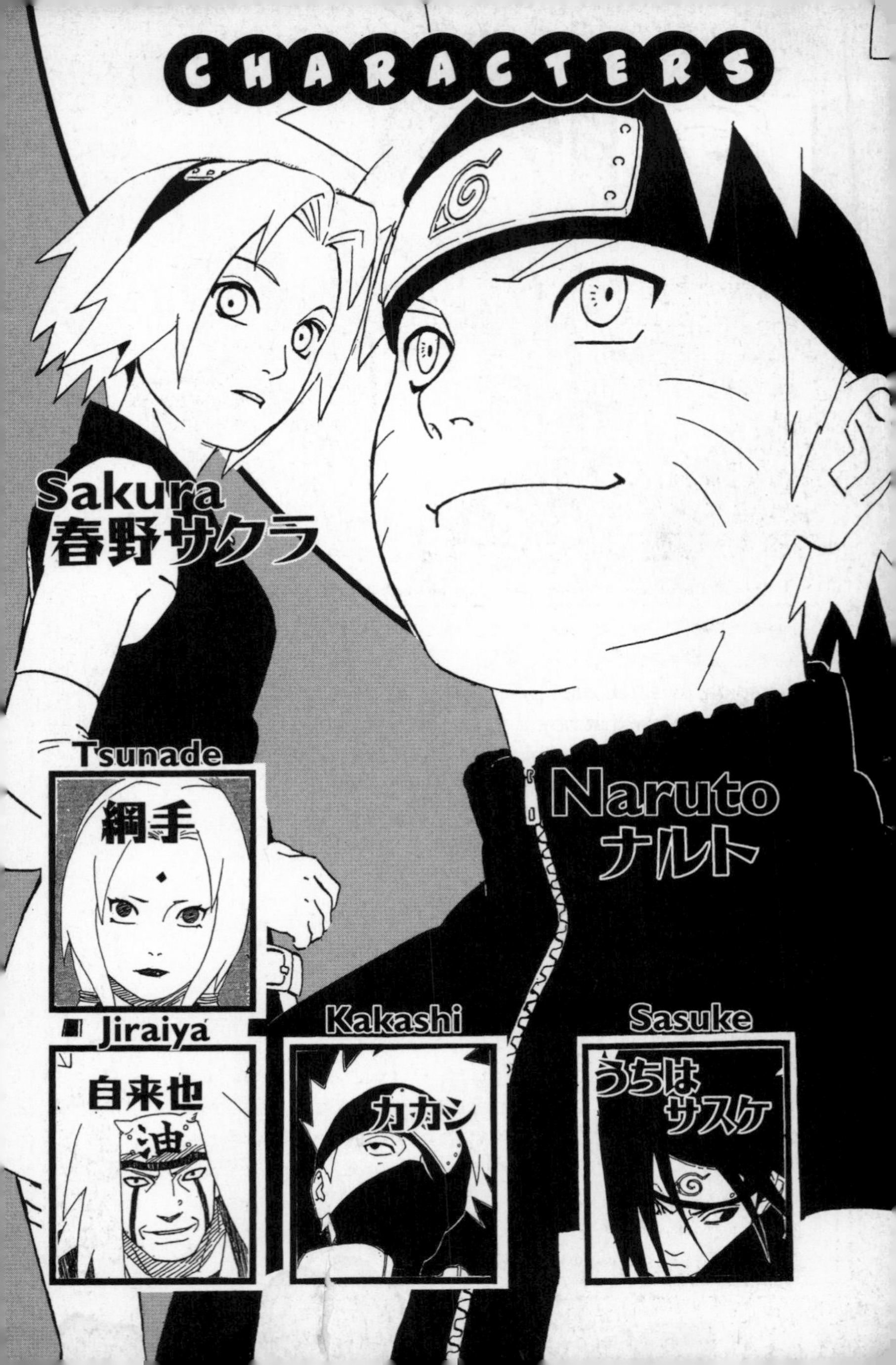
CHARACTERS
Sakura
春野サクラ
Naruto
ナルト
Tsunade
綱手
Jiraiya
自来也
油
Kakashi
カカシ
Sasuke
うちはサスケ

Ebizo
エビゾウ
Granny Chiyo
チヨ
Gaara
我愛羅
Sasori
サソリ
Deidara
デイダラ
Kankuro
カンクロウ

The Story So Far...

Twelve years ago a destructive nine-tailed fox spirit attacked the ninja village of Konohagakure. The Hokage, or village champion, defeated the fox by sealing its soul into the body of a baby boy. Now that boy, Uzumaki Naruto, has grown up to be a ninja-in-training, learning the art of ninjutsu with his teammates Sakura and Sasuke. During the Second Chûnin Exam, Orochimaru, a former student of the Third Hokage, attacks Naruto and the others. He leaves a curse mark upon Sasuke and then vanishes.

During the Third Exam, Orochimaru and company return to launch *Operation Destroy Konoha*, a campaign that ends with the sacrifice of Lord Hokage's life. Following the fierce battle against Orochimaru and Kabuto, Lady Tsunade then becomes the Fifth Hokage.

In the wake of the battle, Konoha suffers yet another loss when Sasuke, tempted by Orochimaru's offer of power, leaves with the Sound Ninja Four. Desperate to save his friend, Naruto enters into a bitter fight with Sasuke, but is ultimately unable to stop him. Amid movement by both Orochimaru and the mysterious organization the Akatsuki, Naruto and the others begin further training!!

NARUTO

VOL. 28
HOMECOMING

CONTENTS

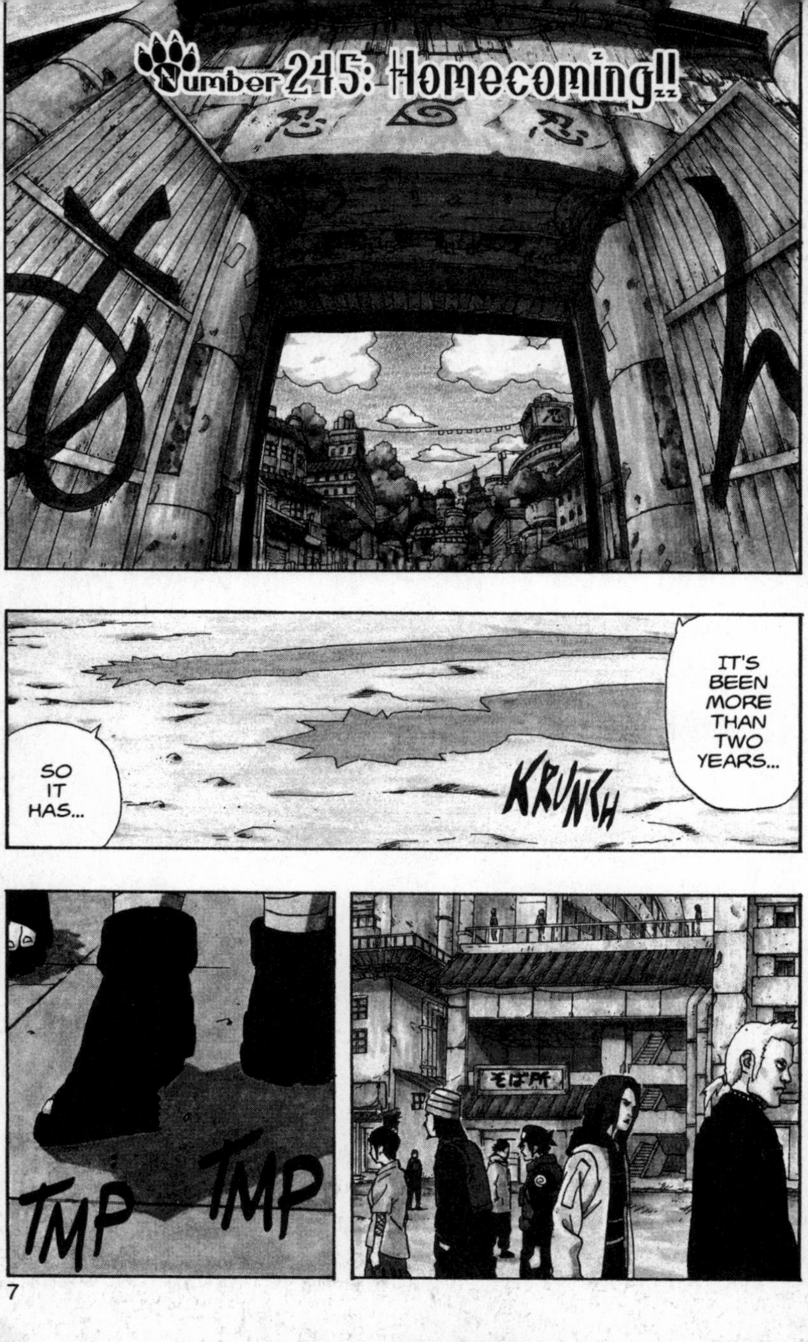
Number 245: Homecoming!!
IT'S BEEN MORE THAN TWO YEARS...
KRUNCH
SO IT HAS...
そば所
TMP TMP

SECOND JUTSU POPULARITY SURVEY!!

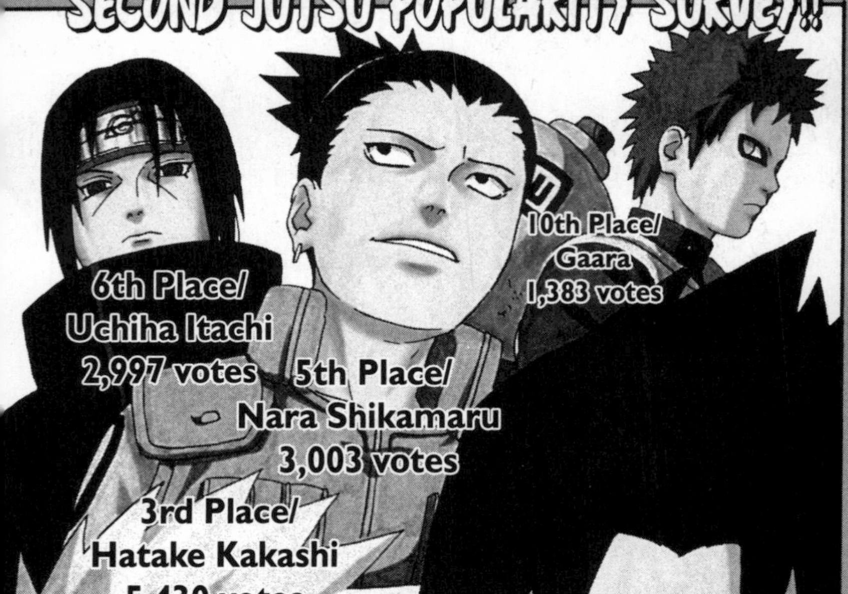
10th Place/
Gaara
1,383 votes
6th Place/
Uchiha Itachi
2,997 votes
5th Place/
Nara Shikamaru
3,003 votes
3rd Place/
Hatake Kakashi
5,430 votes
1st Place/
Uchiha Sasuke
6,647 votes

● The Jutsu Popularity Survey Results ●

1st Place/Rasengan 6,354 votes
2nd Place/Chidori 5,665 votes
3rd Place/Lightning Blade 5,188 votes
4th Place/Tsukuyomi 3,447 votes
5th Place/8 Trigrams 64 Palms 1,624 votes
6th Place/Summoning 1,611 votes
7th Place/Shadow Possession 1,575 votes
8th Place/Sharingan 1,531 votes
9th Place/Byakugan 1,197 votes
10th Place/Mangekyo Sharingan 670 votes
11th Place/Art of Suffocating Darkness 653 votes
12th Place/Ninja Centerfold 617 votes
13th Place/Lions Barrage 616 votes
14th Place/Summoning: Blade Dance 576 votes
15th Place/Mind Transfer Technique 535 votes
16th Place/Reverse Lotus 513 votes
17th Place/Sakura Blizzard* 511 votes
18th Place/Ninja Harem 509 votes
19th Place/Shadow Doppelganger 499 votes
20th Place/One Thousand Years of Death 490 votes

*Sakura's Jutsu from the movie *Ninja Clash in the Land of Snow*

RESULTS OF THE FIFTH CHARACTER AND

Number 245: Homecoming!!

8th Place/ Haruno Sakura 2,394 votes

11th Place/ Temari 1,037 votes

9th Place/ Hyuga Hinata 1,598 votes

2nd Place/ Uzumaki Naruto 5,614 votes

4th Place/ Umino Iruka 4,128 votes

7th Place/ Hyuga Neji 2,497 votes

● More of the Character Popularity Survey Results ●

12th Place/Inuzuka Kiba 788 votes	18th Place/Kimimaro 478 votes	24th Place/Tenten 280 votes
13th Place/Rock Lee 722 votes	19th Place/Yakushi Kabuto 473 votes	25th Place/Tayuya 225 votes
14th Place/Yamanaka Ino 717 votes	20th Place/Gekko Hayate 434 votes	26th Place/Sarutobi Asuma 221 votes
15th Place/Haku 706 votes	21st Place/Aburame Shino 377 votes	27th Place/Orochimaru 211 votes
16th Place/Tsunade 595 votes	22nd Place/Fourth Hokage 345 votes	28th Place/Hoshigaki Kisame 202 votes
17th Place/Might Guy 559 votes	23rd Place/Jiraiya 317 votes	29th Place/Shizune 163 votes
		30th Place/Kankuro 117 votes

This poll was conducted in Japan.

NARUTO -ナルト-

ラ

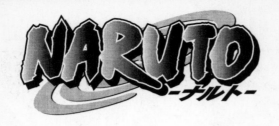

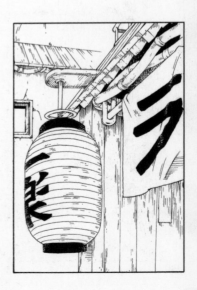

READ THIS WAY

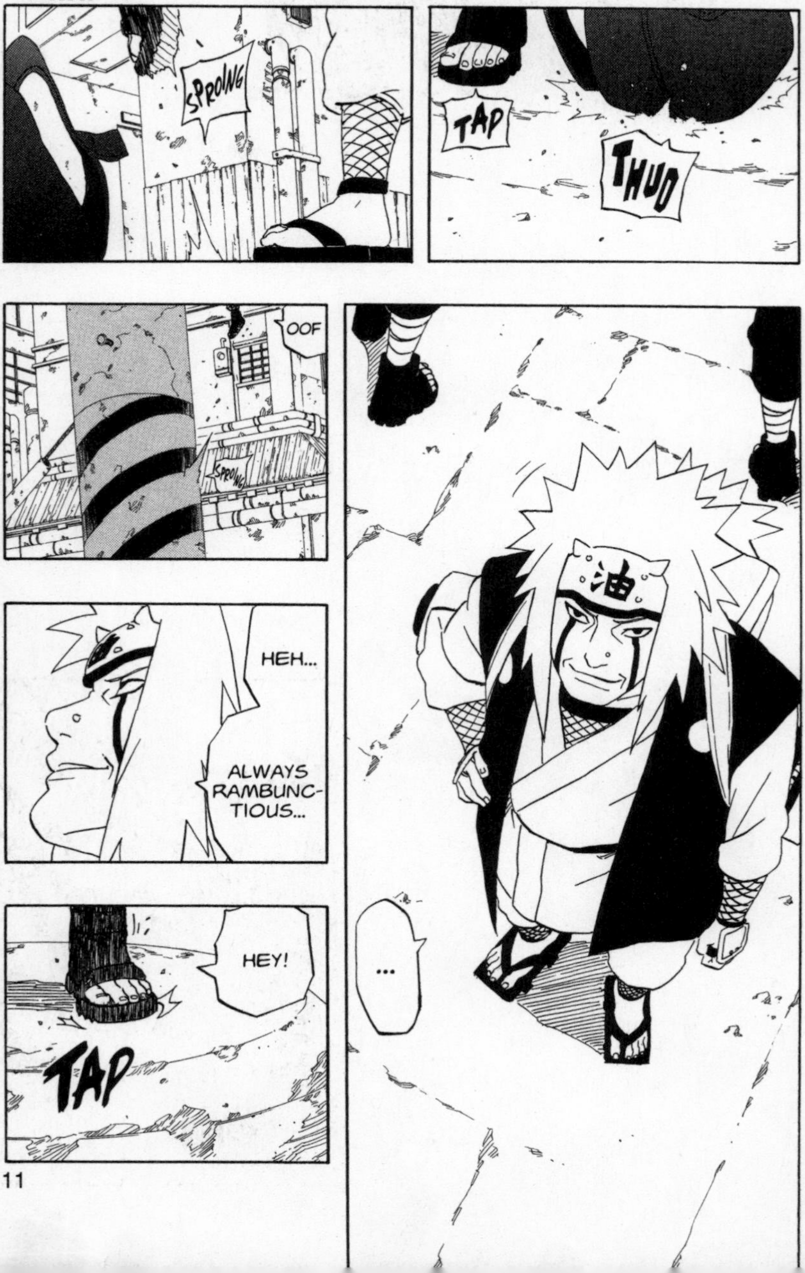
TAP
THUD
SPROING
...
OOF
SPROING
HEH...
ALWAYS RAMBUNCTIOUS...
HEY!
TAP

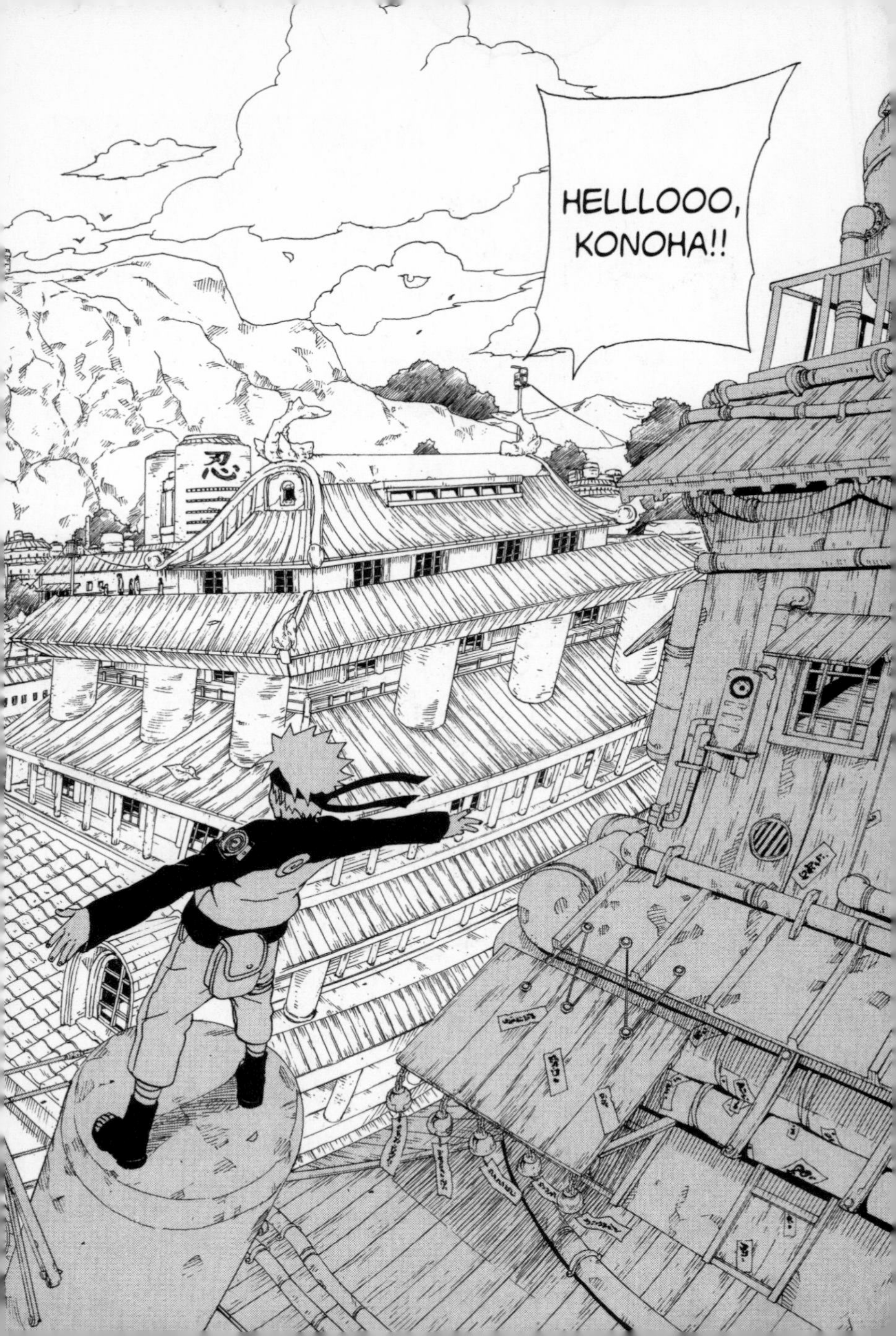
HELLLOOO, KONOHA!!

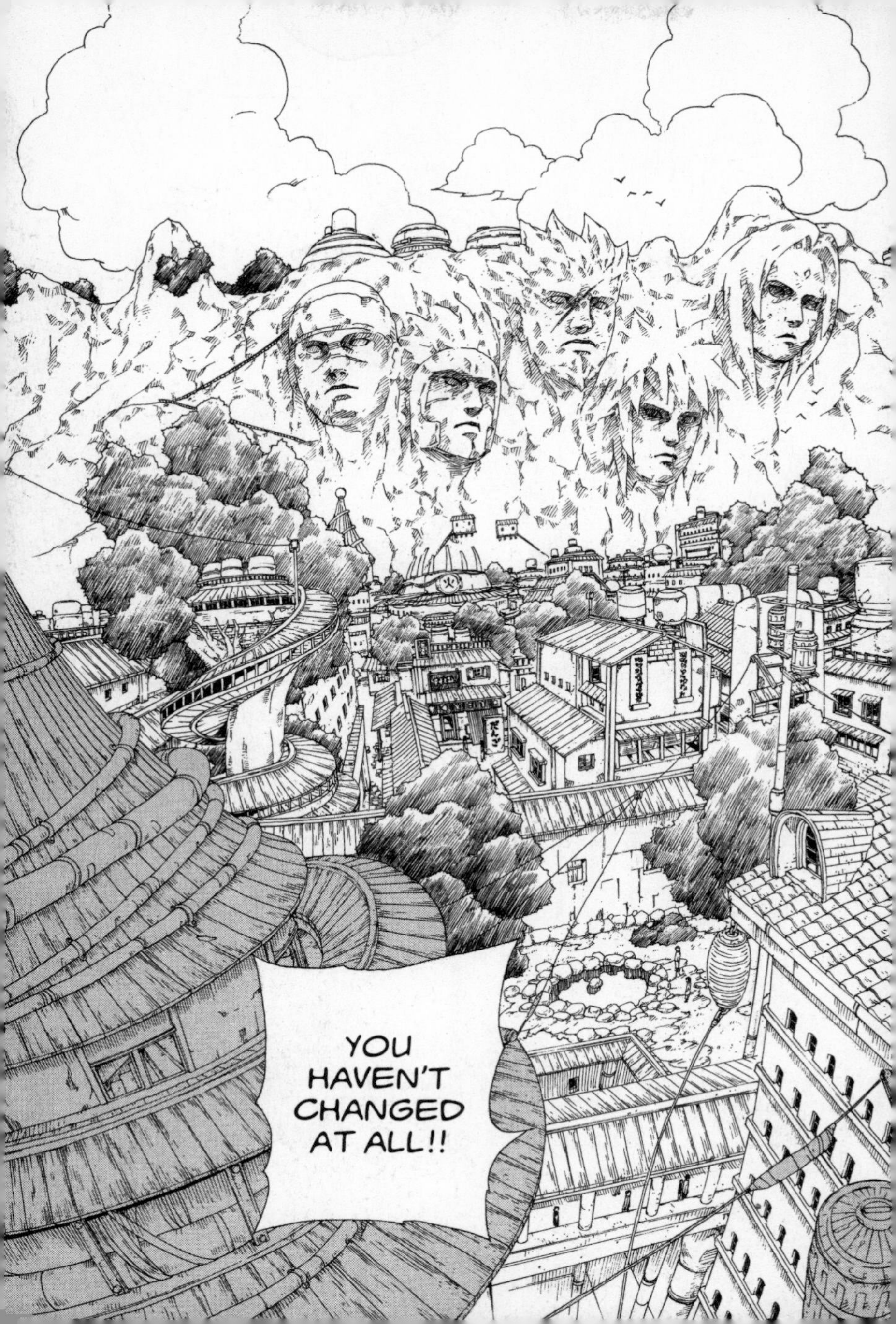
YOU HAVEN'T CHANGED AT ALL!!

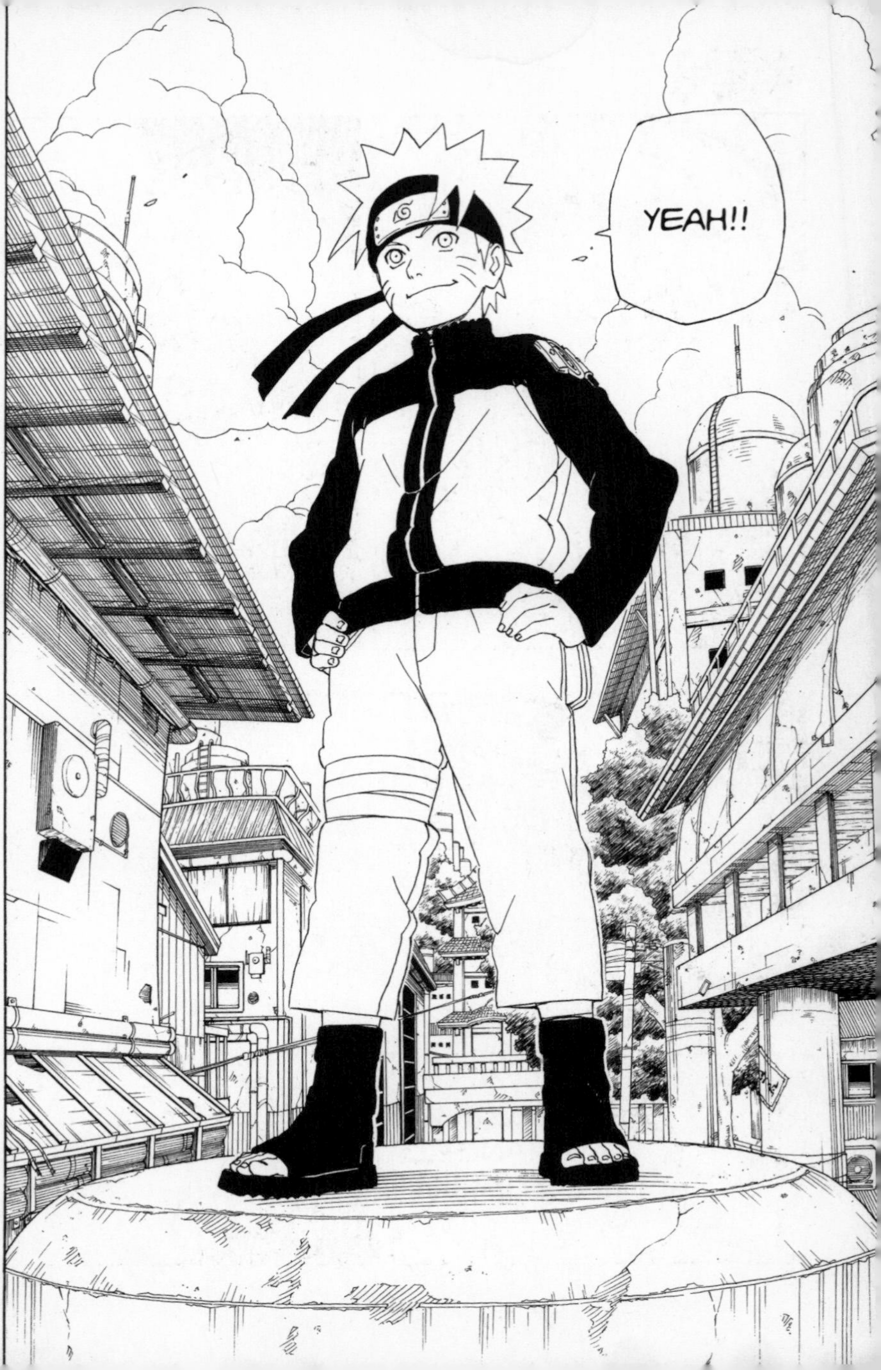
YEAH!!

READ THIS WAY

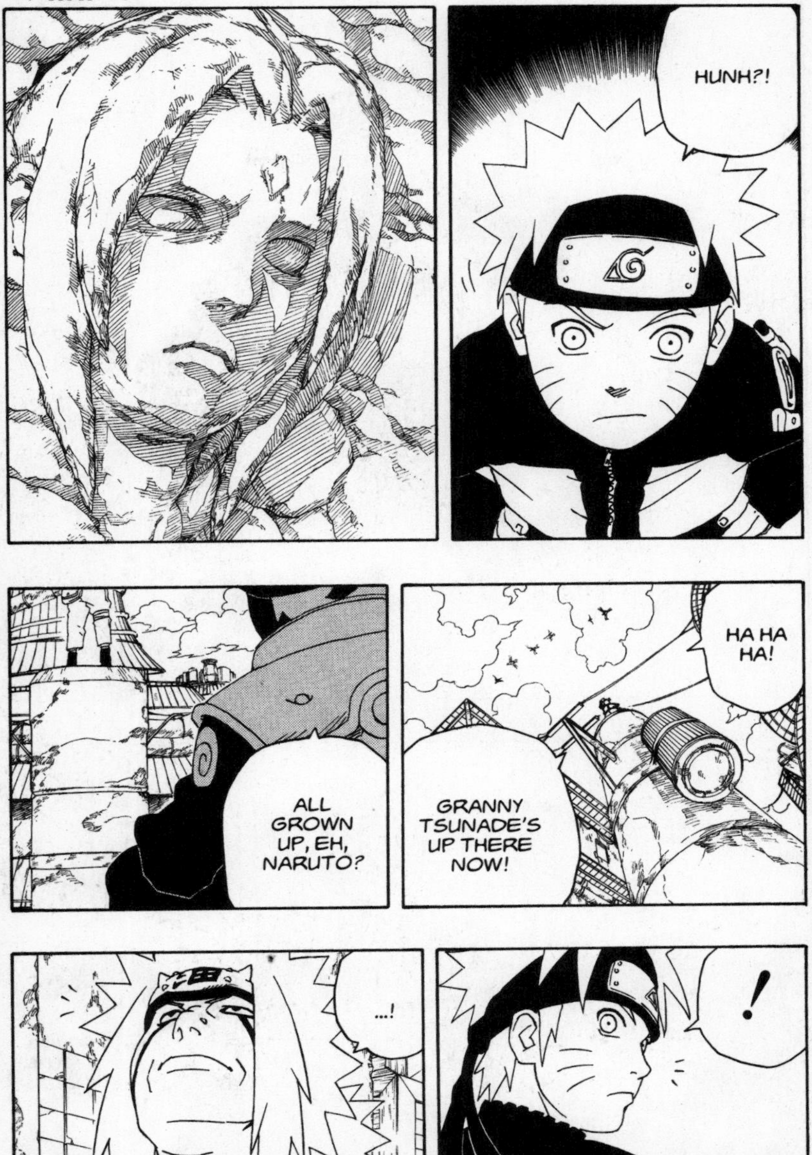
HUNH?!
HA HA HA!
GRANNY TSUNADE'S UP THERE NOW!
ALL GROWN UP, EH, NARUTO?
!
...!

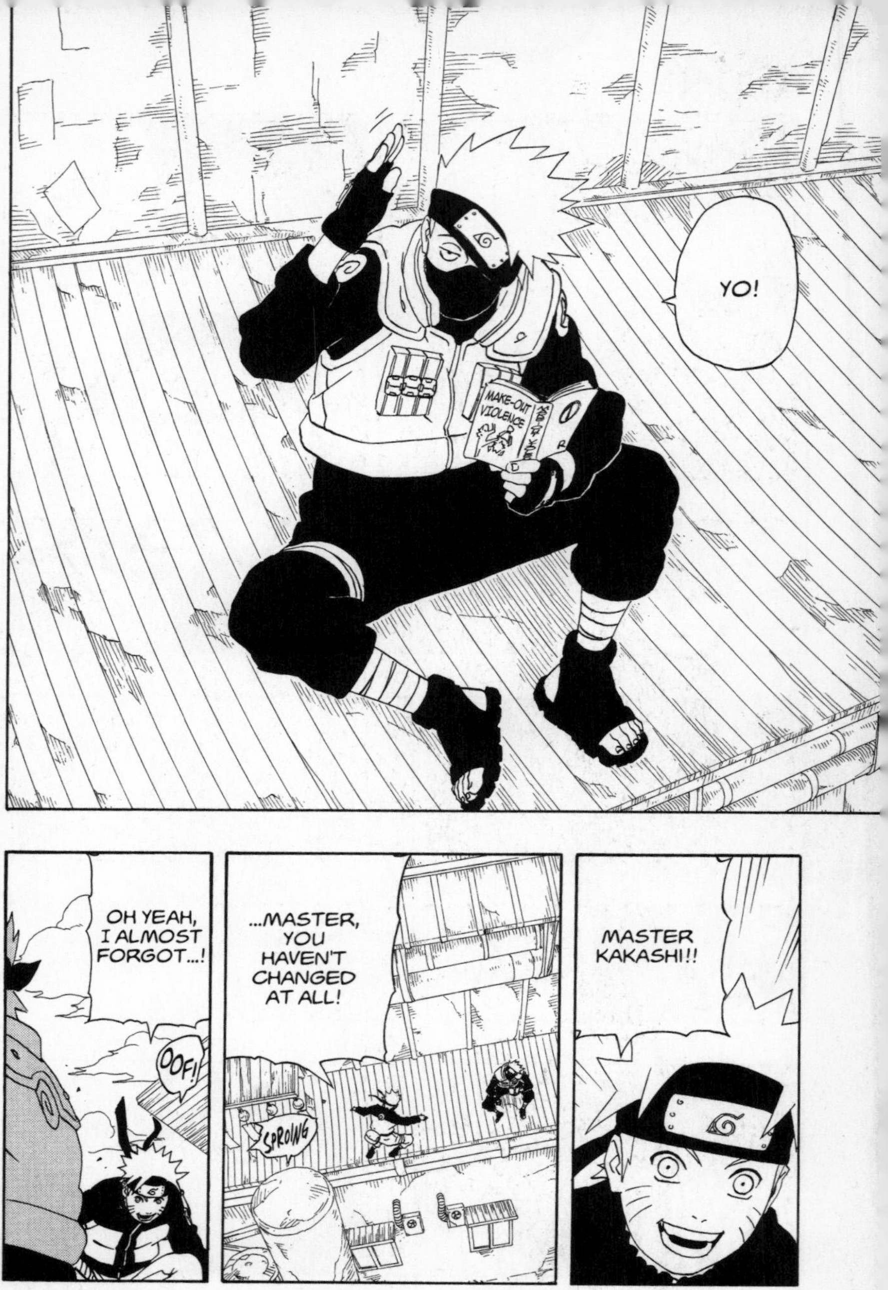
YO!
MAKE-OUT VIOLENCE
MASTER KAKASHI!!
...MASTER, YOU HAVEN'T CHANGED AT ALL!
SPROING
OH YEAH, I ALMOST FORGOT...!
OOF!

SAKURA...

I HAVE SOMETHING FOR YOU!

SHLOOF

?

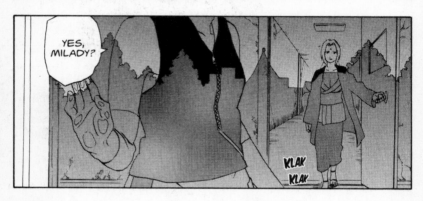

YES, MILADY?

KLAK

KLAK

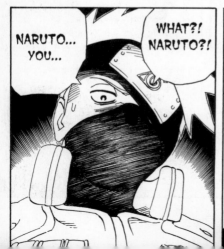

NARUTO... YOU...

WHAT?! NARUTO?!

...NARUTO HAS RE-TURNED!

THAT BRAT...

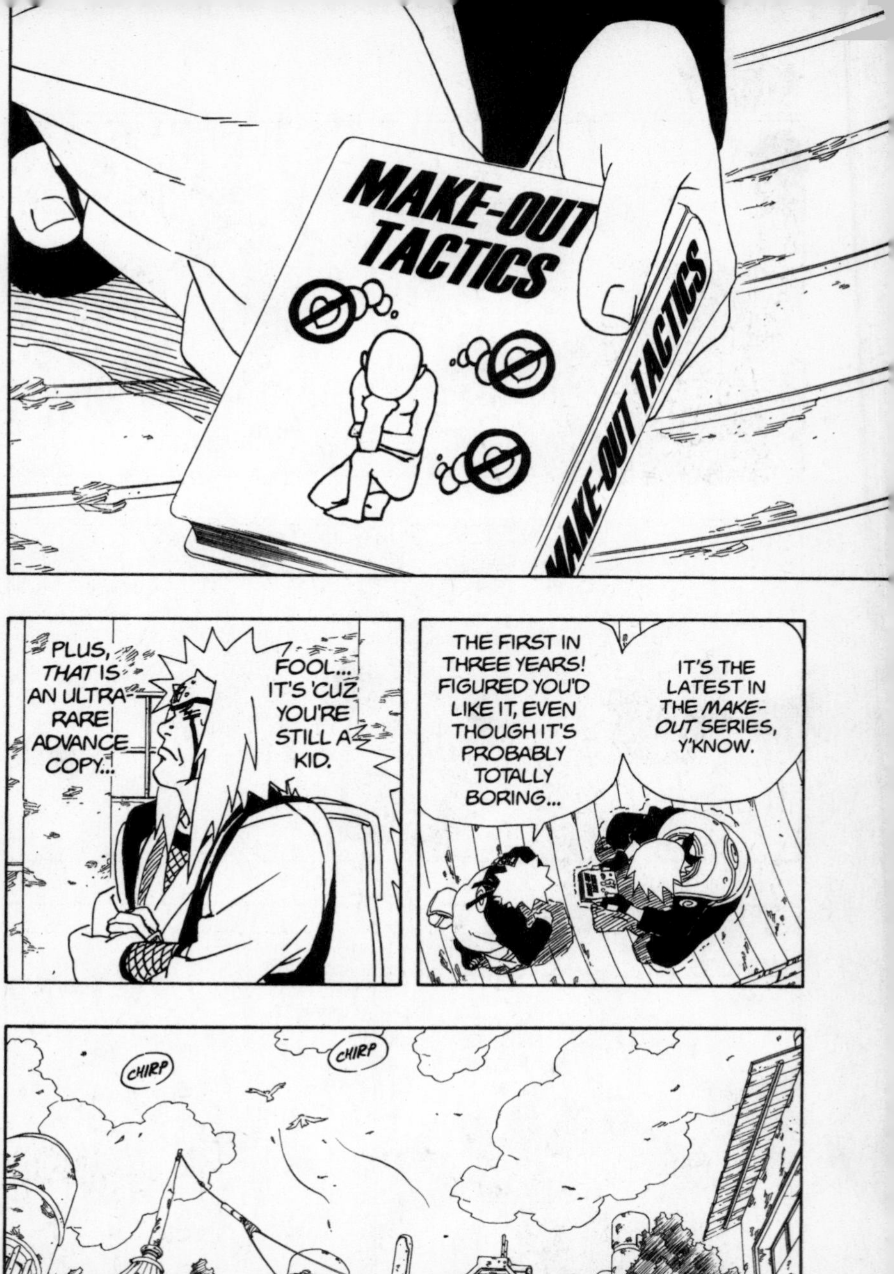
MAKE-OUT TACTICS
MAKE-OUT TACTICS
IT'S THE LATEST IN THE *MAKE-OUT* SERIES, Y'KNOW.
THE FIRST IN THREE YEARS! FIGURED YOU'D LIKE IT, EVEN THOUGH IT'S PROBABLY TOTALLY BORING...
FOOL... IT'S 'CUZ YOU'RE STILL A KID.
PLUS, *THAT* IS AN ULTRA-RARE ADVANCE COPY...
CHIRP
CHIRP

READ THIS WAY

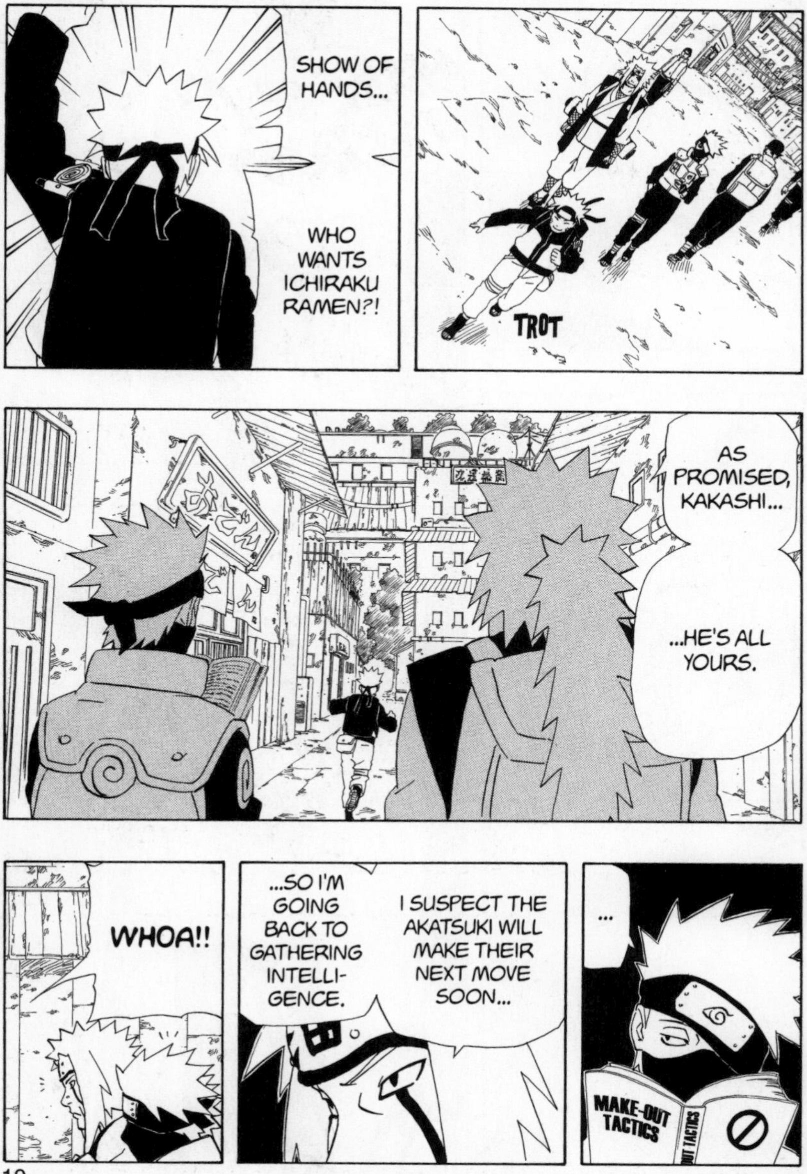
TROT
SHOW OF HANDS...
WHO WANTS ICHIRAKU RAMEN?!
AS PROMISED, KAKASHI...
...HE'S ALL YOURS.
...
I SUSPECT THE AKATSUKI WILL MAKE THEIR NEXT MOVE SOON...
...SO I'M GOING BACK TO GATHERING INTELLI-GENCE.
WHOA!!
MAKE-OUT TACTICS

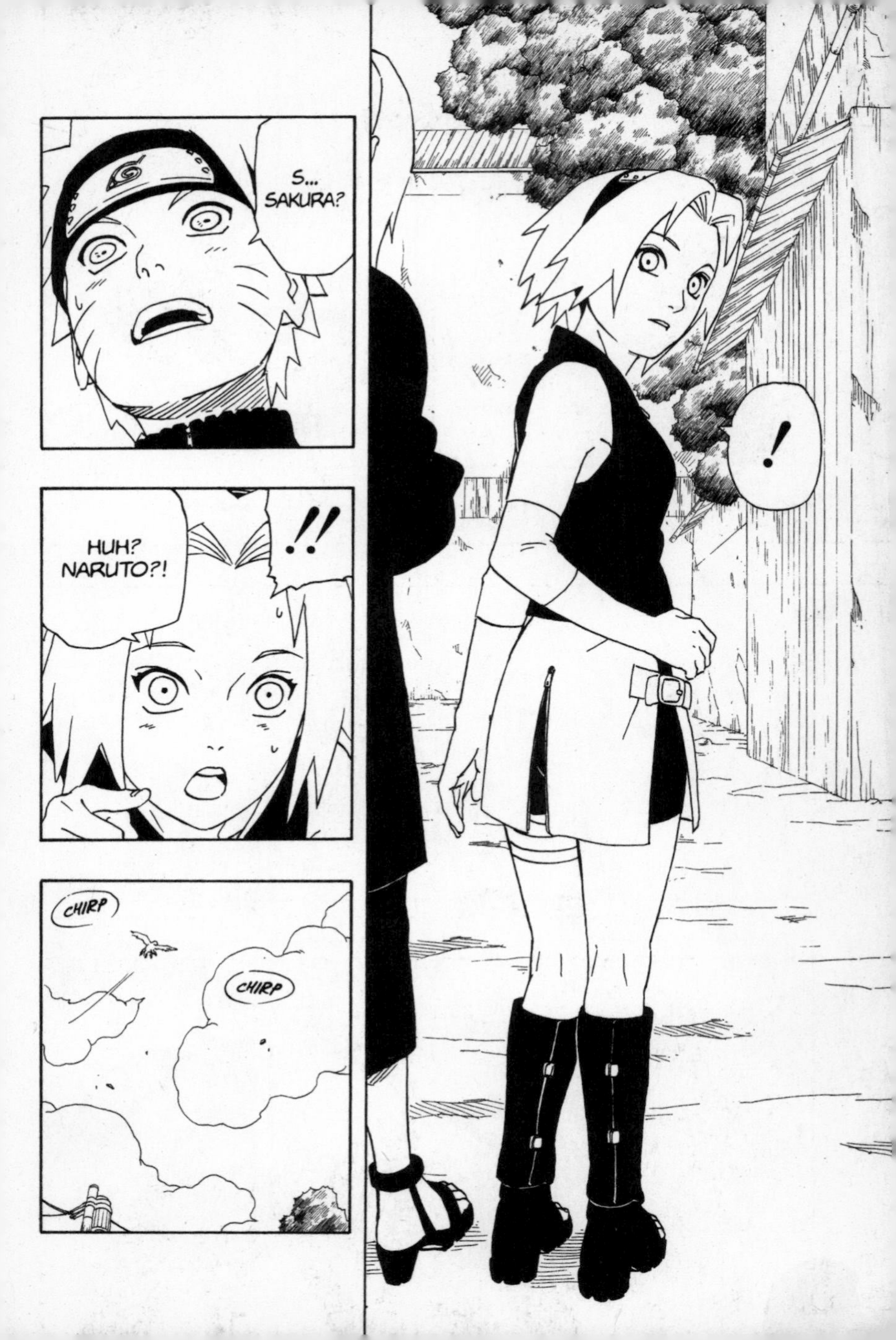
!
S...
SAKURA?
!!
HUH?
NARUTO?!
CHIRP
CHIRP

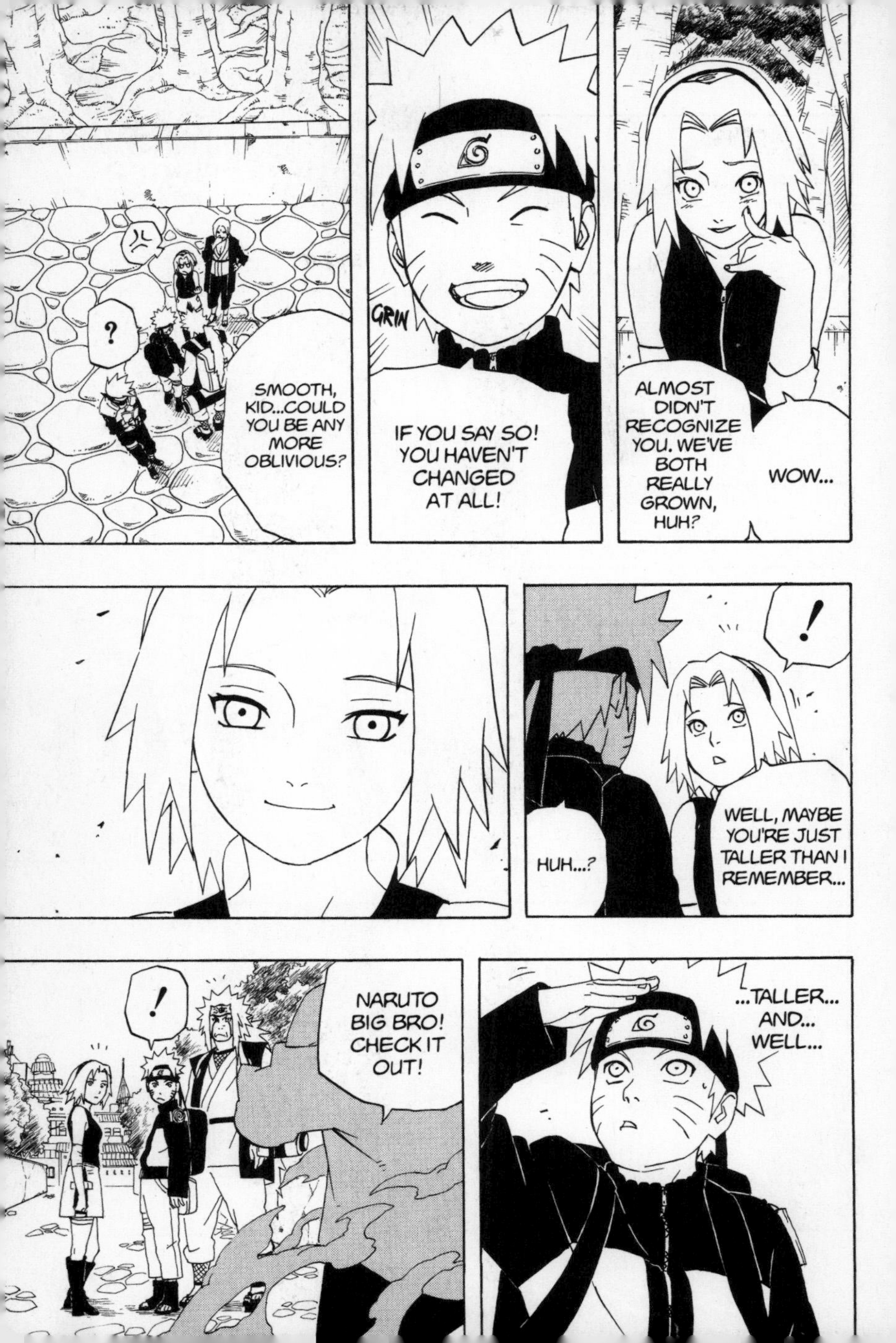
WOW...
ALMOST DIDN'T RECOGNIZE YOU. WE'VE BOTH REALLY GROWN, HUH?
GRIN
IF YOU SAY SO! YOU HAVEN'T CHANGED AT ALL!
?
SMOOTH, KID...COULD YOU BE ANY MORE OBLIVIOUS?
!
WELL, MAYBE YOU'RE JUST TALLER THAN I REMEMBER...
HUH...?
...TALLER... AND... WELL...
NARUTO BIG BRO! CHECK IT OUT!
!

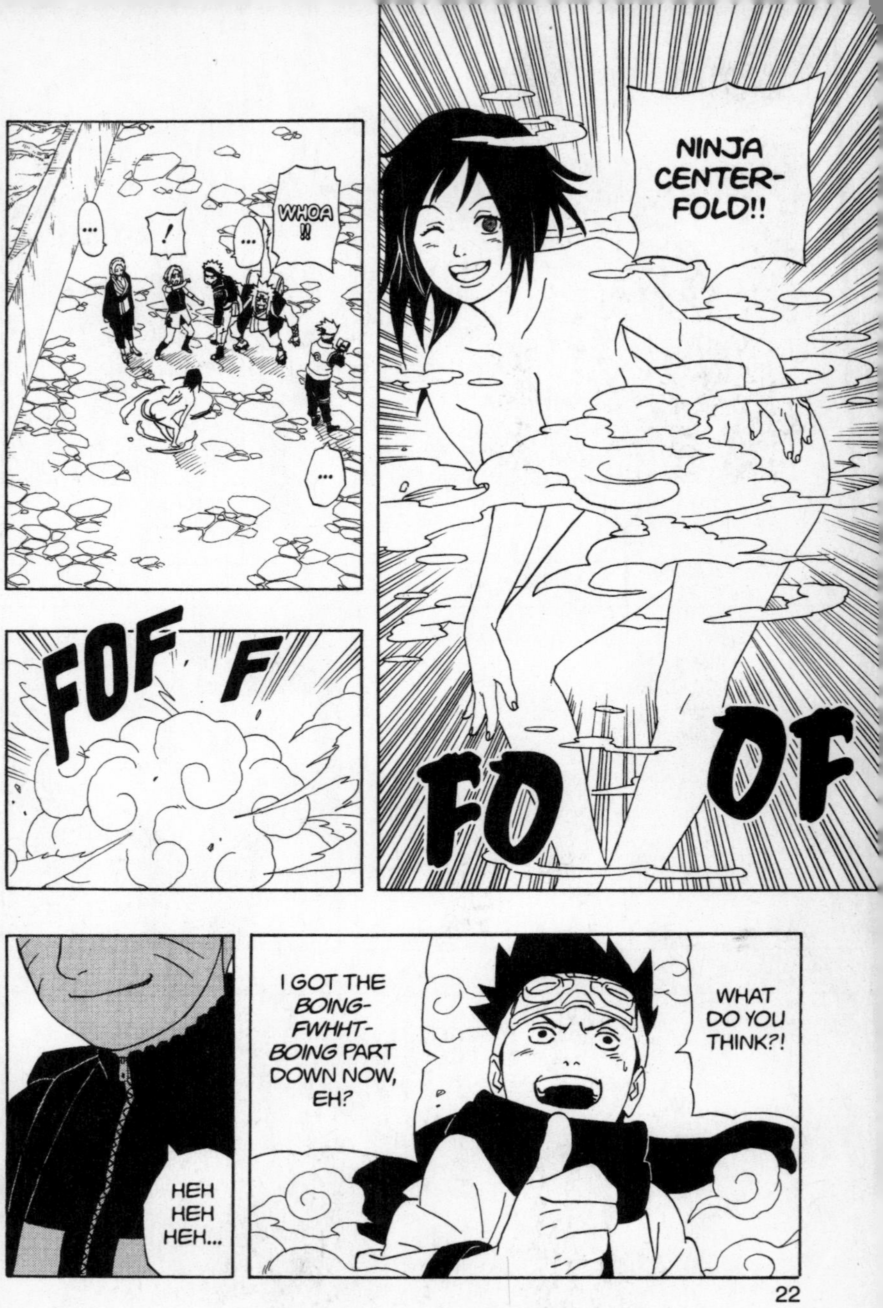
NINJA CENTER-FOLD!!
FO OF
WHOA !!
...
!
...
...
FOF F
WHAT DO YOU THINK?!
I GOT THE BOING-FWHHT-BOING PART DOWN NOW, EH?
HEH HEH HEH...

READ THIS WAY

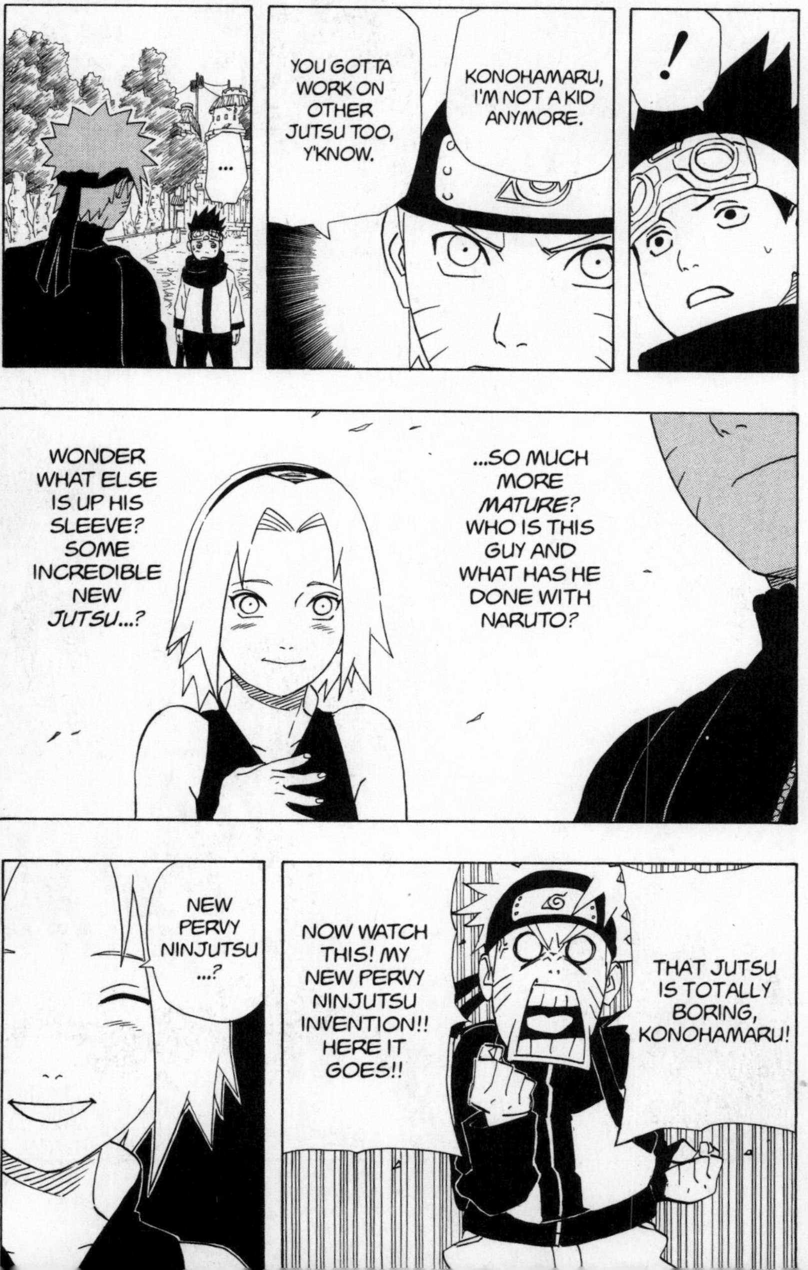
!
KONOHAMARU, I'M NOT A KID ANYMORE.
YOU GOTTA WORK ON OTHER JUTSU TOO, Y'KNOW.
...
...SO MUCH MORE MATURE? WHO IS THIS GUY AND WHAT HAS HE DONE WITH NARUTO?
WONDER WHAT ELSE IS UP HIS SLEEVE? SOME INCREDIBLE NEW JUTSU...?
THAT JUTSU IS TOTALLY BORING, KONOHAMARU!
NOW WATCH THIS! MY NEW PERVY NINJUTSU INVENTION!! HERE IT GOES!!
NEW PERVY NINJUTSU ...?

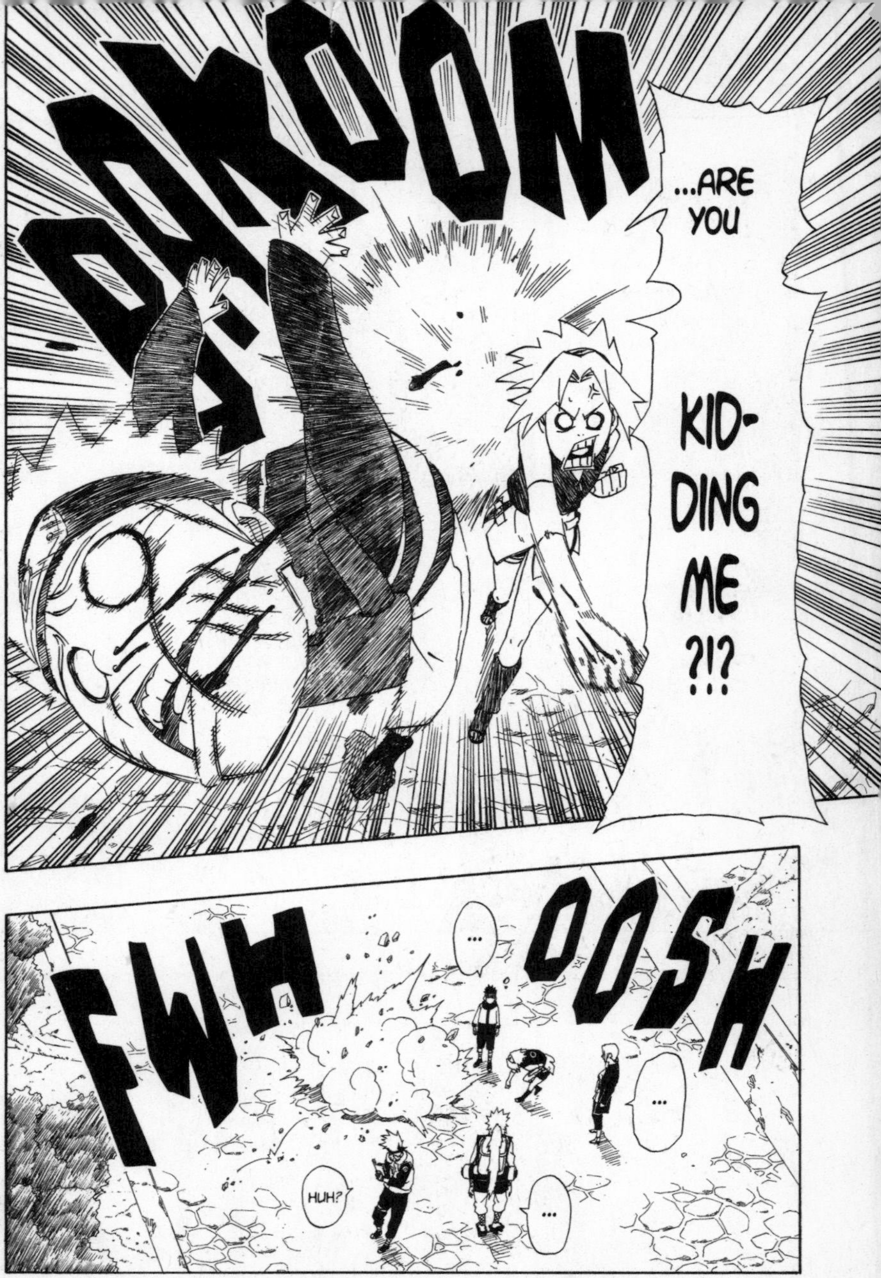
DOKOOM
...ARE YOU KID-DING ME ?!?
FWH OOSH
...
...
...
HUH?

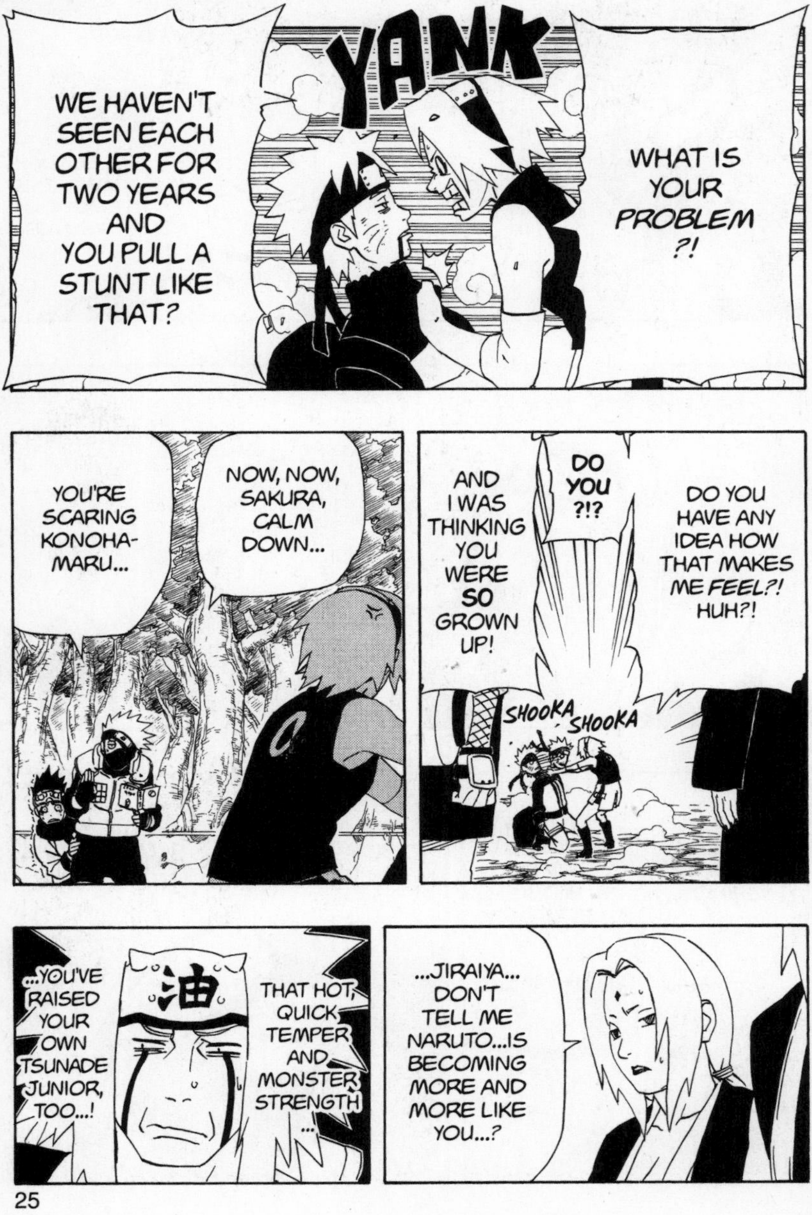
YANK
WHAT IS YOUR PROBLEM?!
WE HAVEN'T SEEN EACH OTHER FOR TWO YEARS AND YOU PULL A STUNT LIKE THAT?
DO YOU HAVE ANY IDEA HOW THAT MAKES ME FEEL?! HUH?!
DO YOU?!?
AND I WAS THINKING YOU WERE SO GROWN UP!
SHOOKA SHOOKA
NOW, NOW, SAKURA, CALM DOWN...
YOU'RE SCARING KONOHA-MARU...
...JIRAIYA... DON'T TELL ME NARUTO...IS BECOMING MORE AND MORE LIKE YOU...?
THAT HOT, QUICK TEMPER AND MONSTER STRENGTH...
...YOU'VE RAISED YOUR OWN TSUNADE JUNIOR, TOO...!

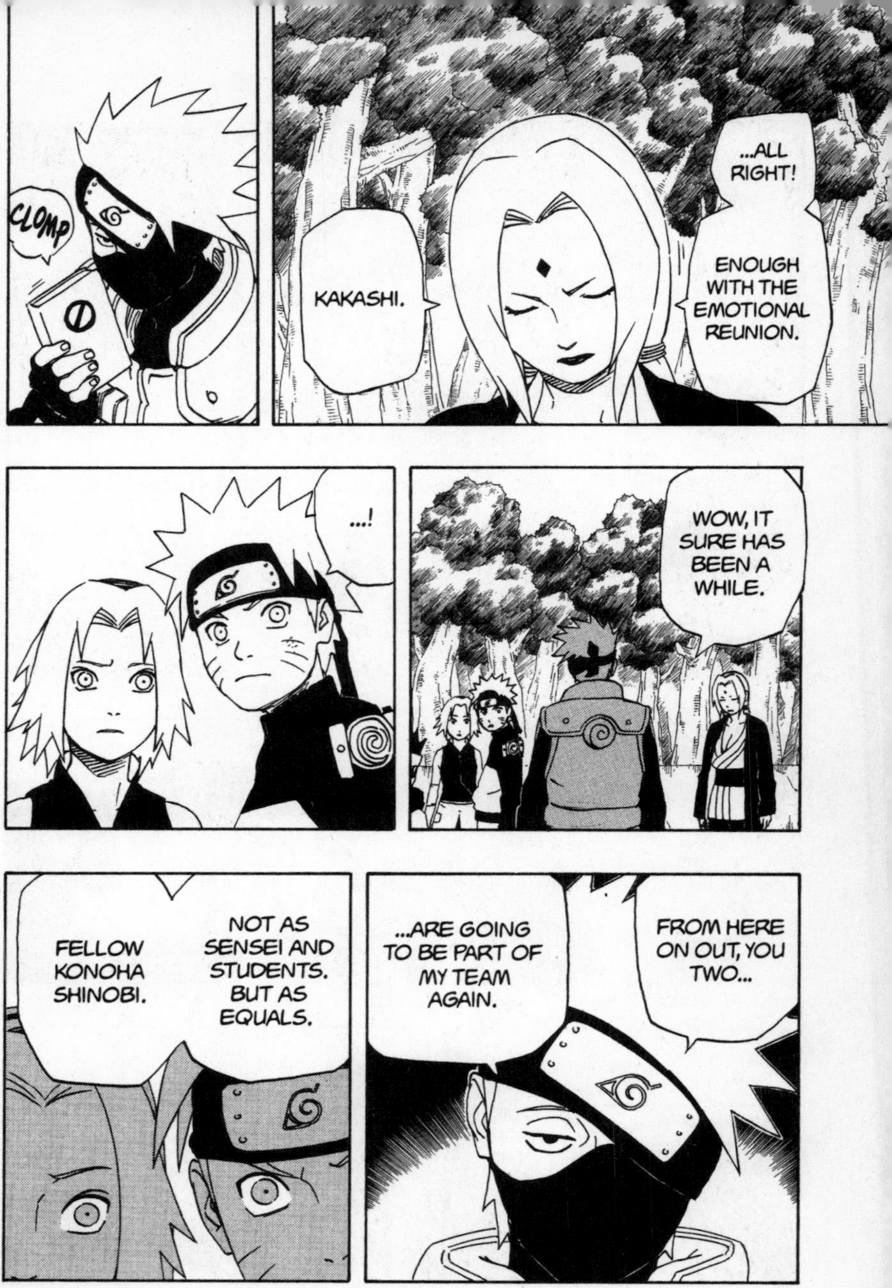
...ALL RIGHT!
ENOUGH WITH THE EMOTIONAL REUNION.
KAKASHI.
CLOMP
WOW, IT SURE HAS BEEN A WHILE.
...!
FROM HERE ON OUT, YOU TWO...
...ARE GOING TO BE PART OF MY TEAM AGAIN.
NOT AS SENSEI AND STUDENTS. BUT AS EQUALS.
FELLOW KONOHA SHINOBI.

READ THIS WAY

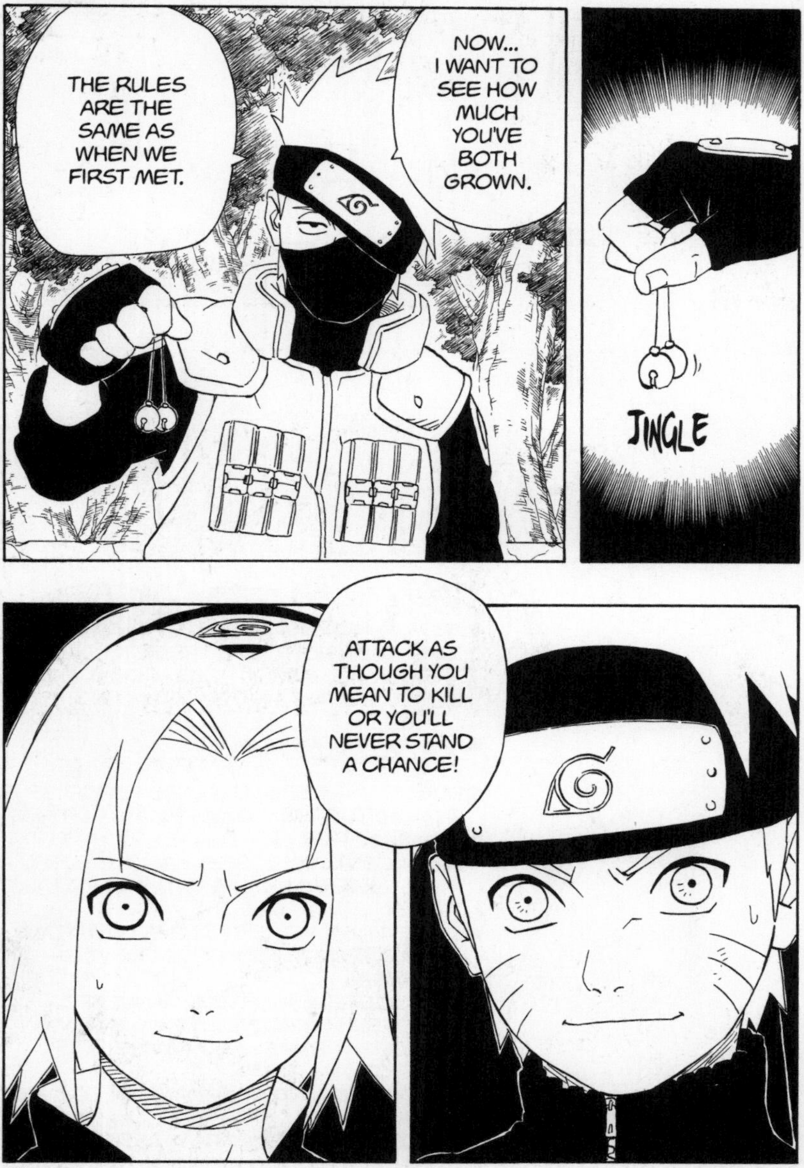
JINGLE
NOW... I WANT TO SEE HOW MUCH YOU'VE BOTH GROWN.
THE RULES ARE THE SAME AS WHEN WE FIRST MET.
ATTACK AS THOUGH YOU MEAN TO KILL OR YOU'LL NEVER STAND A CHANCE!

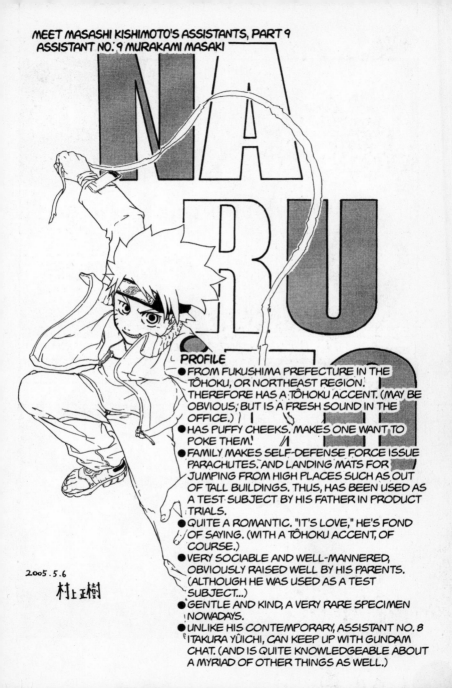

MEET MASASHI KISHIMOTO'S ASSISTANTS, PART 9

ASSISTANT NO. 9 MURAKAMI MASAKI

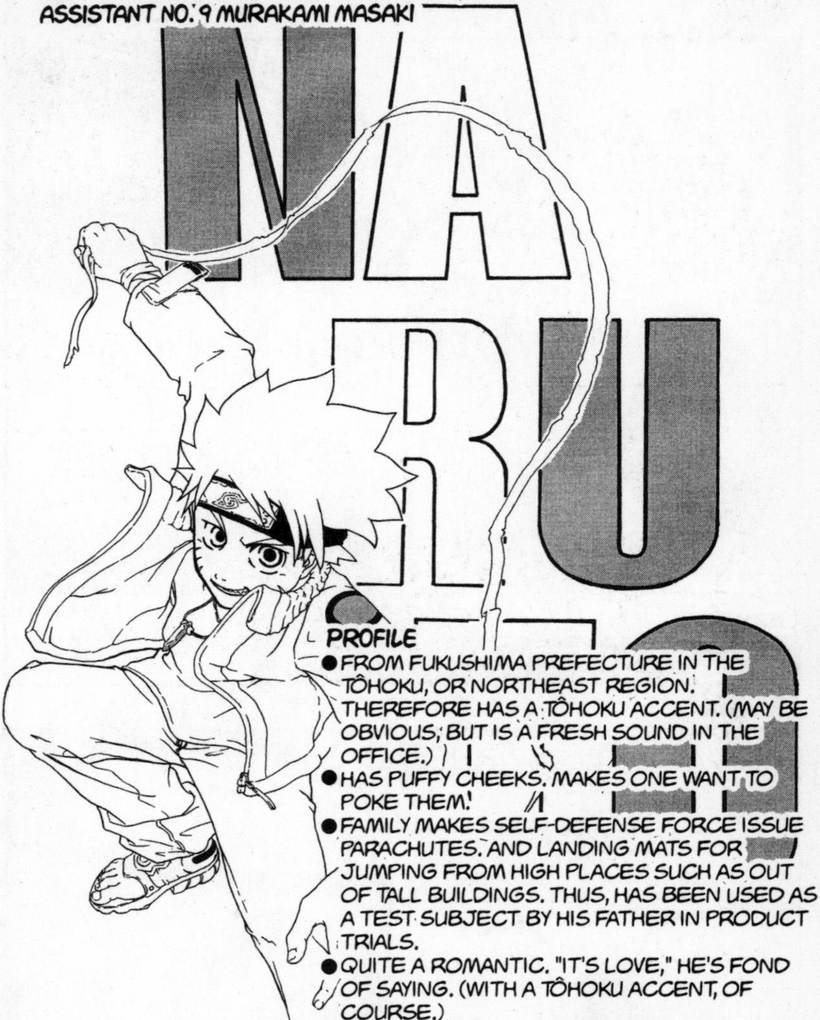
NARUTO
2005.5.6
村上正樹

PROFILE

- FROM FUKUSHIMA PREFECTURE IN THE TÔHOKU, OR NORTHEAST REGION. THEREFORE HAS A TÔHOKU ACCENT. (MAY BE OBVIOUS, BUT IS A FRESH SOUND IN THE OFFICE.)
- HAS PUFFY CHEEKS. MAKES ONE WANT TO POKE THEM!
- FAMILY MAKES SELF-DEFENSE FORCE ISSUE PARACHUTES. AND LANDING MATS FOR JUMPING FROM HIGH PLACES SUCH AS OUT OF TALL BUILDINGS. THUS, HAS BEEN USED AS A TEST SUBJECT BY HIS FATHER IN PRODUCT TRIALS.
- QUITE A ROMANTIC. "IT'S LOVE," HE'S FOND OF SAYING. (WITH A TÔHOKU ACCENT, OF COURSE.)
- VERY SOCIABLE AND WELL-MANNERED, OBVIOUSLY RAISED WELL BY HIS PARENTS. (ALTHOUGH HE WAS USED AS A TEST SUBJECT...)
- GENTLE AND KIND, A VERY RARE SPECIMEN NOWADAYS.
- UNLIKE HIS CONTEMPORARY, ASSISTANT NO. 8 ITAKURA YÛICHI, CAN KEEP UP WITH GUNDAM CHAT. (AND IS QUITE KNOWLEDGEABLE ABOUT A MYRIAD OF OTHER THINGS AS WELL.)

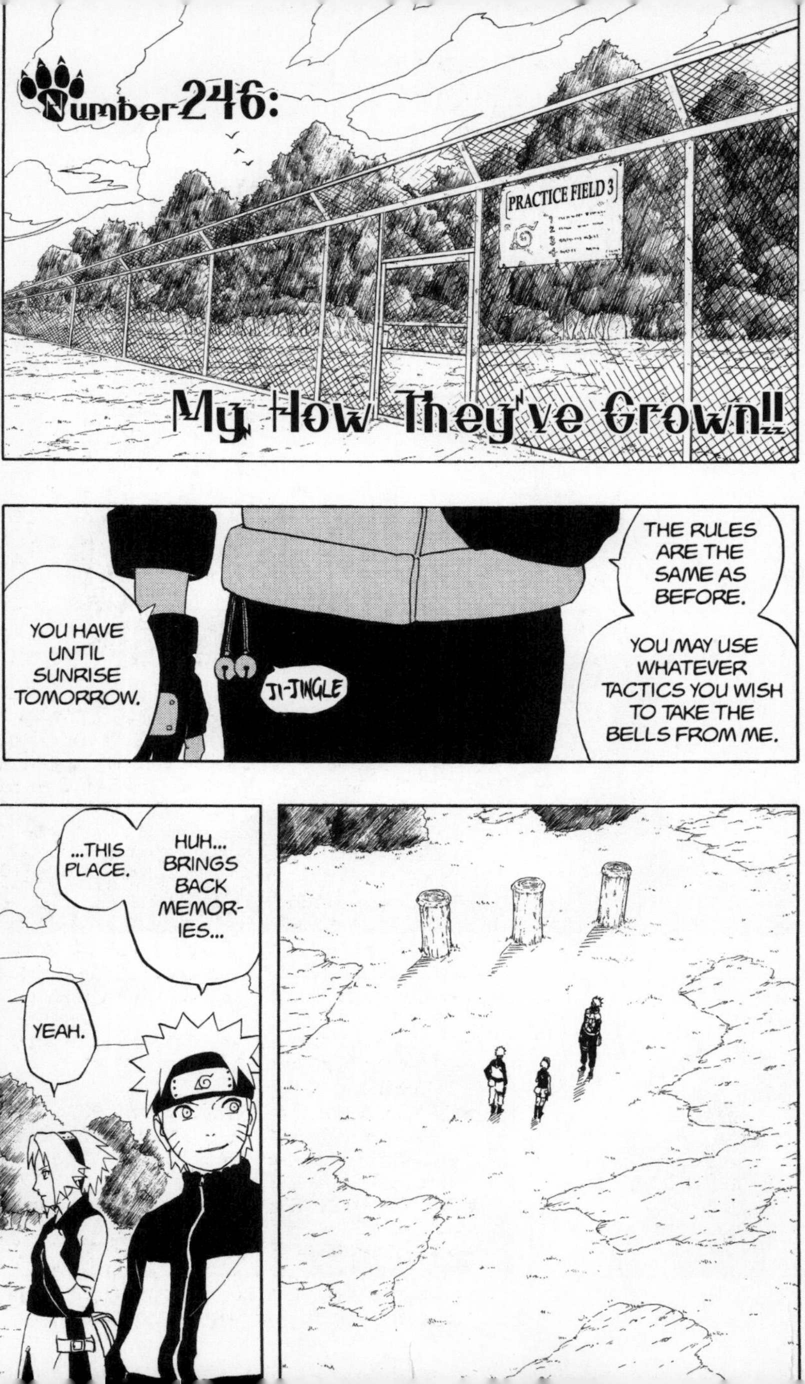
Number 246:
PRACTICE FIELD 3
My How They've Grown!!
THE RULES ARE THE SAME AS BEFORE.
YOU MAY USE WHATEVER TACTICS YOU WISH TO TAKE THE BELLS FROM ME.
JI-JINGLE
YOU HAVE UNTIL SUNRISE TOMORROW.
HUH... BRINGS BACK MEMORIES...
...THIS PLACE.
YEAH.

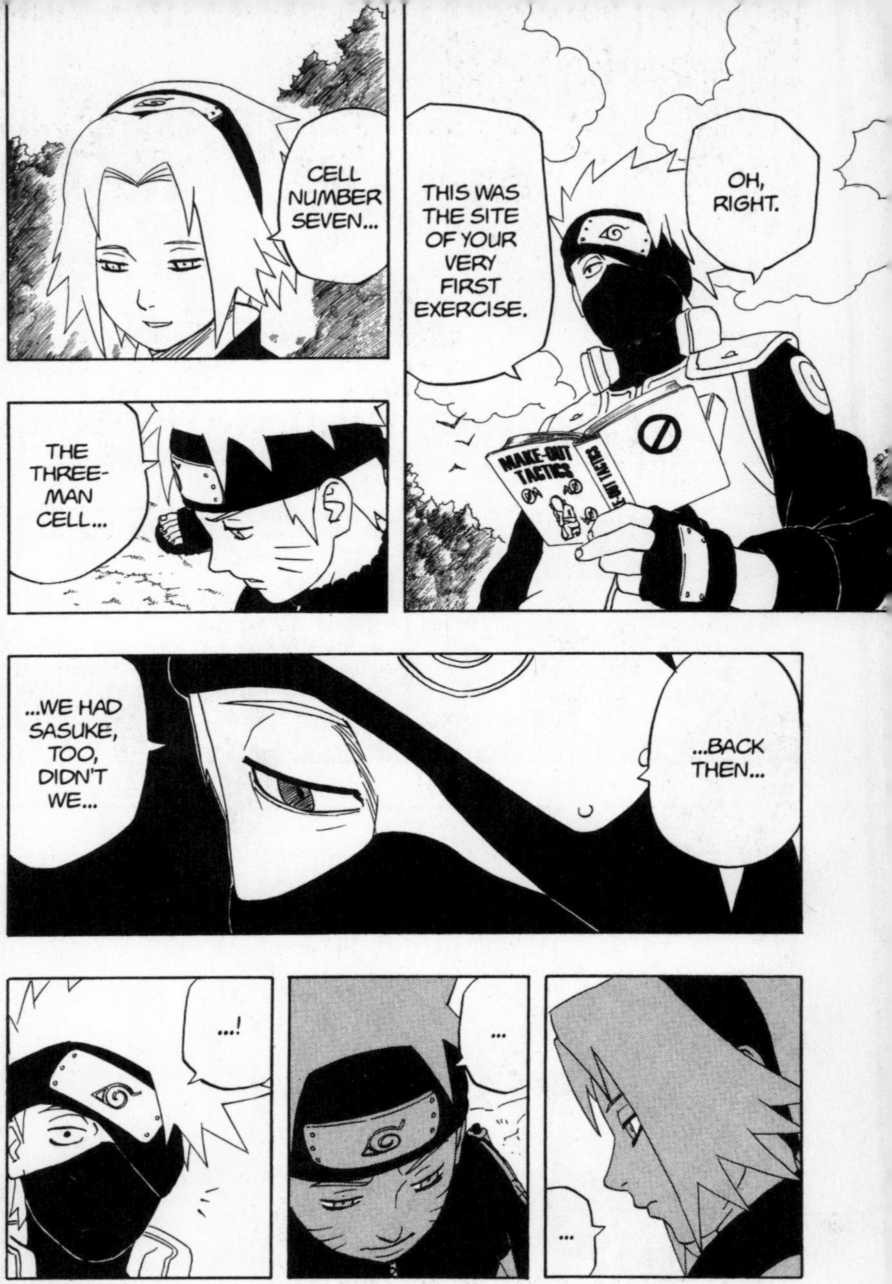
OH, RIGHT.
THIS WAS THE SITE OF YOUR VERY FIRST EXERCISE.
MAKE-OUT TACTICS
CELL NUMBER SEVEN...
THE THREE-MAN CELL...
...BACK THEN...
...WE HAD SASUKE, TOO, DIDN'T WE...
...
...
...!

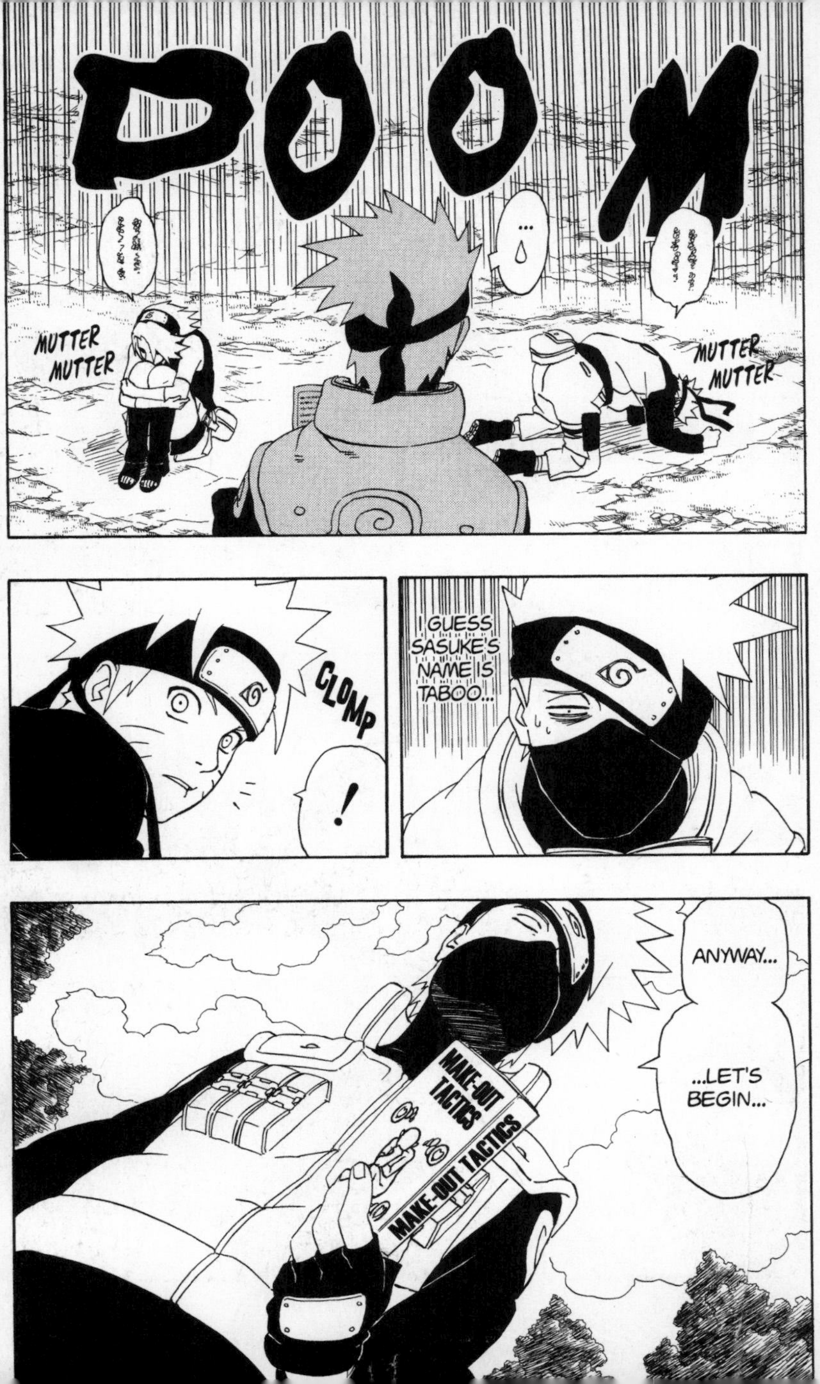
DOOM
MUTTER MUTTER
...
MUTTER MUTTER
I GUESS SASUKE'S NAME IS TABOO...
CLOMP
!
ANYWAY...
...LET'S BEGIN...
MAKE-OUT TACTICS
MAKE-OUT TACTICS

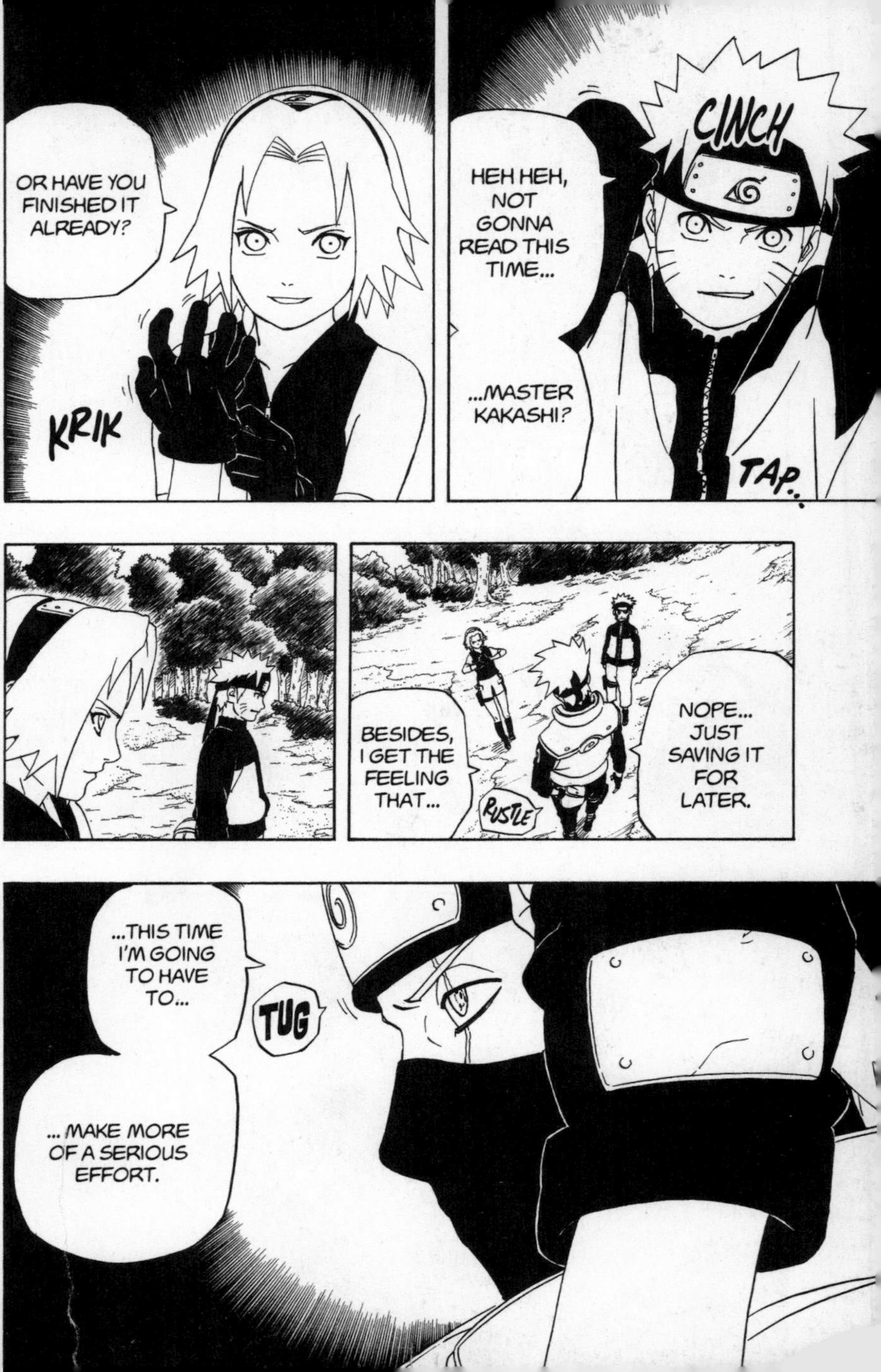
CINCH
HEH HEH, NOT GONNA READ THIS TIME...
...MASTER KAKASHI?
TAP..
OR HAVE YOU FINISHED IT ALREADY?
KRIK
NOPE... JUST SAVING IT FOR LATER.
BESIDES, I GET THE FEELING THAT...
RUSTLE
...THIS TIME I'M GOING TO HAVE TO...
TUG
... MAKE MORE OF A SERIOUS EFFORT.

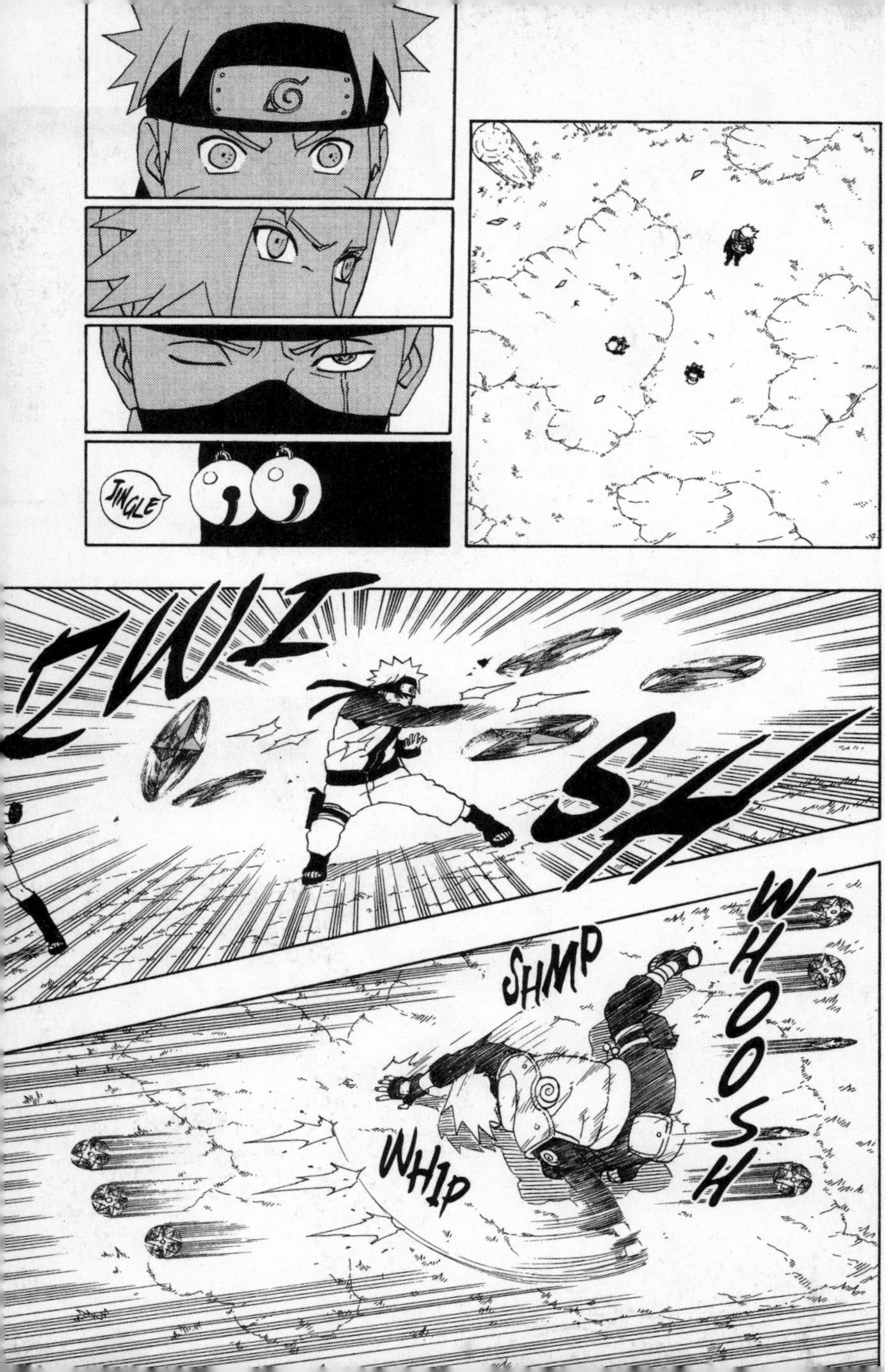
JINGLE
ZWISH
WHOOSH
SHMP
WHIP

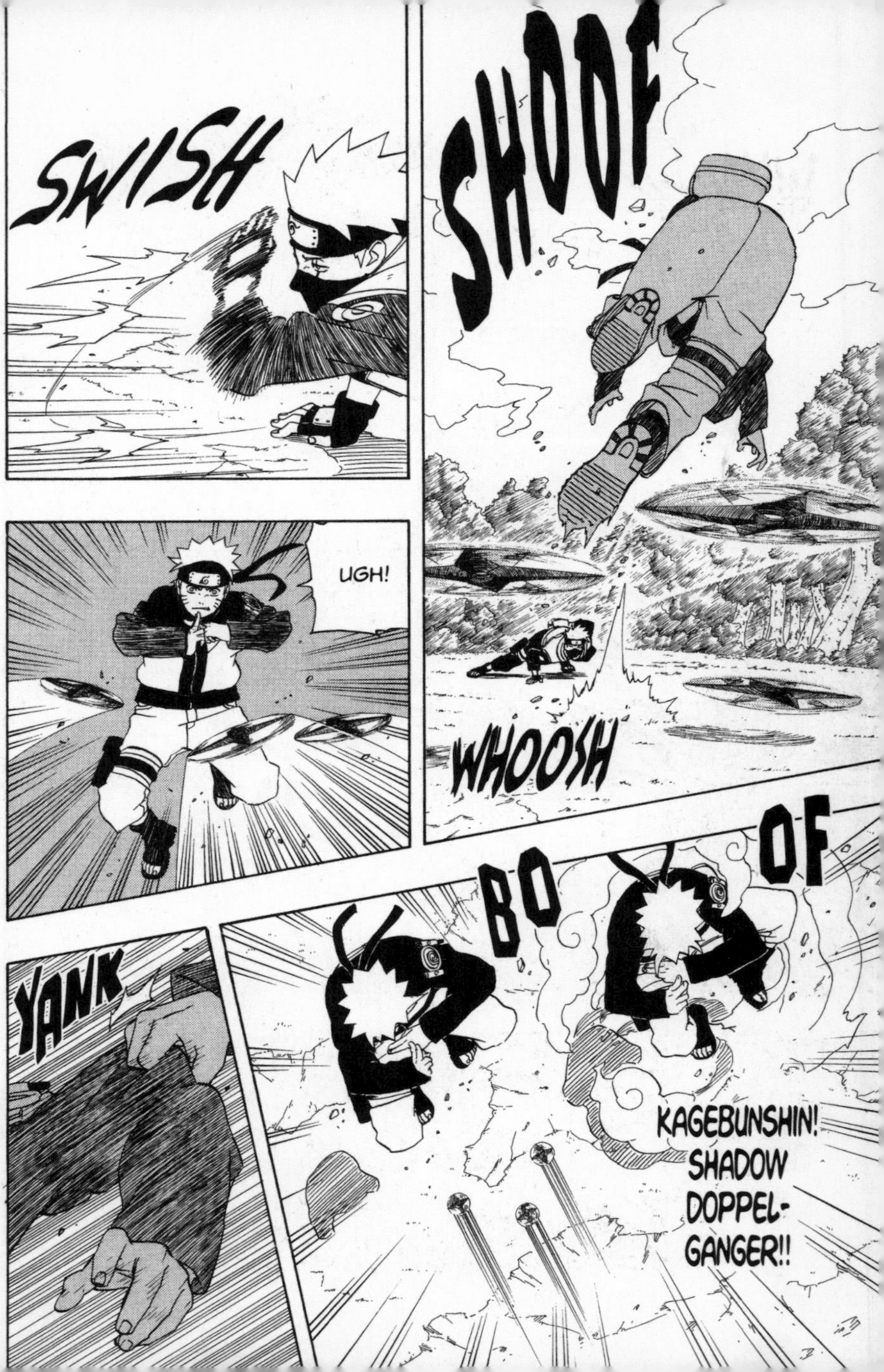
SHOOF
WHOOSH
SWISH
UGH!
BO OF
KAGEBUNSHIN! SHADOW DOPPEL-GANGER!!
YANK

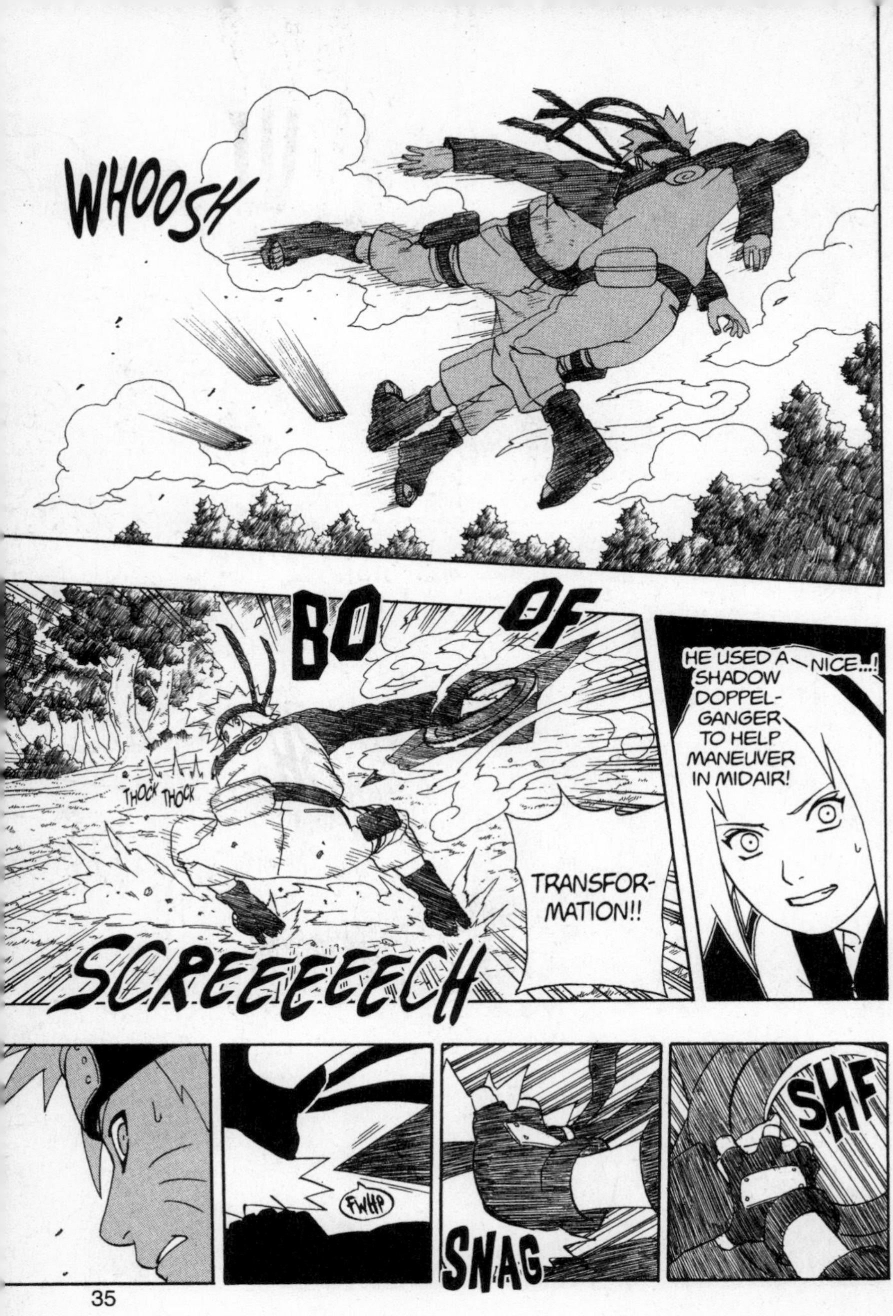
WHOOSH
NICE...!
HE USED A SHADOW DOPPEL-GANGER TO HELP MANEUVER IN MIDAIR!
BOOF
THOCK THOCK
TRANSFOR-MATION!!
SCREEEEEECH
SHF
SNAG
FWHP

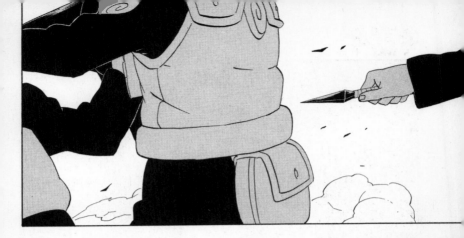

HIS USE OF SHADOW DOPPEL-GANGERS...AND HIS TIMING... THEY'VE BOTH IMPROVED.

HEH... STILL THE IMPATIENT ONE, EH...

...

HEH HEH...

READ THIS WAY

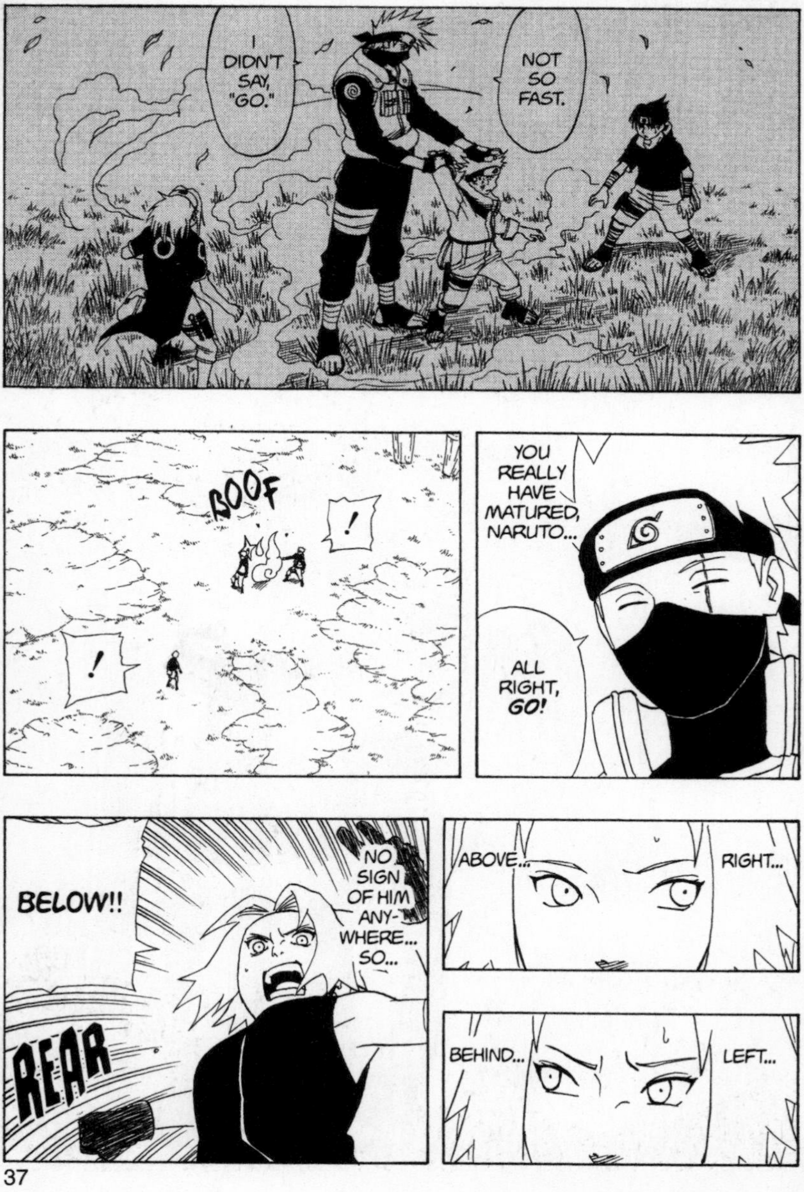
NOT SO FAST.
I DIDN'T SAY, "GO."
YOU REALLY HAVE MATURED, NARUTO...
ALL RIGHT, GO!
BOOF
!
!
RIGHT...
ABOVE...
LEFT...
BEHIND...
NO SIGN OF HIM ANY-WHERE... SO...
BELOW!!
REAR

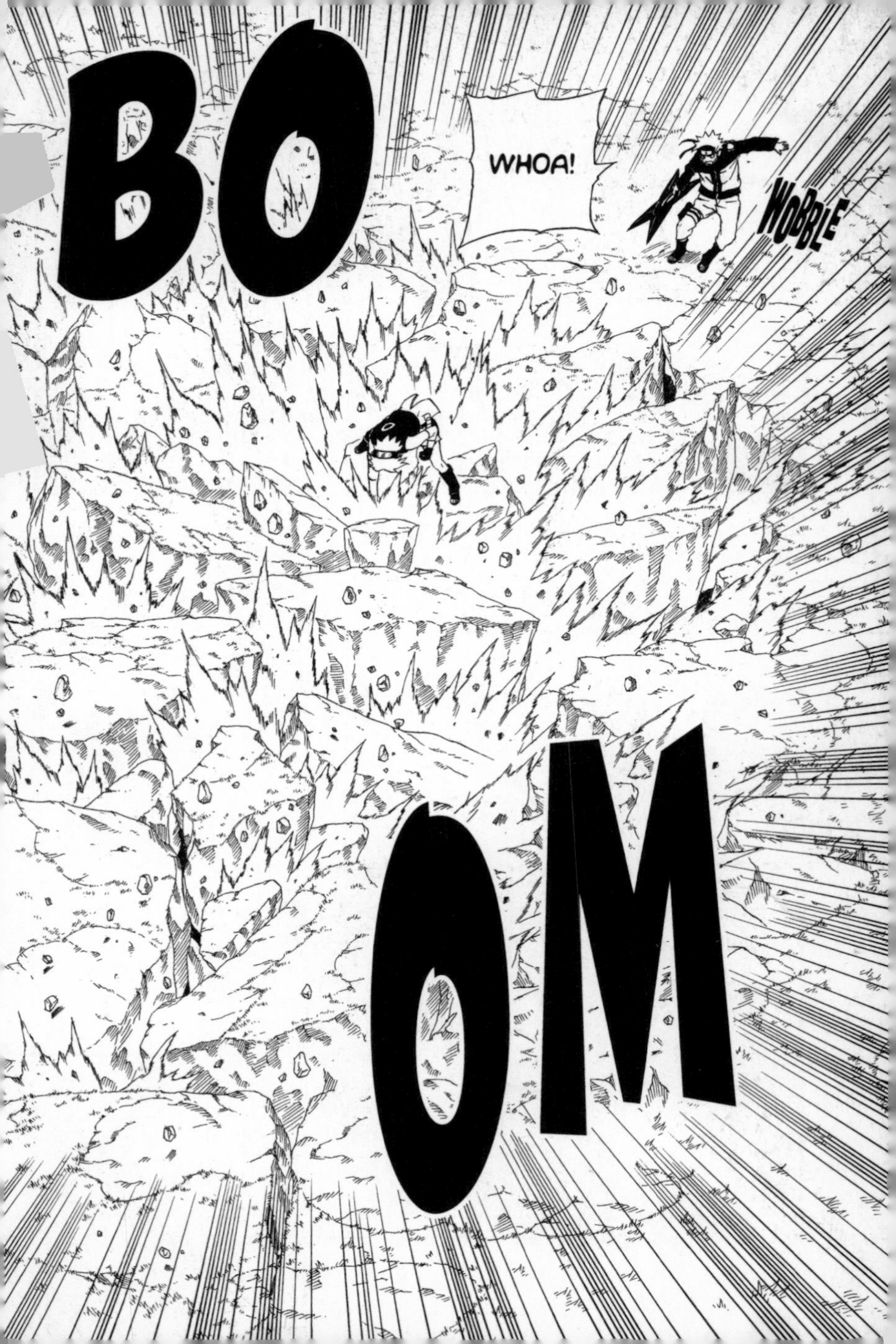
WHOA!
WOBBLE
BOOM

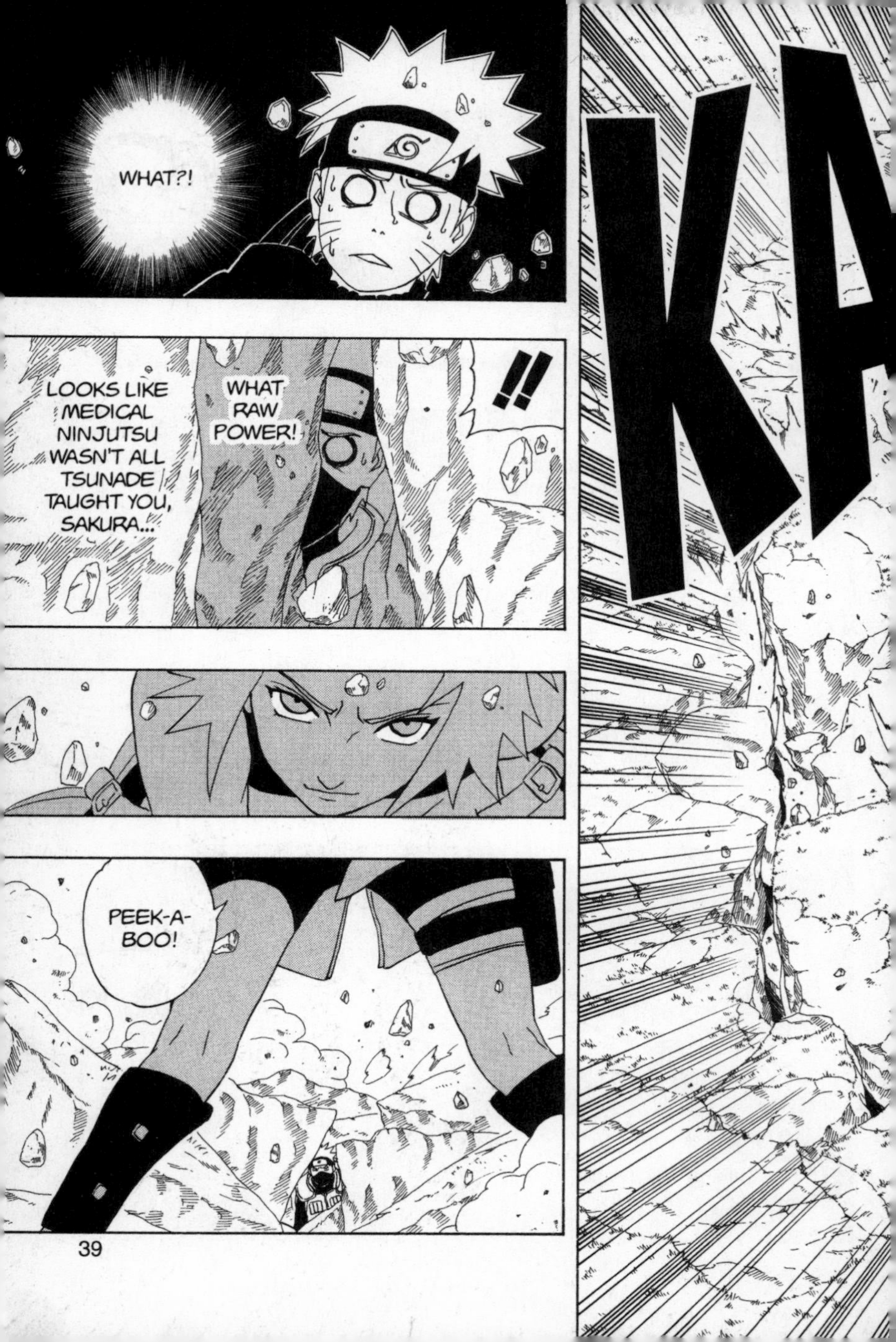
KA
WHAT?!
!!
WHAT RAW POWER!
LOOKS LIKE MEDICAL NINJUTSU WASN'T ALL TSUNADE TAUGHT YOU, SAKURA...
PEEK-A-BOO!

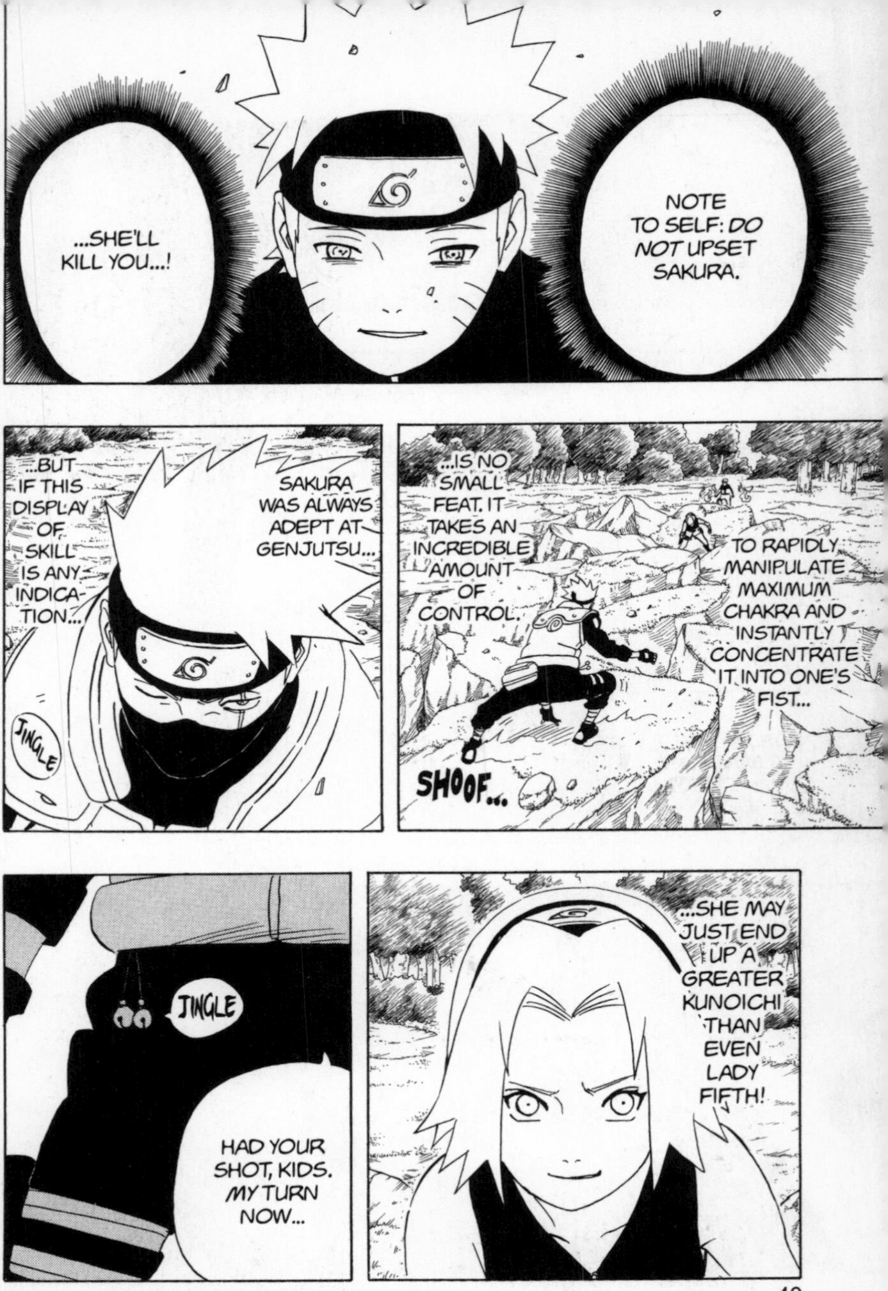
NOTE TO SELF: DO NOT UPSET SAKURA.
...SHE'LL KILL YOU...!
TO RAPIDLY MANIPULATE MAXIMUM CHAKRA AND INSTANTLY CONCENTRATE IT INTO ONE'S FIST...
...IS NO SMALL FEAT. IT TAKES AN INCREDIBLE AMOUNT OF CONTROL.
SHOOF...
SAKURA WAS ALWAYS ADEPT AT GENJUTSU...
...BUT IF THIS DISPLAY OF SKILL IS ANY INDICATION...
JINGLE
...SHE MAY JUST END UP A GREATER KUNOICHI THAN EVEN LADY FIFTH!
JINGLE
HAD YOUR SHOT, KIDS. MY TURN NOW...

READ THIS WAY

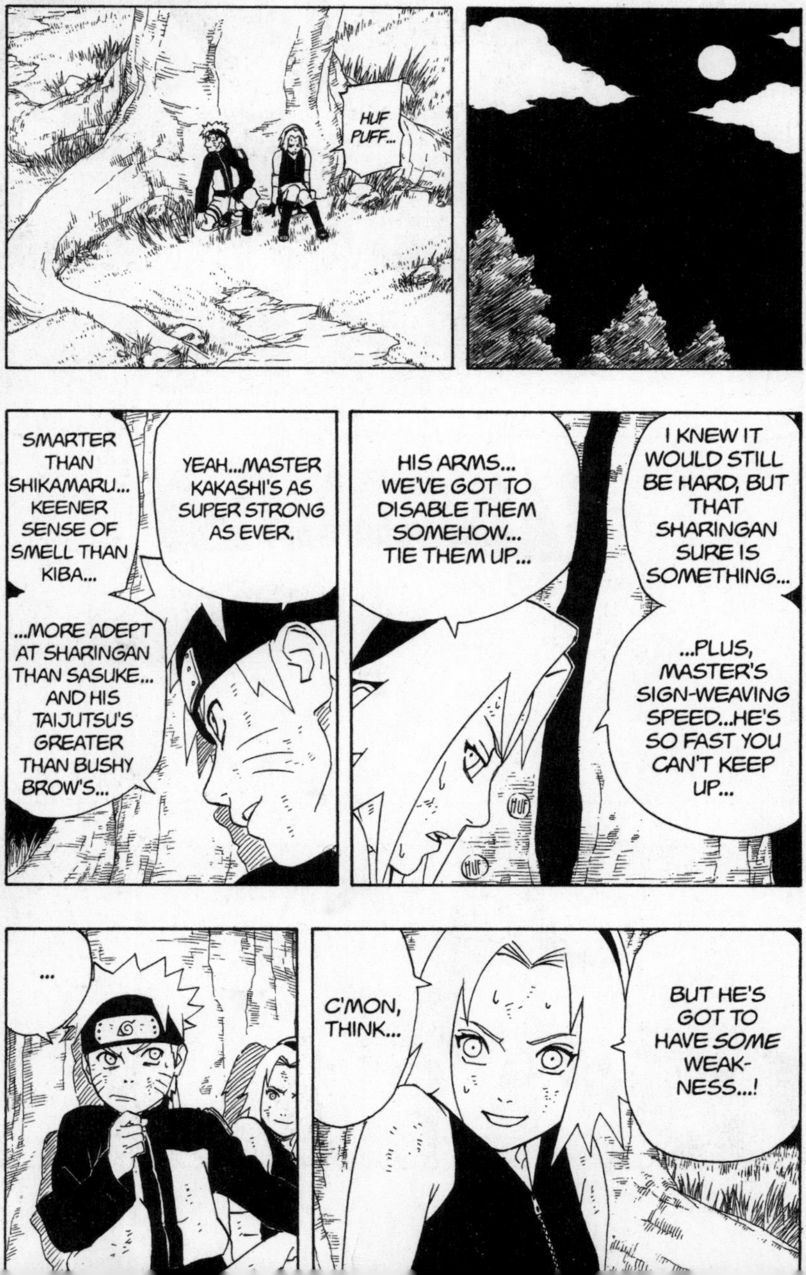
HUF PUFF...
I KNEW IT WOULD STILL BE HARD, BUT THAT SHARINGAN SURE IS SOMETHING...
...PLUS, MASTER'S SIGN-WEAVING SPEED...HE'S SO FAST YOU CAN'T KEEP UP...
HIS ARMS... WE'VE GOT TO DISABLE THEM SOMEHOW... TIE THEM UP...
HUF
HUF
YEAH...MASTER KAKASHI'S AS SUPER STRONG AS EVER.
SMARTER THAN SHIKAMARU... KEENER SENSE OF SMELL THAN KIBA...
...MORE ADEPT AT SHARINGAN THAN SASUKE... AND HIS TAIJUTSU'S GREATER THAN BUSHY BROW'S...
BUT HE'S GOT TO HAVE *SOME* WEAK-NESS...!
C'MON, THINK...
...

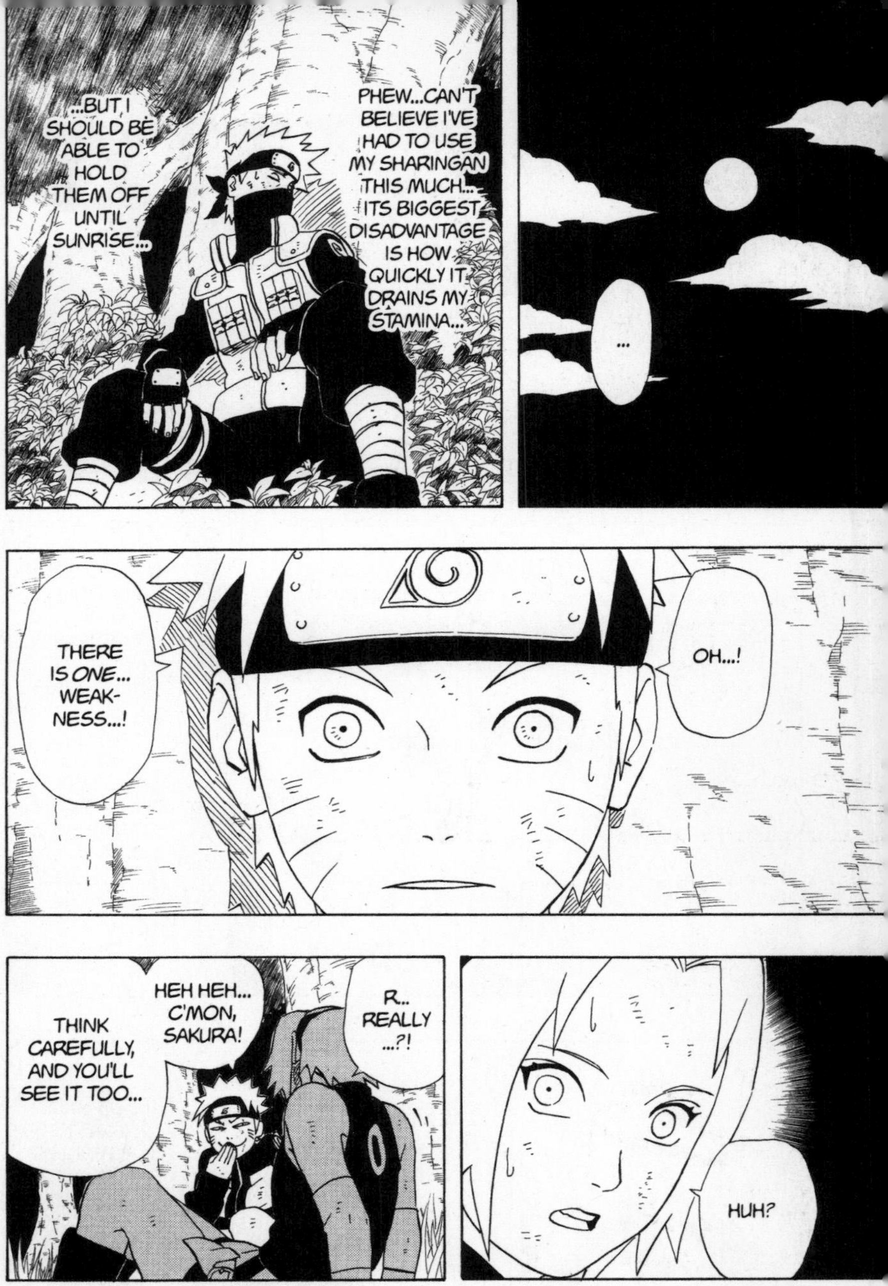
...
PHEW...CAN'T BELIEVE I'VE HAD TO USE MY SHARINGAN THIS MUCH... ITS BIGGEST DISADVANTAGE IS HOW QUICKLY IT DRAINS MY STAMINA...
...BUT I SHOULD BE ABLE TO HOLD THEM OFF UNTIL SUNRISE...
OH...!
THERE IS *ONE*... WEAKNESS...!
HUH?
R.. REALLY ...?!
HEH HEH... C'MON, SAKURA!
THINK CAREFULLY, AND YOU'LL SEE IT TOO...

READ THIS WAY

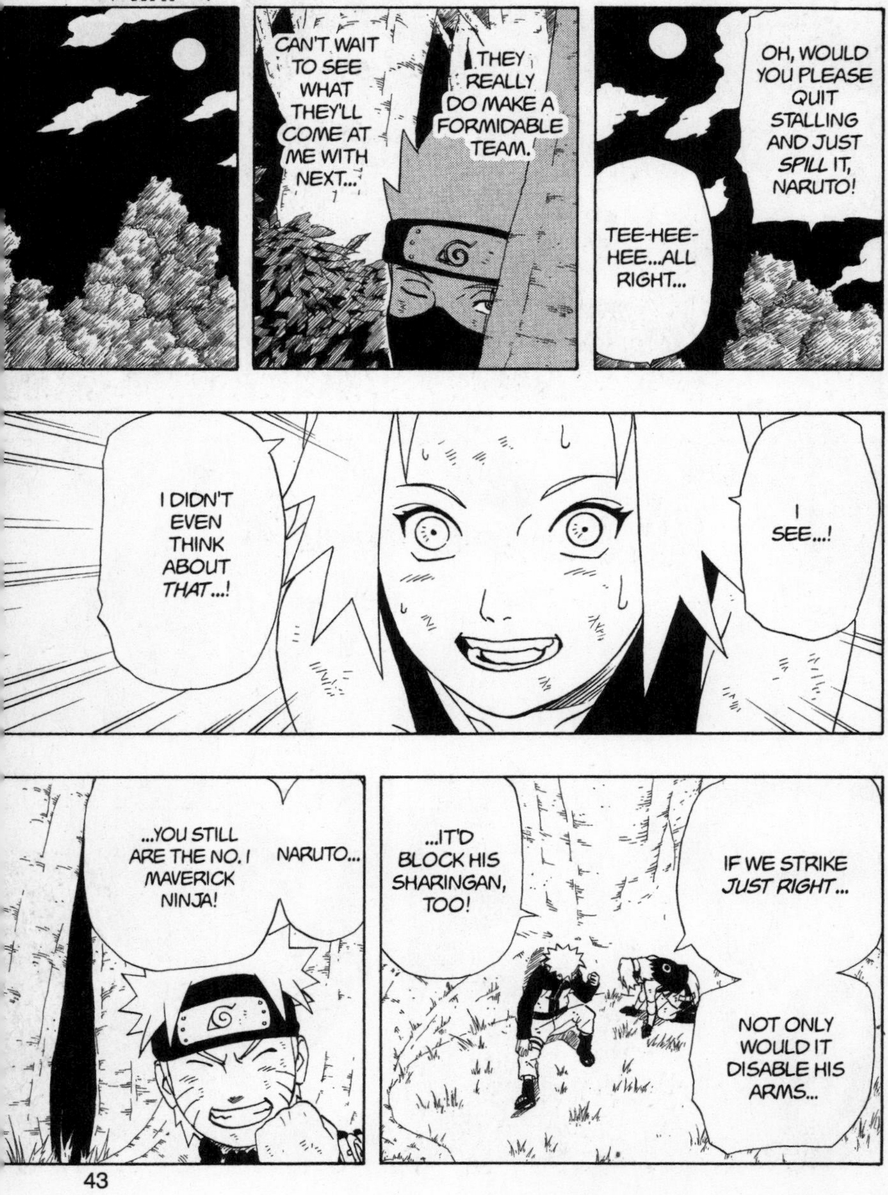

OH, WOULD YOU PLEASE QUIT STALLING AND JUST *SPILL* IT, NARUTO!
TEE-HEE-HEE...ALL RIGHT...
THEY REALLY DO MAKE A FORMIDABLE TEAM.
CAN'T WAIT TO SEE WHAT THEY'LL COME AT ME WITH NEXT...
I SEE...!
I DIDN'T EVEN THINK ABOUT *THAT*...!
IF WE STRIKE *JUST RIGHT*...
NOT ONLY WOULD IT DISABLE HIS ARMS...
...IT'D BLOCK HIS SHARINGAN, TOO!
NARUTO...
...YOU STILL ARE THE NO. 1 MAVERICK NINJA!

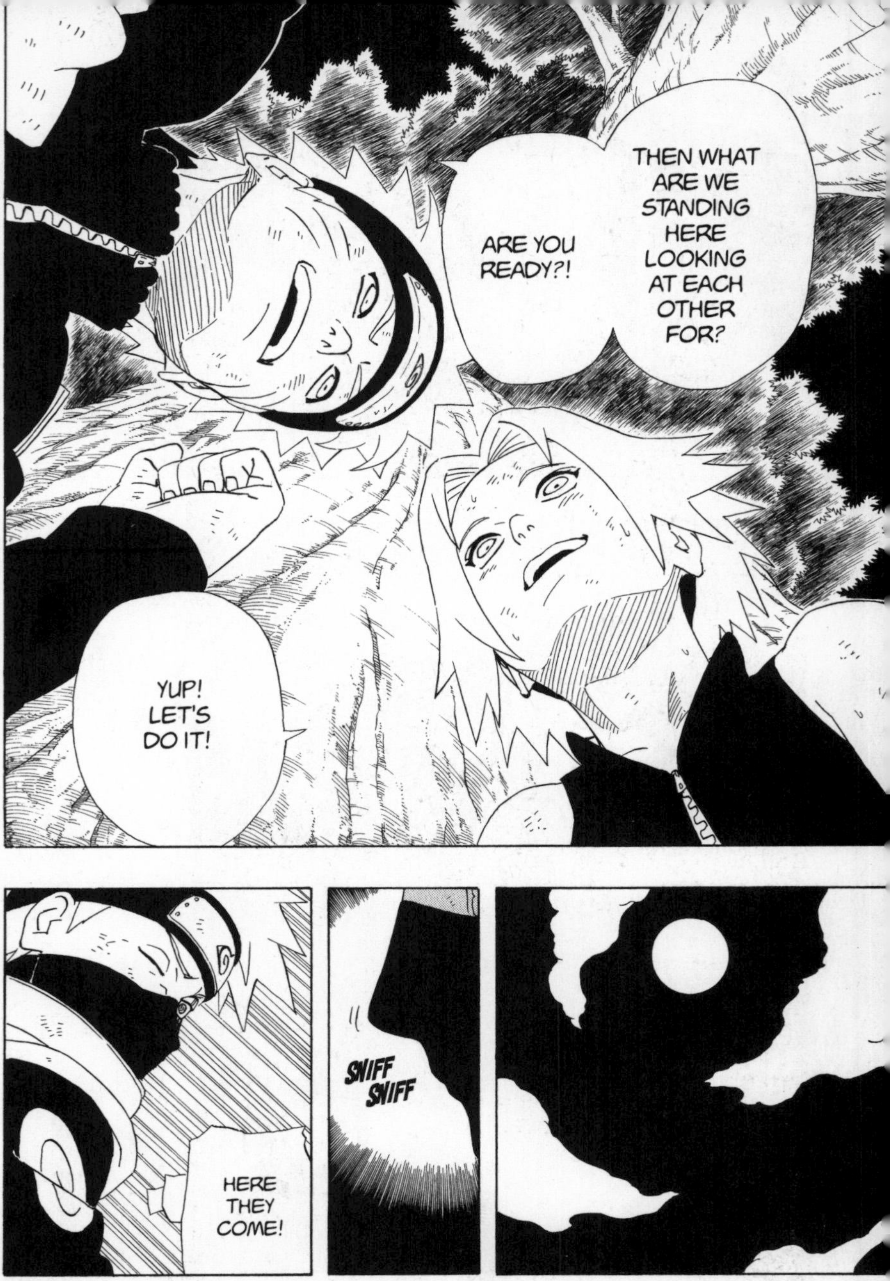
THEN WHAT ARE WE STANDING HERE LOOKING AT EACH OTHER FOR?
ARE YOU READY?!
YUP! LET'S DO IT!
SNIFF SNIFF
HERE THEY COME!

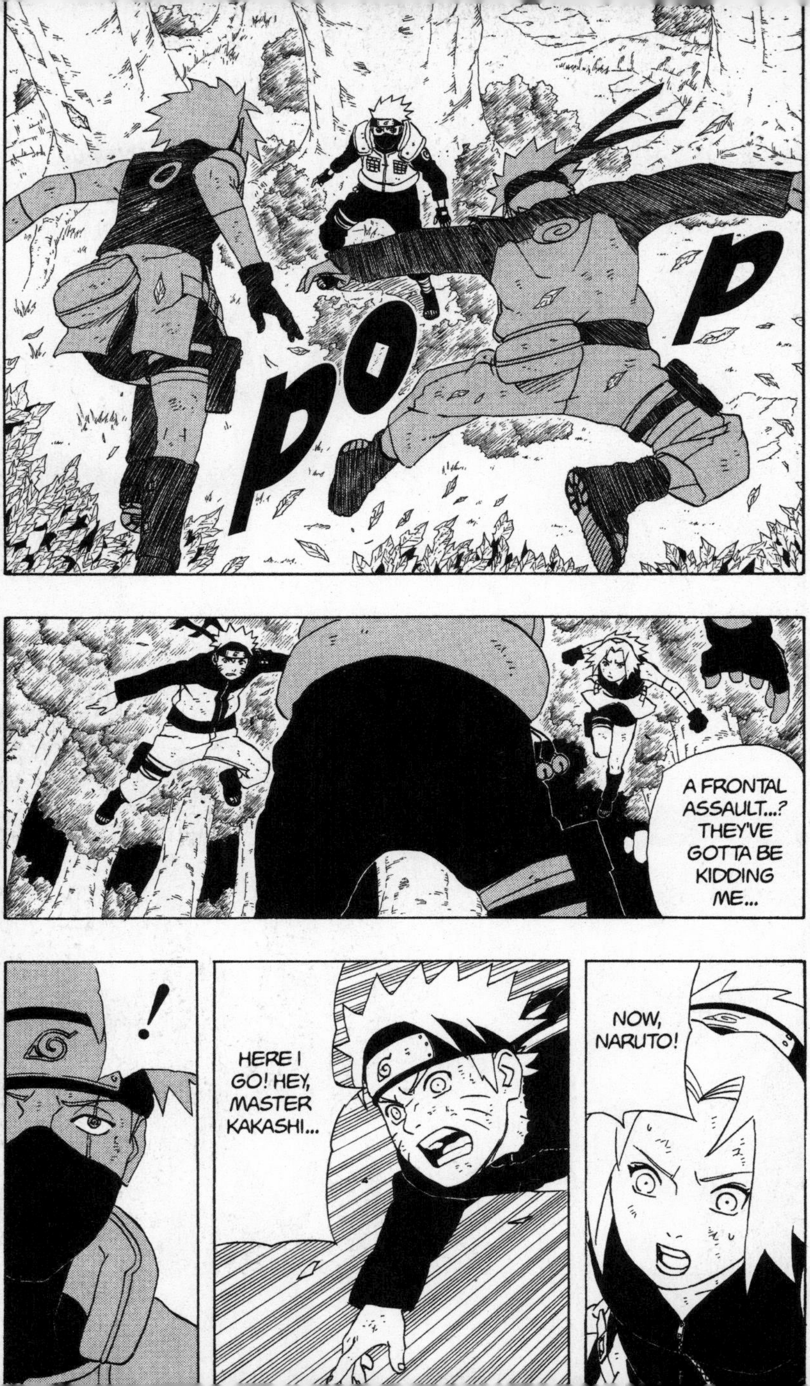
POP
A FRONTAL ASSAULT...? THEY'VE GOTTA BE KIDDING ME...
NOW, NARUTO!
HERE I GO! HEY, MASTER KAKASHI...
!

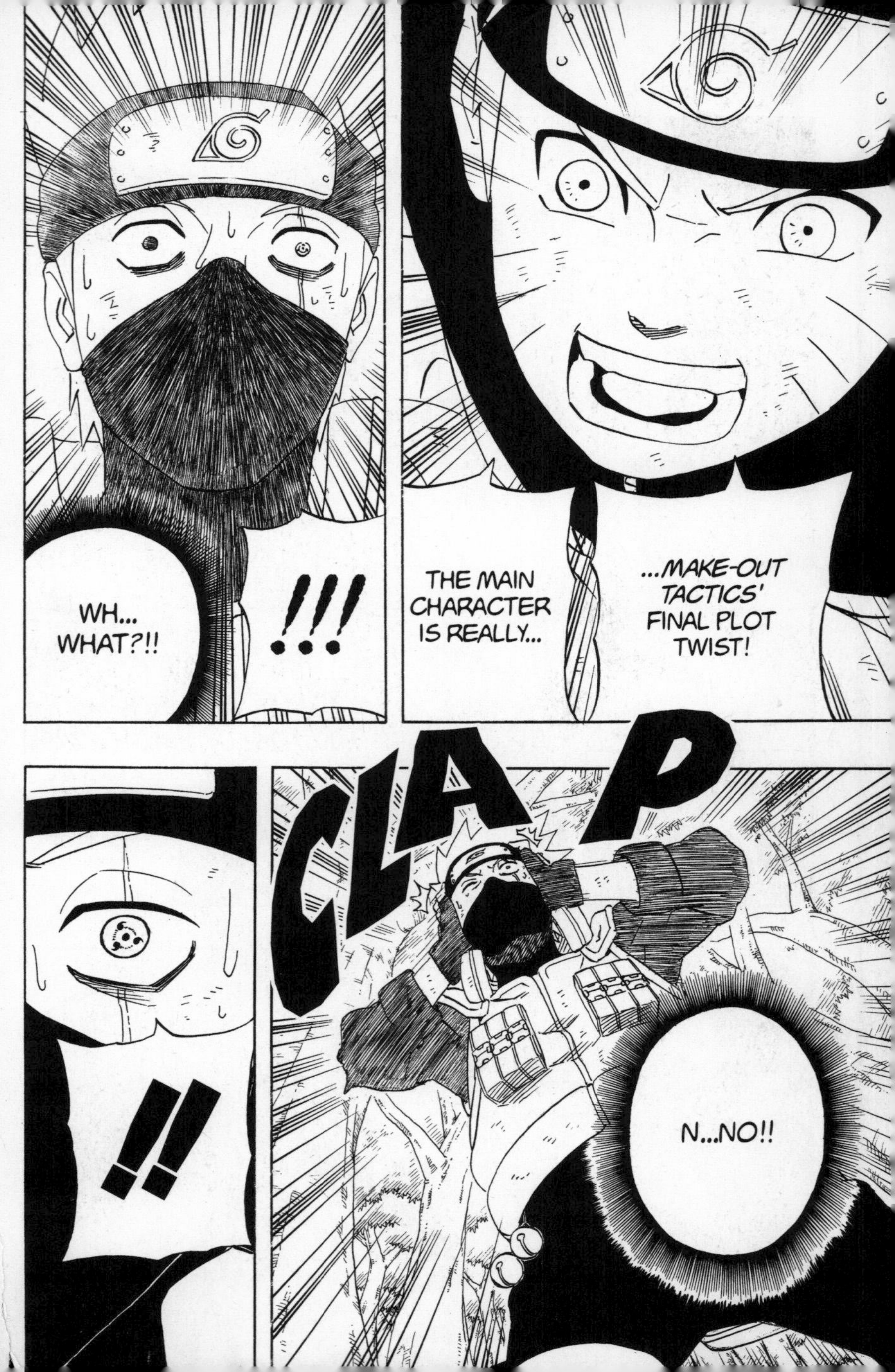
...MAKE-OUT TACTICS' FINAL PLOT TWIST!
THE MAIN CHARACTER IS REALLY...
!!!
WH... WHAT?!!
CLAP
N...NO!!
!!

READ THIS WAY

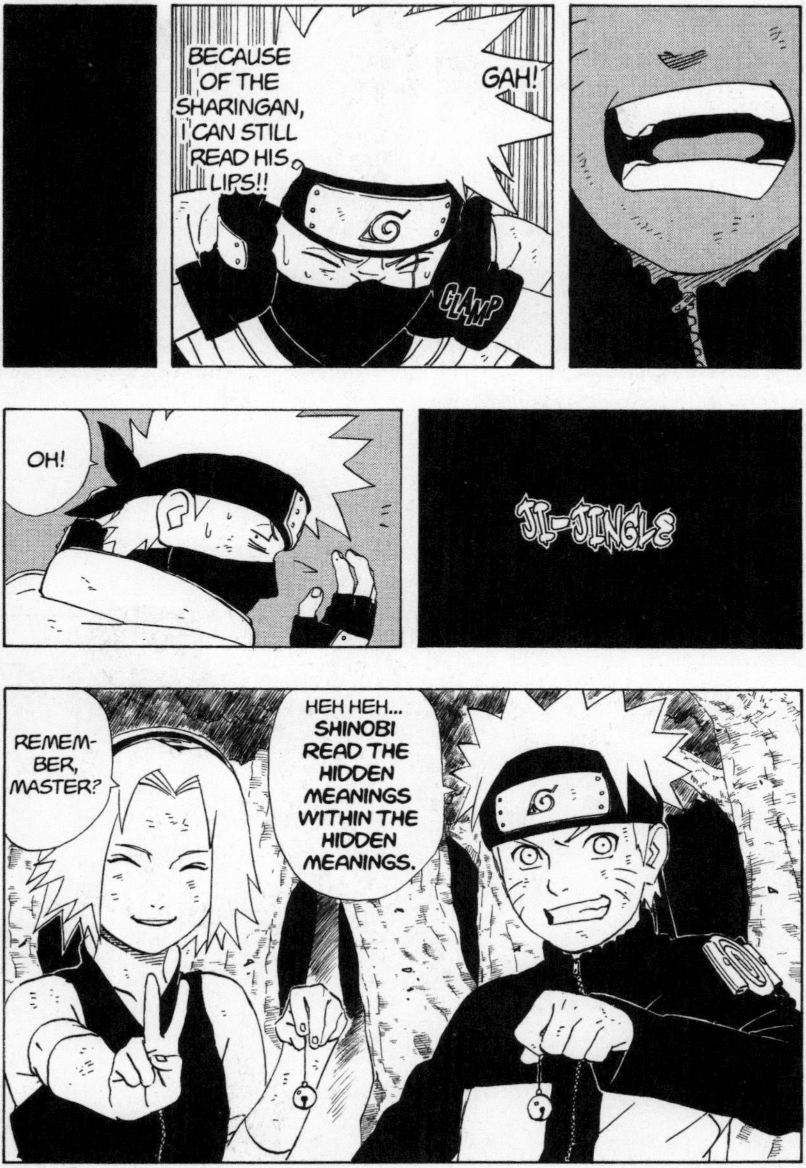
BECAUSE OF THE SHARINGAN, I CAN STILL READ HIS LIPS!!
GAH!
CLAMP
JI-JINGLE
OH!
HEH HEH... SHINOBI READ THE HIDDEN MEANINGS WITHIN THE HIDDEN MEANINGS.
REMEM-BER, MASTER?

THE WORLD OF KISHIMOTO MASASHI
MY PERSONAL HISTORY, VIDEO GAMES PART I

SOMETIMES, IF I DRAW TOO LONG, I START THINKING, "HAVE I EVER SPENT TIME IN MY LIFE DOING ANYTHING OTHER THAN DRAWING PICTURES?"

AND THEN IT COMES TO ME. YES, THERE IS ONE OTHER THING.

WHICH IS...VIDEO GAMES.

EVER SINCE I WAS A KID, I LOVED PLAYING VIDEO GAMES ALMOST AS MUCH AS I LOVED DRAWING. MY FRIENDS ALL DID, TOO... AND EVEN MY FOLKS, SO I DON'T THINK OF MYSELF AS AN EXCEPTION... BUT IN ANY CASE, I LOVED VIDEO GAMES AND PLAYED THEM A LOT. OF COURSE, THE STANDARD GAME PLATFORM AT THE TIME WAS THE FAMILY COMPUTER, A.K.A. THE FAMICOM.

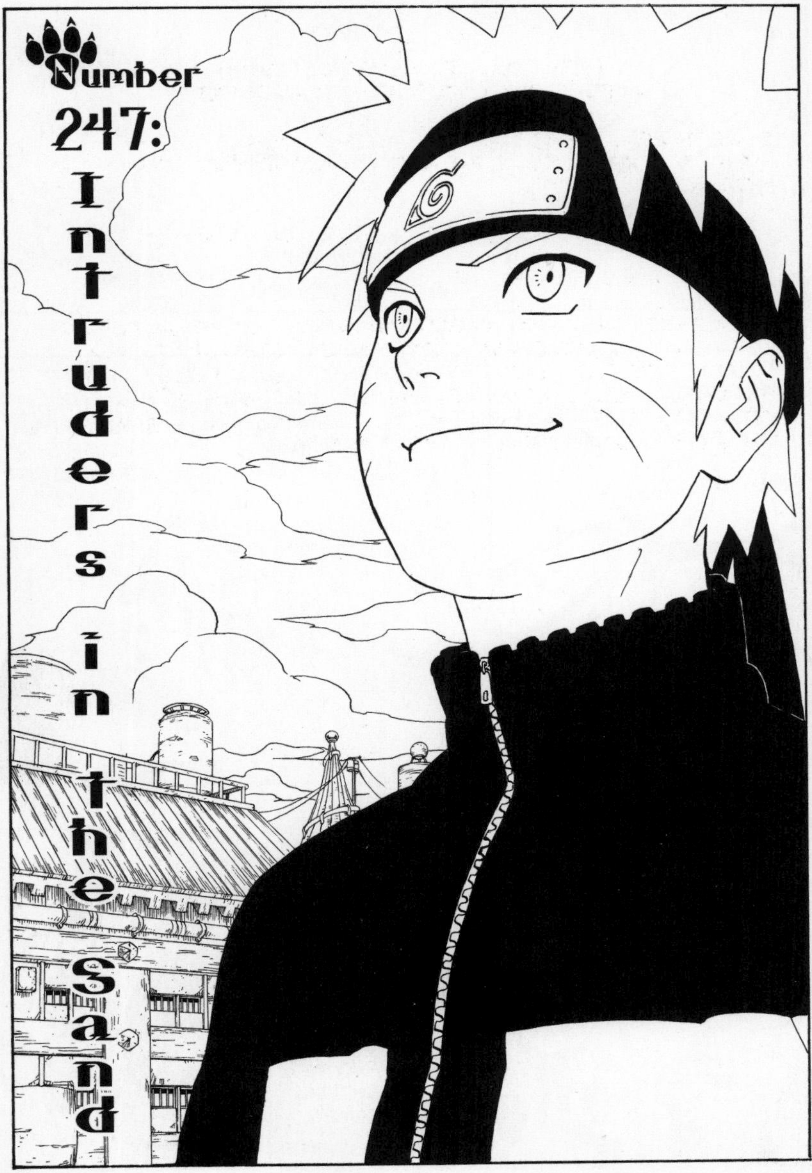
Number 247: Intruders in the Sand

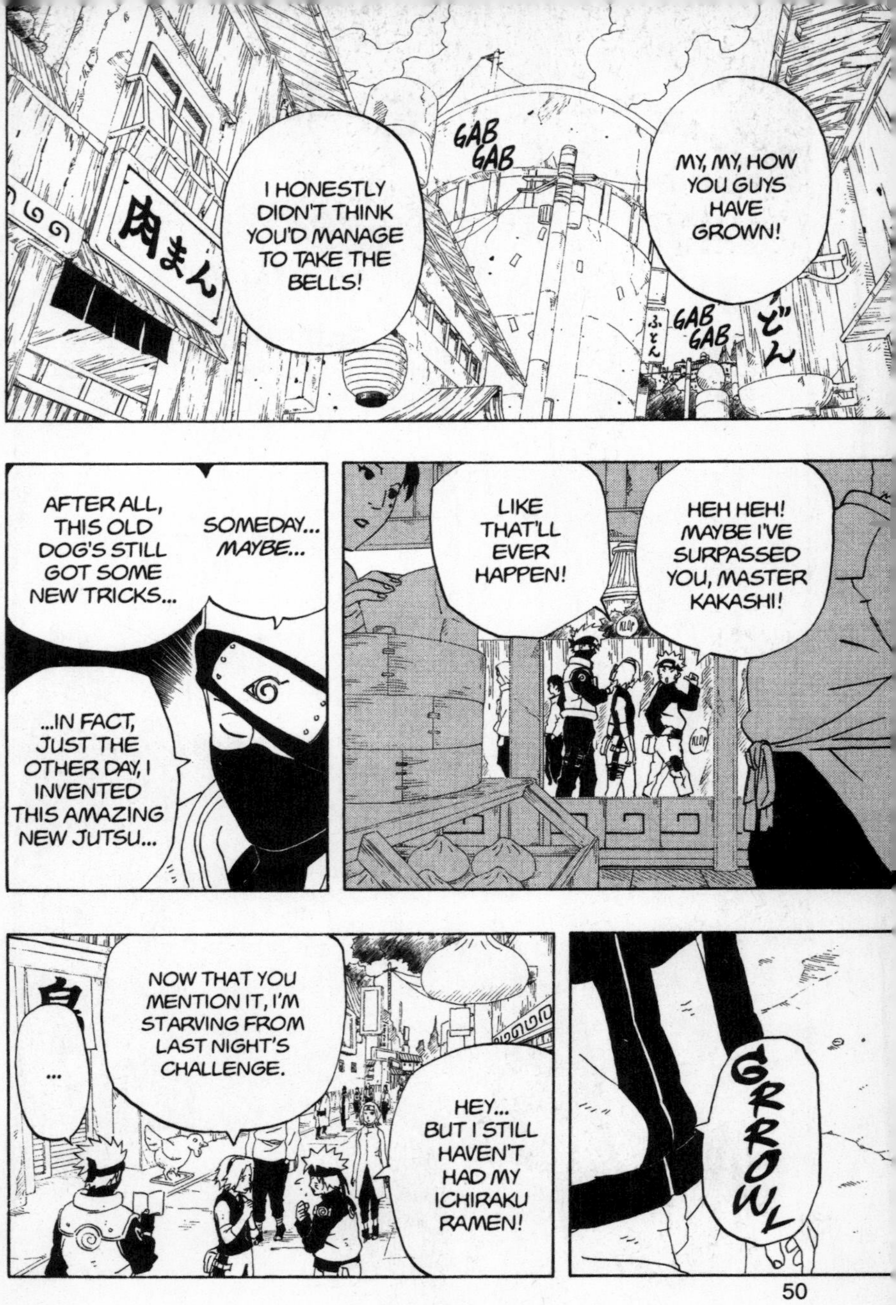
MY, MY, HOW YOU GUYS HAVE GROWN!
GAB GAB
GAB GAB
I HONESTLY DIDN'T THINK YOU'D MANAGE TO TAKE THE BELLS!
どん
ふとん
肉まん
HEH HEH! MAYBE I'VE SURPASSED YOU, MASTER KAKASHI!
LIKE THAT'LL EVER HAPPEN!
KLOP
KLOP
SOMEDAY... MAYBE...
AFTER ALL, THIS OLD DOG'S STILL GOT SOME NEW TRICKS...
...IN FACT, JUST THE OTHER DAY, I INVENTED THIS AMAZING NEW JUTSU...
GRROWL
HEY... BUT I STILL HAVEN'T HAD MY ICHIRAKU RAMEN!
NOW THAT YOU MENTION IT, I'M STARVING FROM LAST NIGHT'S CHALLENGE.
...

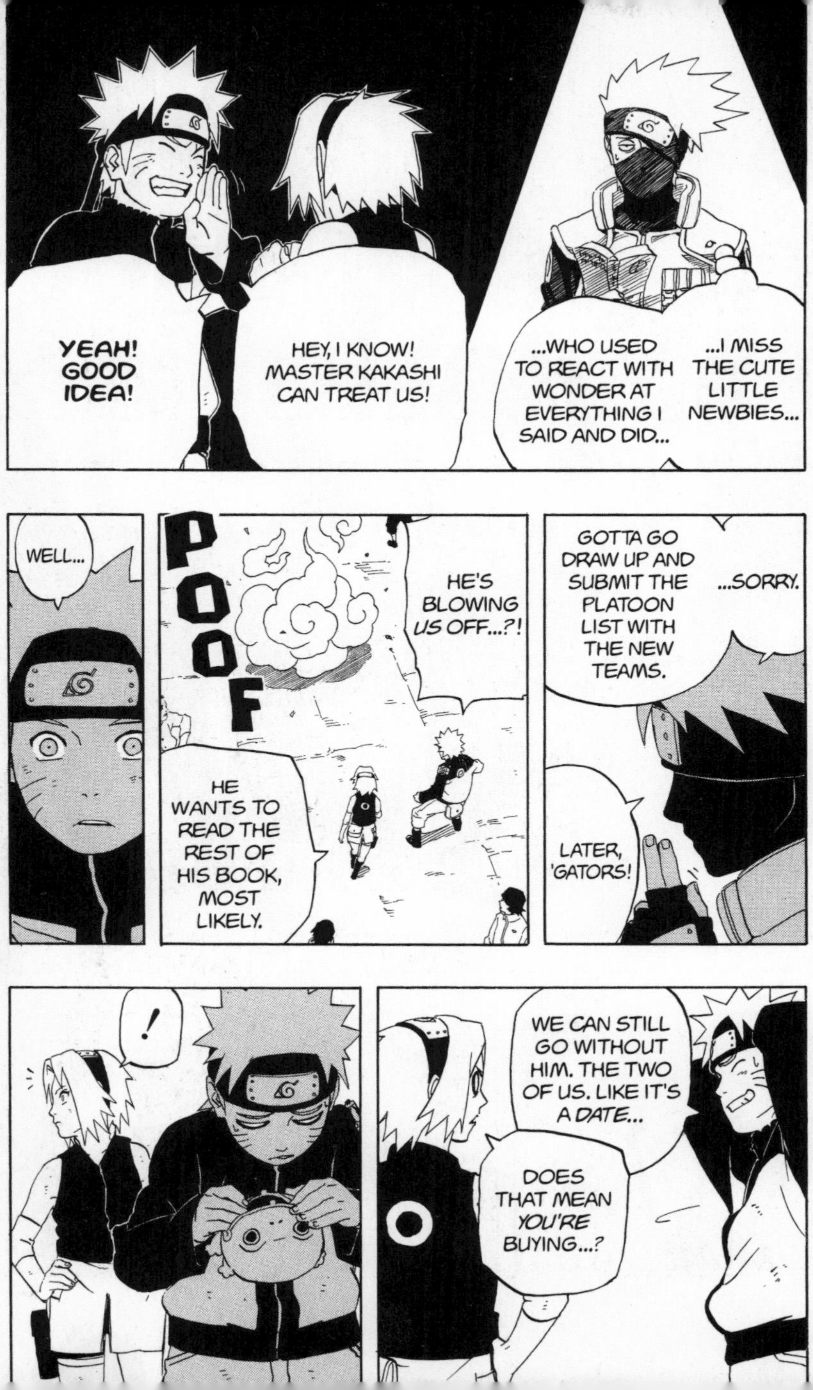
...I MISS THE CUTE LITTLE NEWBIES...
...WHO USED TO REACT WITH WONDER AT EVERYTHING I SAID AND DID...
HEY, I KNOW! MASTER KAKASHI CAN TREAT US!
YEAH! GOOD IDEA!
...SORRY.
GOTTA GO DRAW UP AND SUBMIT THE PLATOON LIST WITH THE NEW TEAMS.
LATER, 'GATORS!
POOF
HE'S BLOWING US OFF...?!
HE WANTS TO READ THE REST OF HIS BOOK, MOST LIKELY.
WELL...
WE CAN STILL GO WITHOUT HIM. THE TWO OF US. LIKE IT'S A DATE...
DOES THAT MEAN YOU'RE BUYING...?
!

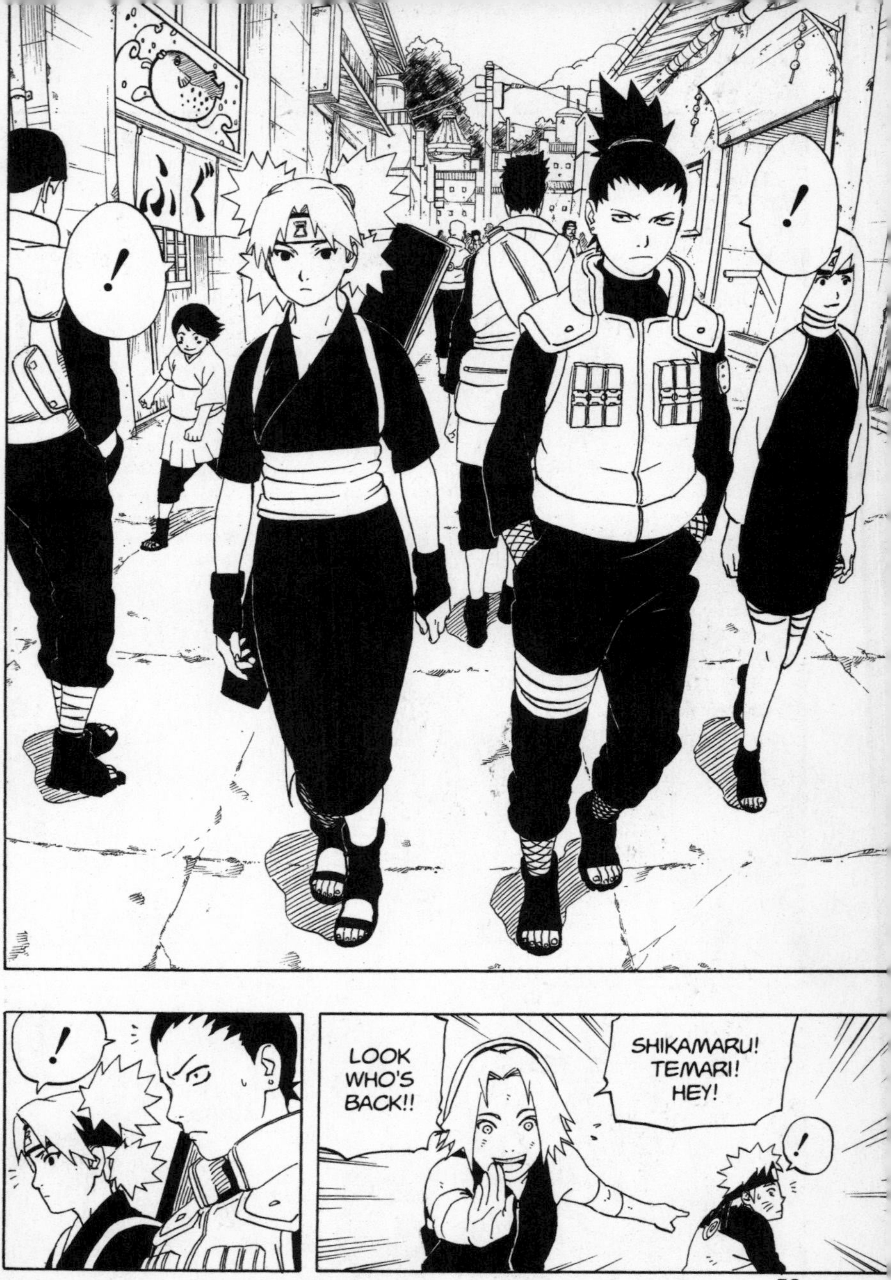
!
ふぐ
!
SHIKAMARU! TEMARI! HEY!
LOOK WHO'S BACK!!
!
!

READ THIS WAY

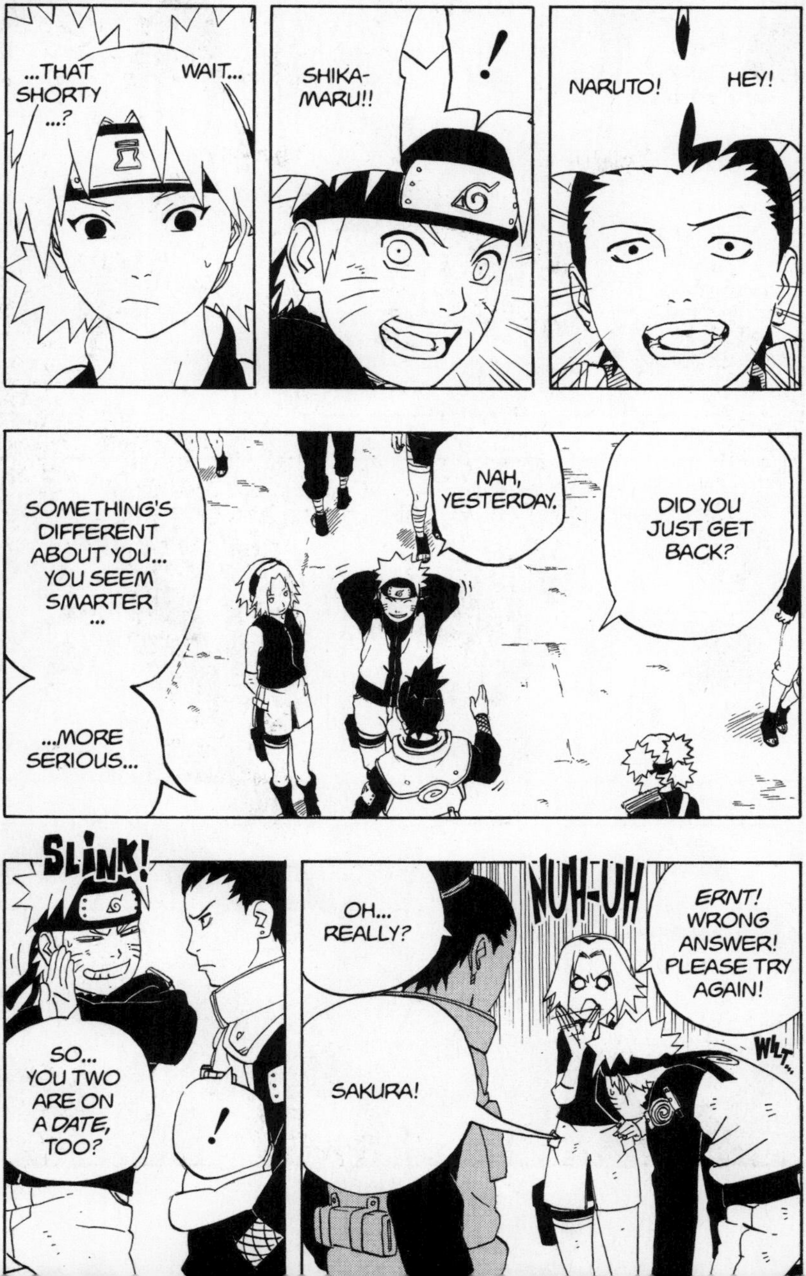
HEY!
NARUTO!
!
SHIKA-MARU!!
WAIT...
...THAT SHORTY ...?
DID YOU JUST GET BACK?
NAH, YESTERDAY.
SOMETHING'S DIFFERENT ABOUT YOU... YOU SEEM SMARTER ...
...MORE SERIOUS...
ERNT! WRONG ANSWER! PLEASE TRY AGAIN!
NUH-UH
OH... REALLY?
WLT...
SAKURA!
SLINK!
SO... YOU TWO ARE ON A DATE, TOO?
!

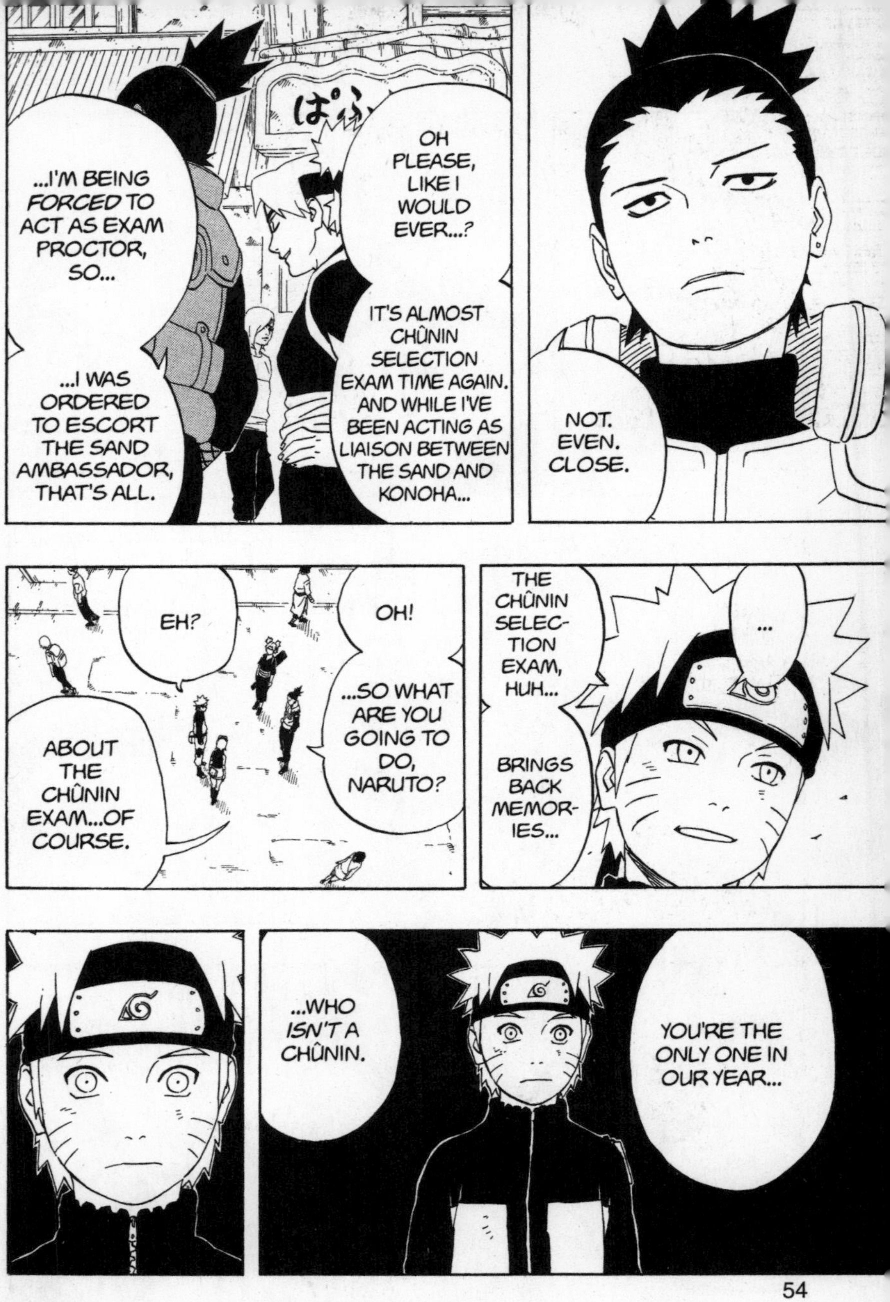
NOT. EVEN. CLOSE.
OH PLEASE, LIKE I WOULD EVER...?
IT'S ALMOST CHÛNIN SELECTION EXAM TIME AGAIN. AND WHILE I'VE BEEN ACTING AS LIAISON BETWEEN THE SAND AND KONOHA...
...I'M BEING FORCED TO ACT AS EXAM PROCTOR, SO...
...I WAS ORDERED TO ESCORT THE SAND AMBASSADOR, THAT'S ALL.
...
THE CHÛNIN SELECTION EXAM, HUH...
BRINGS BACK MEMORIES...
OH!
...SO WHAT ARE YOU GOING TO DO, NARUTO?
EH?
ABOUT THE CHÛNIN EXAM...OF COURSE.
YOU'RE THE ONLY ONE IN OUR YEAR...
...WHO ISN'T A CHÛNIN.

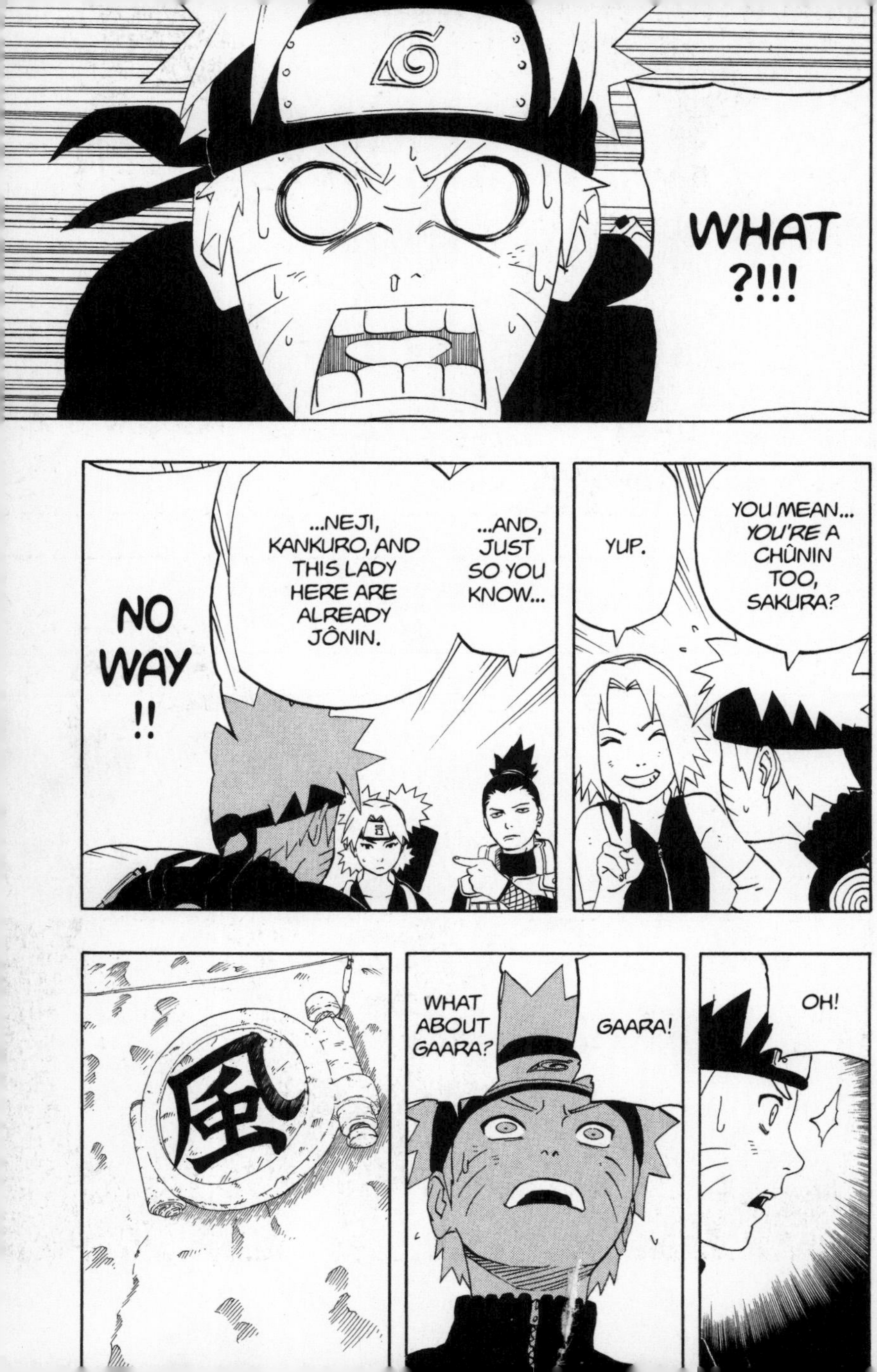
WHAT ?!!!
YOU MEAN... YOU'RE A CHÛNIN TOO, SAKURA?
YUP.
...AND, JUST SO YOU KNOW...
...NEJI, KANKURO, AND THIS LADY HERE ARE ALREADY JÔNIN.
NO WAY !!
OH!
GAARA!
WHAT ABOUT GAARA?

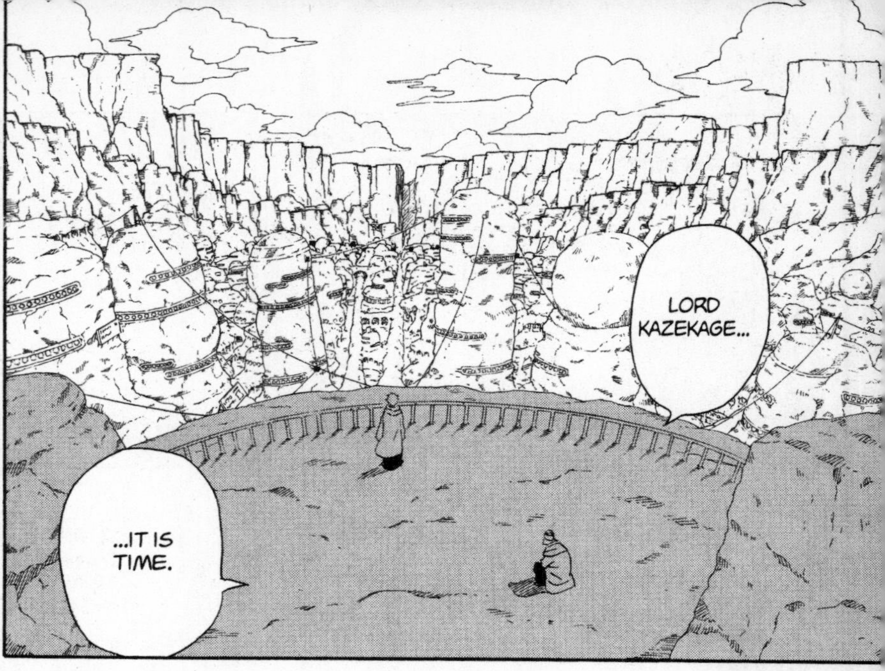
LORD KAZEKAGE...
...IT IS TIME.
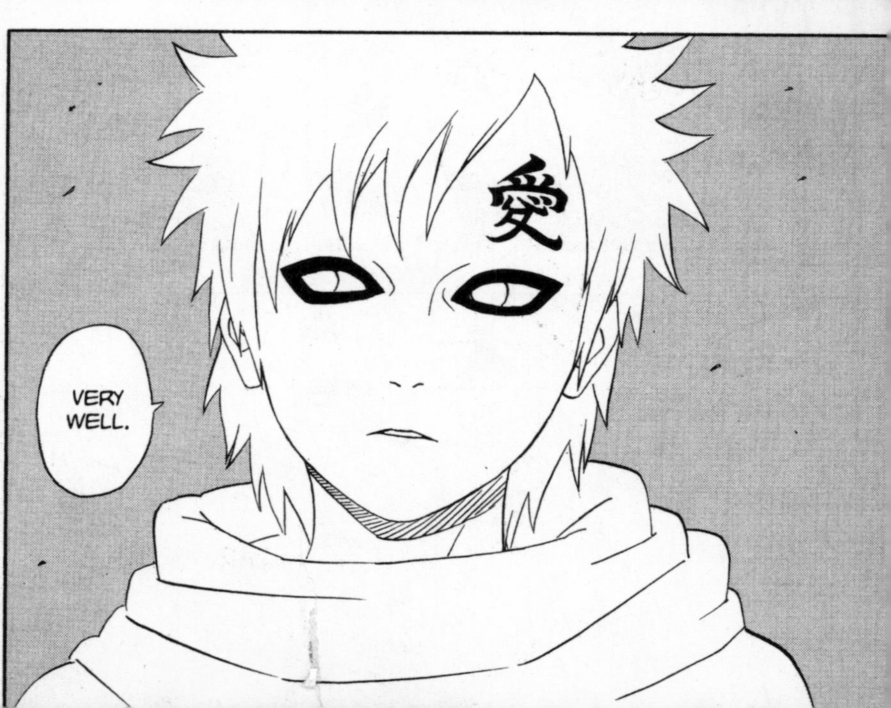
VERY WELL.

READ THIS WAY

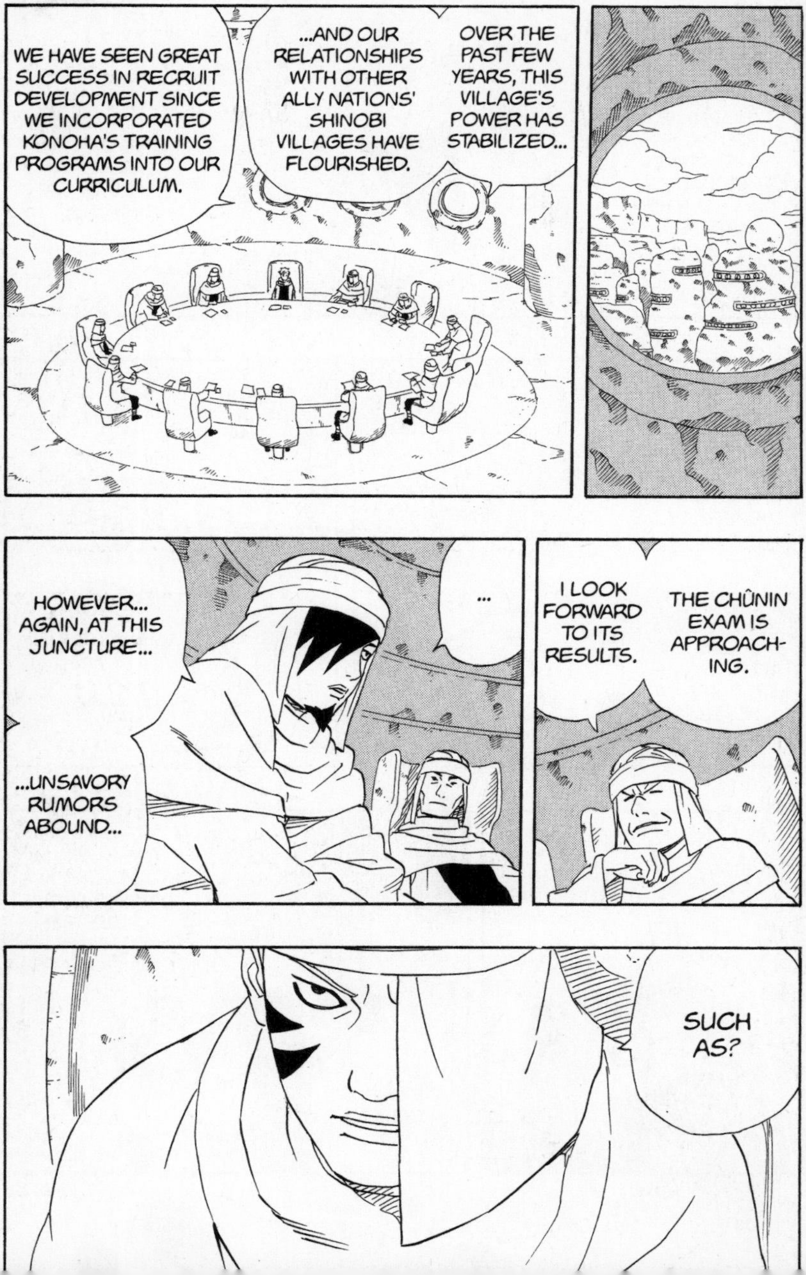
OVER THE PAST FEW YEARS, THIS VILLAGE'S POWER HAS STABILIZED...
...AND OUR RELATIONSHIPS WITH OTHER ALLY NATIONS' SHINOBI VILLAGES HAVE FLOURISHED.
WE HAVE SEEN GREAT SUCCESS IN RECRUIT DEVELOPMENT SINCE WE INCORPORATED KONOHA'S TRAINING PROGRAMS INTO OUR CURRICULUM.
THE CHÛNIN EXAM IS APPROACH-ING.
I LOOK FORWARD TO ITS RESULTS.
...
HOWEVER... AGAIN, AT THIS JUNCTURE...
...UNSAVORY RUMORS ABOUND...
SUCH AS?

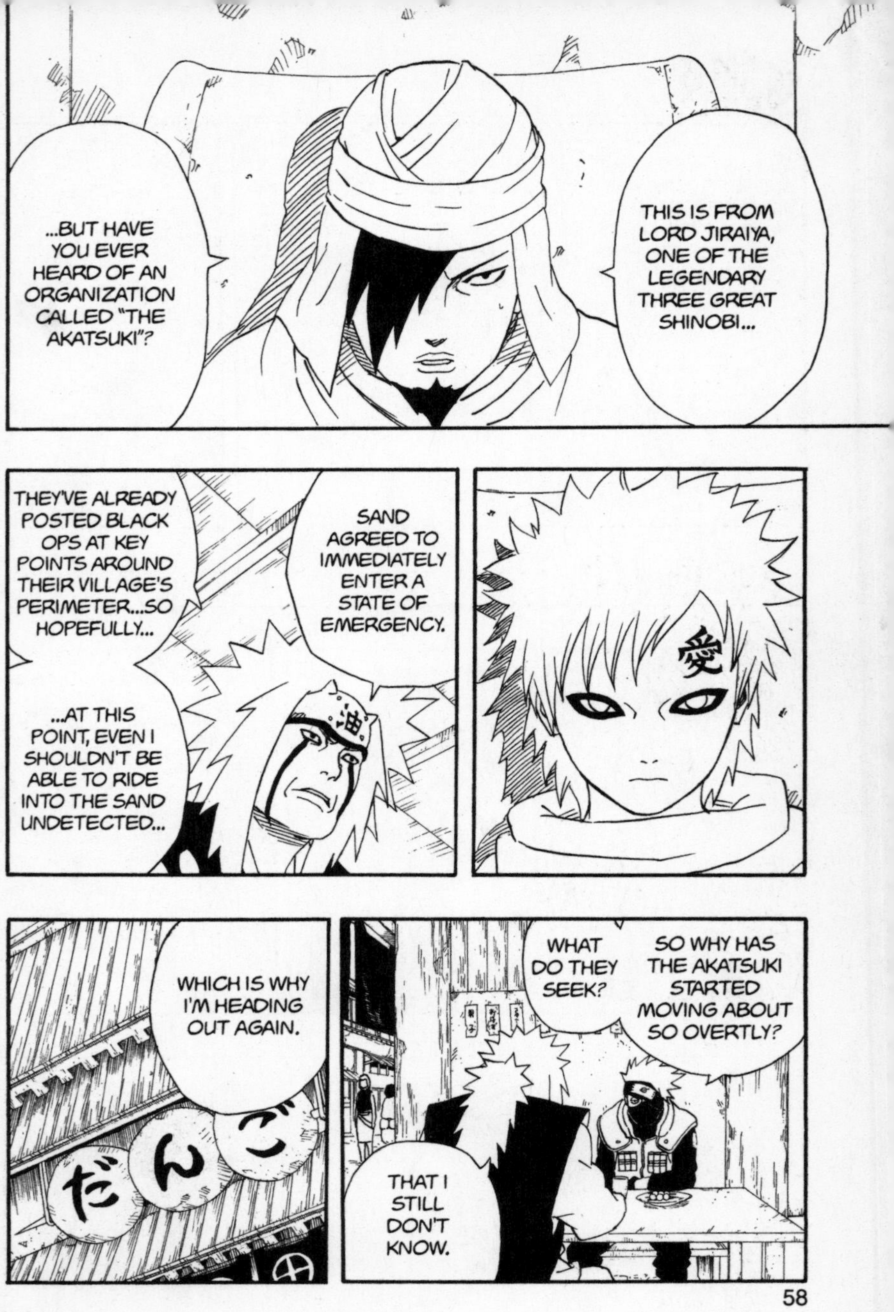
THIS IS FROM LORD JIRAIYA, ONE OF THE LEGENDARY THREE GREAT SHINOBI...
...BUT HAVE YOU EVER HEARD OF AN ORGANIZATION CALLED "THE AKATSUKI"?
SAND AGREED TO IMMEDIATELY ENTER A STATE OF EMERGENCY.
THEY'VE ALREADY POSTED BLACK OPS AT KEY POINTS AROUND THEIR VILLAGE'S PERIMETER...SO HOPEFULLY...
...AT THIS POINT, EVEN I SHOULDN'T BE ABLE TO RIDE INTO THE SAND UNDETECTED...
SO WHY HAS THE AKATSUKI STARTED MOVING ABOUT SO OVERTLY?
WHAT DO THEY SEEK?
THAT I STILL DON'T KNOW.
WHICH IS WHY I'M HEADING OUT AGAIN.
だんご

READ THIS WAY

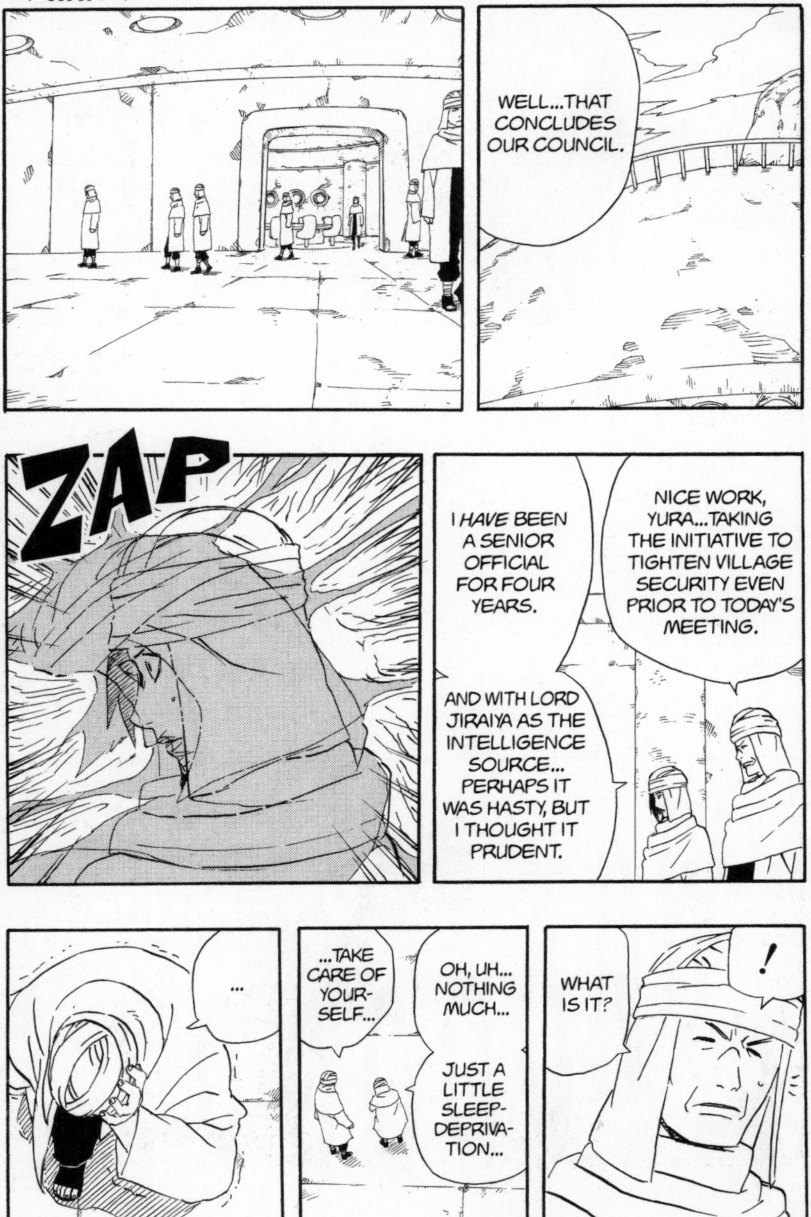

WELL...THAT CONCLUDES OUR COUNCIL.
NICE WORK, YURA...TAKING THE INITIATIVE TO TIGHTEN VILLAGE SECURITY EVEN PRIOR TO TODAY'S MEETING.
I *HAVE* BEEN A SENIOR OFFICIAL FOR FOUR YEARS.
AND WITH LORD JIRAIYA AS THE INTELLIGENCE SOURCE... PERHAPS IT WAS HASTY, BUT I THOUGHT IT PRUDENT.
ZAP
!
WHAT IS IT?
OH, UH... NOTHING MUCH...
JUST A LITTLE SLEEP-DEPRIVATION...
...TAKE CARE OF YOURSELF...
...

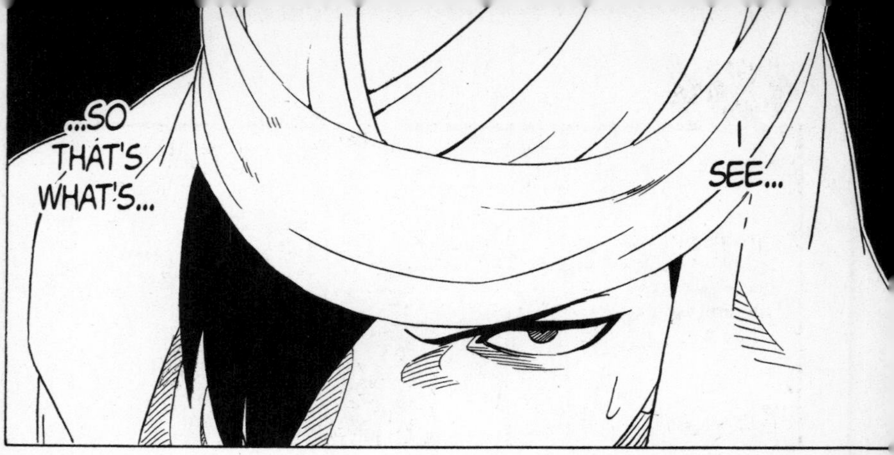
I SEE...
...SO THAT'S WHAT'S...

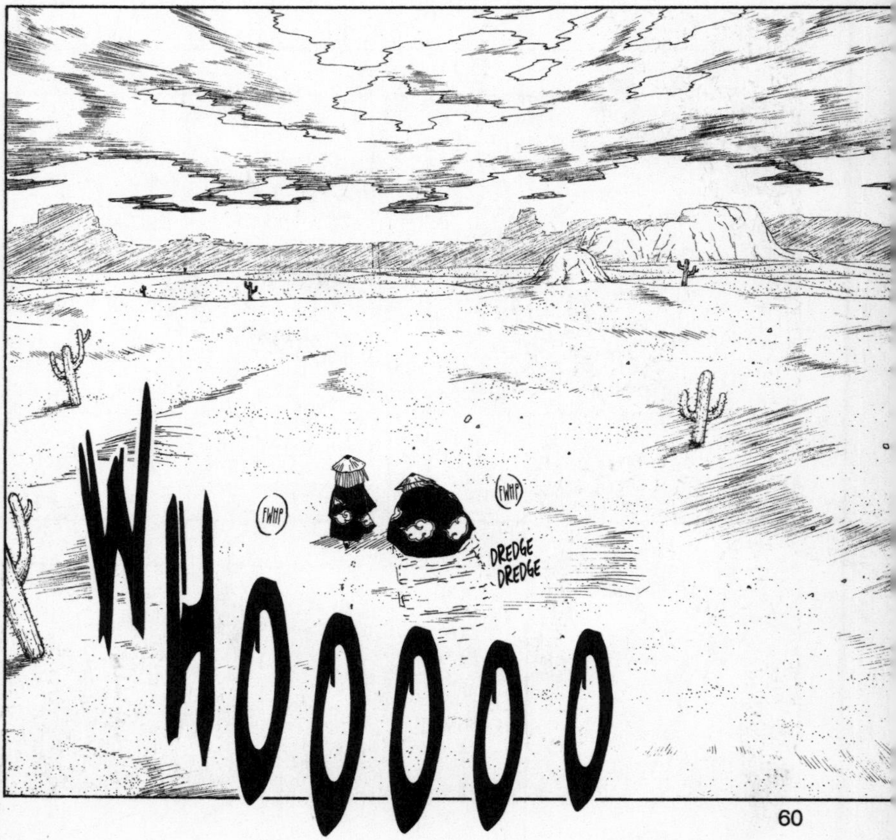
FWHP
DREDGE DREDGE
FWHP
WHOOOOO

READ THIS WAY

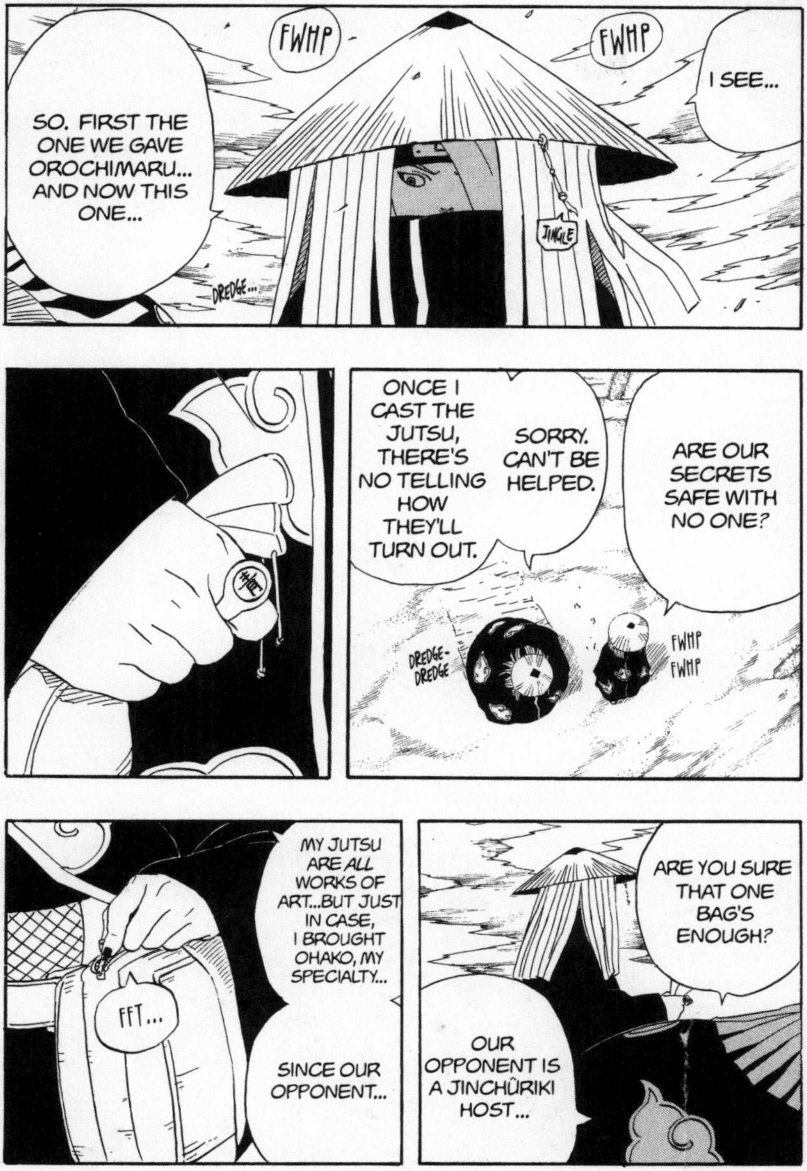

I SEE...
FWHP
FWHP
SO. FIRST THE ONE WE GAVE OROCHIMARU... AND NOW THIS ONE...
JINGLE
DREDGE...
ARE OUR SECRETS SAFE WITH NO ONE?
SORRY. CAN'T BE HELPED.
ONCE I CAST THE JUTSU, THERE'S NO TELLING HOW THEY'LL TURN OUT.
FWHP FWHP
DREDGE-DREDGE
ARE YOU SURE THAT ONE BAG'S ENOUGH?
OUR OPPONENT IS A JINCHŪRIKI HOST...
MY JUTSU ARE ALL WORKS OF ART...BUT JUST IN CASE, I BROUGHT OHAKO, MY SPECIALTY...
SINCE OUR OPPONENT...
FFT...

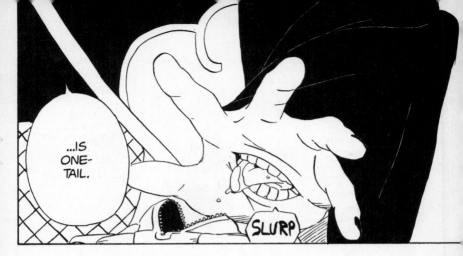

...IS ONE-TAIL.

SLURP

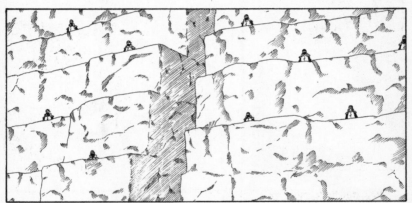

...THOSE ARE...!

BLACK COATS WITH RED CLOUD PATTERNS...

KRUNCH

DREDGE-DREDGE...

KRUNCH

WHAT THE...?

READ THIS WAY

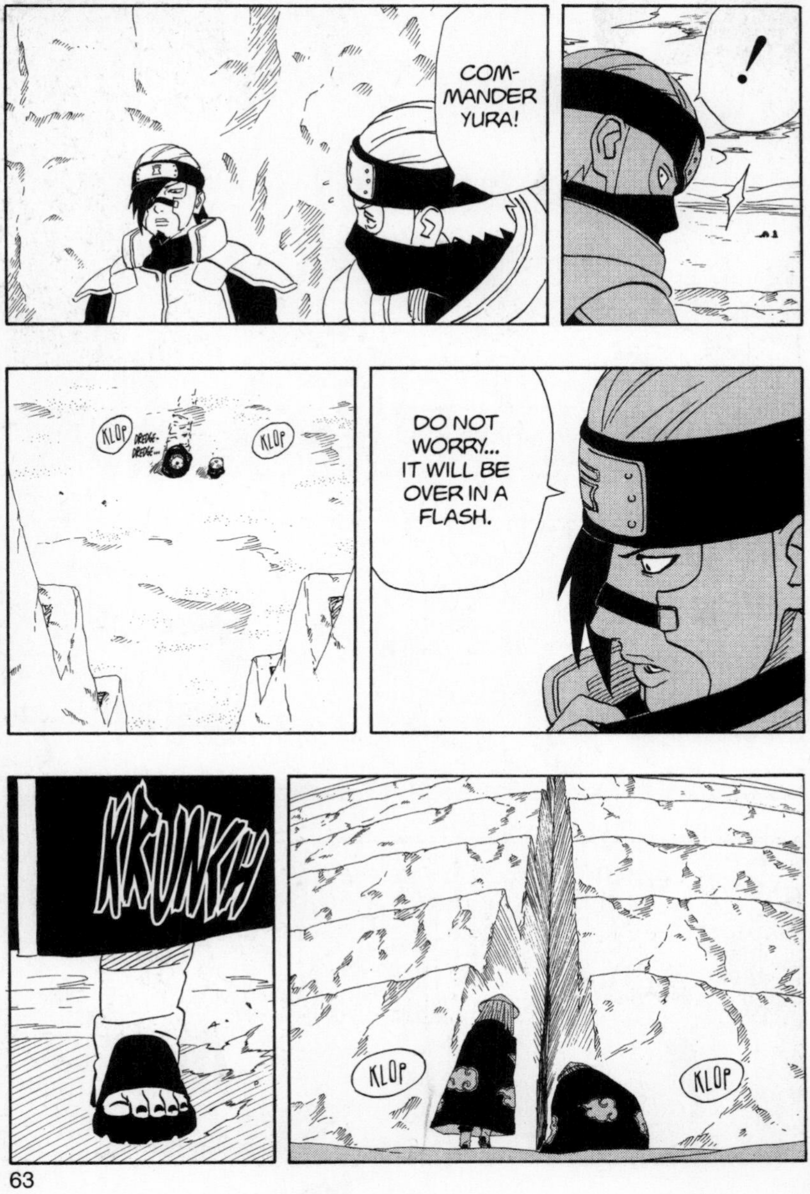

!
COM-MANDER YURA!
DO NOT WORRY... IT WILL BE OVER IN A FLASH.
KLOP
DREDGE-DREDGE...
KLOP
KLOP
KLOP
KRUNKCH

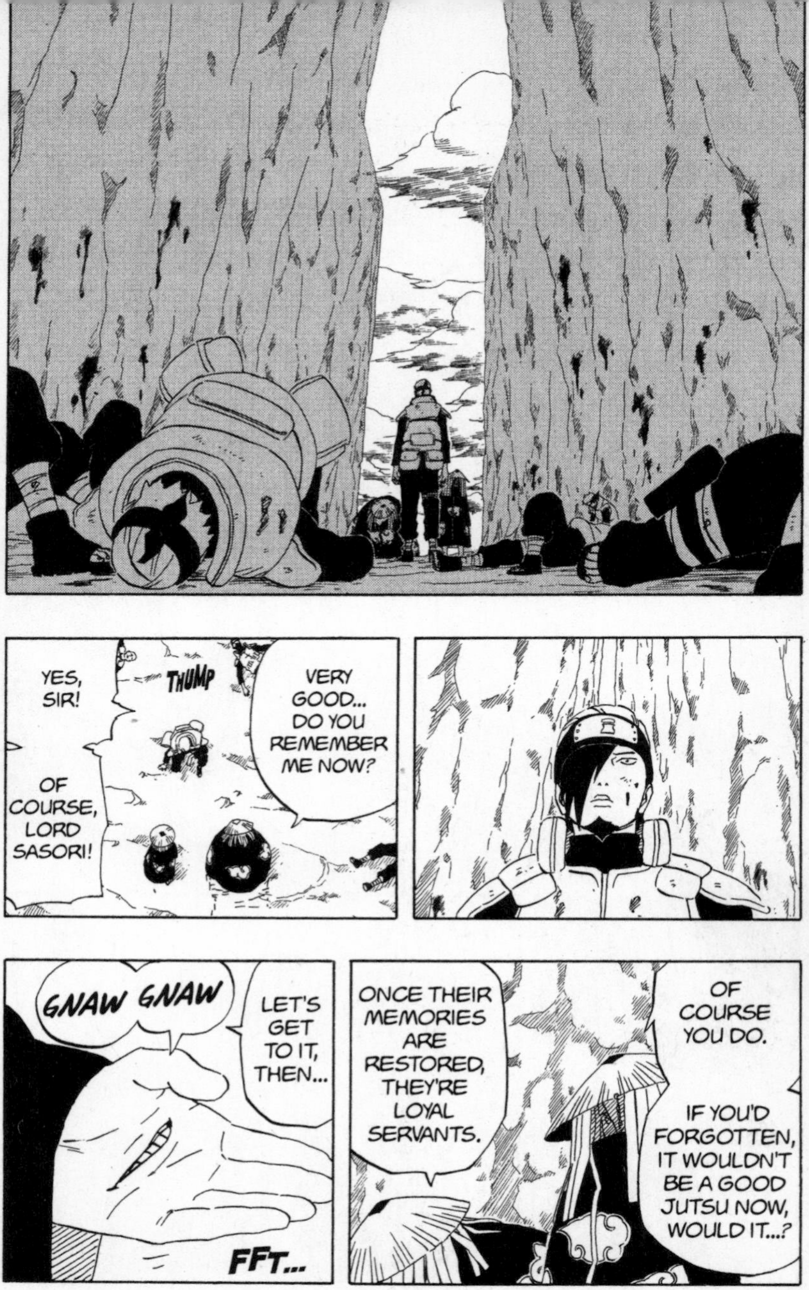
VERY GOOD... DO YOU REMEMBER ME NOW?
THUMP
YES, SIR!
OF COURSE, LORD SASORI!
OF COURSE YOU DO.
IF YOU'D FORGOTTEN, IT WOULDN'T BE A GOOD JUTSU NOW, WOULD IT...?
ONCE THEIR MEMORIES ARE RESTORED, THEY'RE LOYAL SERVANTS.
LET'S GET TO IT, THEN...
GNAW GNAW
FFT...

READ THIS WAY

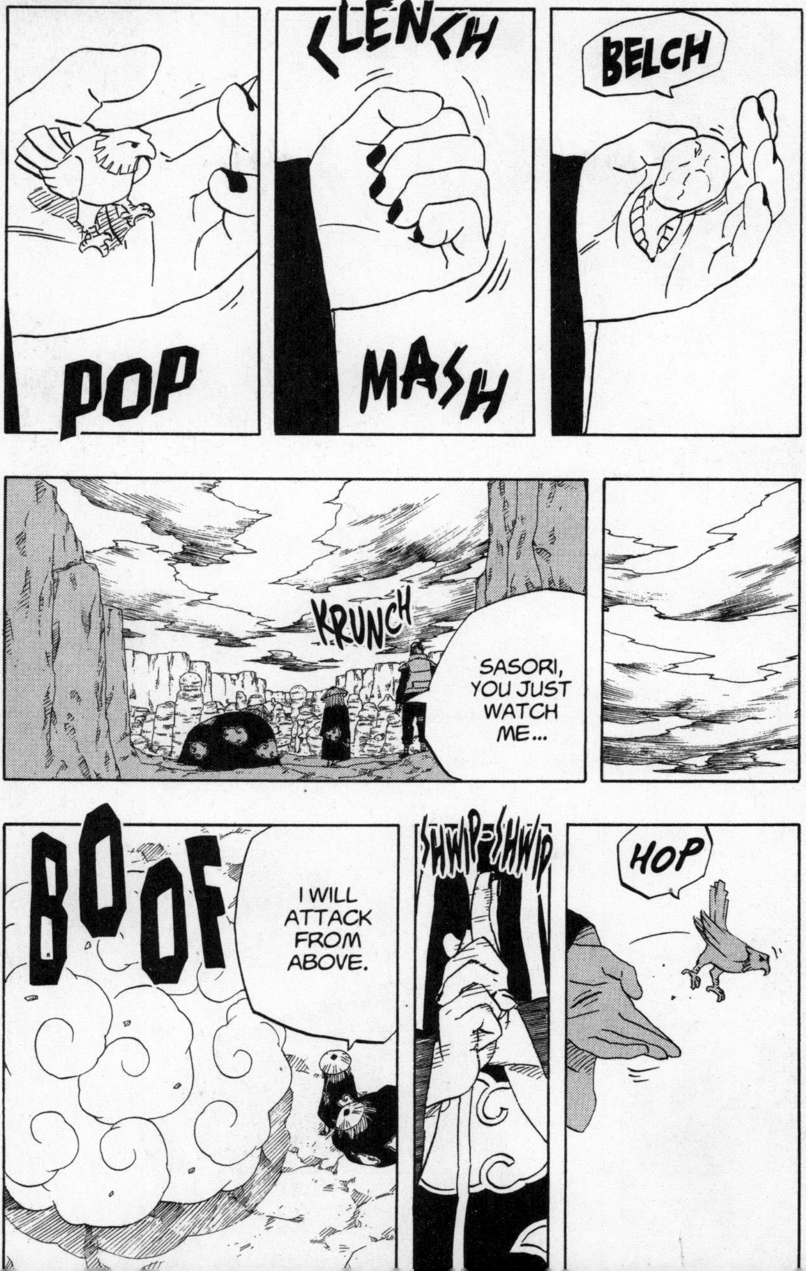

BELCH
CLENCH
MASH
POP
SASORI, YOU JUST WATCH ME...
KRUNCH
HOP
SHWIP SHWIP
I WILL ATTACK FROM ABOVE.
BOOF

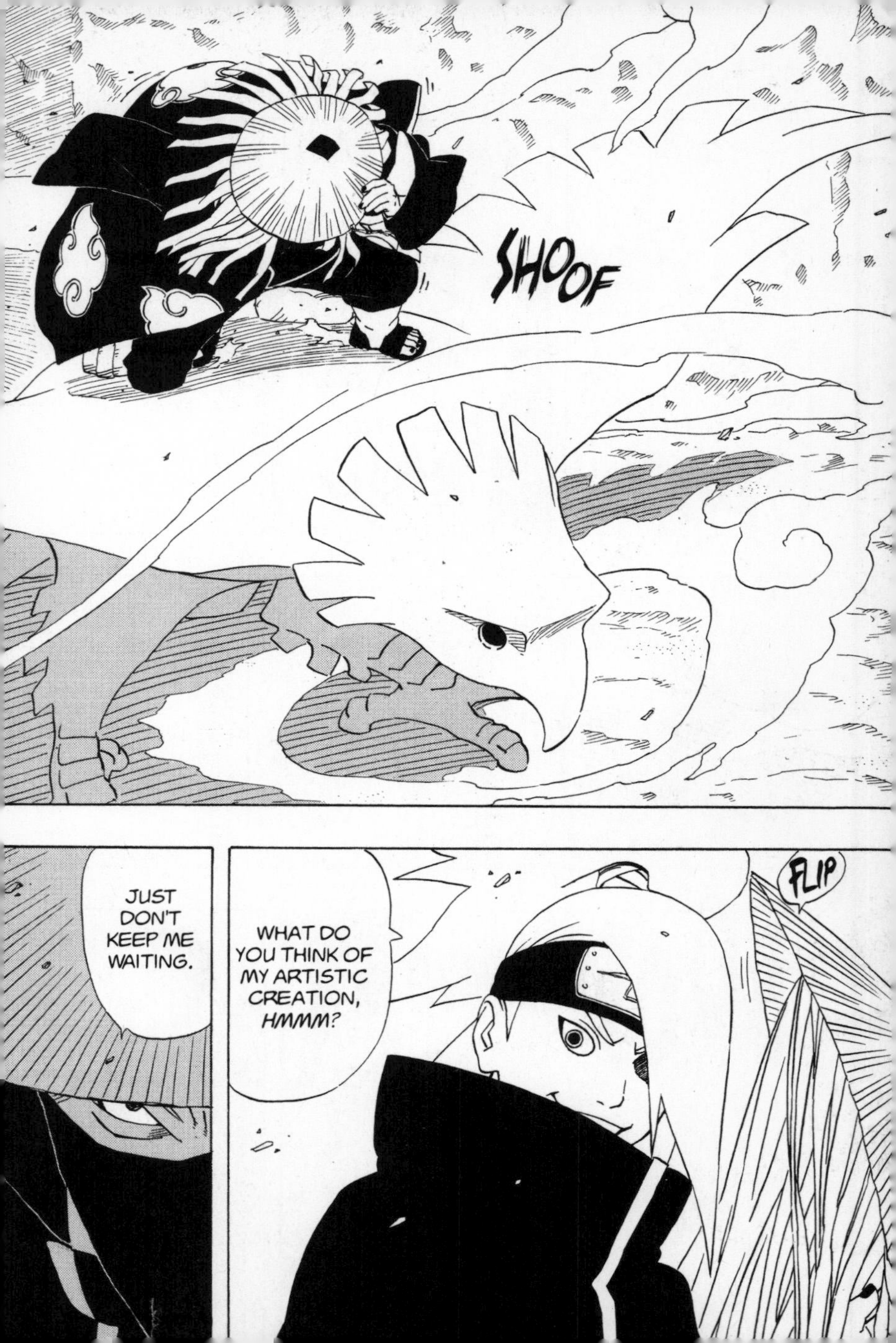
SHOOF
FLIP
WHAT DO YOU THINK OF MY ARTISTIC CREATION, HMMM?
JUST DON'T KEEP ME WAITING.

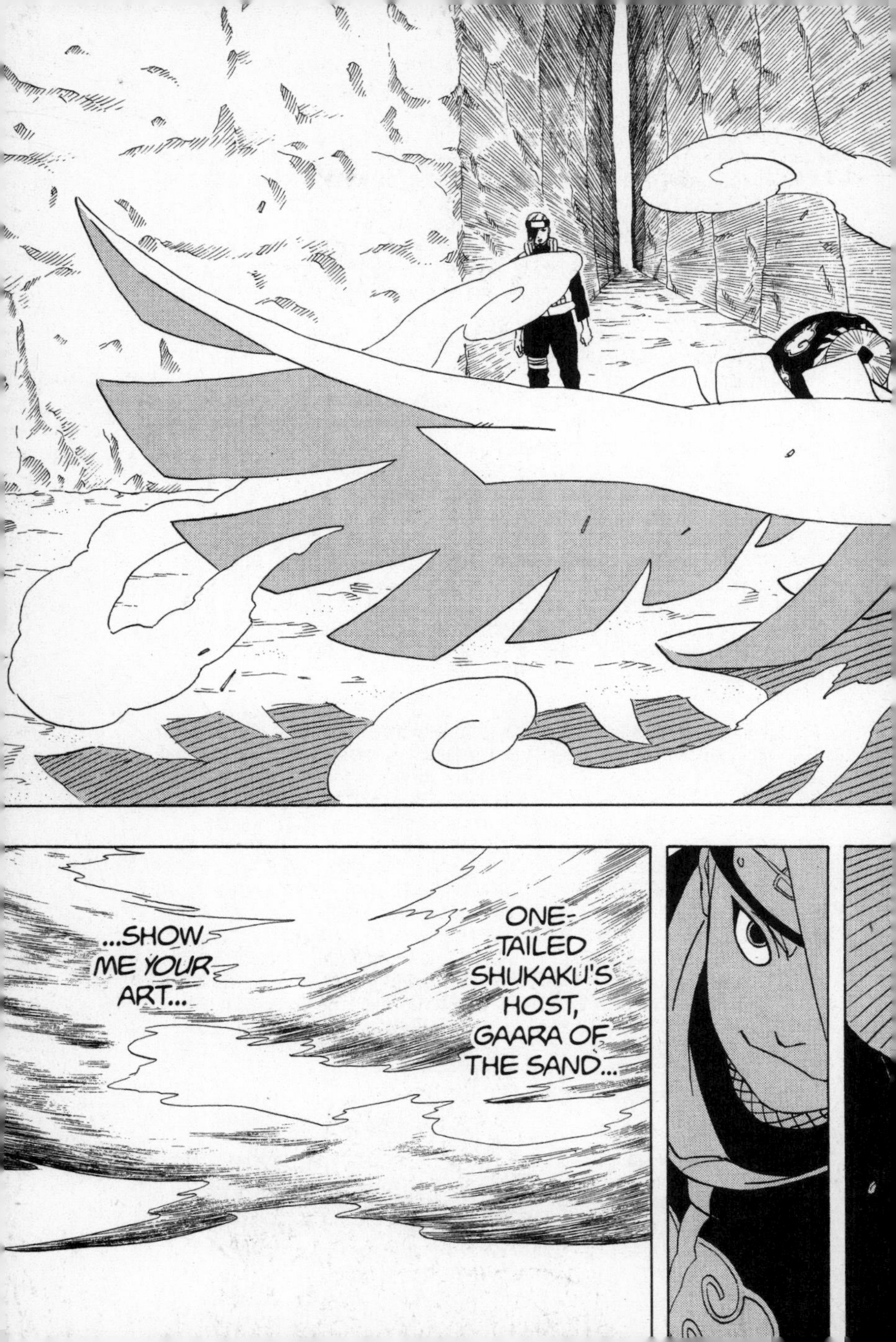
ONE-TAILED SHUKAKU'S HOST, GAARA OF THE SAND...
...SHOW ME YOUR ART...

THE WORLD OF KISHIMOTO MASASHI
MY PERSONAL HISTORY, VIDEO GAMES PART 2

AS I PREVIOUSLY WROTE IN VOLUME 25, I ESPECIALLY LIKED CARTRIDGE GAMES, SUCH AS "THE LEGEND OF ZELDA," "ZELDA 2: ADVENTURE OF LINK," "THE MYSTERIOUS CASTLE MURASAME," "KID ICARUS," "CASTLEVANIA," AND "METROID." YOU COULD SAVE AND RELOAD THESE GAMES, WHICH, FOR ME BACK THEN, WAS TREMENDOUSLY APPEALING. RECENTLY, MANY OF THESE GAMES WERE RE-RELEASED FOR THE GAME BOY, SO I DECIDED TO TRY THEM OUT AGAIN... I WAS PLEASANTLY SURPRISED TO DISCOVER THEY WERE STILL QUITE FUN. IN FACT, I BEAT THEM ALL (ALTHOUGH BECAUSE I DON'T HAVE A LOT OF FREE TIME, I WAS ONLY PLAYING THEM SPORADICALLY).

MOST OF MY CURRENT ASSISTANTS ARE ALSO OF THE FAMICOM GENERATION, SO WE OFTEN REMINISCE ABOUT THAT ERA, HAVING DISCUSSIONS LIKE, "REMEMBER HOW WE HAD TO 'RIOT' WITH JUST TWO CHARACTERS," OR "IN MISSISSIPPI ["MURDER ON THE MISSISSIPPI"], REMEMBER HOW YOU COULD KILL WITH JUST A SINGLE KNIFE THRUST," AND SO ON. AT SOME POINT, THE CONVERSATION WOULD ALWAYS TURN TO EITHER TO *DRAGON QUEST* OR THE *FINAL FANTASY* SERIES (I BET IT'S TRUE FOR YOU ALL AS WELL). WITH ONLY PARTIAL ALLEGIANCES--I.E. FF FANS WHO STILL LIKE DQ AND DQ FANS WHO STILL OWN FF GAMES--THERE EMERGE SOME BIZARRE COMMENTS. AS THE TALK GETS MORE AND MORE HEATED, SOMEONE WILL INVARIABLY SHOUT OUT, "SO WHAT ABOUT YOU, KISHIMOTO-SAN?"

AND MY REPLY WOULD BE, "I LOVE TORIYAMA-SENSEI'S ART, AND THE VERY FIRST GAME I EVER BOUGHT WAS DRAGON QUEST, SO I WANT TO SAY I'M A DQ FAN... BUT I WAS ALSO DRAWN TO FF BECAUSE OF ITS GLITCHES, LIKE THE ABILITY TO LEVEL-UP BY ATTACKING ONE'S ALLIES IN FFII AND TO CANCEL ATTACKS BY PRESSING THE A AND B BUTTONS SIMULTANEOUSLY. IN FFIV, THE LITTLE TWINS PALOM AND POROM MADE ME CRY EVEN THOUGH IT WAS A GAME. THE TRANSITION FROM PIXEL ART TO POLYGONAL 3D, COMPUTER GRAPHICS IN FFVII WAS SO GROUNDBREAKING THAT I CAN'T DENY THAT I LOVE FF AS WELL. SO AM I A FF MANIAC? ...YET DQ WAS SO BALANCED TOO. I LOVED HOW PRINCE SAMANTORIA OF DQII--WHO ALWAYS DIED SO EASILY--WAS ABLE TO MASTER THE ZAORIKU, OR REVIVE SPELL. AND EVEN THOUGH THE "SPELL OF RESURRECTION" WAS REALLY LONG, THE MUSIC THAT PLAYED DURING THE PASSWORD SCREEN BECAME MY FAVORITE OF THE DQ SERIES. BUT THEN, DQI~III'S "LEGEND OF THE HERO LOTO", IS A THREE-PART WORK THAT REALLY WAS A CLASSIC FOR ME TOO.

...SO IT'S REALLY HARD FOR ME TO CHOOSE BETWEEN THE TWO. AND MY ASSISTANTS, TOO, THEY ALWAYS END UP GIVING VAGUE ANSWERS AS WELL. SO THE DEBATE IS USUALLY SETTLED WITH MUTUAL ADMIRATION FOR AND AGREEMENT ABOUT HOW INCREDIBLE THE COLLABORATION PROJECT GAME "CHRONO TRIGGER" WAS. WE ALL JUST LOVE VIDEO GAMES.

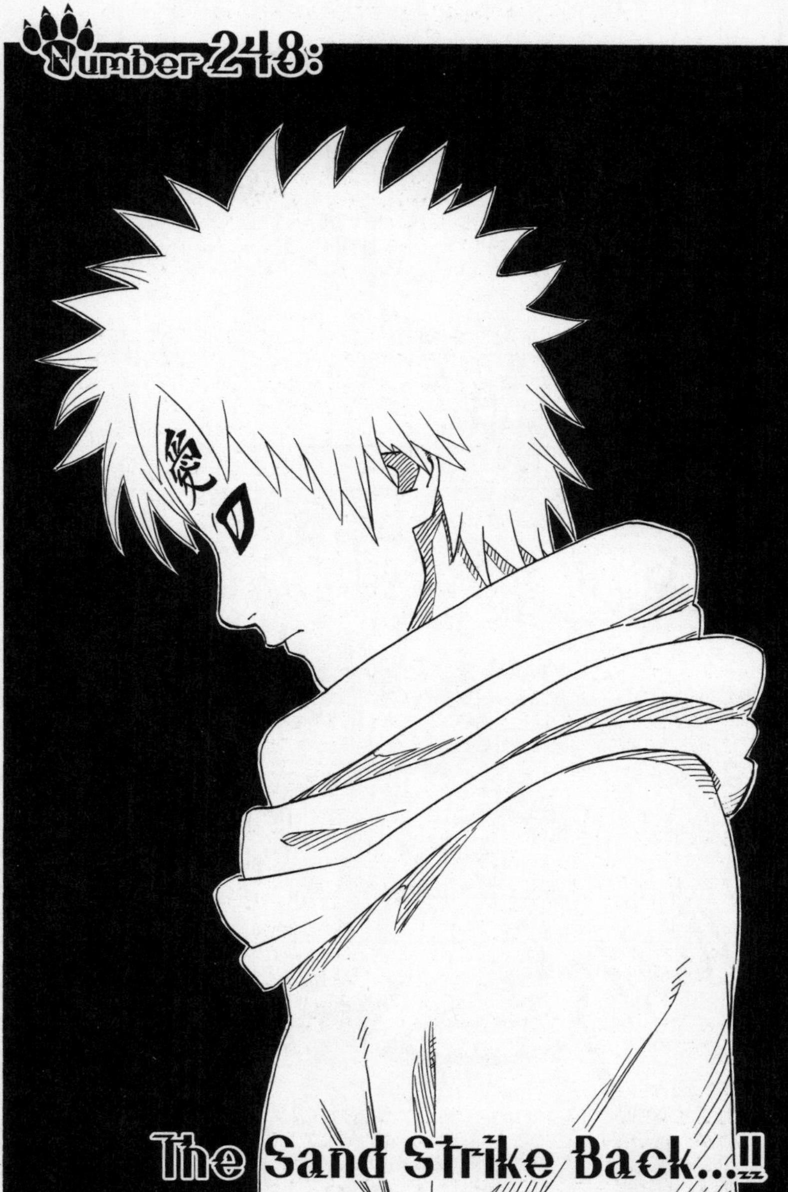
Number 248:
The Sand Strike Back...!!

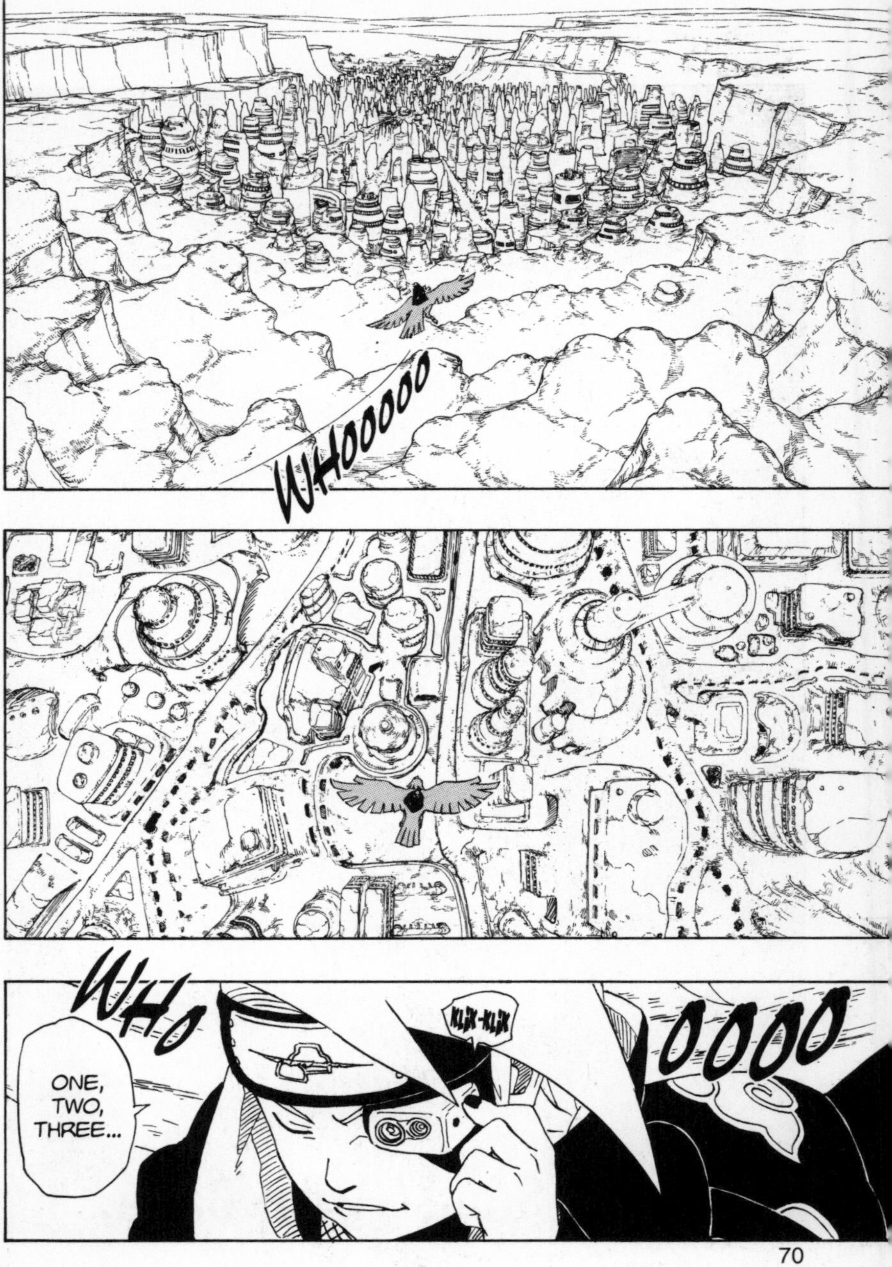
WHOOOOOO
WHO
OOOO
KLIK-KLIK
ONE, TWO, THREE...

READ THIS WAY

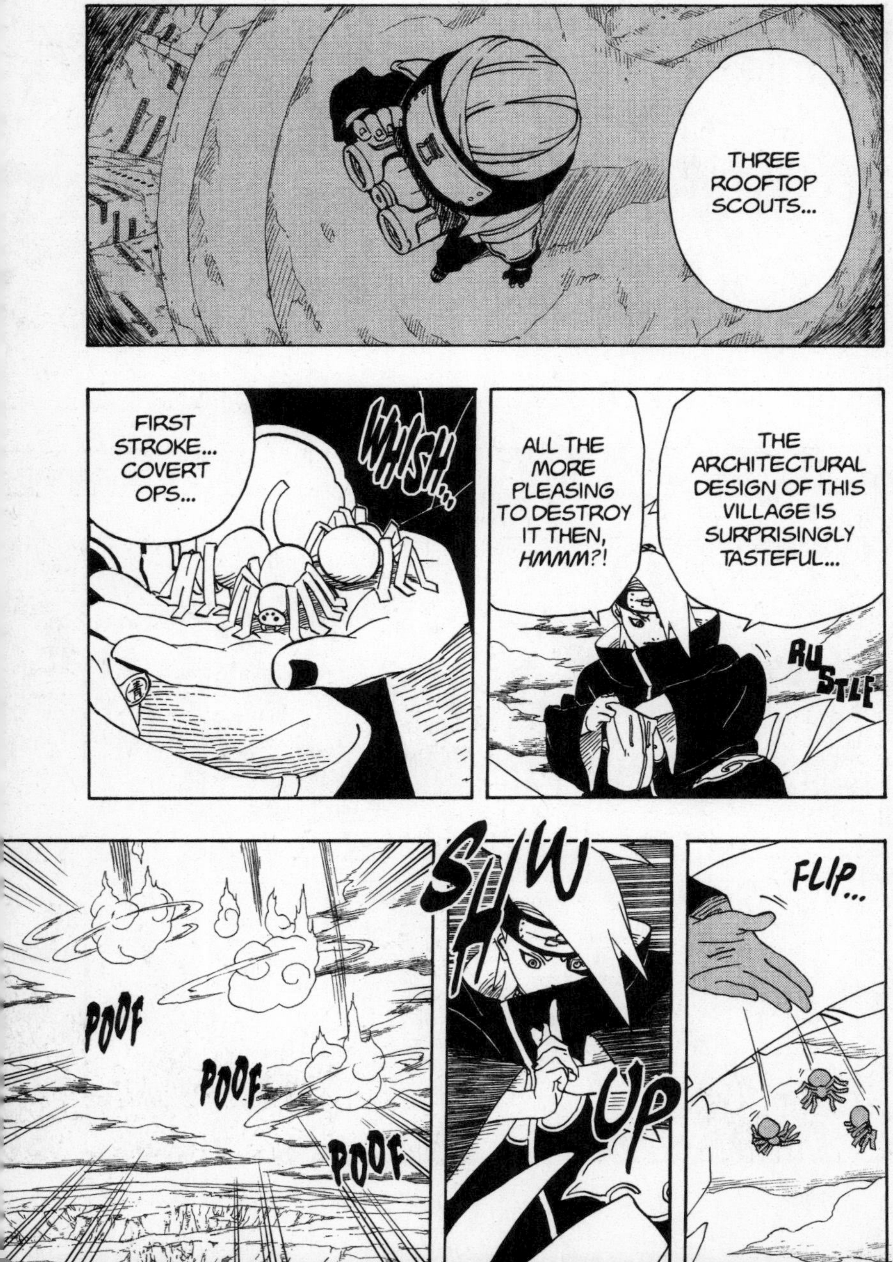
THREE ROOFTOP SCOUTS...
THE ARCHITECTURAL DESIGN OF THIS VILLAGE IS SURPRISINGLY TASTEFUL...
ALL THE MORE PLEASING TO DESTROY IT THEN, *HMMM*?!
RUSTLE
WHISH...
FIRST STROKE... COVERT OPS...
FLIP...
SHWUP
POOF
POOF
POOF

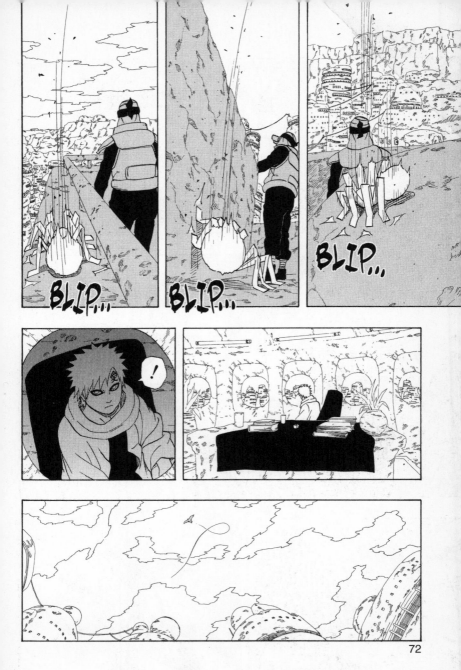

BLIP...

BLIP...

BLIP...

READ THIS WAY

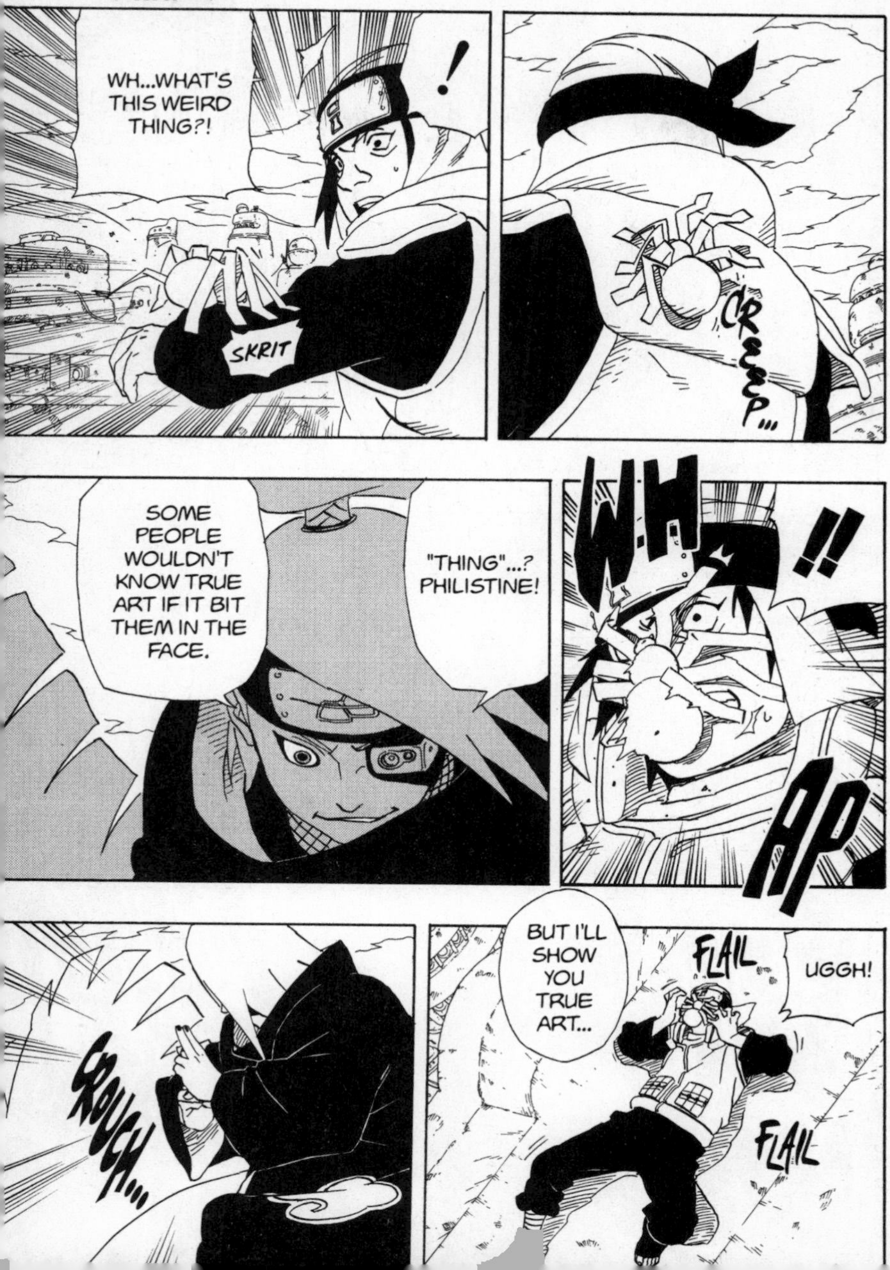
CREEP...
!
WH...WHAT'S THIS WEIRD THING?!
SKRIT
WH!!
AP
"THING"...? PHILISTINE!
SOME PEOPLE WOULDN'T KNOW TRUE ART IF IT BIT THEM IN THE FACE.
UGGH!
FLAIL
BUT I'LL SHOW YOU TRUE ART...
FLAIL
CROUCH...

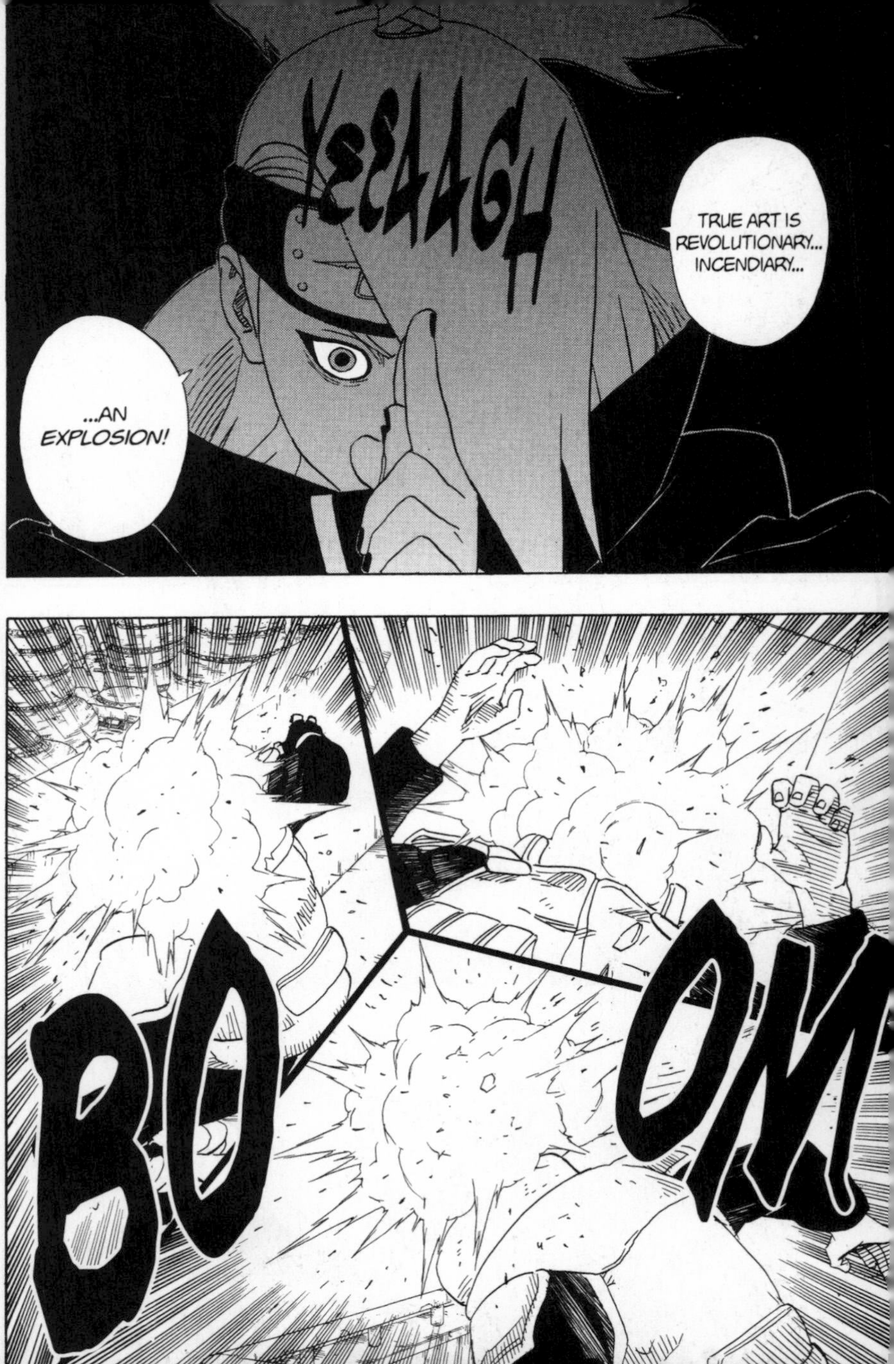
YEEAAGH
TRUE ART IS REVOLUTIONARY... INCENDIARY...
...AN EXPLOSION!
BOOM

READ THIS WAY

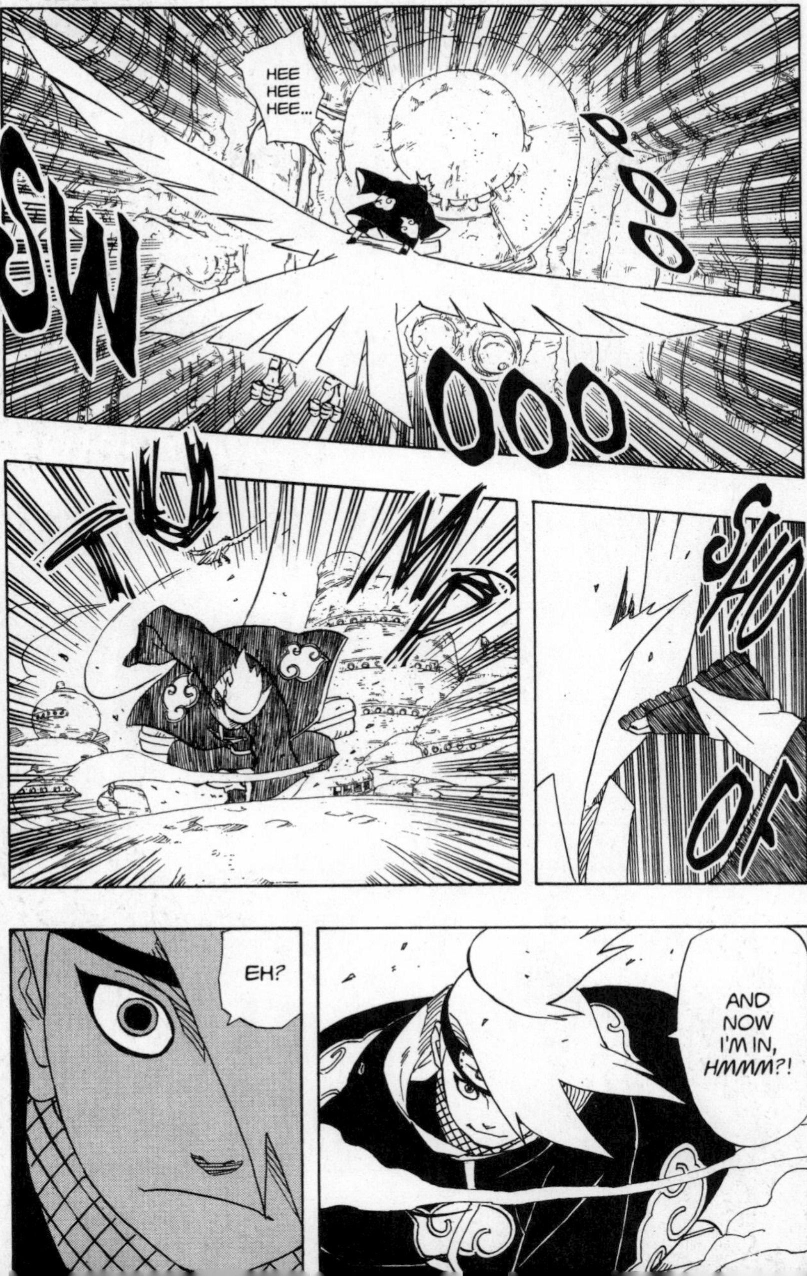
HEE HEE HEE...
SW
OOO
DOOO
SHO
OF
THUMP
AND NOW I'M IN, HMMM?!
EH?

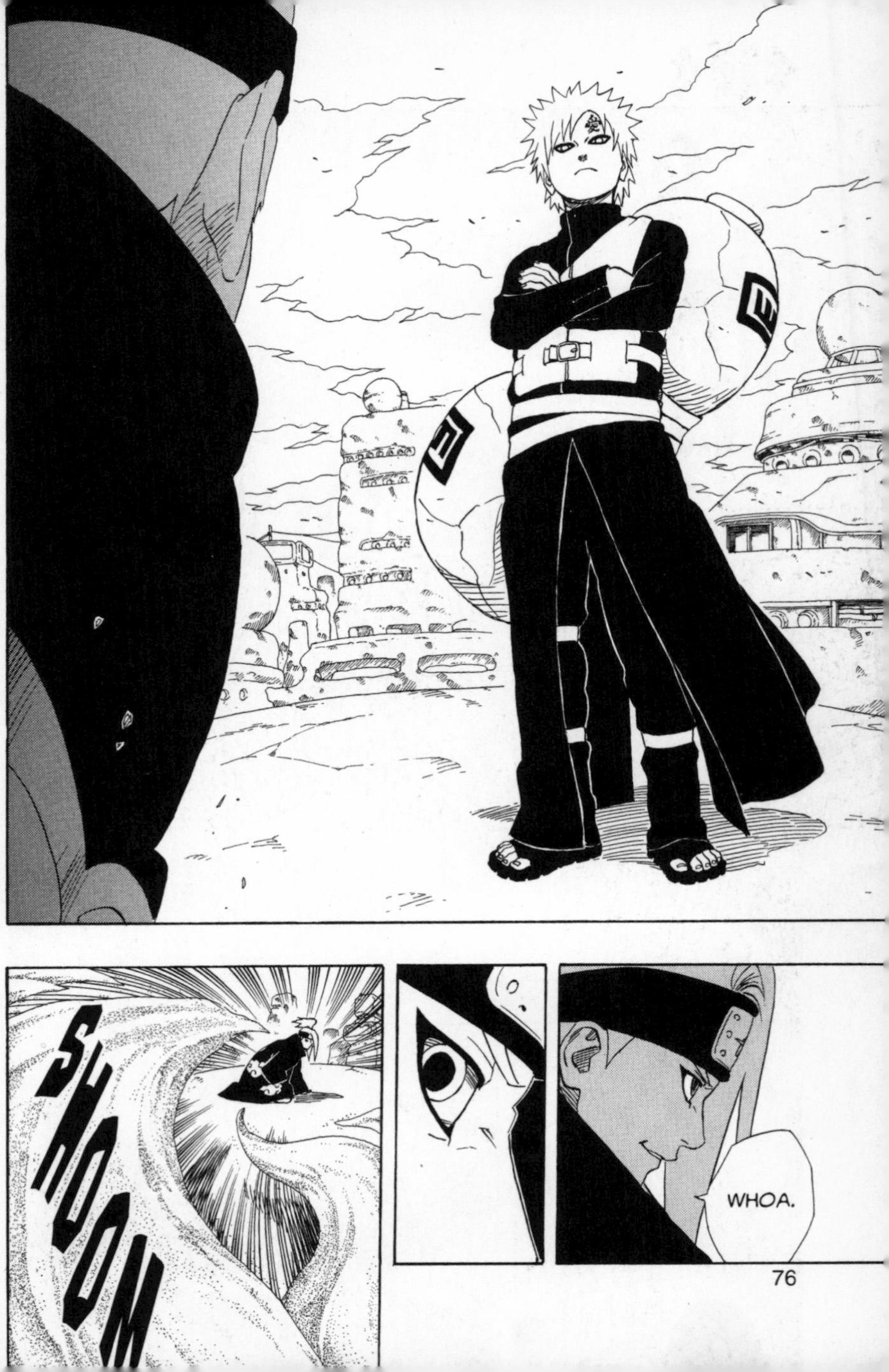
WHOA.
SHOOM

READ THIS WAY

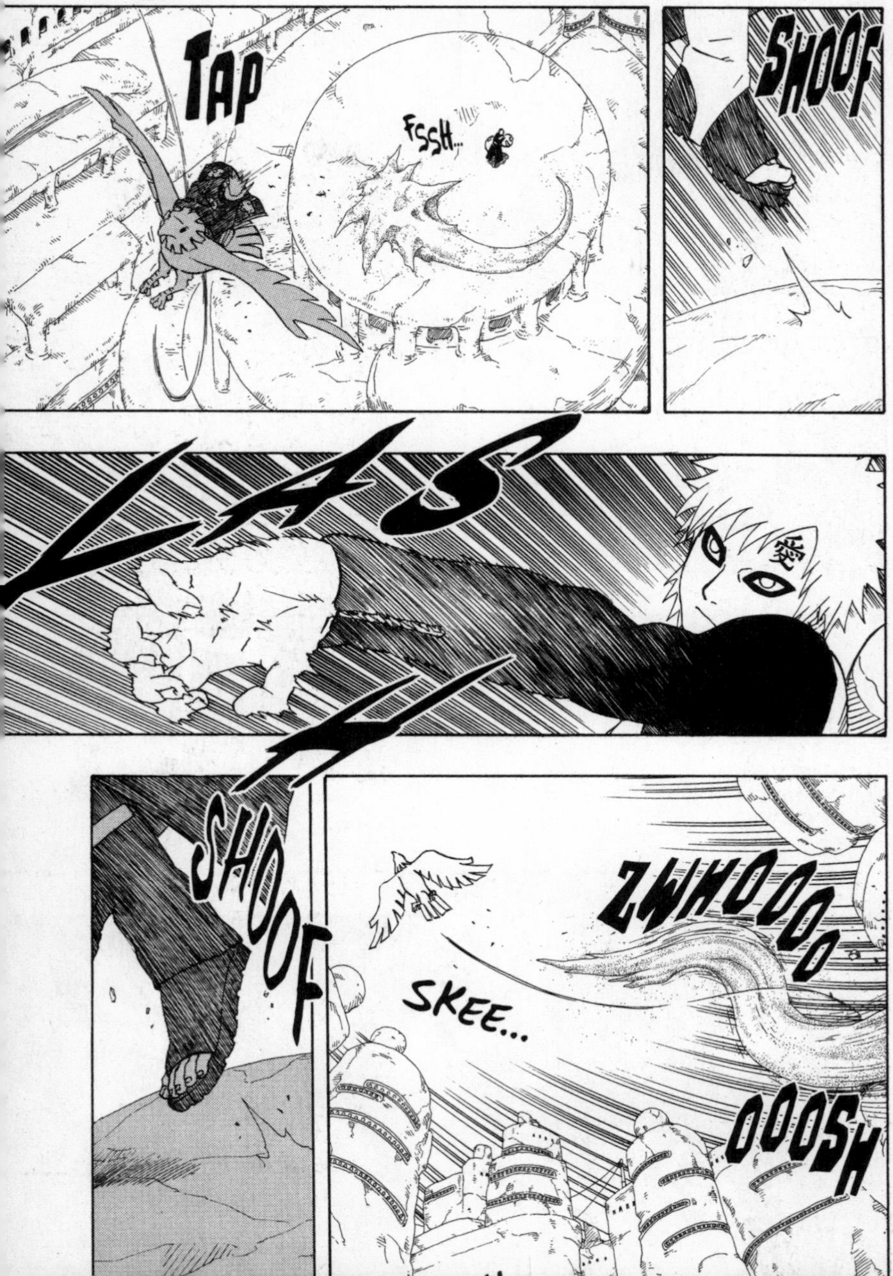
SHOOF
TAP
FSSH...
SKEE...
ZWHOOOO
OOOSH
SHOOF

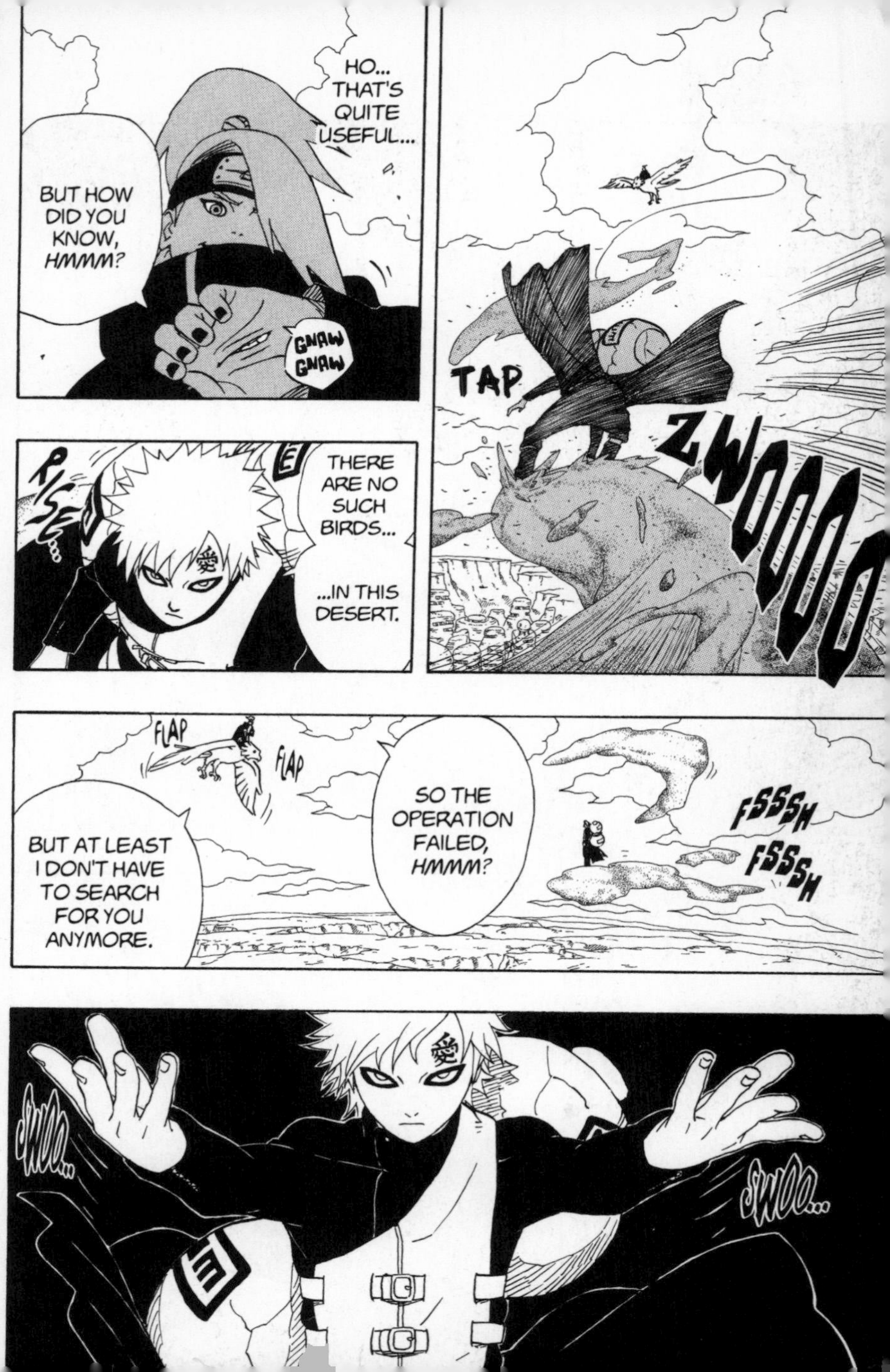
TAP
ZWOOOO
HO... THAT'S QUITE USEFUL...
BUT HOW DID YOU KNOW, HMMM?
GNAW GNAW
THERE ARE NO SUCH BIRDS...
...IN THIS DESERT.
RISE
FSSSH
FSSSH
SO THE OPERATION FAILED, HMMM?
FLAP
FLAP
BUT AT LEAST I DON'T HAVE TO SEARCH FOR YOU ANYMORE.
SWOO...
SWOO...

READ THIS WAY

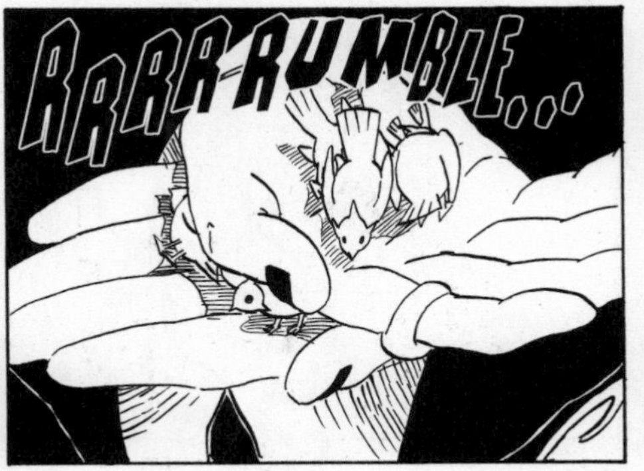
RRRR RUMBLE...

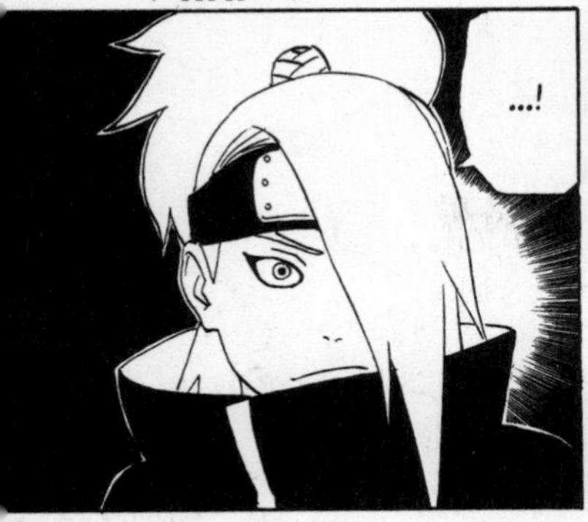
...!

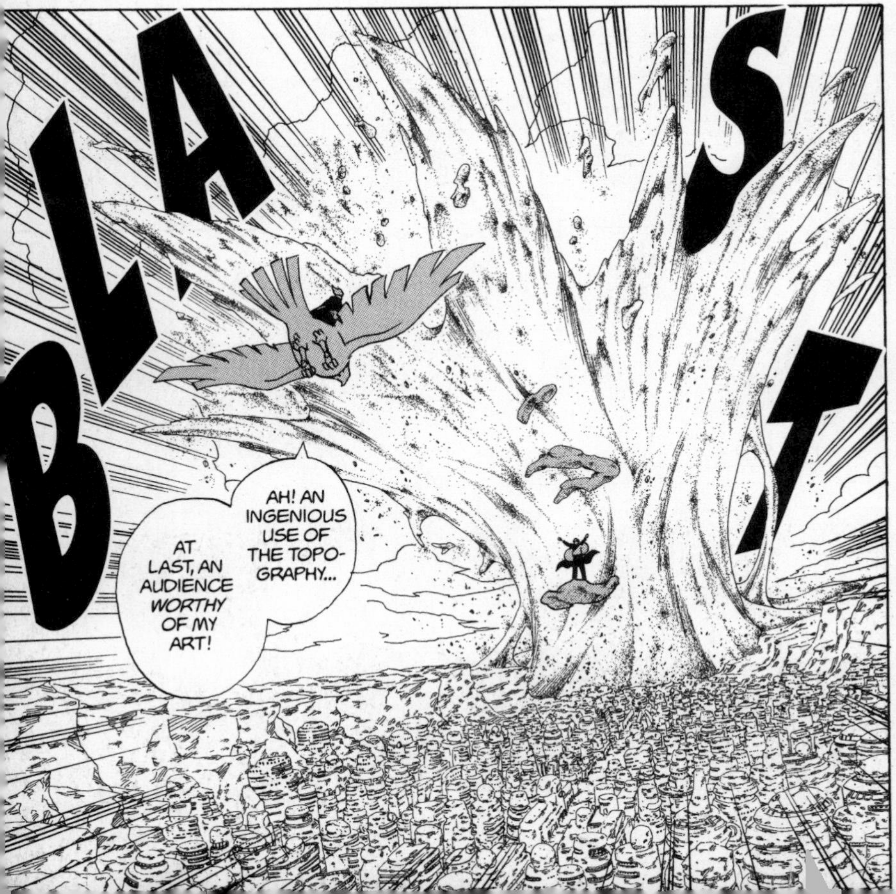
BLAST
AH! AN INGENIOUS USE OF THE TOPOGRAPHY...
AT LAST, AN AUDIENCE WORTHY OF MY ART!

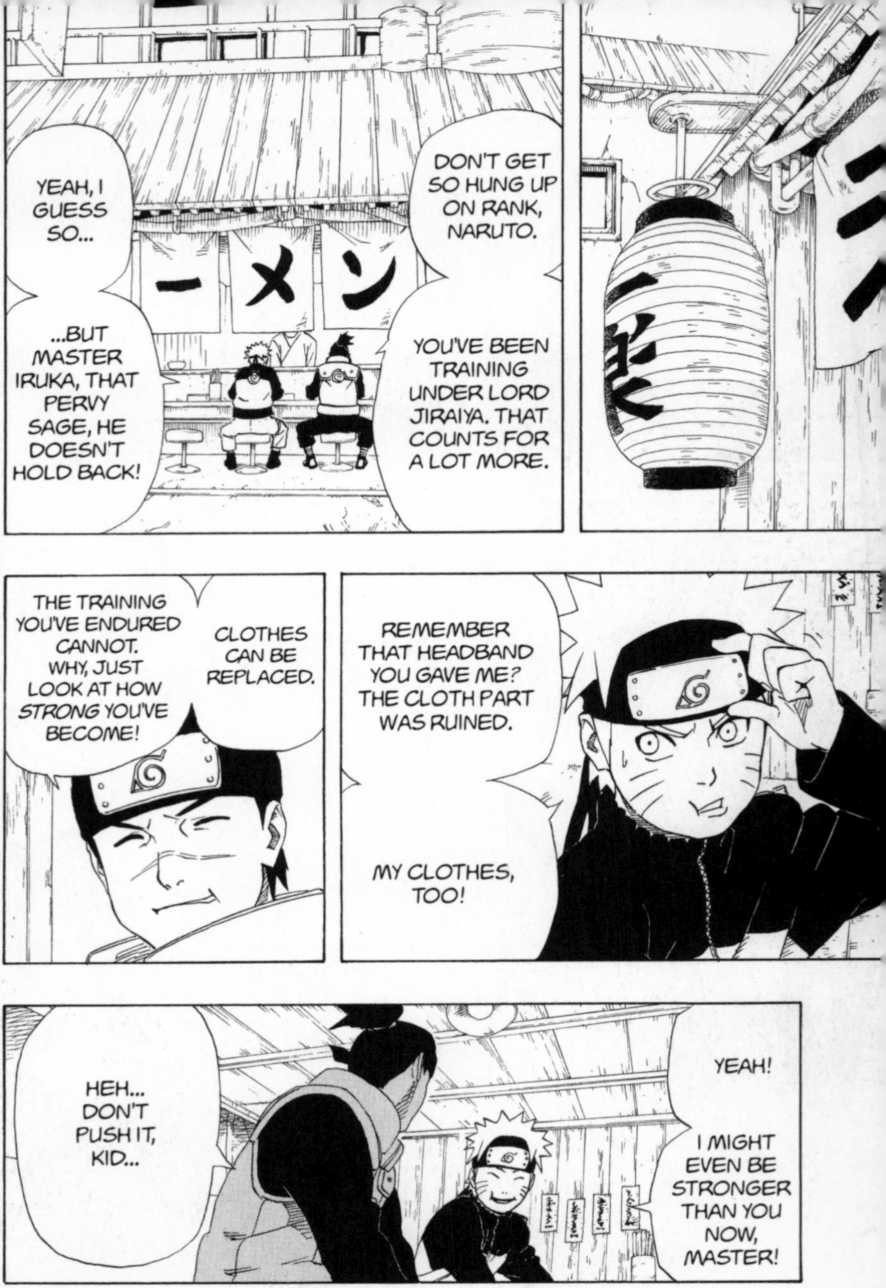
DON'T GET SO HUNG UP ON RANK, NARUTO.
YEAH, I GUESS SO...
...BUT MASTER IRUKA, THAT PERVY SAGE, HE DOESN'T HOLD BACK!
YOU'VE BEEN TRAINING UNDER LORD JIRAIYA. THAT COUNTS FOR A LOT MORE.
REMEMBER THAT HEADBAND YOU GAVE ME? THE CLOTH PART WAS RUINED.
MY CLOTHES, TOO!
CLOTHES CAN BE REPLACED.
THE TRAINING YOU'VE ENDURED CANNOT. WHY, JUST LOOK AT HOW *STRONG* YOU'VE BECOME!
YEAH!
I MIGHT EVEN BE STRONGER THAN YOU NOW, MASTER!
HEH... DON'T PUSH IT, KID...

READ THIS WAY

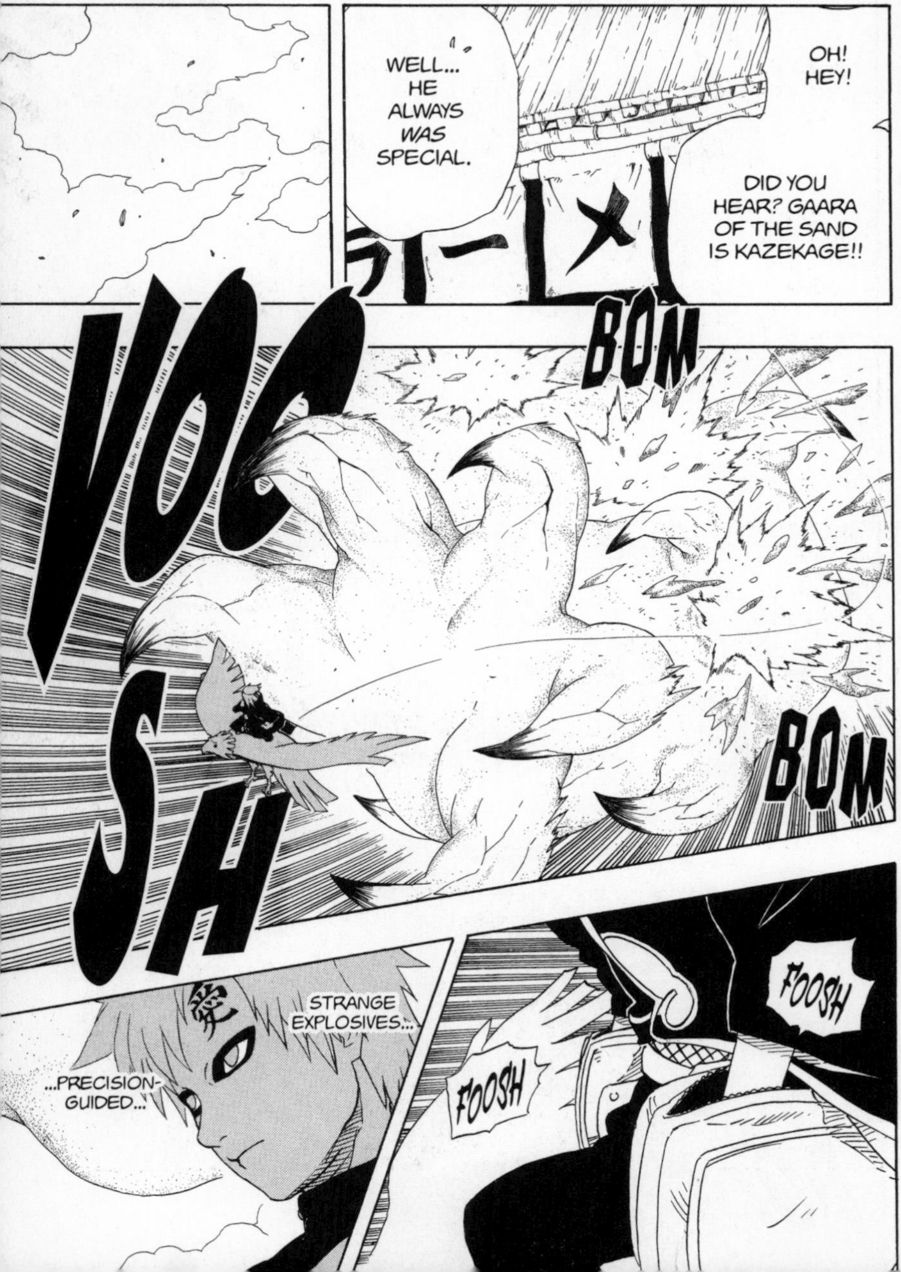
OH! HEY!
DID YOU HEAR? GAARA OF THE SAND IS KAZEKAGE!!
WELL... HE ALWAYS WAS SPECIAL.
BOM
BOM
VOOSH
FOOSH
FOOSH
STRANGE EXPLOSIVES...
...PRECISION-GUIDED...

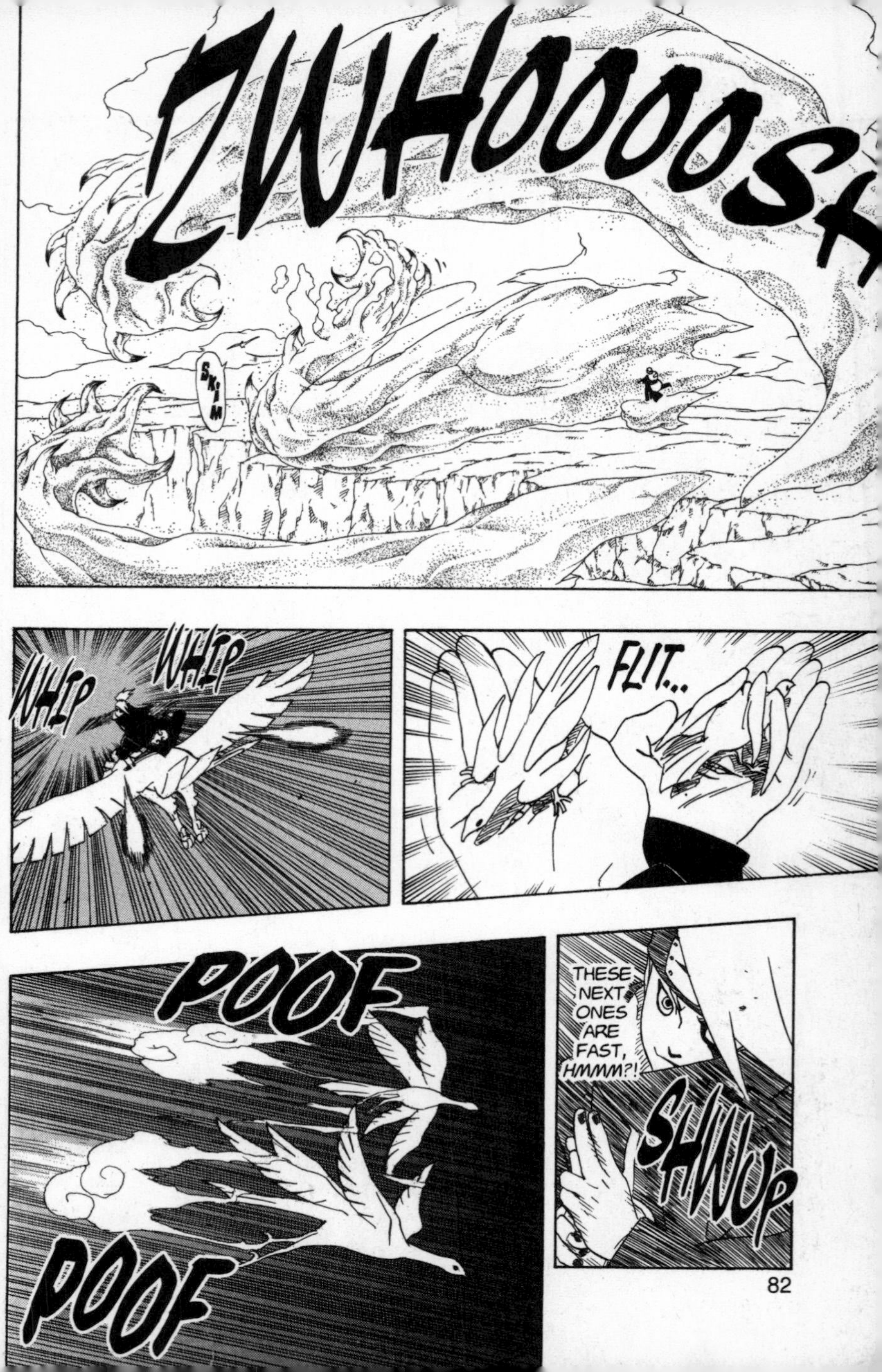
ZWHOOOOSH
SKIM
FLIT...
WHIP
WHIP
THESE NEXT ONES ARE FAST, HMMM?!
SHWOOP
POOF
POOF

READ THIS WAY

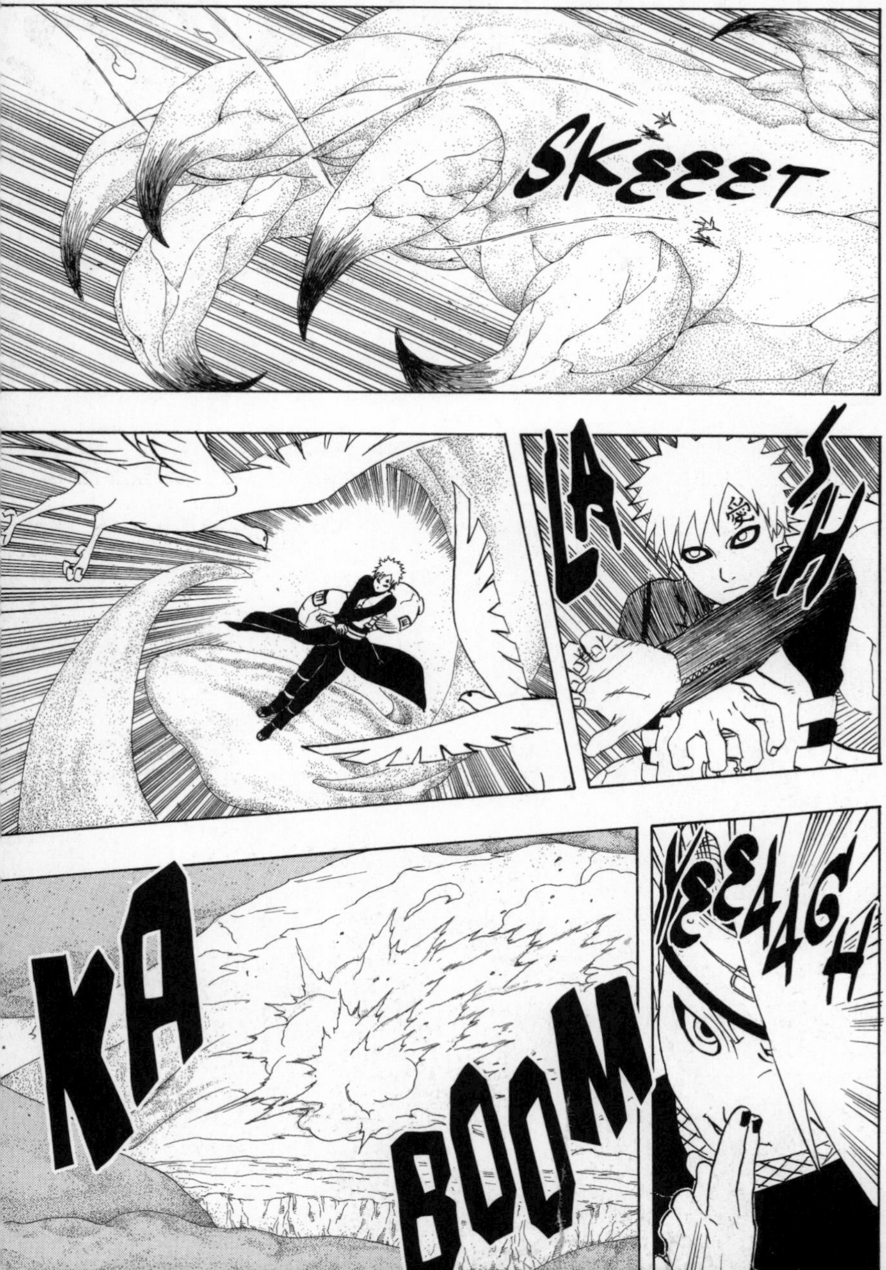
SKEEET
LA
SH
YEEAAGH
KA
BOOM

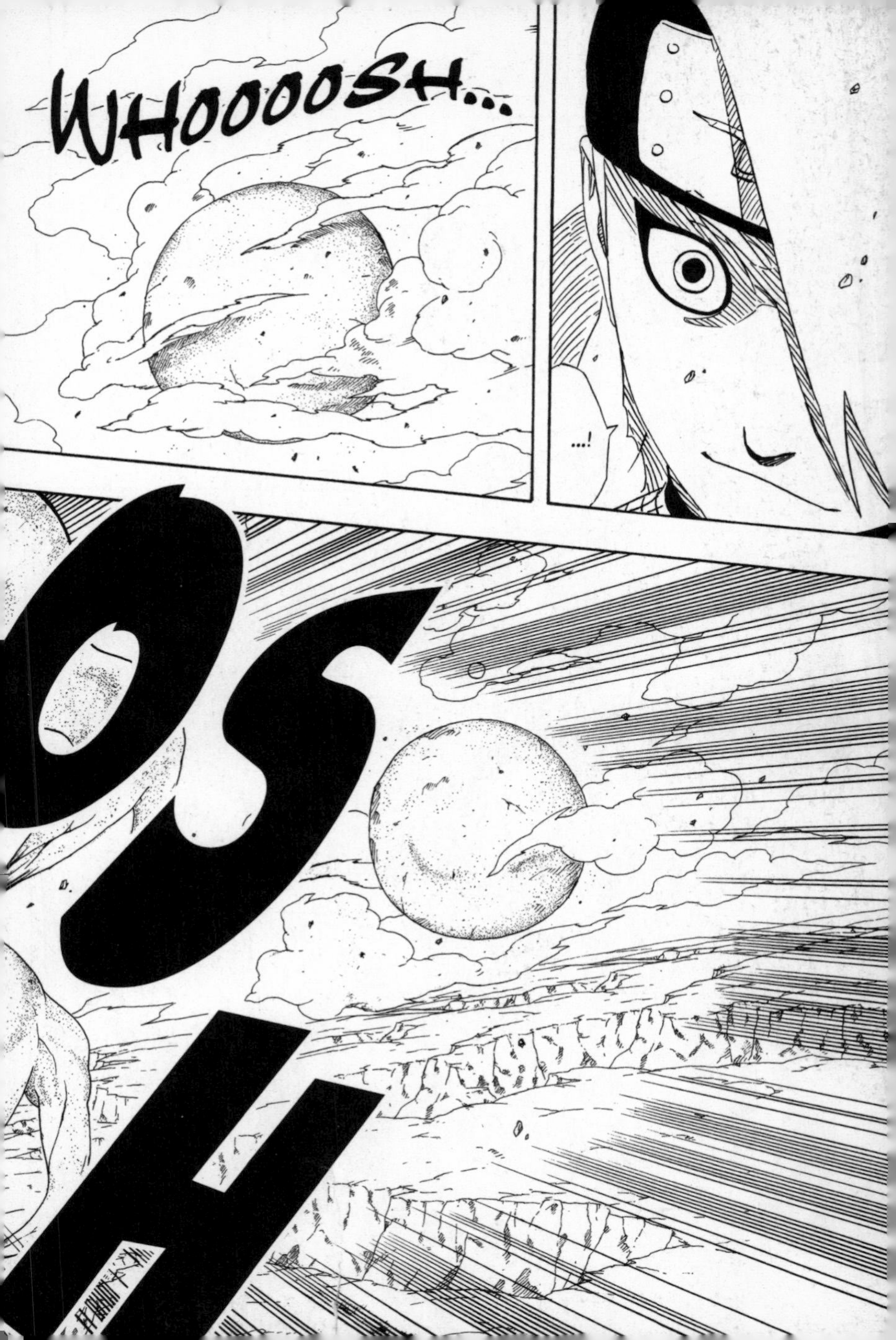
...!
WHOOOOSH...
OSH

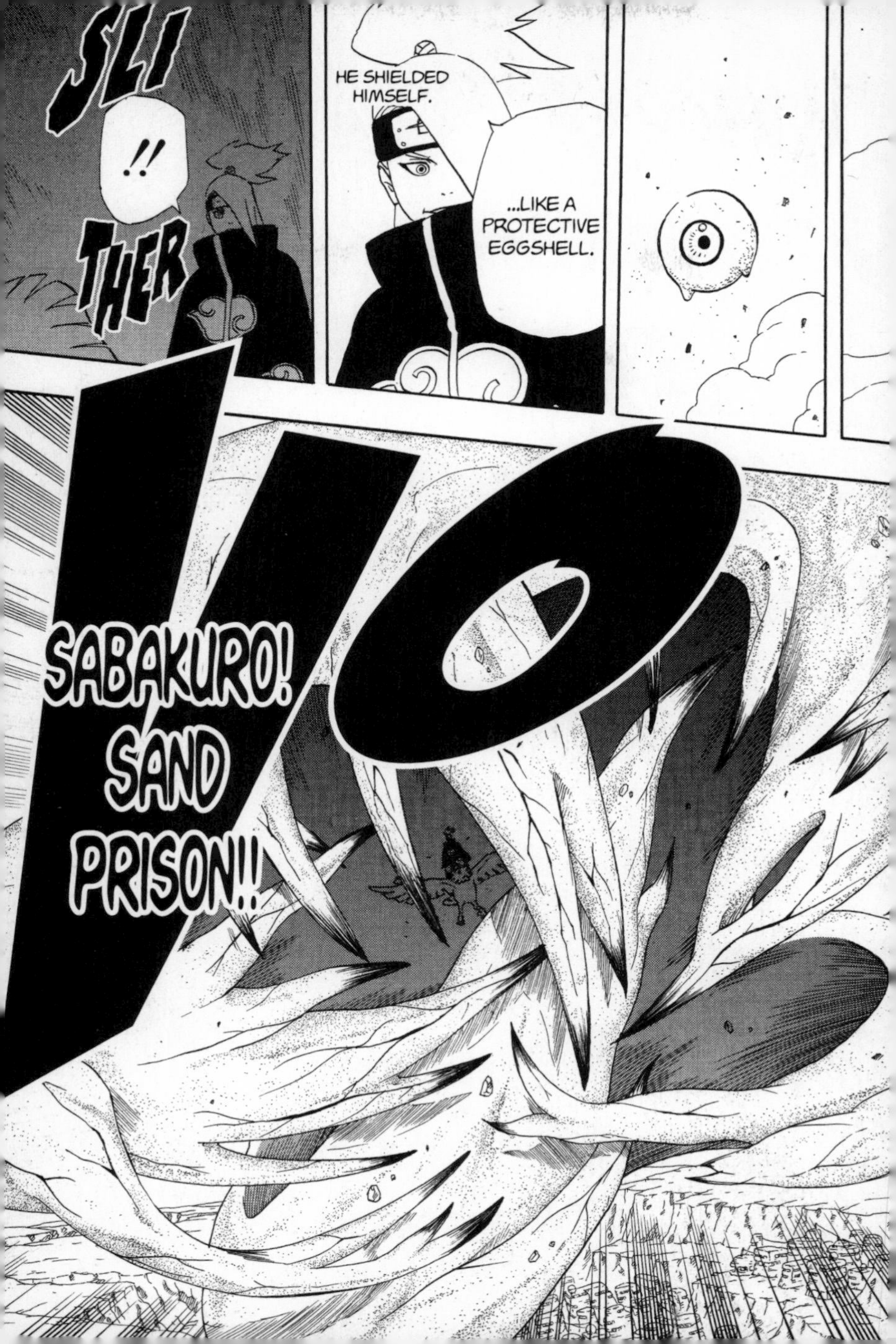
HE SHIELDED HIMSELF.
...LIKE A PROTECTIVE EGGSHELL.
SLI THER
!!
VO
SABAKURO! SAND PRISON!!

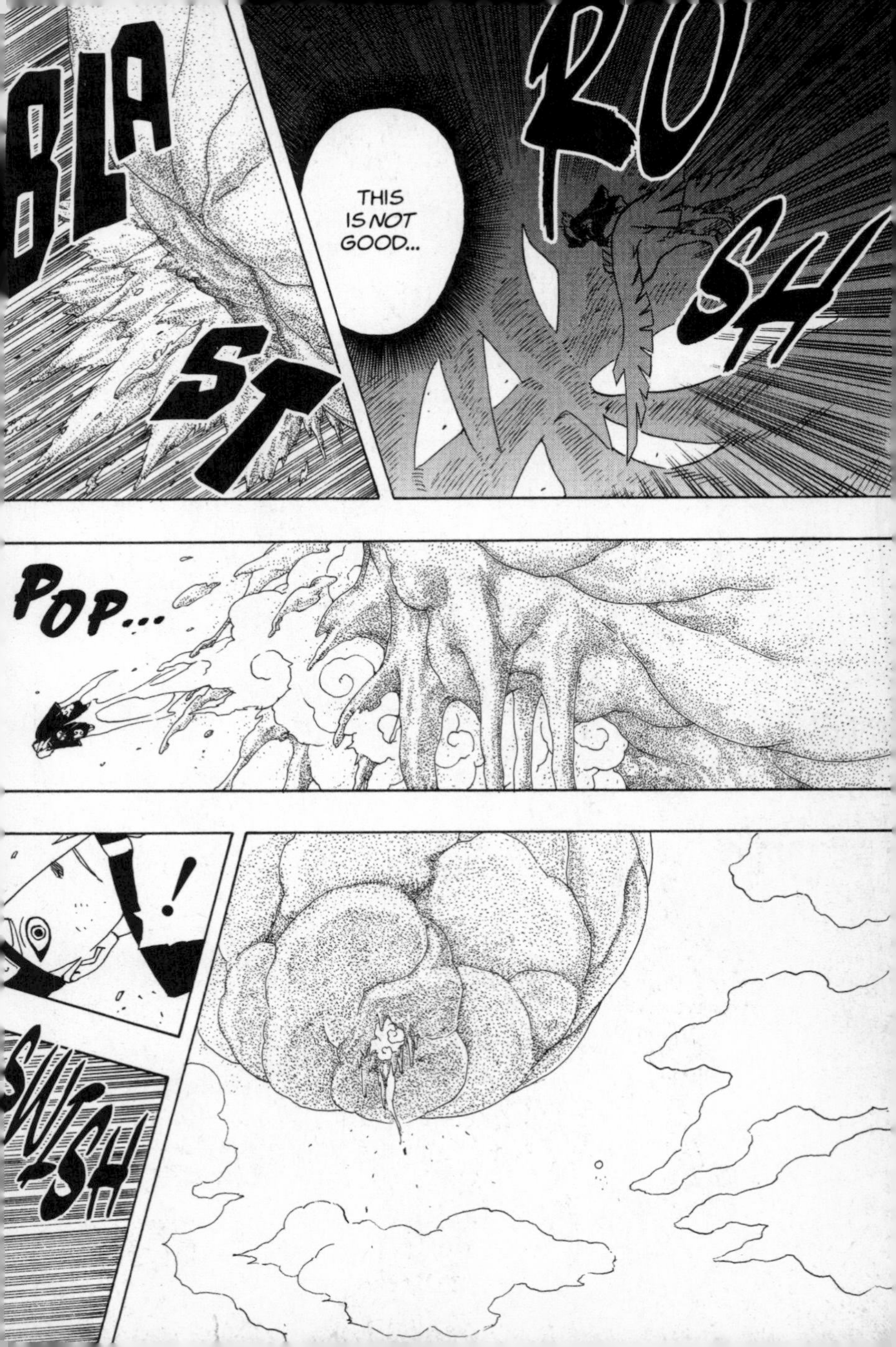
RUSH
THIS IS NOT GOOD...
BLAST
POP...
!
SWISH

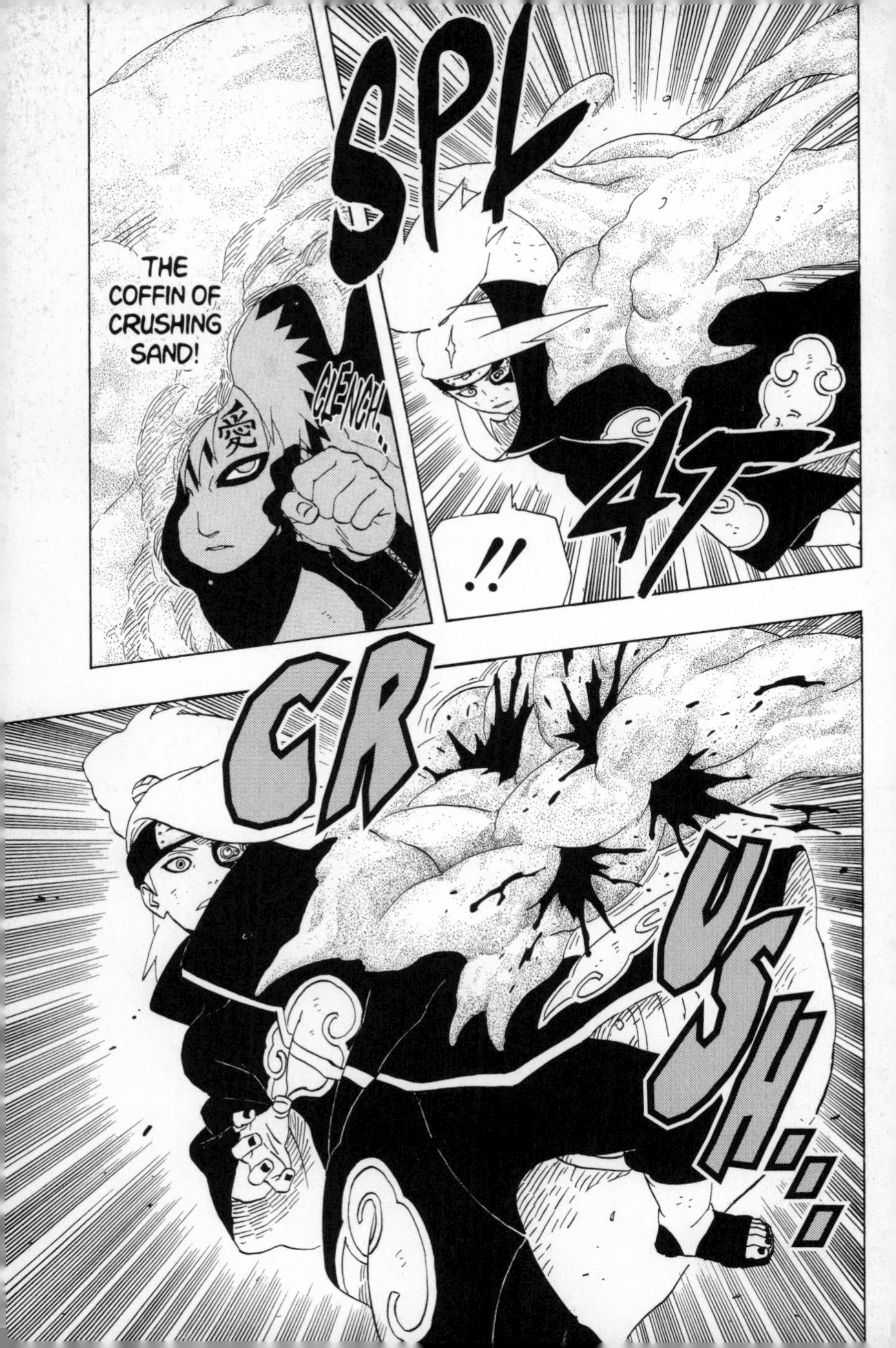
SPLAT
!!
THE COFFIN OF CRUSHING SAND!
CLENCH...
CRUSH...

NARUTO

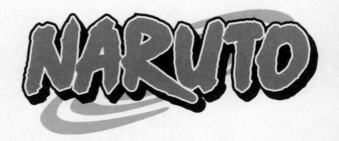

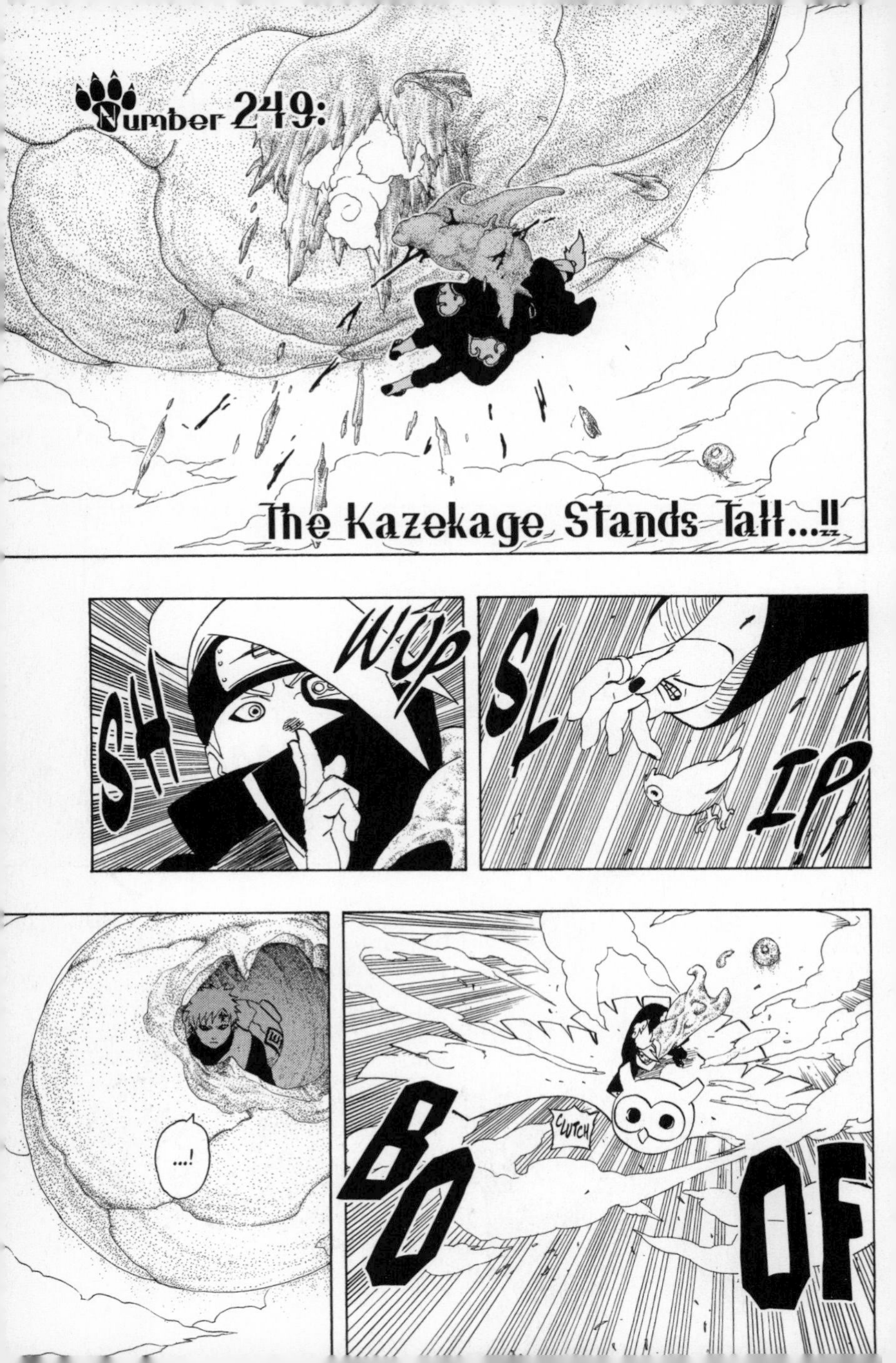

Number 249:
The Kazekage Stands Tall...!!
SLIP
WUP
SH
CLUTCH
BOOF
...!

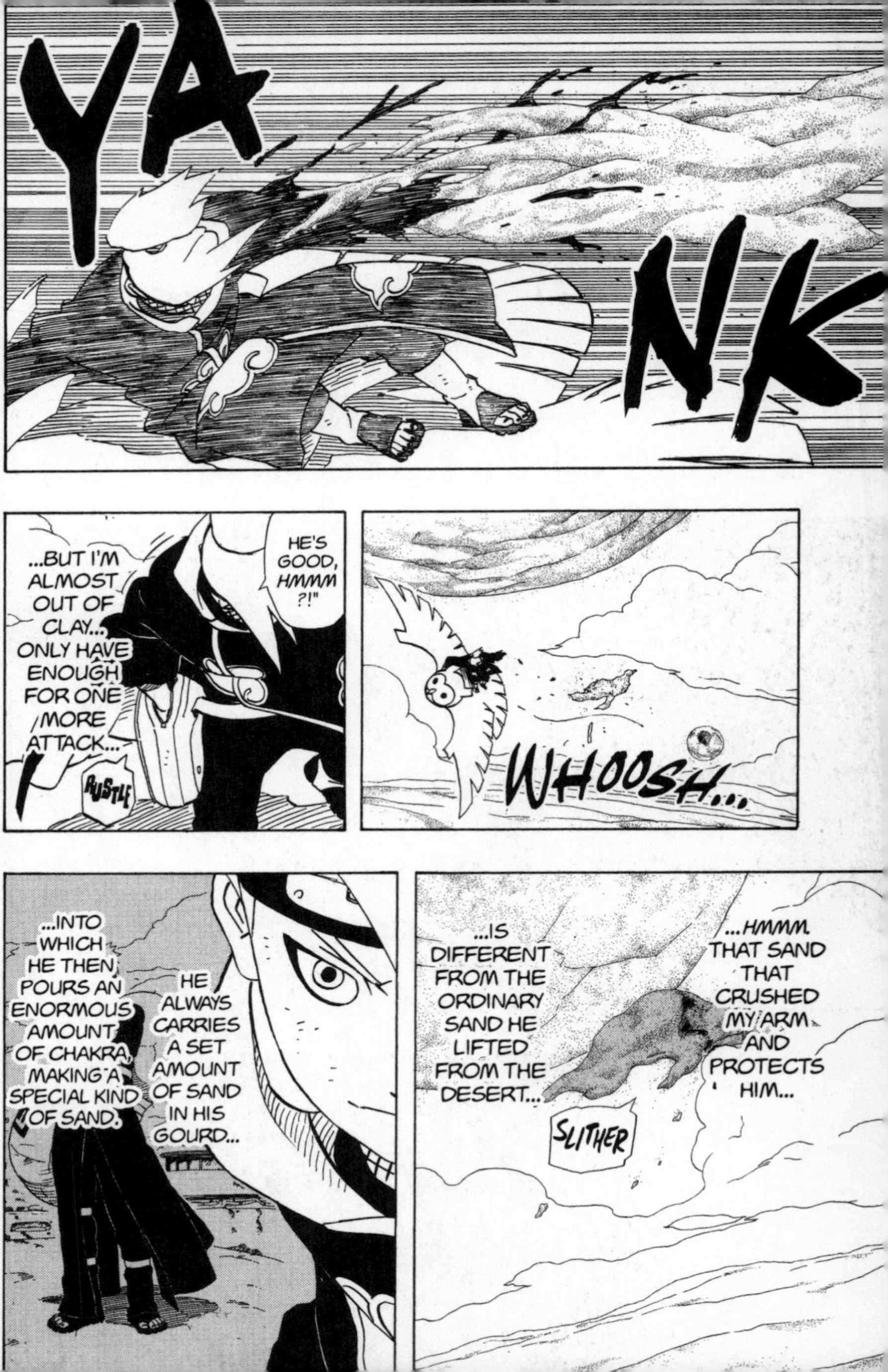
YANK
WHOOSH...
HE'S GOOD, HMMM ?!"
...BUT I'M ALMOST OUT OF CLAY... ONLY HAVE ENOUGH FOR ONE MORE ATTACK...
RUSTLE
...HMMM THAT SAND THAT CRUSHED MY ARM AND PROTECTS HIM...
...IS DIFFERENT FROM THE ORDINARY SAND HE LIFTED FROM THE DESERT...
SLITHER
HE ALWAYS CARRIES A SET AMOUNT OF SAND IN HIS GOURD...
...INTO WHICH HE THEN POURS AN ENORMOUS AMOUNT OF CHAKRA, MAKING A SPECIAL KIND OF SAND.

READ THIS WAY

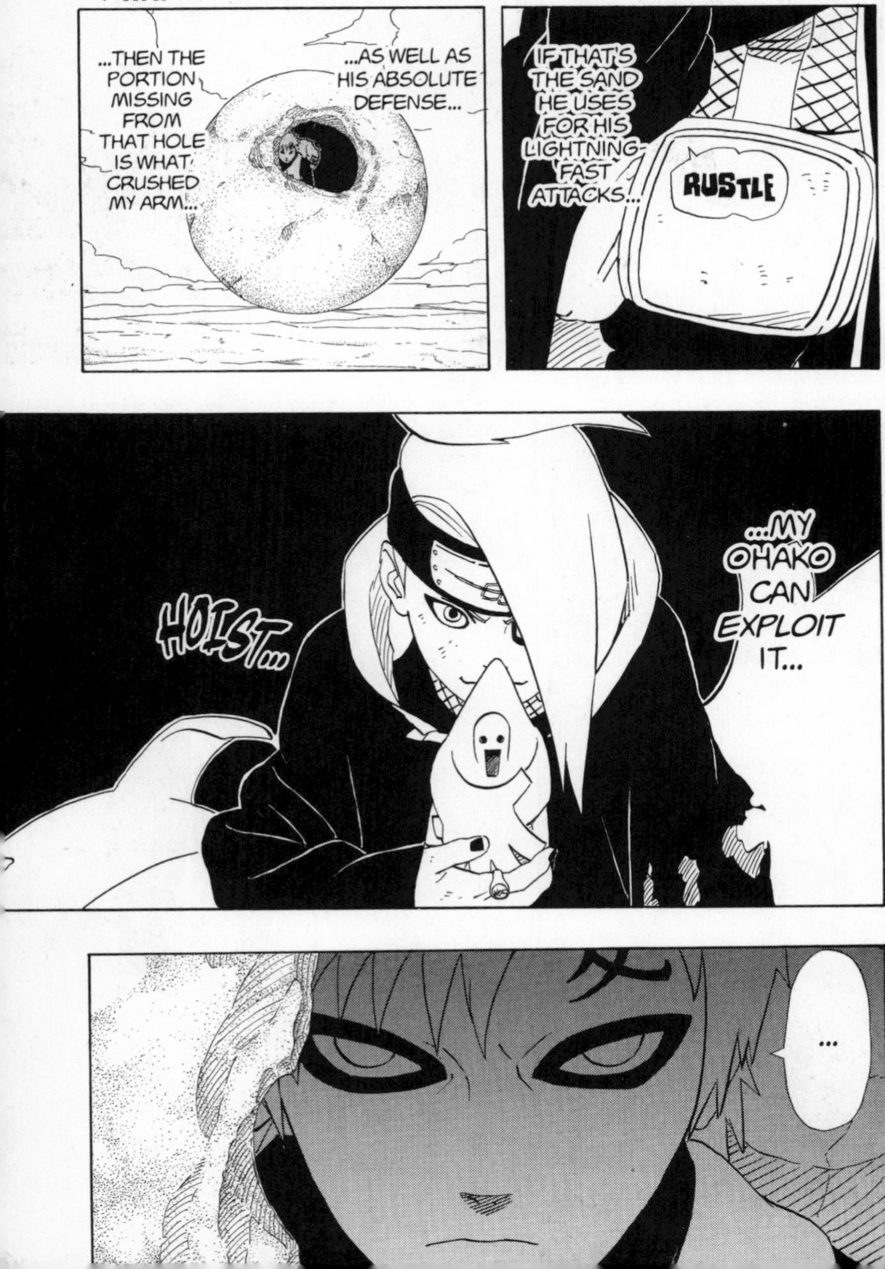
IF THAT'S THE SAND HE USES FOR HIS LIGHTNING-FAST ATTACKS...
RUSTLE
...THEN THE PORTION MISSING FROM THAT HOLE IS WHAT CRUSHED MY ARM...
...AS WELL AS HIS ABSOLUTE DEFENSE...
...MY OHAKO CAN EXPLOIT IT...
HOIST...
...

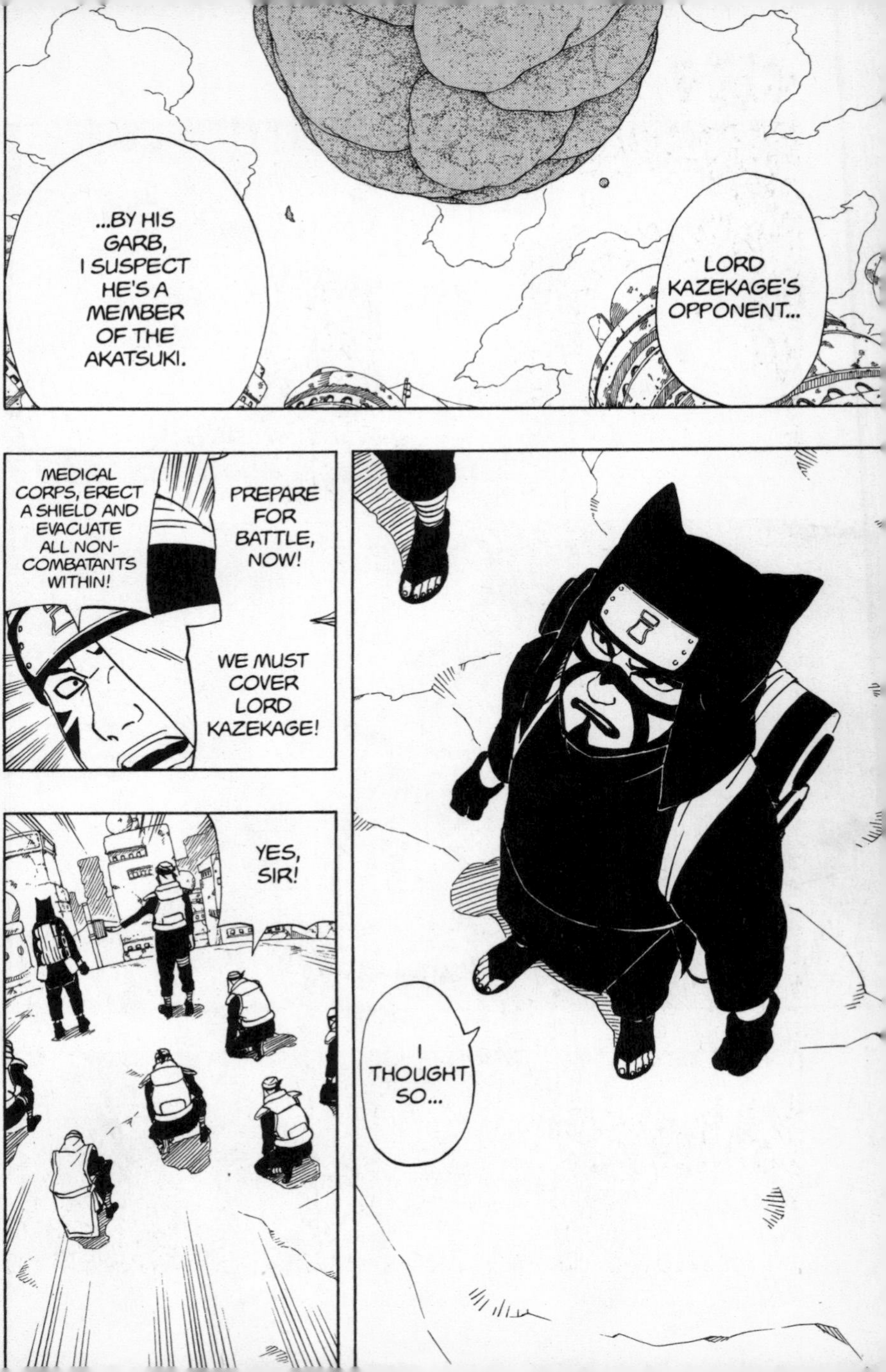
LORD KAZEKAGE'S OPPONENT...
...BY HIS GARB, I SUSPECT HE'S A MEMBER OF THE AKATSUKI.
I THOUGHT SO...
PREPARE FOR BATTLE, NOW!
MEDICAL CORPS, ERECT A SHIELD AND EVACUATE ALL NON-COMBATANTS WITHIN!
WE MUST COVER LORD KAZEKAGE!
YES, SIR!

READ THIS WAY

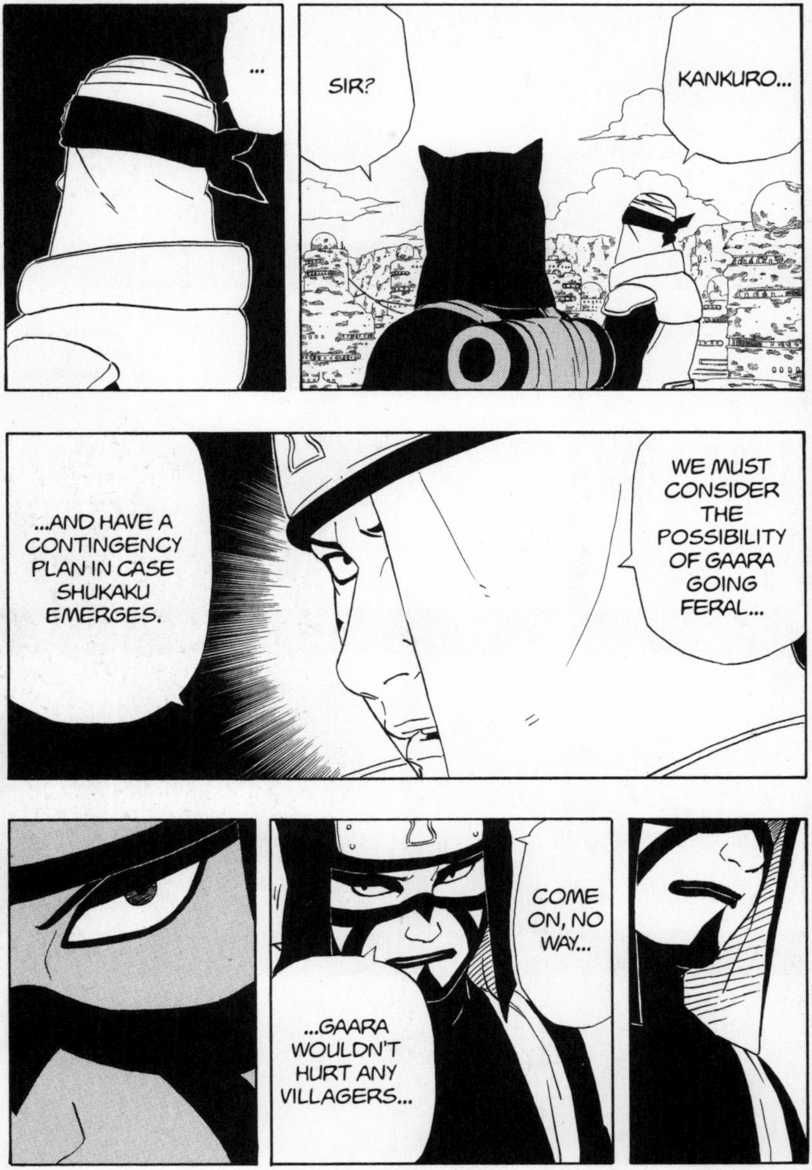
KANKURO...
SIR?
...
WE MUST CONSIDER THE POSSIBILITY OF GAARA GOING FERAL...
...AND HAVE A CONTINGENCY PLAN IN CASE SHUKAKU EMERGES.
COME ON, NO WAY...
...GAARA WOULDN'T HURT ANY VILLAGERS...

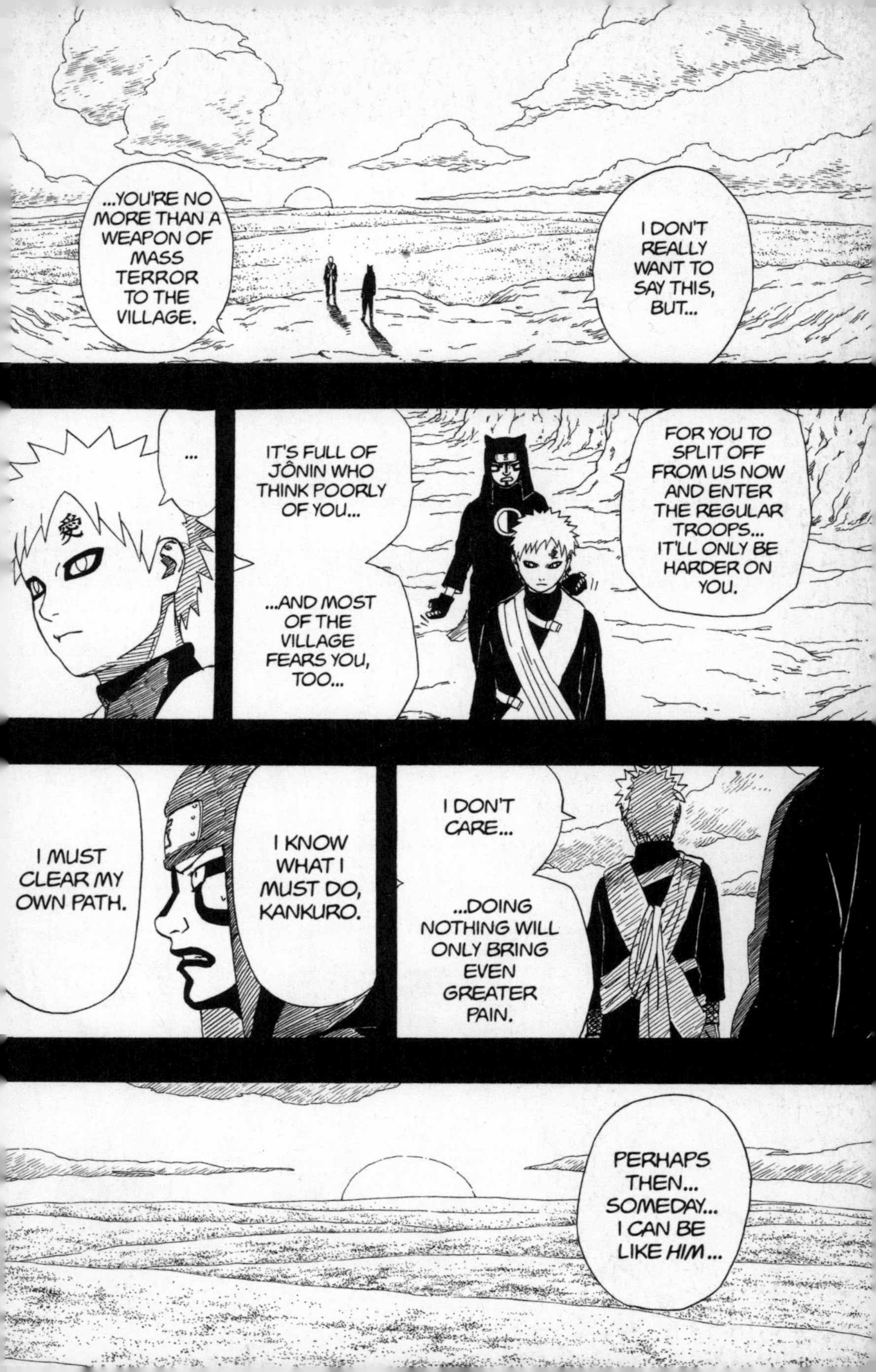
I DON'T REALLY WANT TO SAY THIS, BUT...
...YOU'RE NO MORE THAN A WEAPON OF MASS TERROR TO THE VILLAGE.
FOR YOU TO SPLIT OFF FROM US NOW AND ENTER THE REGULAR TROOPS... IT'LL ONLY BE HARDER ON YOU.
IT'S FULL OF JÔNIN WHO THINK POORLY OF YOU...
...AND MOST OF THE VILLAGE FEARS YOU, TOO...
...
I DON'T CARE...
...DOING NOTHING WILL ONLY BRING EVEN GREATER PAIN.
I KNOW WHAT I MUST DO, KANKURO.
I MUST CLEAR MY OWN PATH.
PERHAPS THEN... SOMEDAY... I CAN BE LIKE *HIM*...

READ THIS WAY

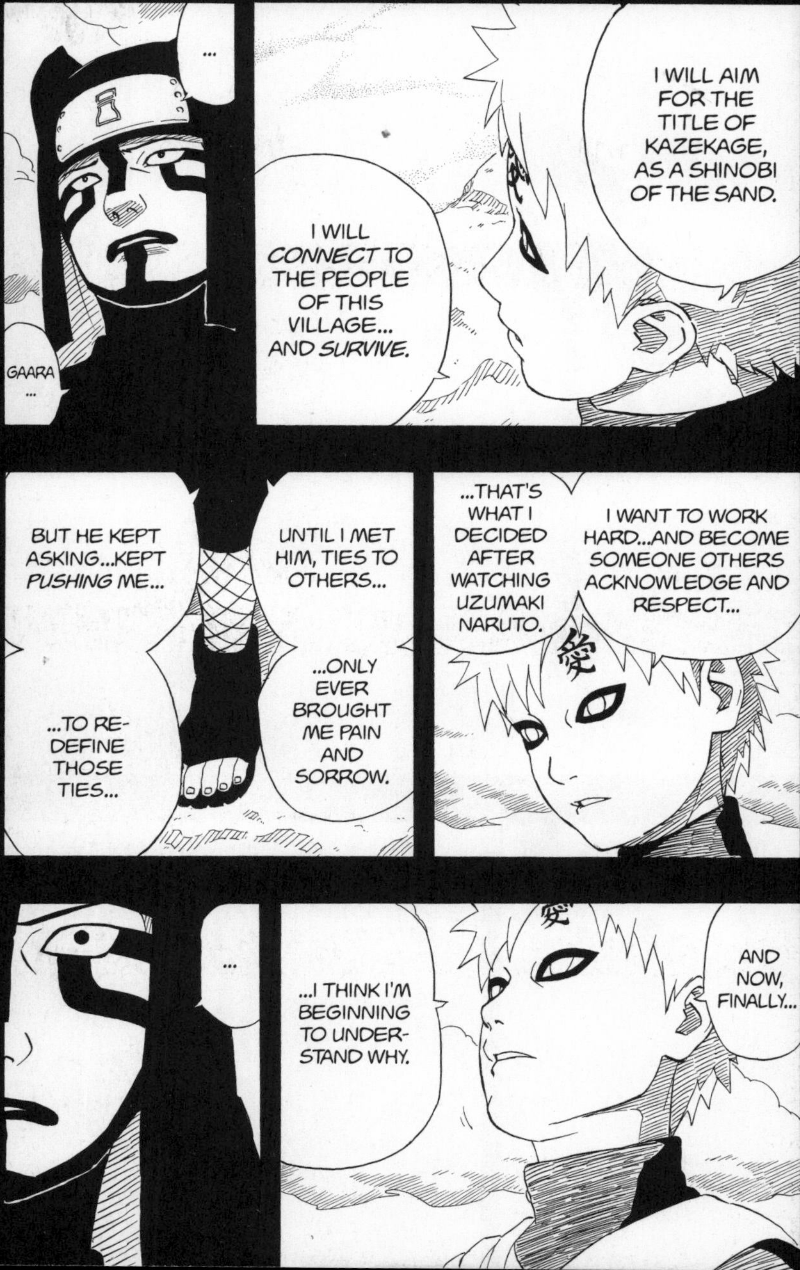
I WILL AIM FOR THE TITLE OF KAZEKAGE, AS A SHINOBI OF THE SAND.
I WILL *CONNECT* TO THE PEOPLE OF THIS VILLAGE... AND *SURVIVE.*
...
GAARA ...
I WANT TO WORK HARD...AND BECOME SOMEONE OTHERS ACKNOWLEDGE AND RESPECT...
...THAT'S WHAT I DECIDED AFTER WATCHING UZUMAKI NARUTO.
UNTIL I MET HIM, TIES TO OTHERS...
...ONLY EVER BROUGHT ME PAIN AND SORROW.
BUT HE KEPT ASKING...KEPT *PUSHING ME...*
...TO RE-DEFINE THOSE TIES...
AND NOW, FINALLY...
...I THINK I'M BEGINNING TO UNDER-STAND WHY.
...

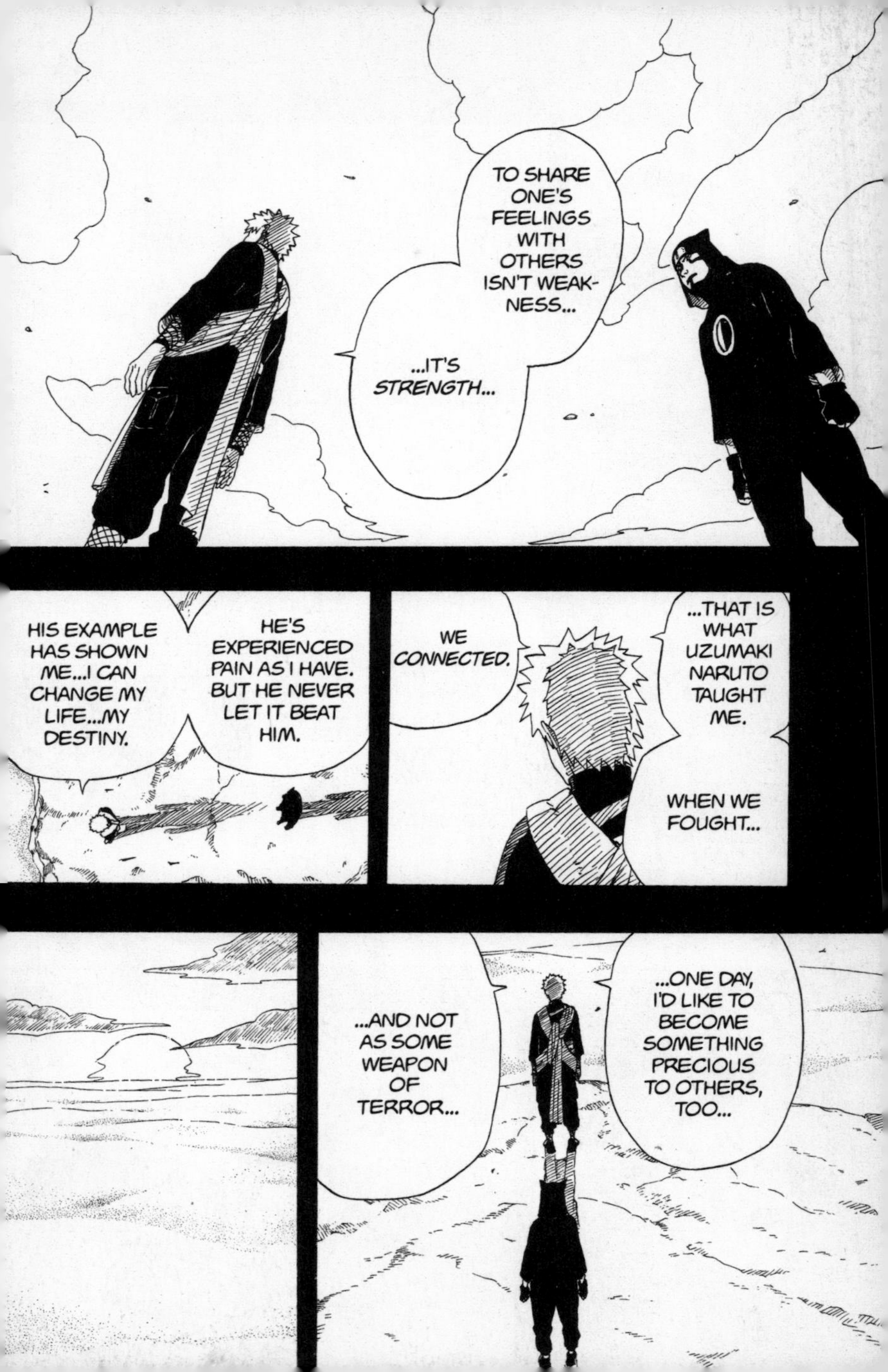
TO SHARE ONE'S FEELINGS WITH OTHERS ISN'T WEAK- NESS...
...IT'S STRENGTH...
...THAT IS WHAT UZUMAKI NARUTO TAUGHT ME.
WHEN WE FOUGHT...
WE CONNECTED.
HE'S EXPERIENCED PAIN AS I HAVE. BUT HE NEVER LET IT BEAT HIM.
HIS EXAMPLE HAS SHOWN ME...I CAN CHANGE MY LIFE...MY DESTINY.
...ONE DAY, I'D LIKE TO BECOME SOMETHING PRECIOUS TO OTHERS, TOO...
...AND NOT AS SOME WEAPON OF TERROR...

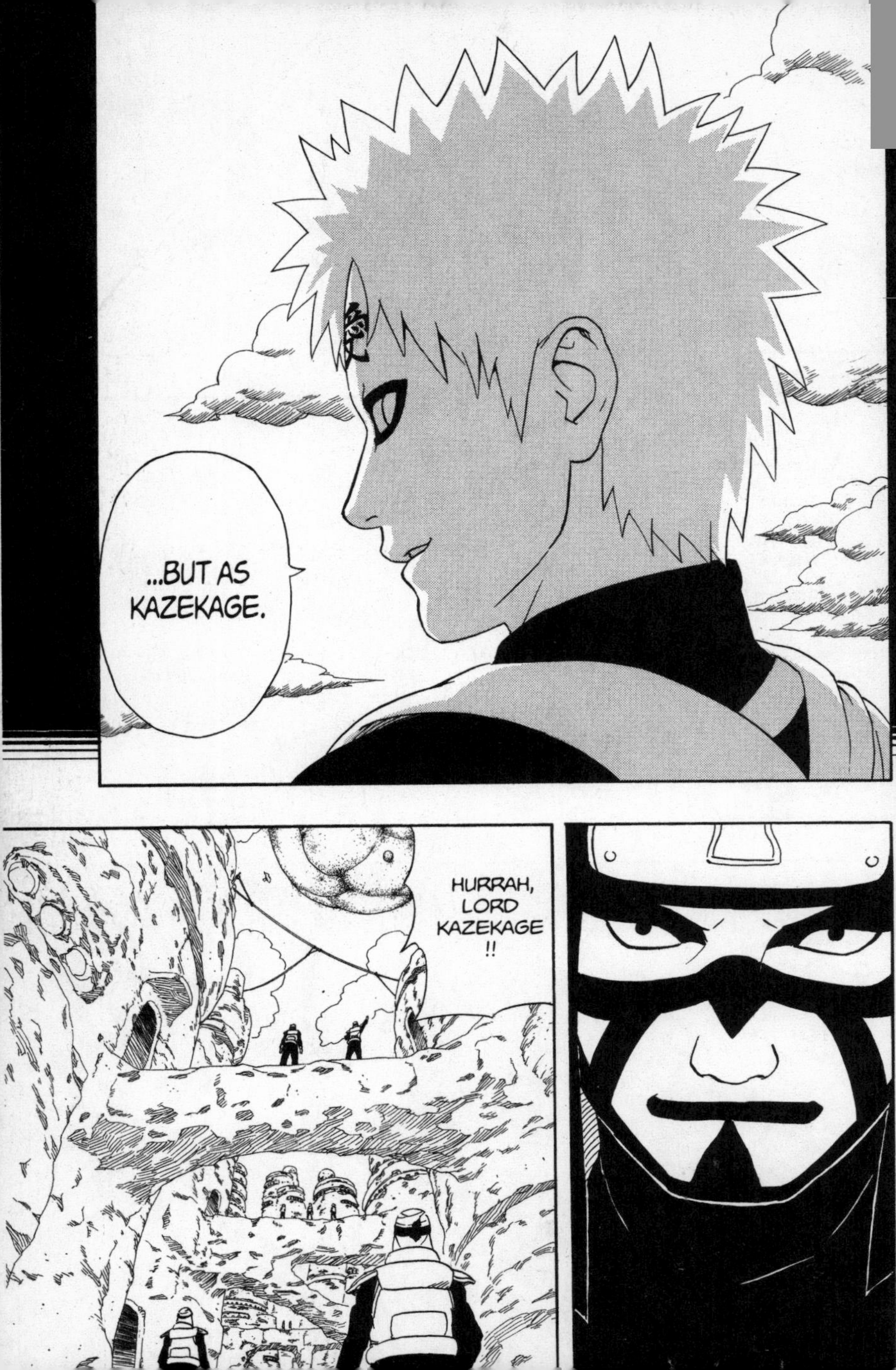
...BUT AS KAZEKAGE.
HURRAH, LORD KAZEKAGE!!

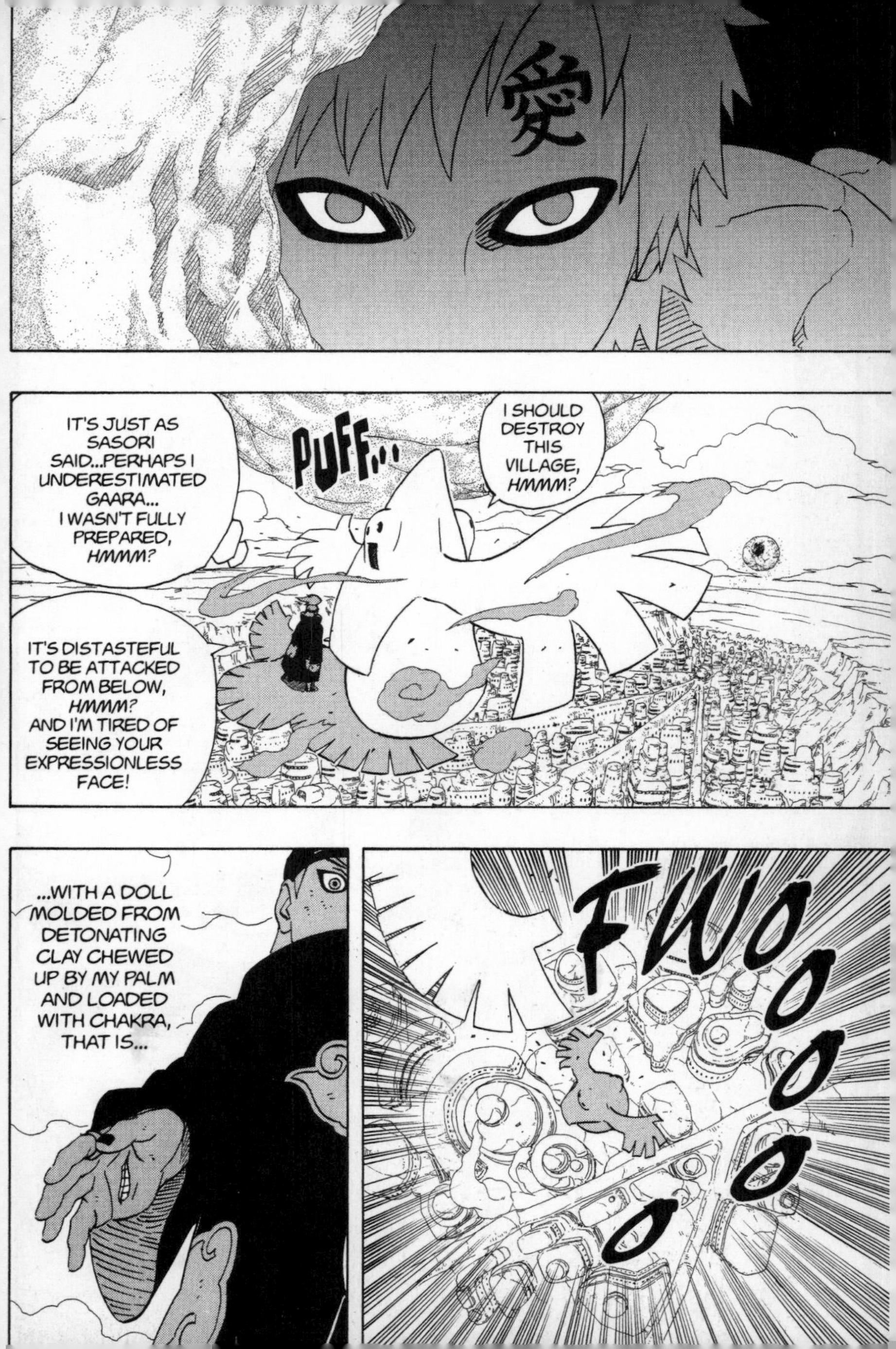
I SHOULD DESTROY THIS VILLAGE, HMMM?
PUFF...
IT'S JUST AS SASORI SAID...PERHAPS I UNDERESTIMATED GAARA... I WASN'T FULLY PREPARED, HMMM?
IT'S DISTASTEFUL TO BE ATTACKED FROM BELOW, HMMM? AND I'M TIRED OF SEEING YOUR EXPRESSIONLESS FACE!
FWOOOOO
...WITH A DOLL MOLDED FROM DETONATING CLAY CHEWED UP BY MY PALM AND LOADED WITH CHAKRA, THAT IS...

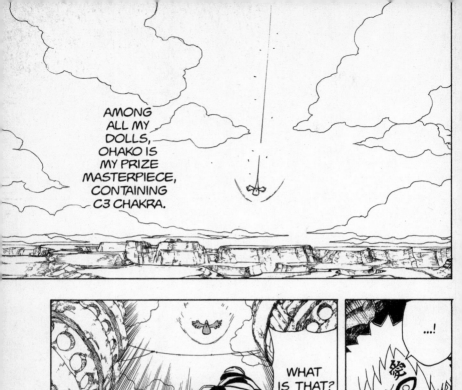

AMONG ALL MY DOLLS, OHAKO IS MY PRIZE MASTERPIECE, CONTAINING C3 CHAKRA.

WHAT IS THAT?

....!

!!

TOO LATE!

NOT GOOD. RUN !!

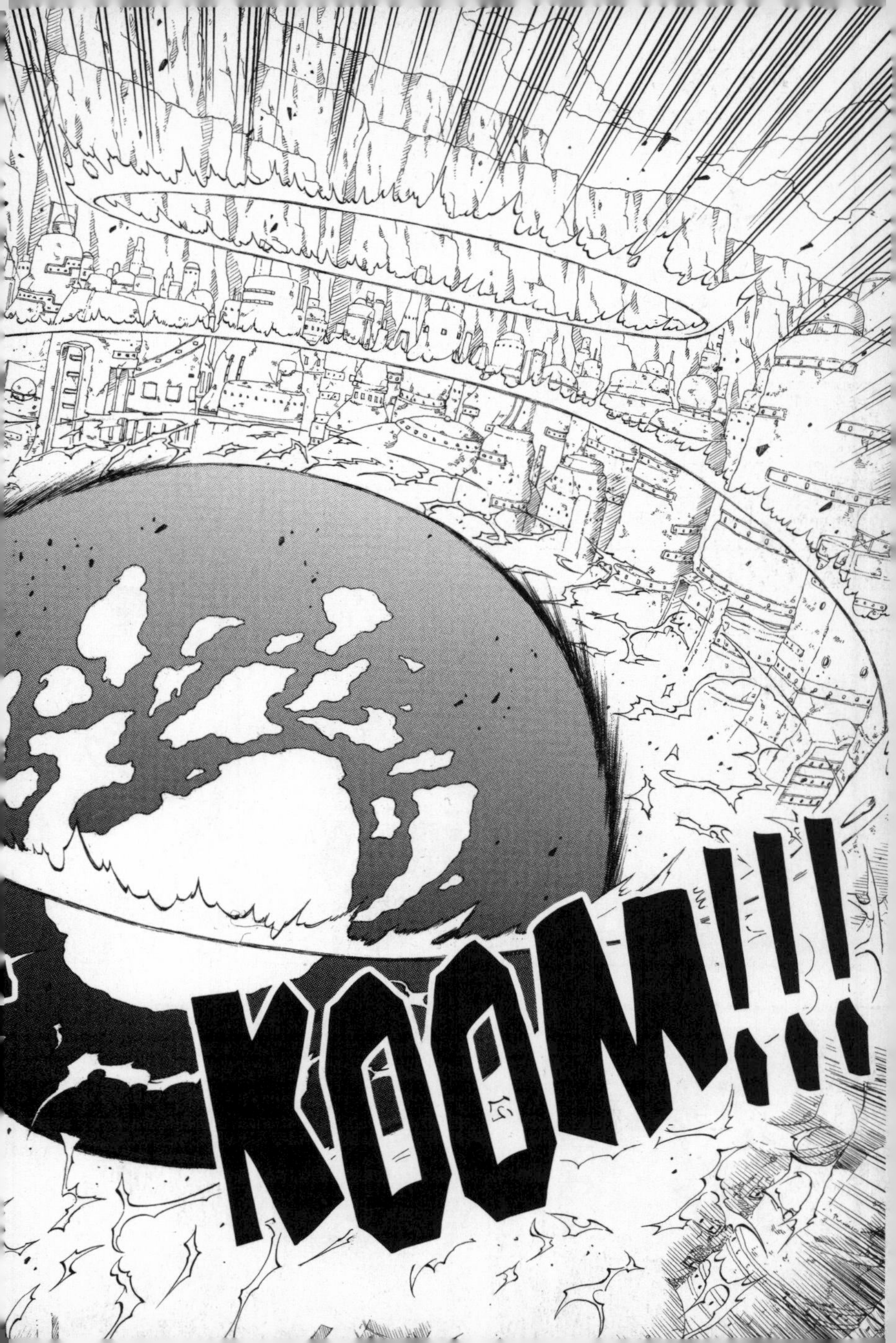
KOOM!!!

READ THIS WAY

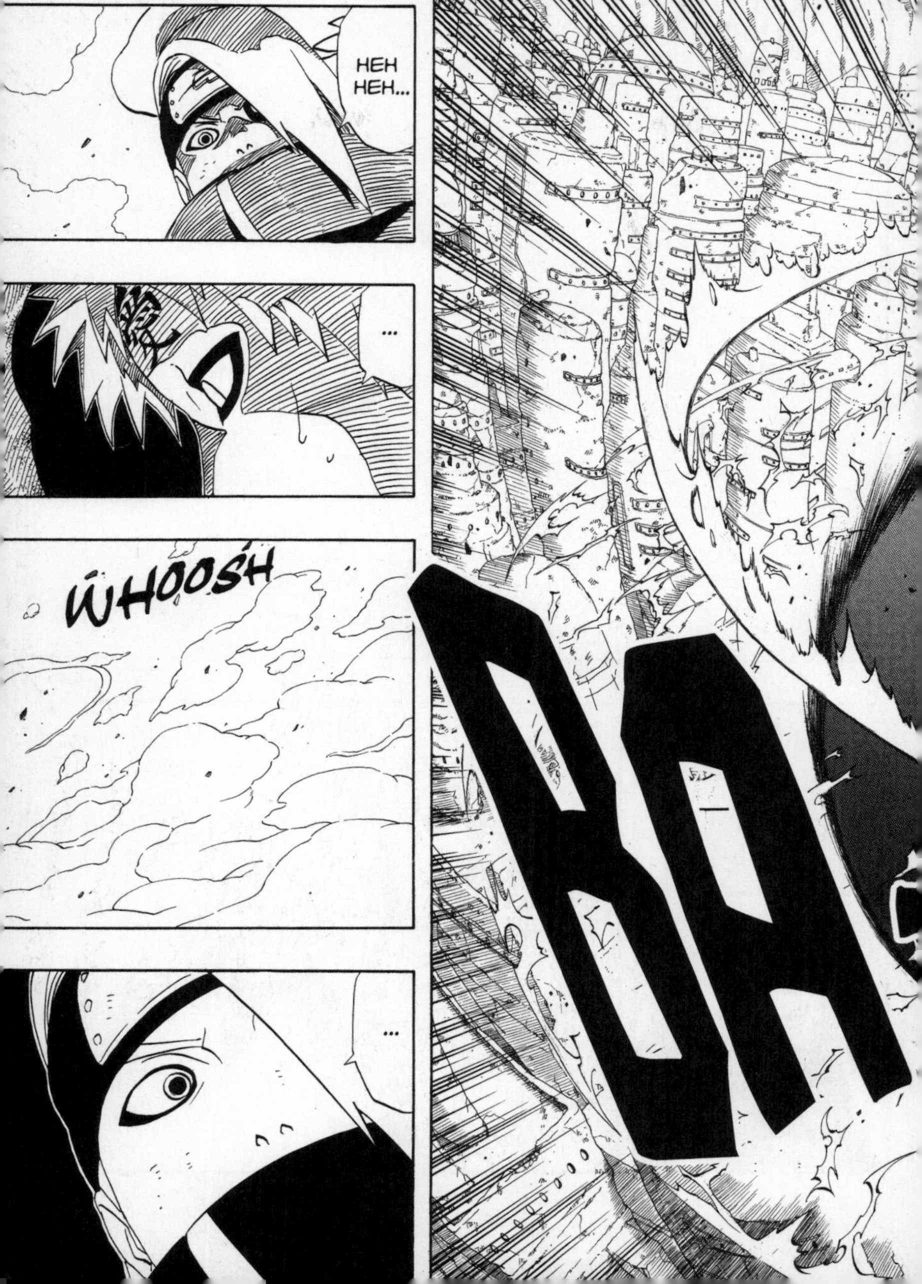
HEH HEH...
...
WHOOSH
...

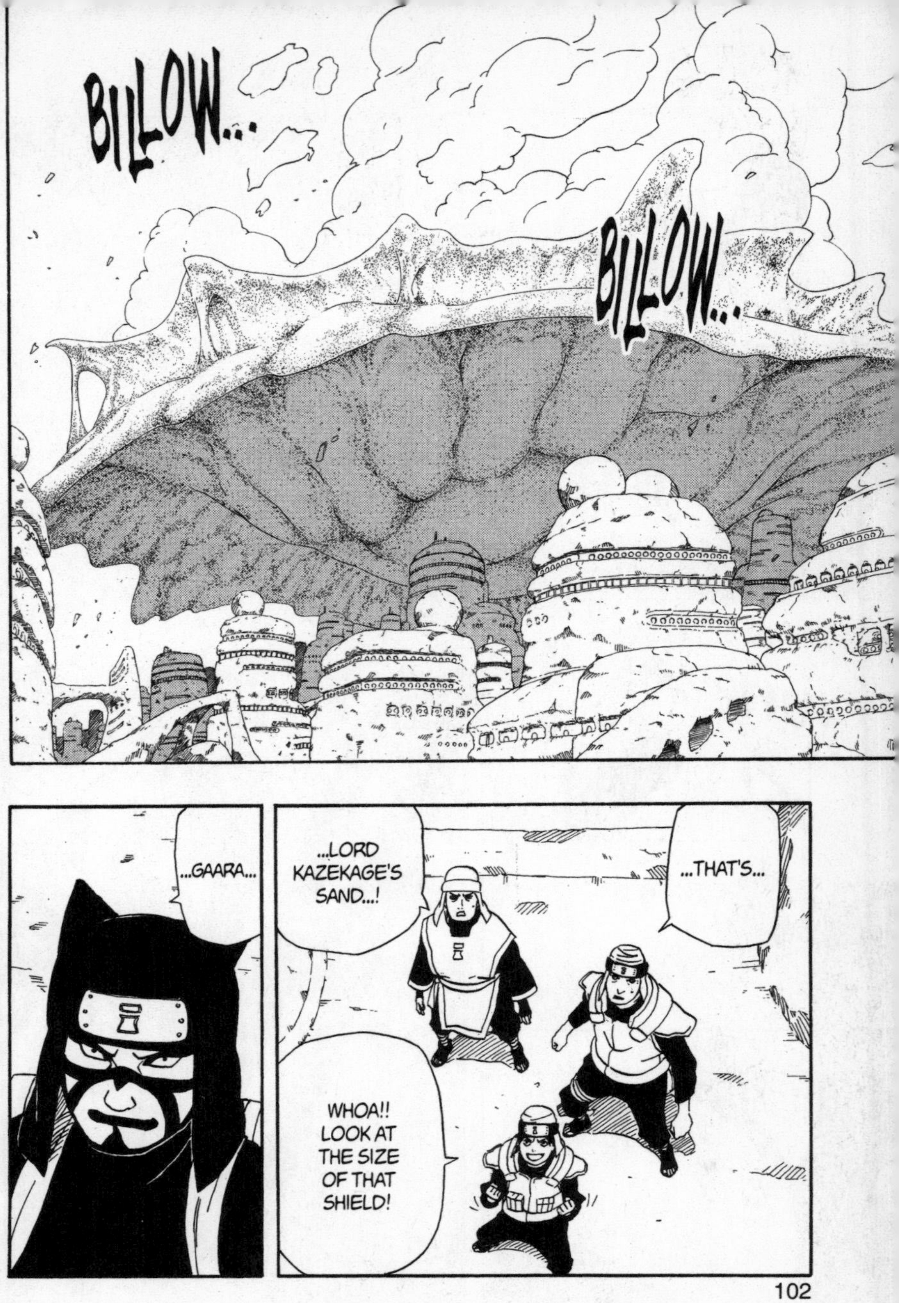
BILLOW...
BILLOW...
...THAT'S...
...LORD KAZEKAGE'S SAND...!
WHOA!! LOOK AT THE SIZE OF THAT SHIELD!
...GAARA...

READ THIS WAY

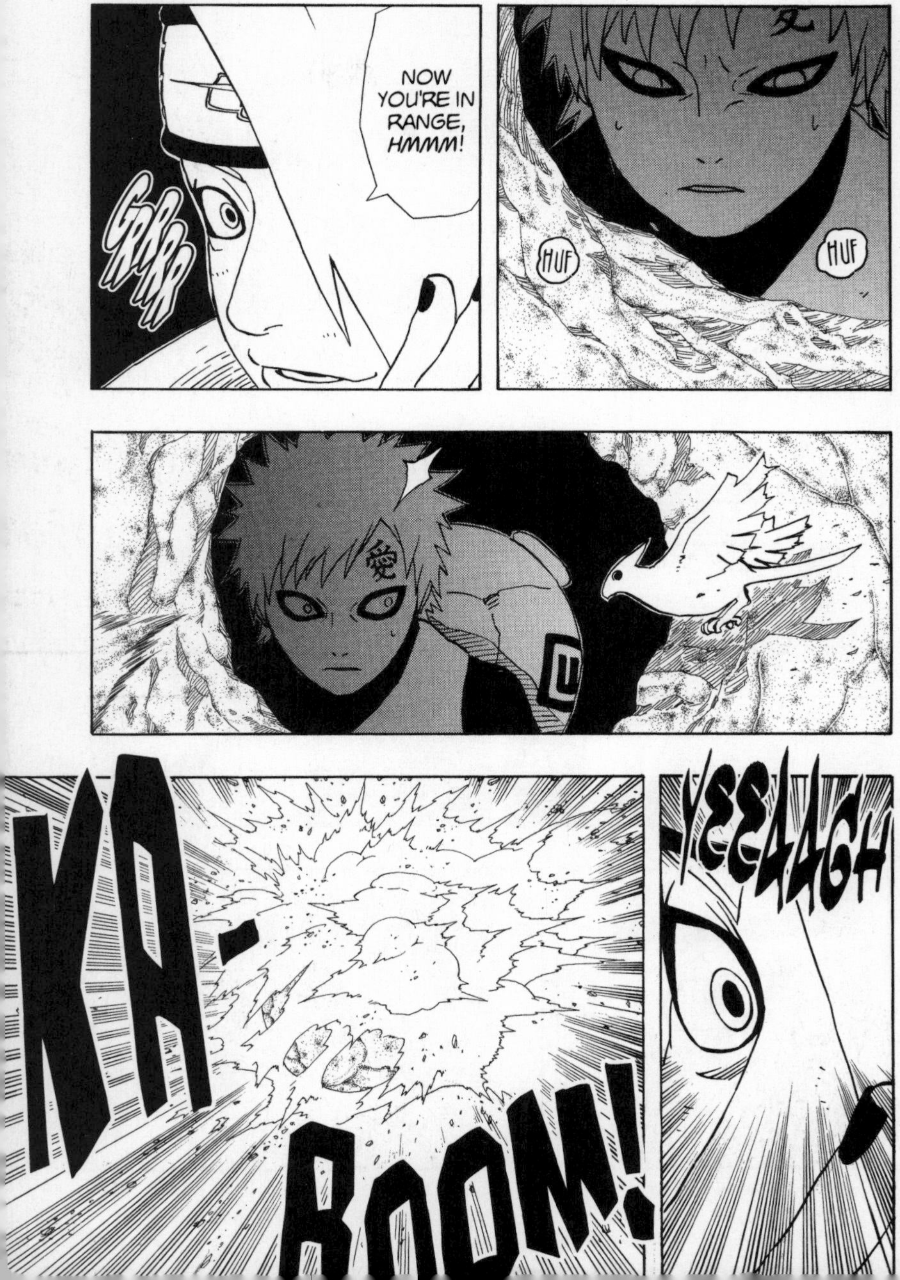
HUF
HUF
GRRR
NOW YOU'RE IN RANGE, HMMM!
YEEAAGH
KA-BOOM!

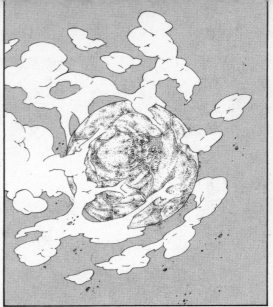

SWIFT AND RESILIENT...

FLAP FLAP

...IF SOMEWHAT PREDICTABLE!

...

HUF HUF

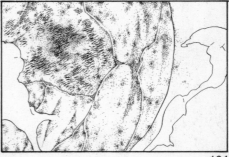

READ THIS WAY

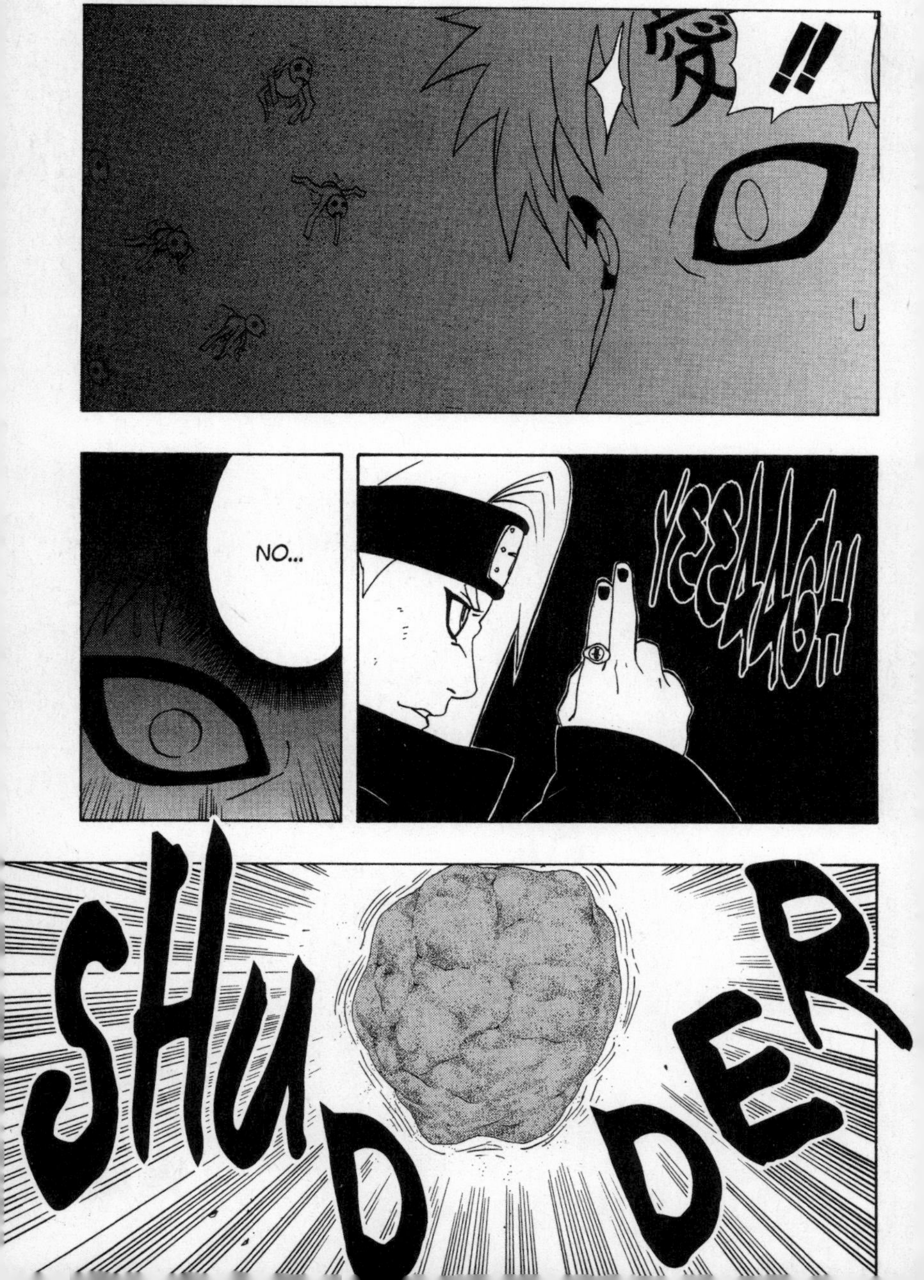
!!
NO...
YEEAAGH
SHUDDER

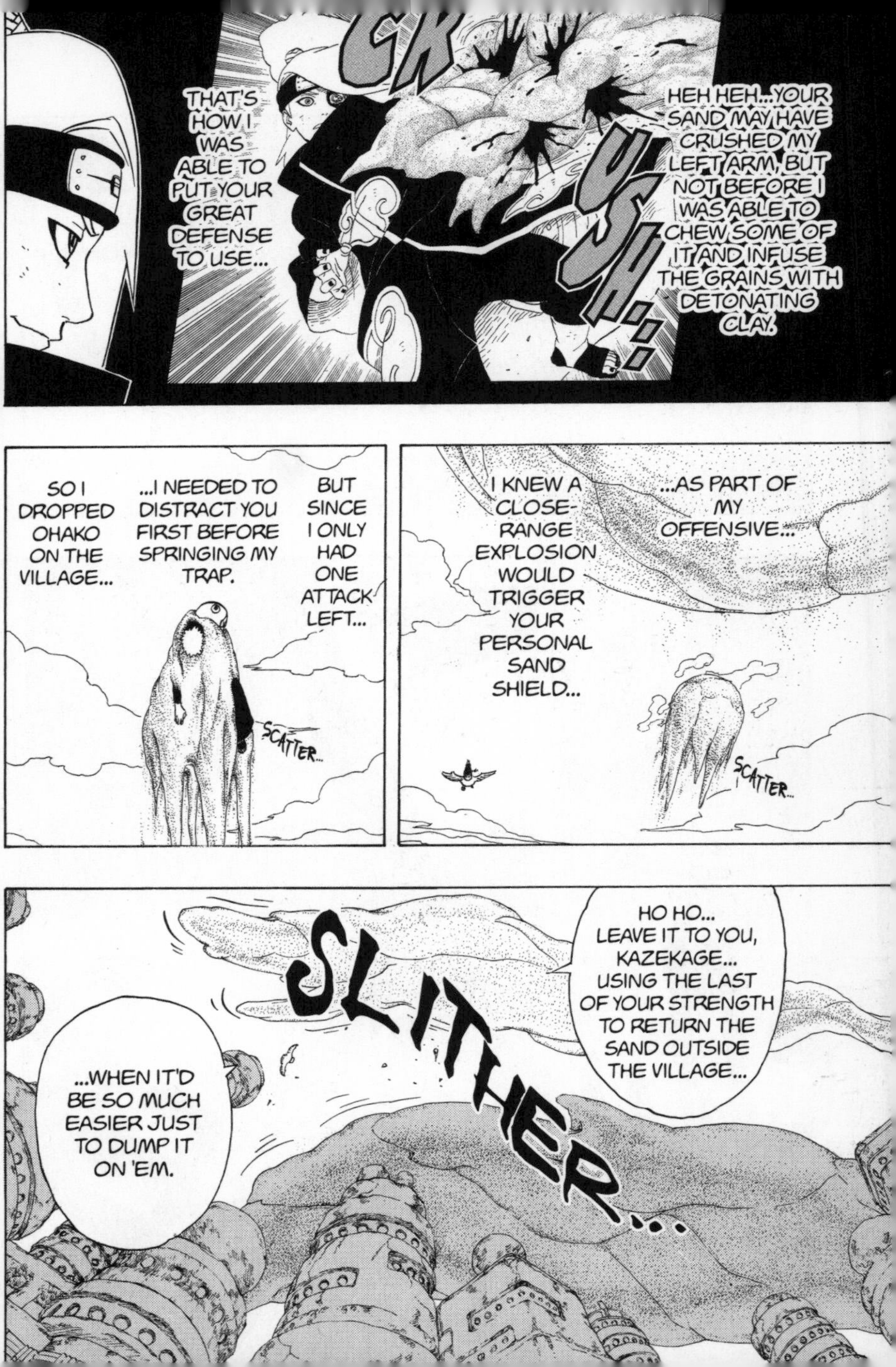

HEH HEH... YOUR SAND MAY HAVE CRUSHED MY LEFT ARM, BUT NOT BEFORE I WAS ABLE TO CHEW SOME OF IT AND INFUSE THE GRAINS WITH DETONATING CLAY.
CR
USH...
THAT'S HOW I WAS ABLE TO PUT YOUR GREAT DEFENSE TO USE...
...AS PART OF MY OFFENSIVE...
I KNEW A CLOSE-RANGE EXPLOSION WOULD TRIGGER YOUR PERSONAL SAND SHIELD...
SCATTER...
BUT SINCE I ONLY HAD ONE ATTACK LEFT...
...I NEEDED TO DISTRACT YOU FIRST BEFORE SPRINGING MY TRAP.
SO I DROPPED OHAKO ON THE VILLAGE...
SCATTER...
HO HO... LEAVE IT TO YOU, KAZEKAGE... USING THE LAST OF YOUR STRENGTH TO RETURN THE SAND OUTSIDE THE VILLAGE...
SLITHER...
...WHEN IT'D BE SO MUCH EASIER JUST TO DUMP IT ON 'EM.

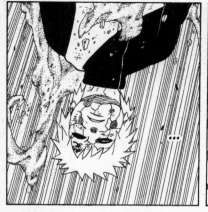

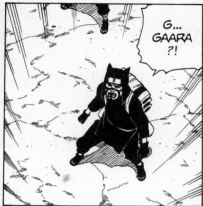

READ THIS WAY

G... GAARA ?!
...
SHOOM
SNARING YOU ALIVE WAS THE HARD PART...
...AND A MOST SATISFYING END TO THIS MASTER-PIECE...

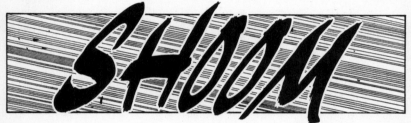

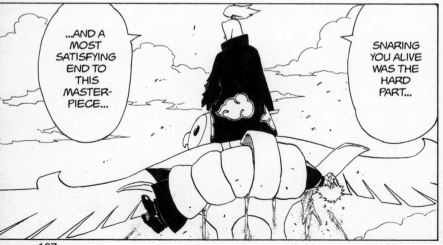

NARUTO

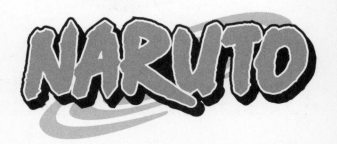

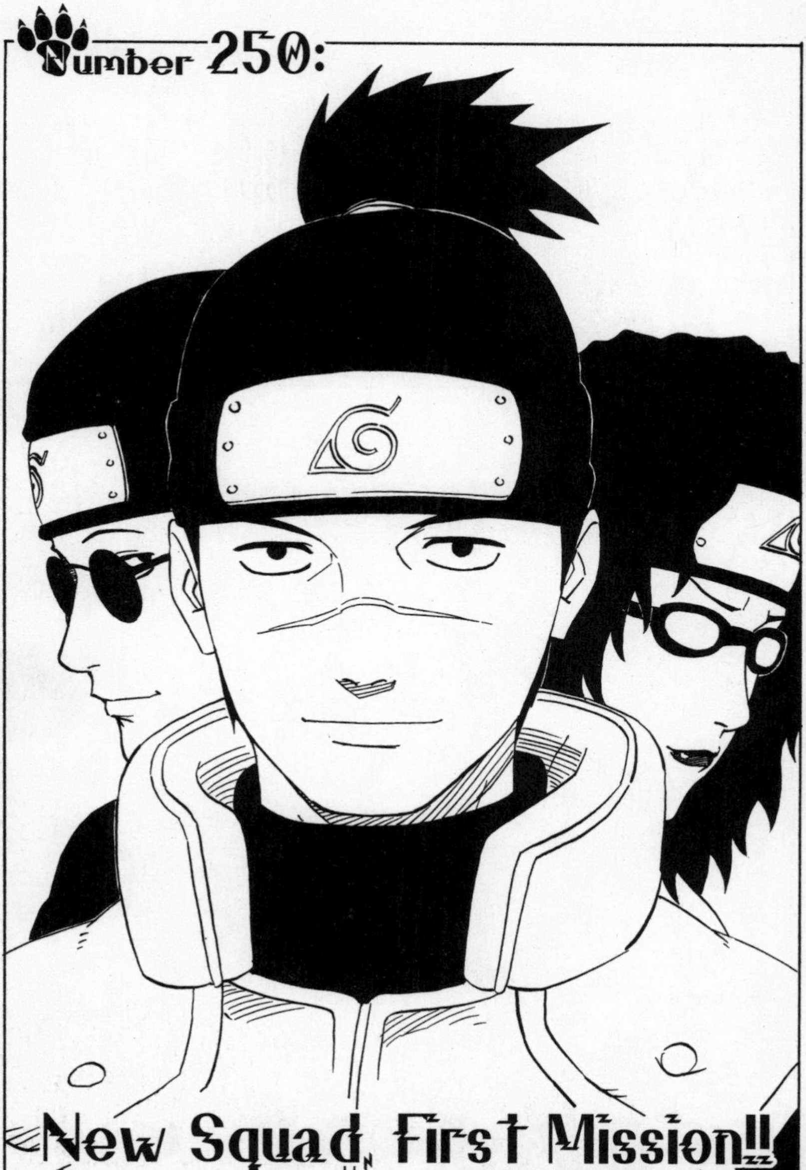
Number 250:
New Squad, First Mission!!

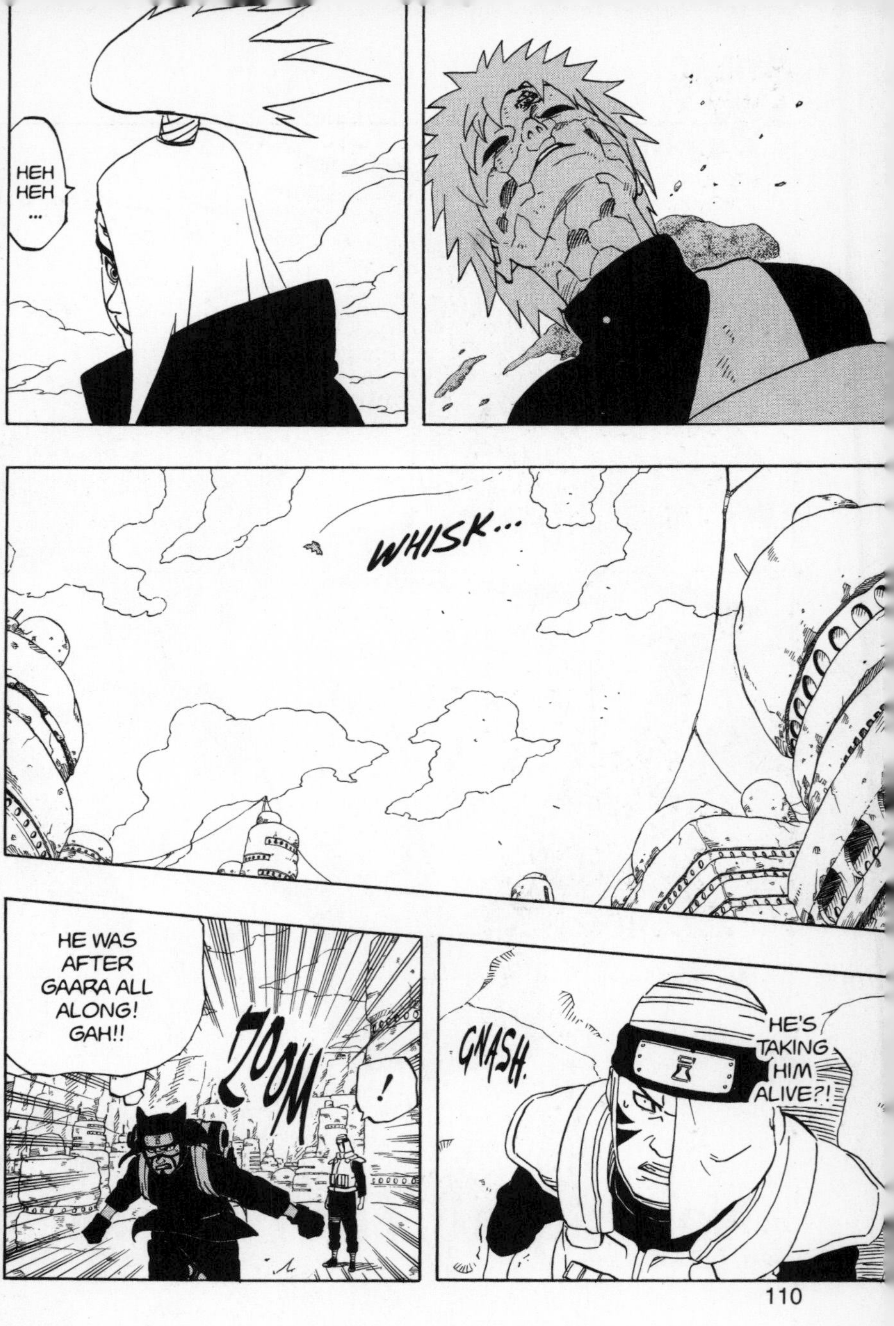
HEH HEH ...
WHISK...
GNASH.
HE'S TAKING HIM ALIVE?!
HE WAS AFTER GAARA ALL ALONG! GAH!!
ZOOM
!

READ THIS WAY

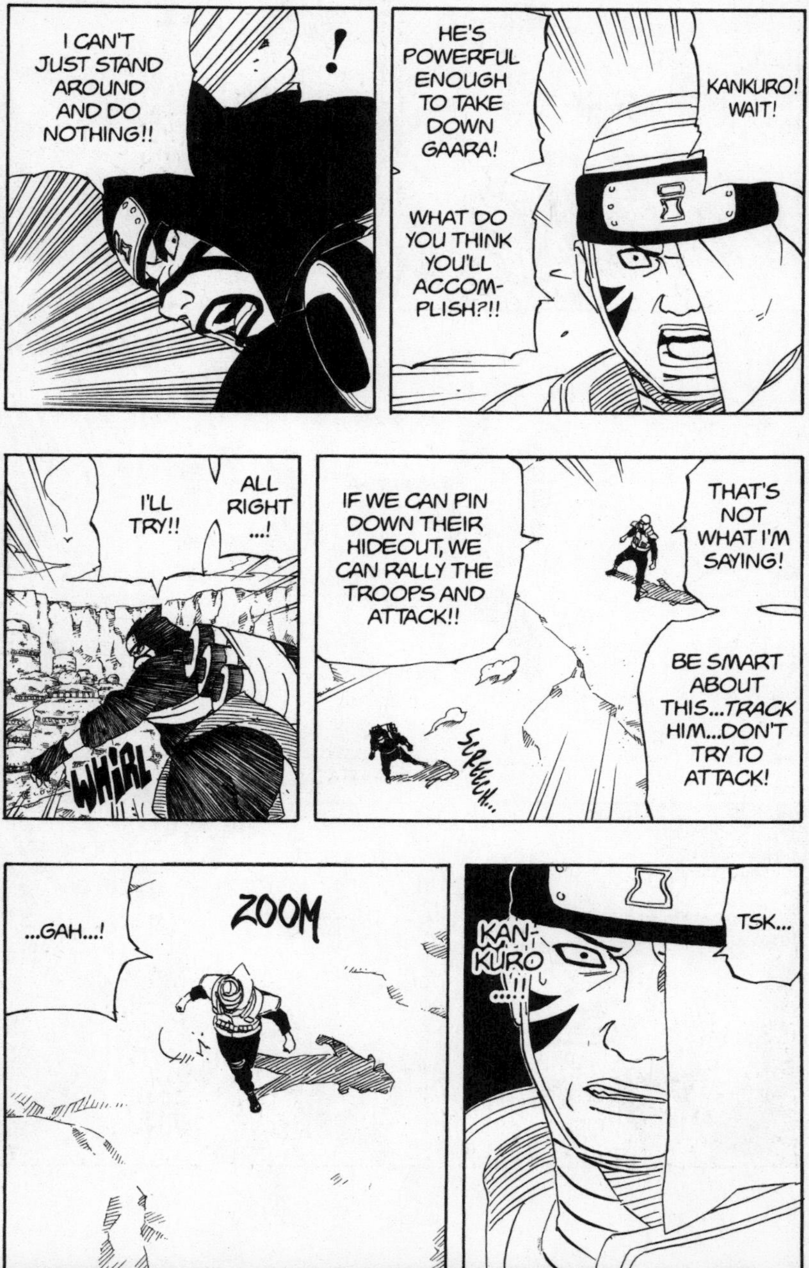
KANKURO! WAIT!
HE'S POWERFUL ENOUGH TO TAKE DOWN GAARA!
WHAT DO YOU THINK YOU'LL ACCOMPLISH?!!
!
I CAN'T JUST STAND AROUND AND DO NOTHING!!
THAT'S NOT WHAT I'M SAYING!
IF WE CAN PIN DOWN THEIR HIDEOUT, WE CAN RALLY THE TROOPS AND ATTACK!!
BE SMART ABOUT THIS...*TRACK* HIM...DON'T TRY TO ATTACK!
SCREECH...
ALL RIGHT ...!
I'LL TRY!!
WHIRL
TSK...
KAN-KURO ...!!
ZOOM
...GAH...!

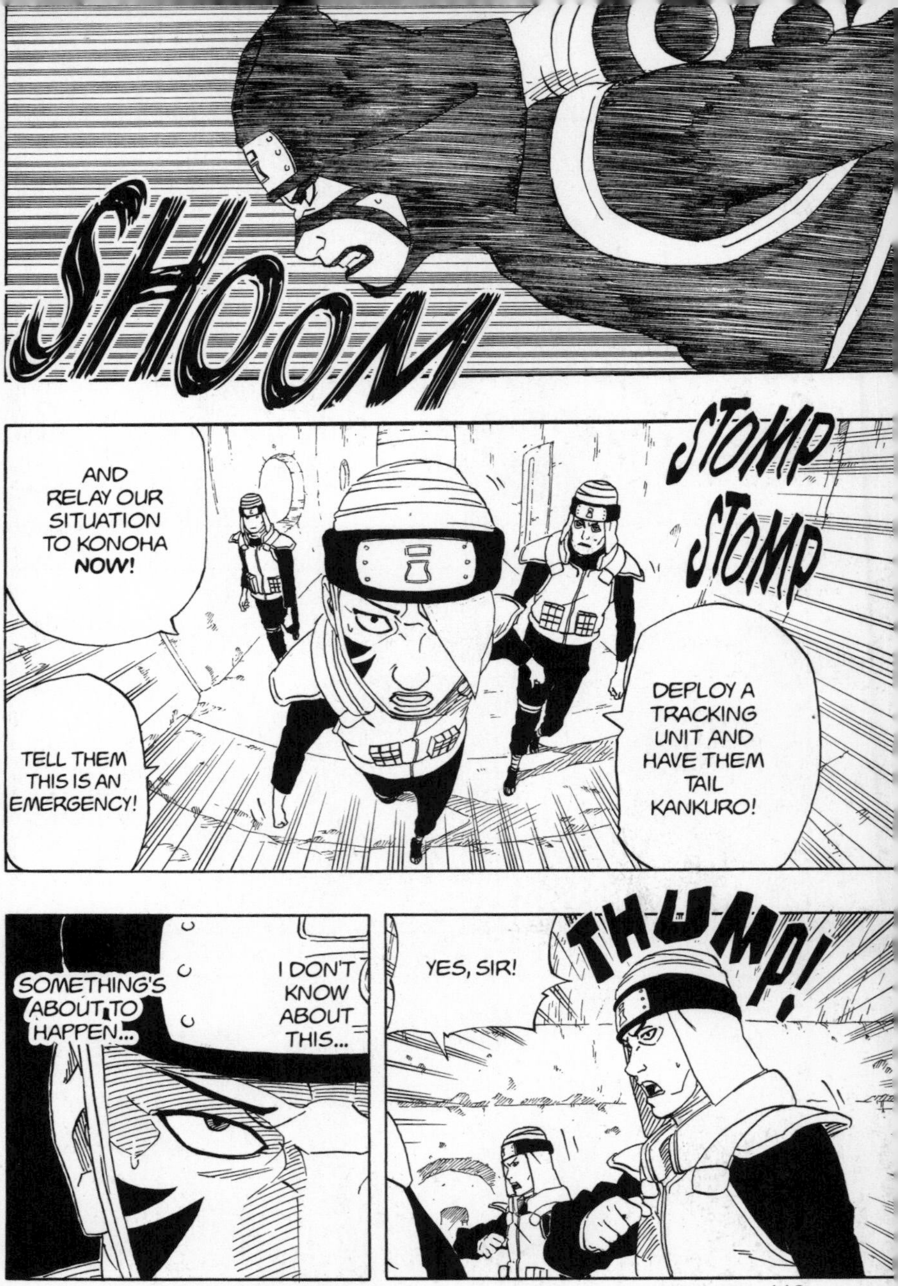
SHOOM
STOMP STOMP
DEPLOY A TRACKING UNIT AND HAVE THEM TAIL KANKURO!
AND RELAY OUR SITUATION TO KONOHA NOW!
TELL THEM THIS IS AN EMERGENCY!
THUMP!
YES, SIR!
I DON'T KNOW ABOUT THIS...
SOMETHING'S ABOUT TO HAPPEN...

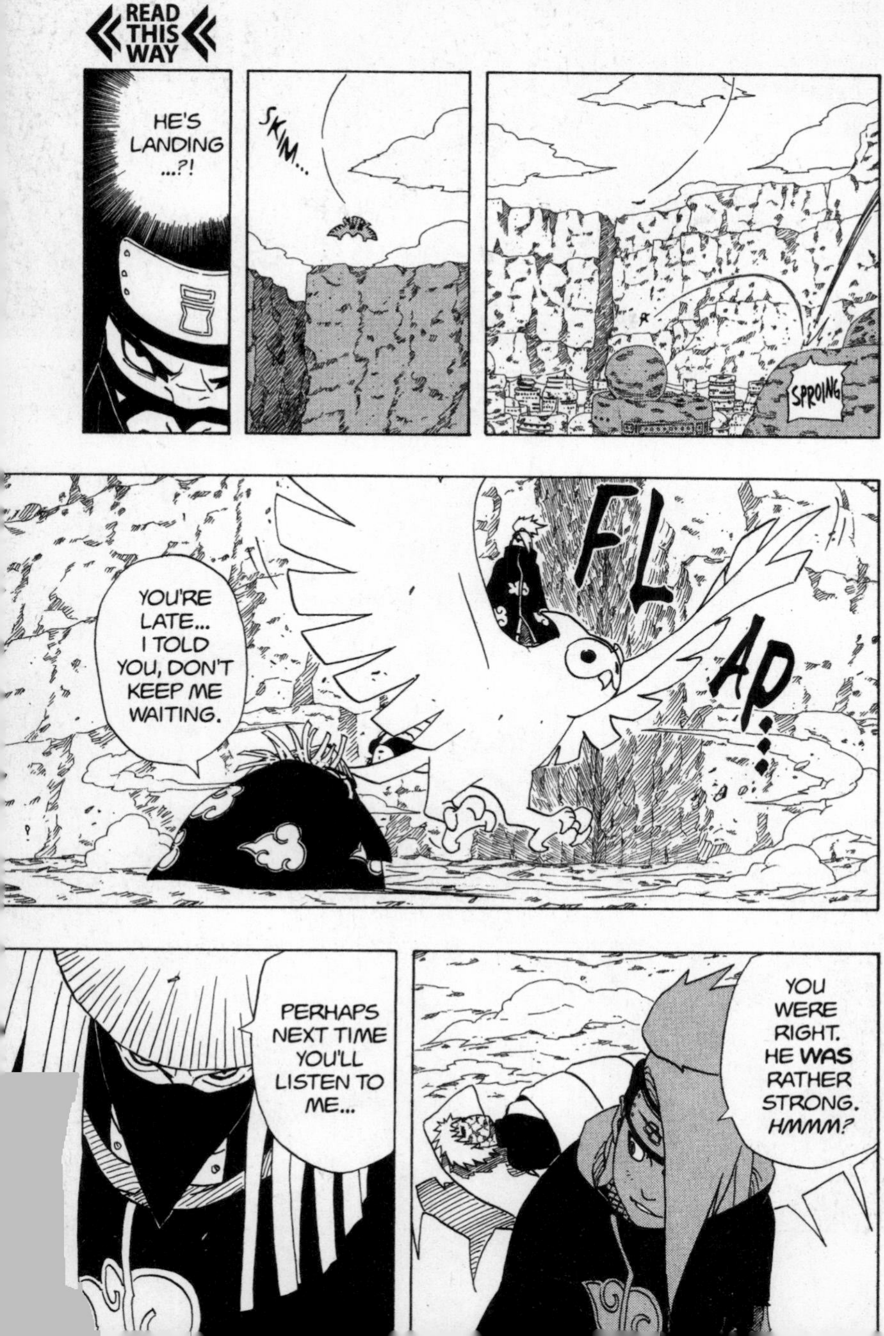
READ THIS WAY
SPROING
SKIM...
HE'S LANDING ...?!
FLAP...
YOU'RE LATE... I TOLD YOU, DON'T KEEP ME WAITING.
YOU WERE RIGHT. HE WAS RATHER STRONG. HMMM?
PERHAPS NEXT TIME YOU'LL LISTEN TO ME...

NO... THIS CAN'T BE...

...WH... WHAT...?!

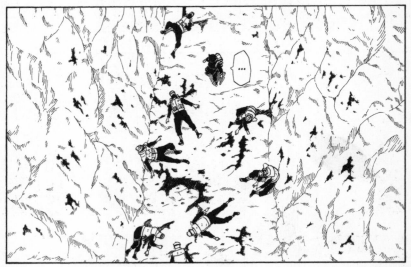

SHOOF

GRRR

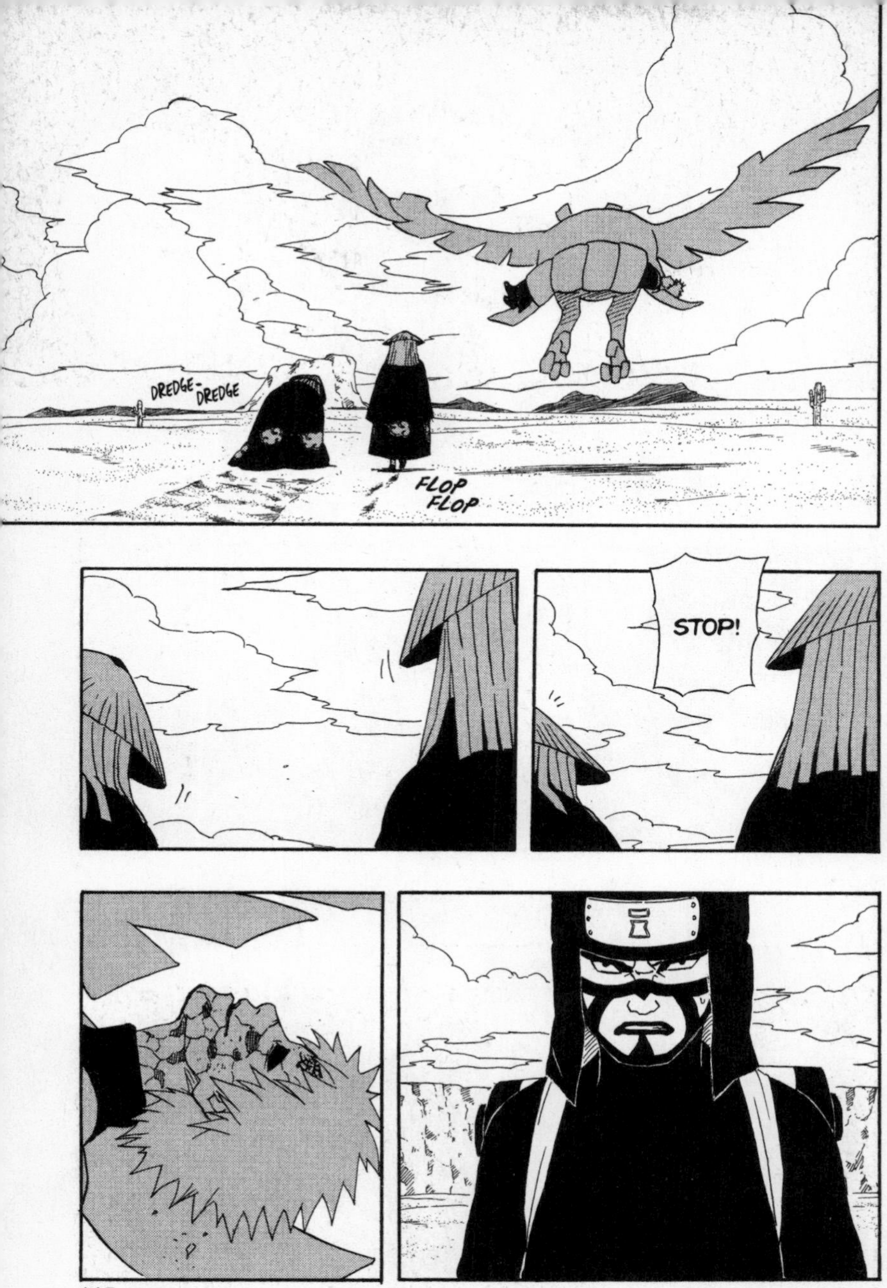
DREDGE-DREDGE
FLOP FLOP
STOP!

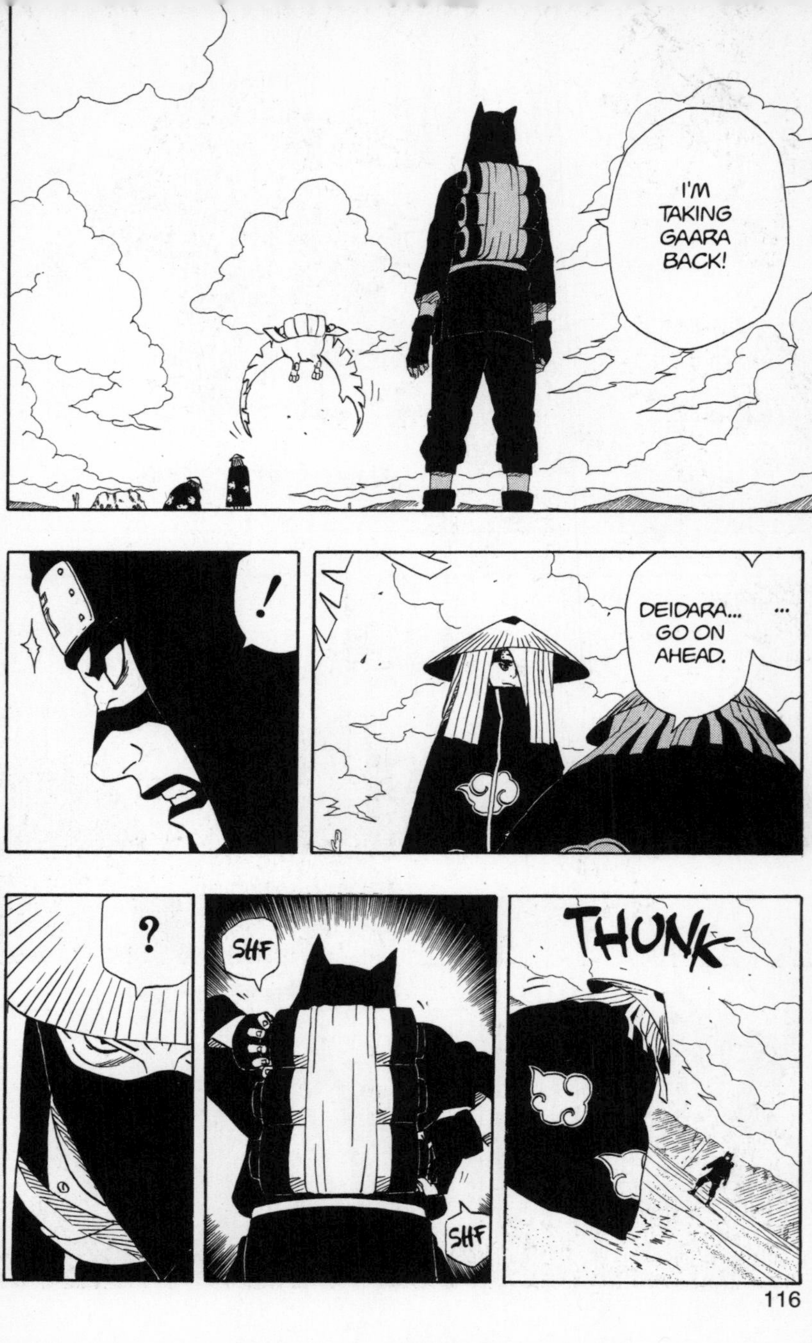
I'M TAKING GAARA BACK!
...
DEIDARA... GO ON AHEAD.
!
THUNK
SHF
SHF
?

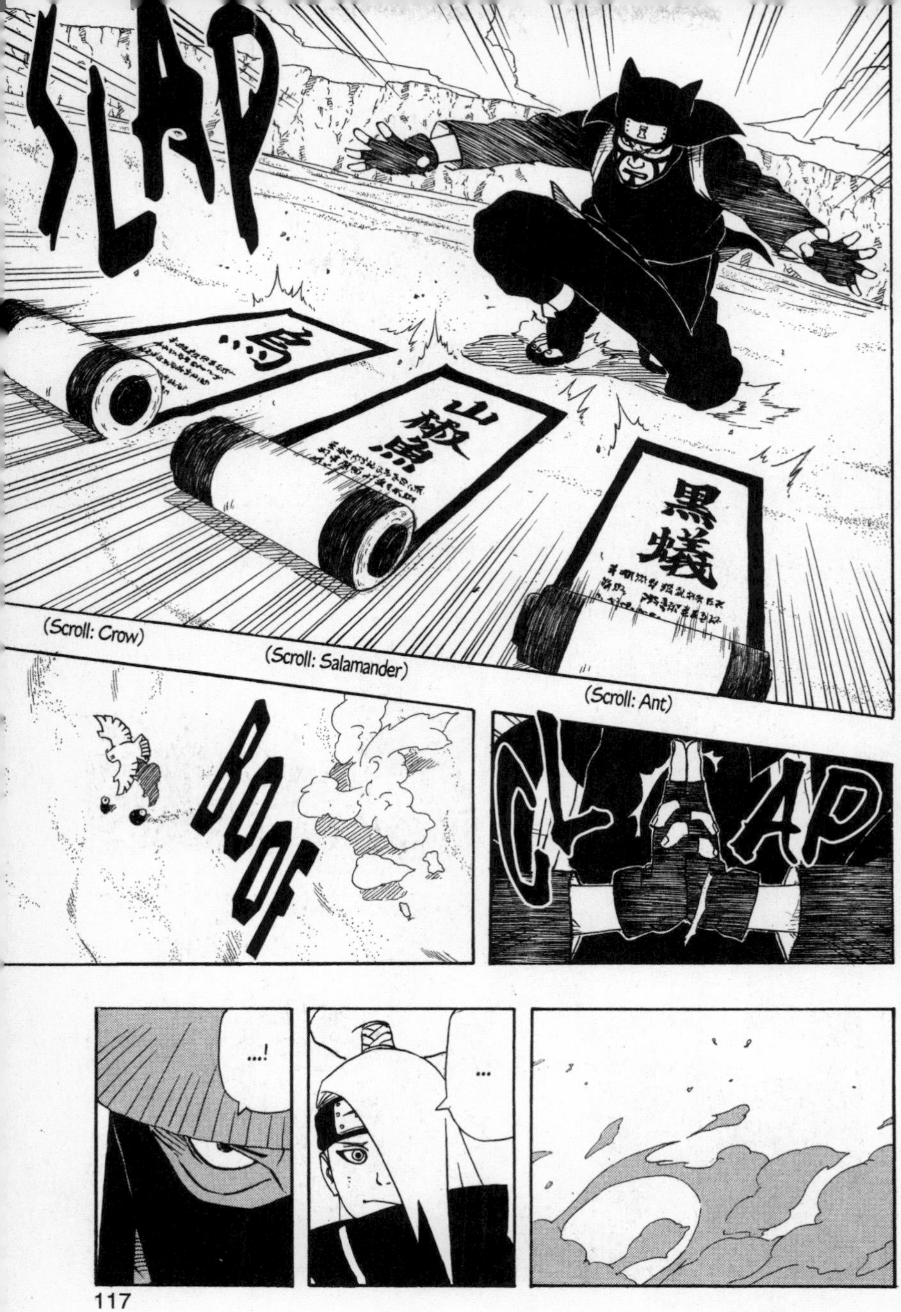
SLAP
烏
(Scroll: Crow)
山椒魚
(Scroll: Salamander)
黒蟻
(Scroll: Ant)
CLAP
BOOF
...
...!

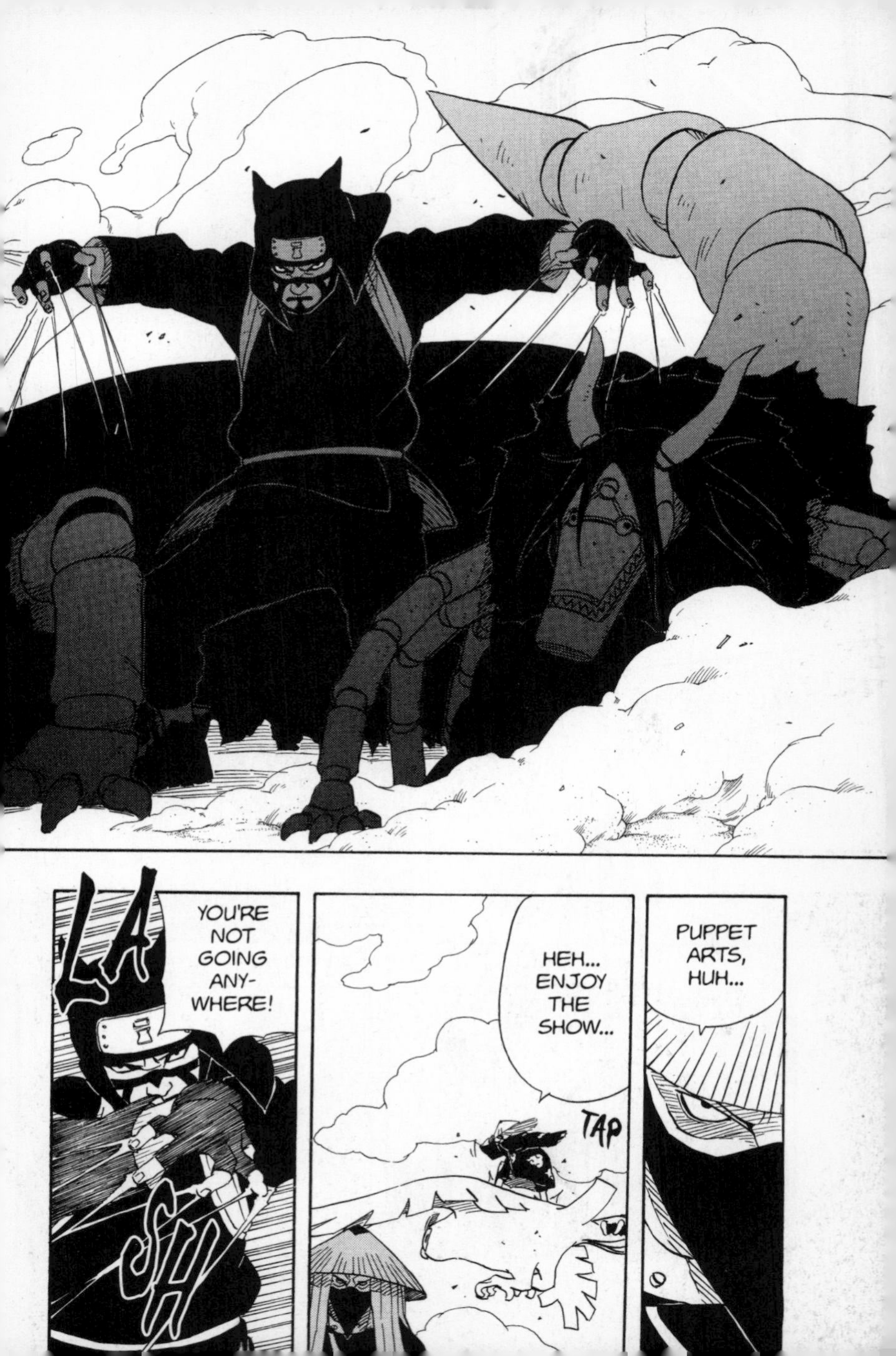
PUPPET ARTS, HUH...
HEH... ENJOY THE SHOW...
TAP
YOU'RE NOT GOING ANY-WHERE!
LA
SH

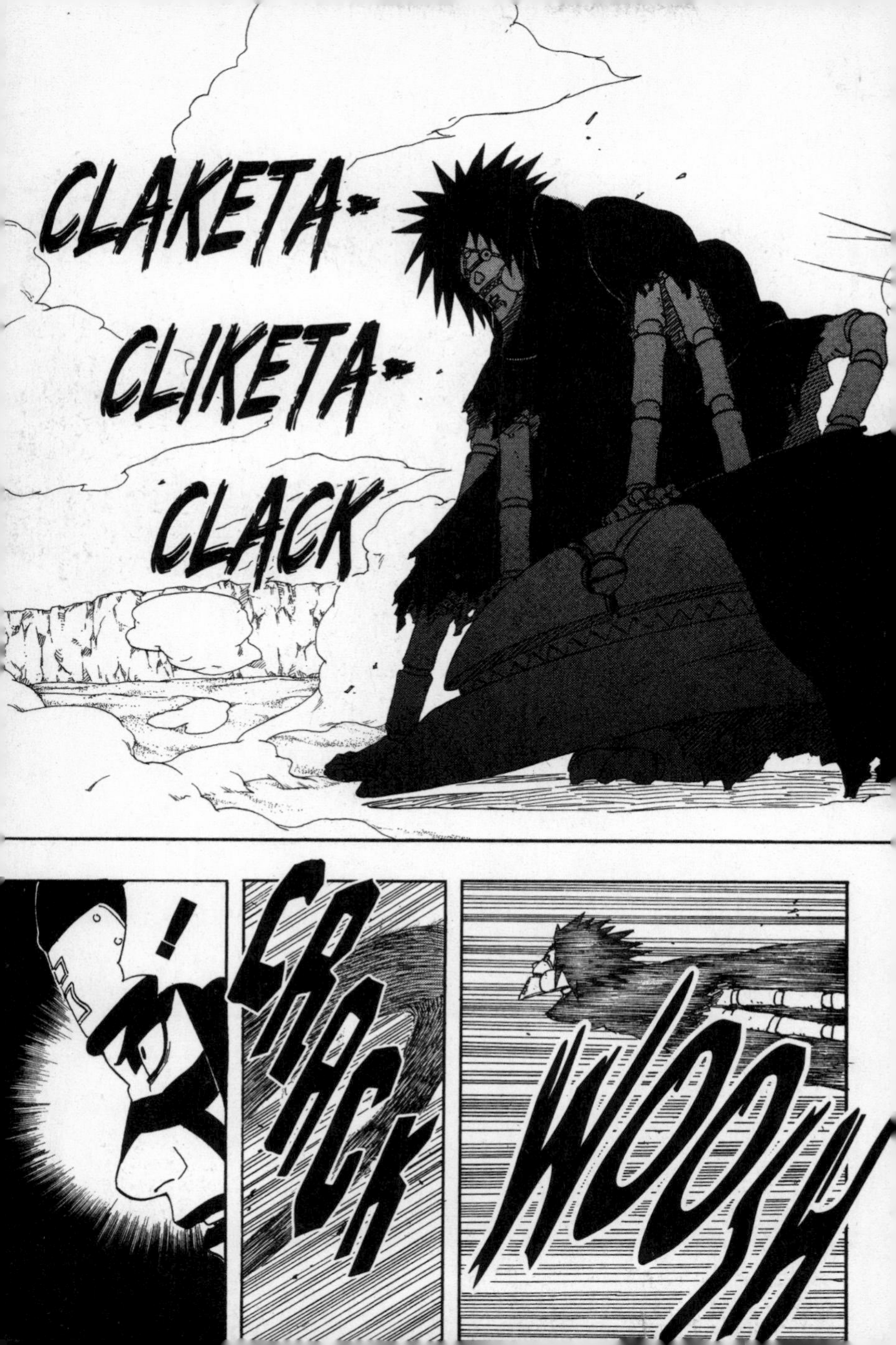
CLAKETA-
CLIKETA-
CLACK
WHOOSH
CRACK
!

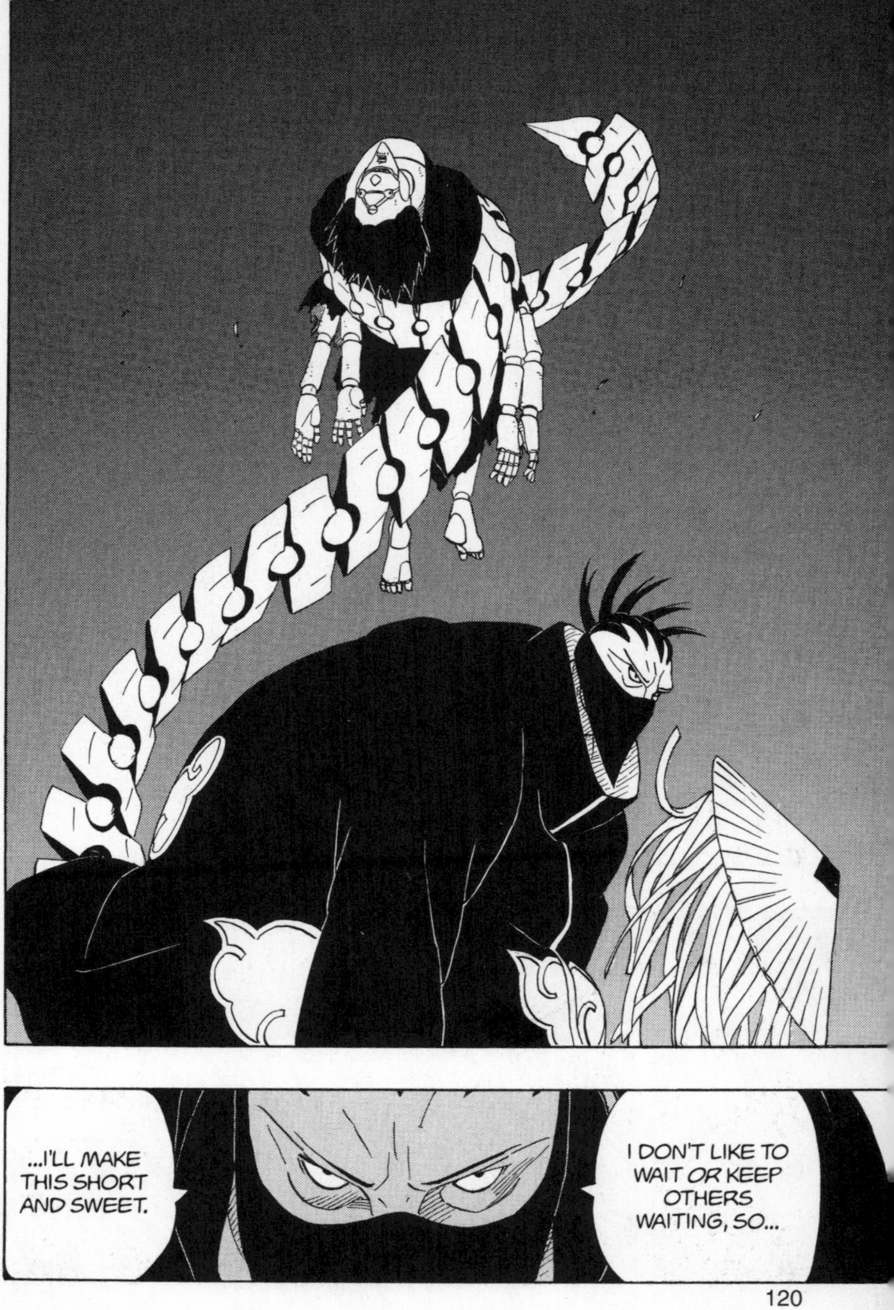
I DON'T LIKE TO WAIT OR KEEP OTHERS WAITING, SO...
...I'LL MAKE THIS SHORT AND SWEET.

READ THIS WAY

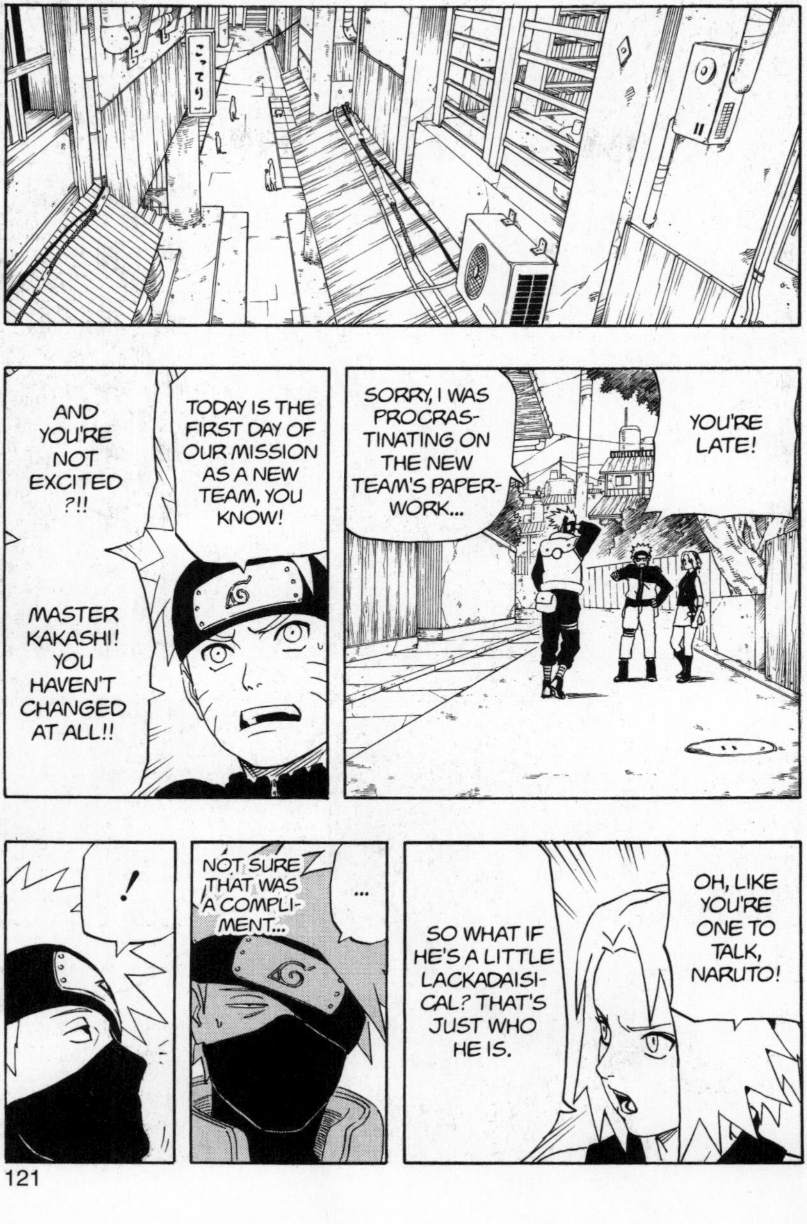

こってり
YOU'RE LATE!
SORRY, I WAS PROCRAS-TINATING ON THE NEW TEAM'S PAPER-WORK...
TODAY IS THE FIRST DAY OF OUR MISSION AS A NEW TEAM, YOU KNOW!
AND YOU'RE NOT EXCITED?!!
MASTER KAKASHI! YOU HAVEN'T CHANGED AT ALL!!
OH, LIKE YOU'RE ONE TO TALK, NARUTO!
SO WHAT IF HE'S A LITTLE LACKADAISI-CAL? THAT'S JUST WHO HE IS.
...
NOT SURE THAT WAS A COMPLI-MENT...
!

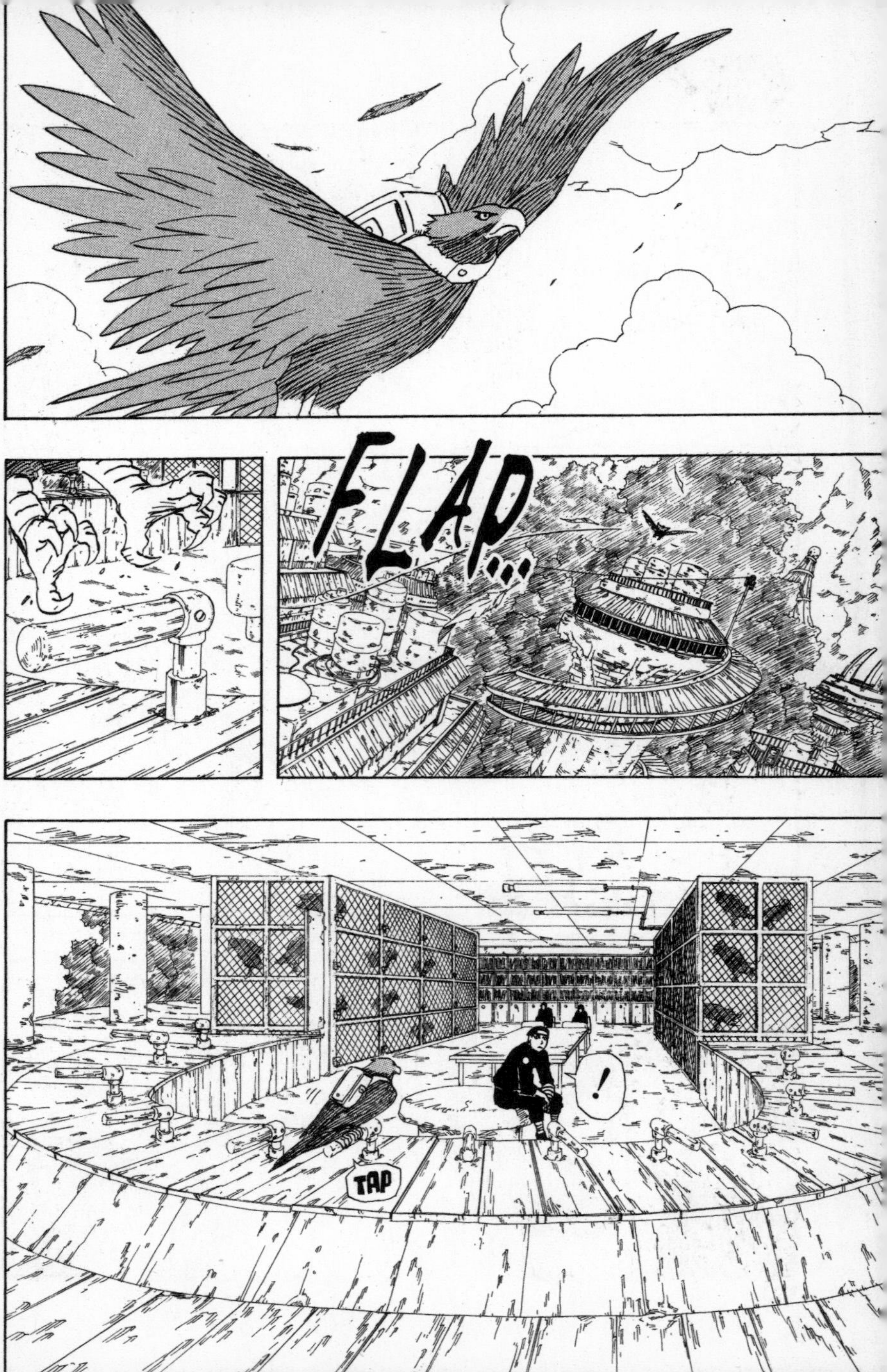
FLAP...
TAP
!

READ THIS WAY

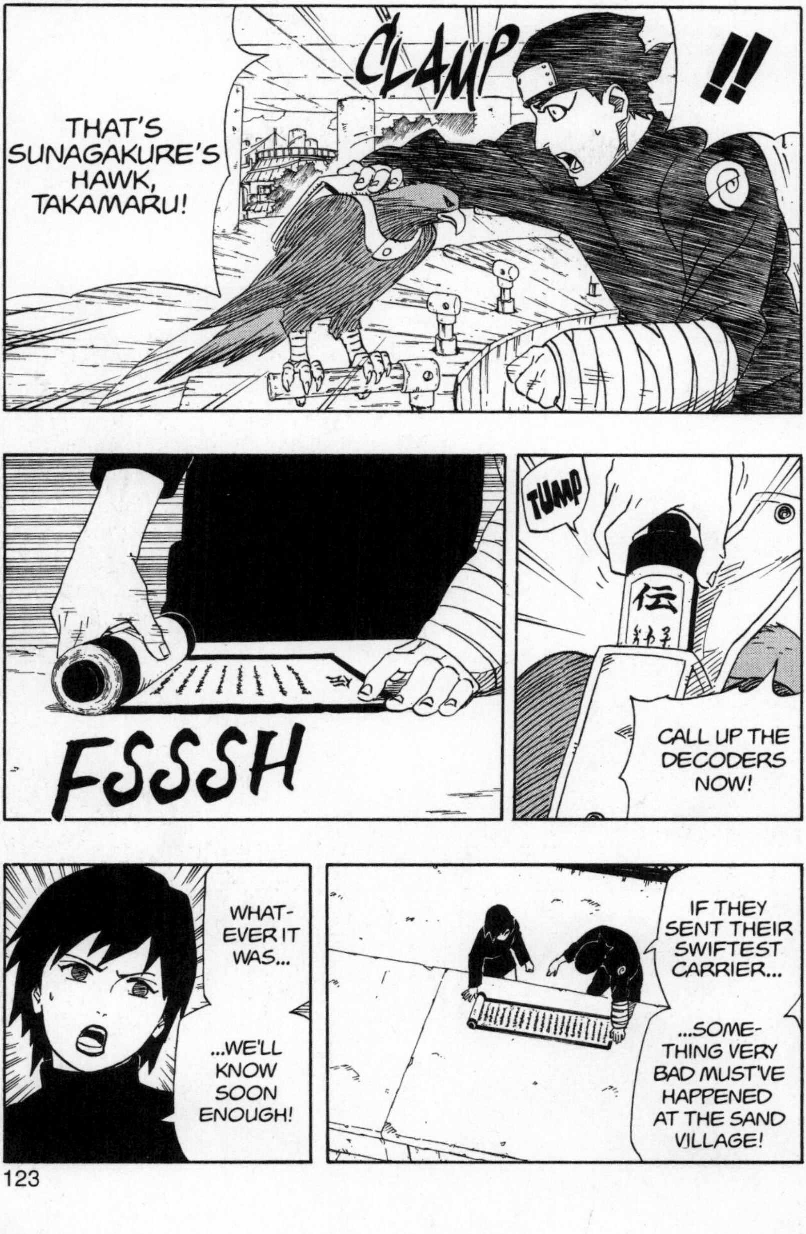
CLAMP
!!
THAT'S SUNAGAKURE'S HAWK, TAKAMARU!
TUMP
伝
CALL UP THE DECODERS NOW!
FSSSH
IF THEY SENT THEIR SWIFTEST CARRIER...
...SOME-THING VERY BAD MUST'VE HAPPENED AT THE SAND VILLAGE!
WHAT-EVER IT WAS...
...WE'LL KNOW SOON ENOUGH!

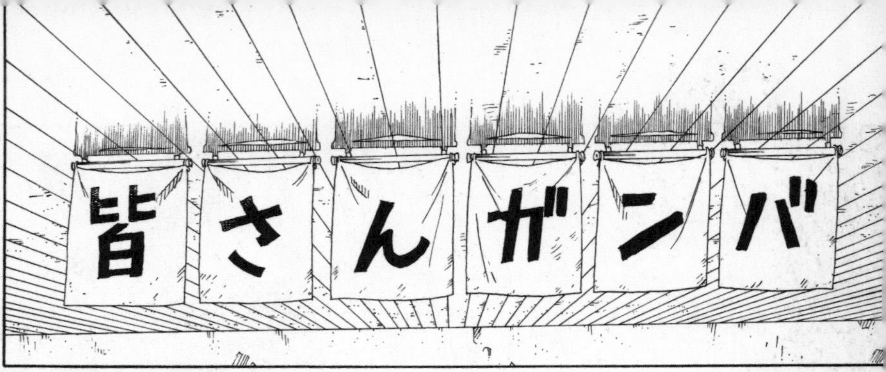
皆さんガンバ

(Banner: Everyone, Good Luck)

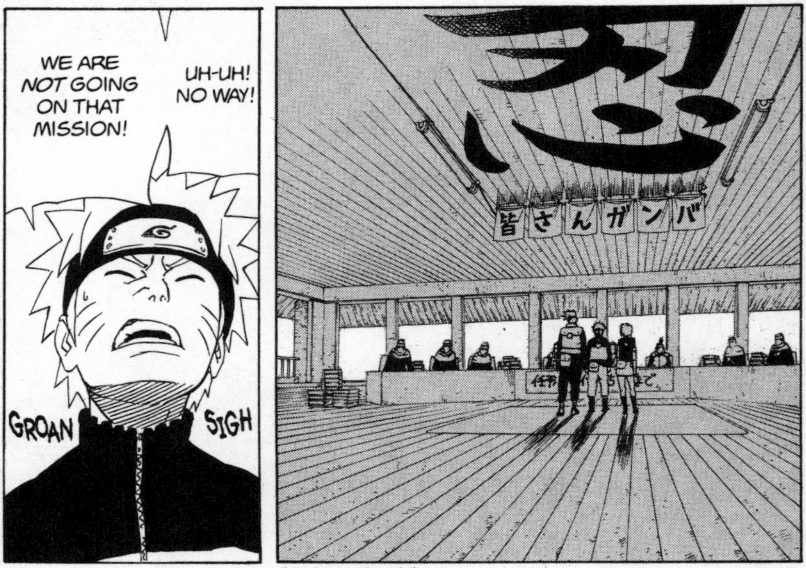
忍
皆さんガンバ
UH-UH! NO WAY!
WE ARE NOT GOING ON THAT MISSION!
SIGH
GROAN

(Ceiling: Shinobi)

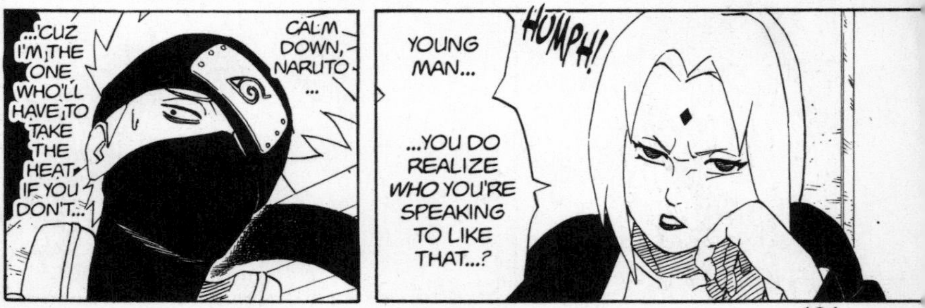
HUMPH!
YOUNG MAN...
...YOU DO REALIZE WHO YOU'RE SPEAKING TO LIKE THAT...?
CALM DOWN, NARUTO...
...CUZ I'M THE ONE WHO'LL HAVE TO TAKE THE HEAT IF YOU DON'T...

READ THIS WAY

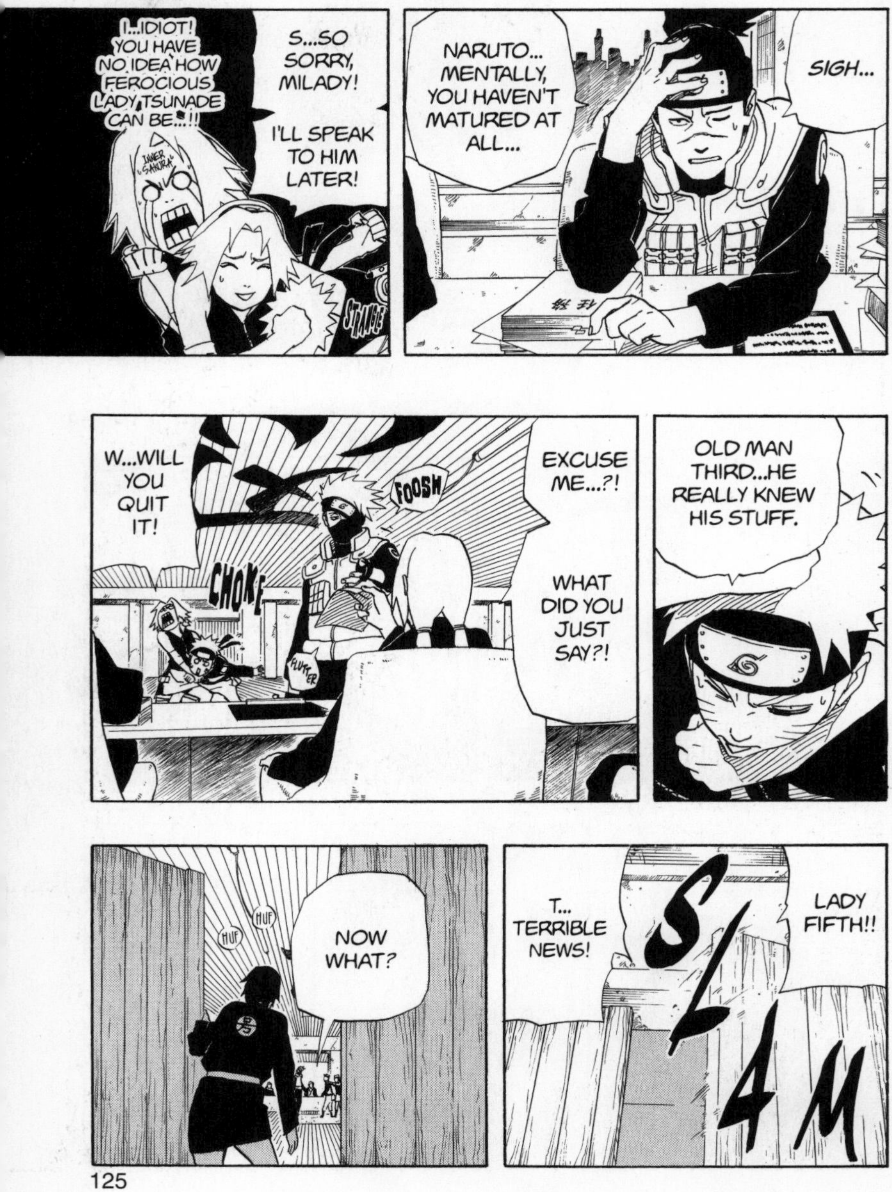
SIGH...
NARUTO... MENTALLY, YOU HAVEN'T MATURED AT ALL...
S...SO SORRY, MILADY!
I'LL SPEAK TO HIM LATER!
I...IDIOT! YOU HAVE NO IDEA HOW FEROCIOUS LADY TSUNADE CAN BE...!!!
INNER SAKURA
STRANGE
OLD MAN THIRD...HE REALLY KNEW HIS STUFF.
EXCUSE ME...?!
WHAT DID YOU JUST SAY?!
FOOSH
W...WILL YOU QUIT IT!
CHOKE
FLUTTER
LADY FIFTH!!
SLAM
T... TERRIBLE NEWS!
NOW WHAT?
HUF
HUF

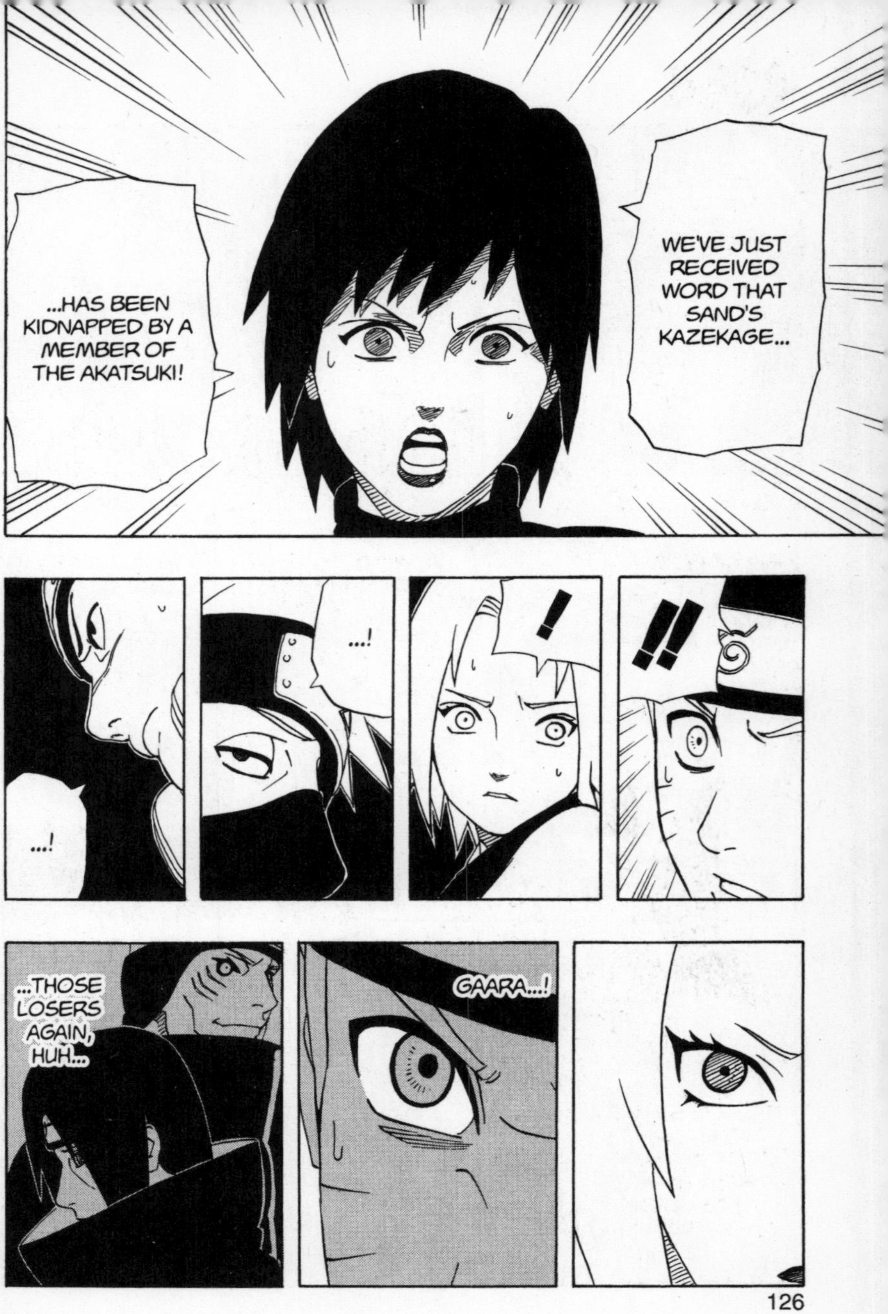
WE'VE JUST RECEIVED WORD THAT SAND'S KAZEKAGE...
...HAS BEEN KIDNAPPED BY A MEMBER OF THE AKATSUKI!
!!
!
...!
...!
GAARA...!
...THOSE LOSERS AGAIN, HUH...

READ THIS WAY

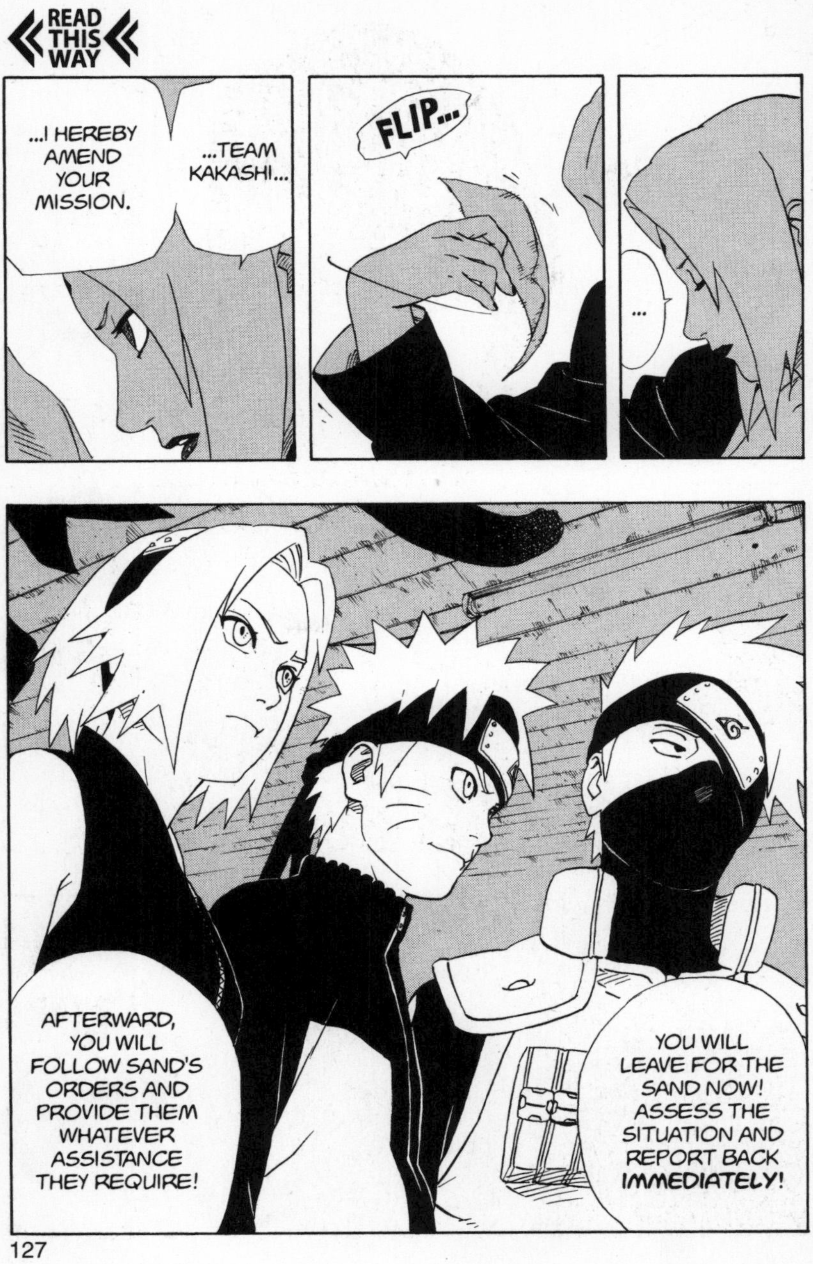
...
FLIP...
...TEAM KAKASHI...
...I HEREBY AMEND YOUR MISSION.
YOU WILL LEAVE FOR THE SAND NOW! ASSESS THE SITUATION AND REPORT BACK **IMMEDIATELY**!
AFTERWARD, YOU WILL FOLLOW SAND'S ORDERS AND PROVIDE THEM WHATEVER ASSISTANCE THEY REQUIRE!

NARUTO

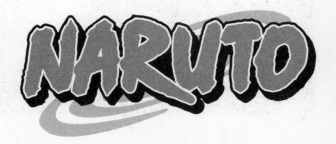

Number 251: To the Sand...!!

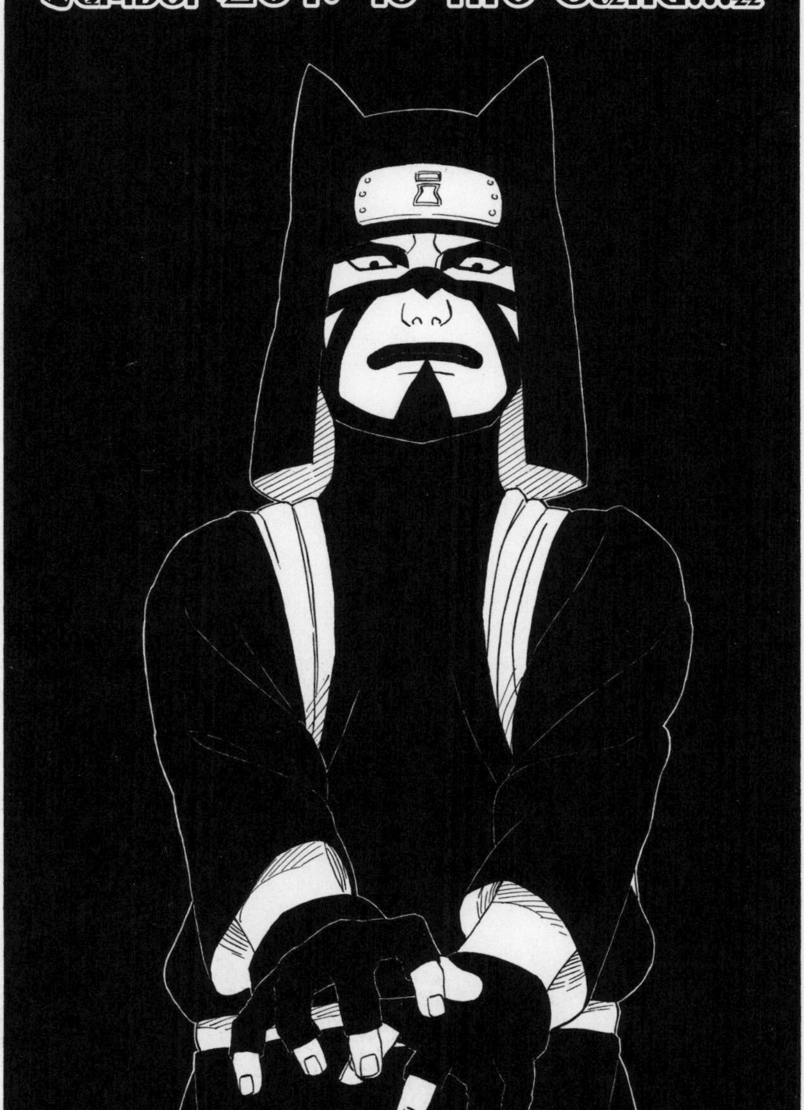

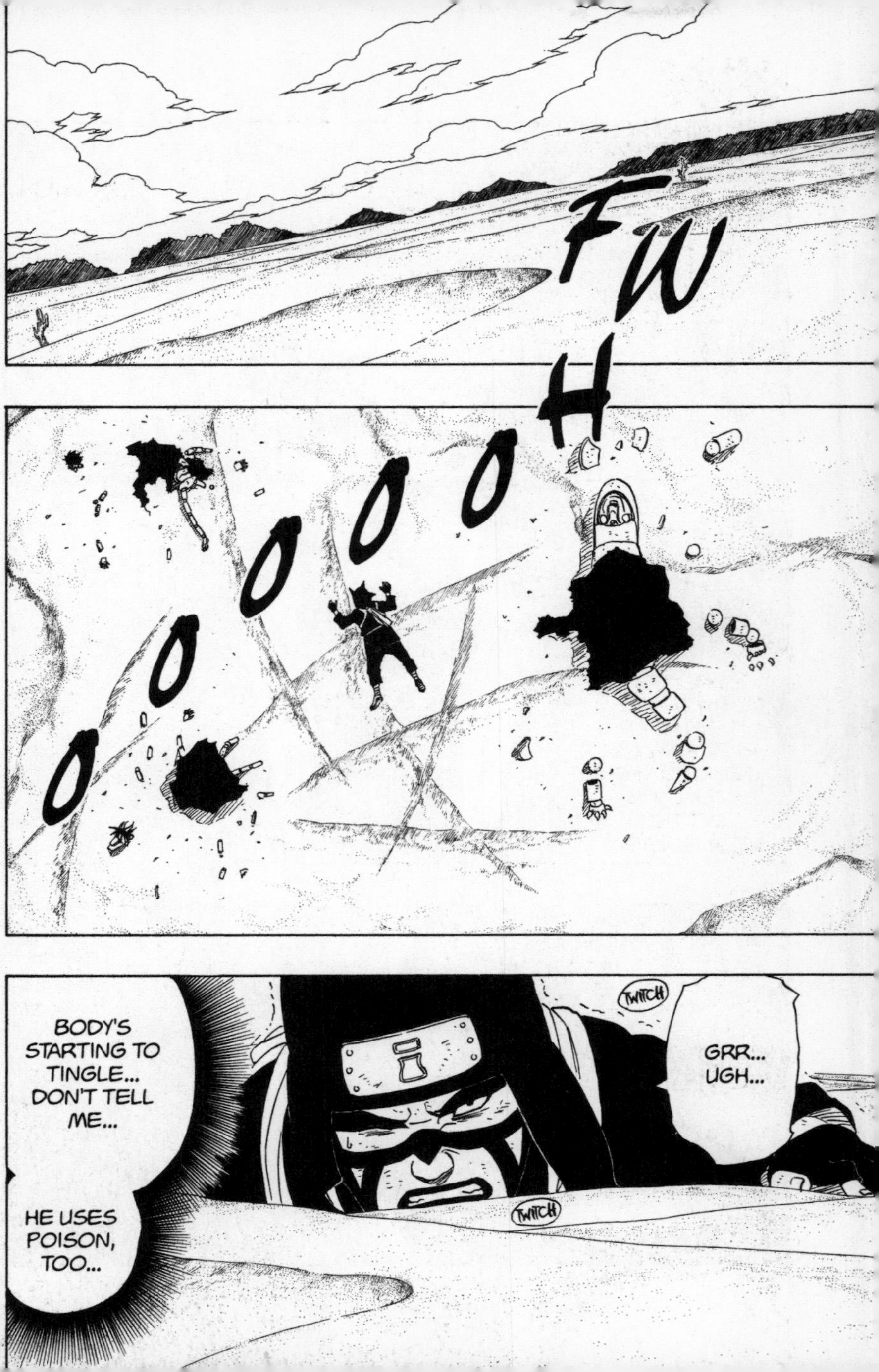
FWHOOOOO
TWITCH
GRR... UGH...
BODY'S STARTING TO TINGLE... DON'T TELL ME...
TWITCH
HE USES POISON, TOO...

READ THIS WAY

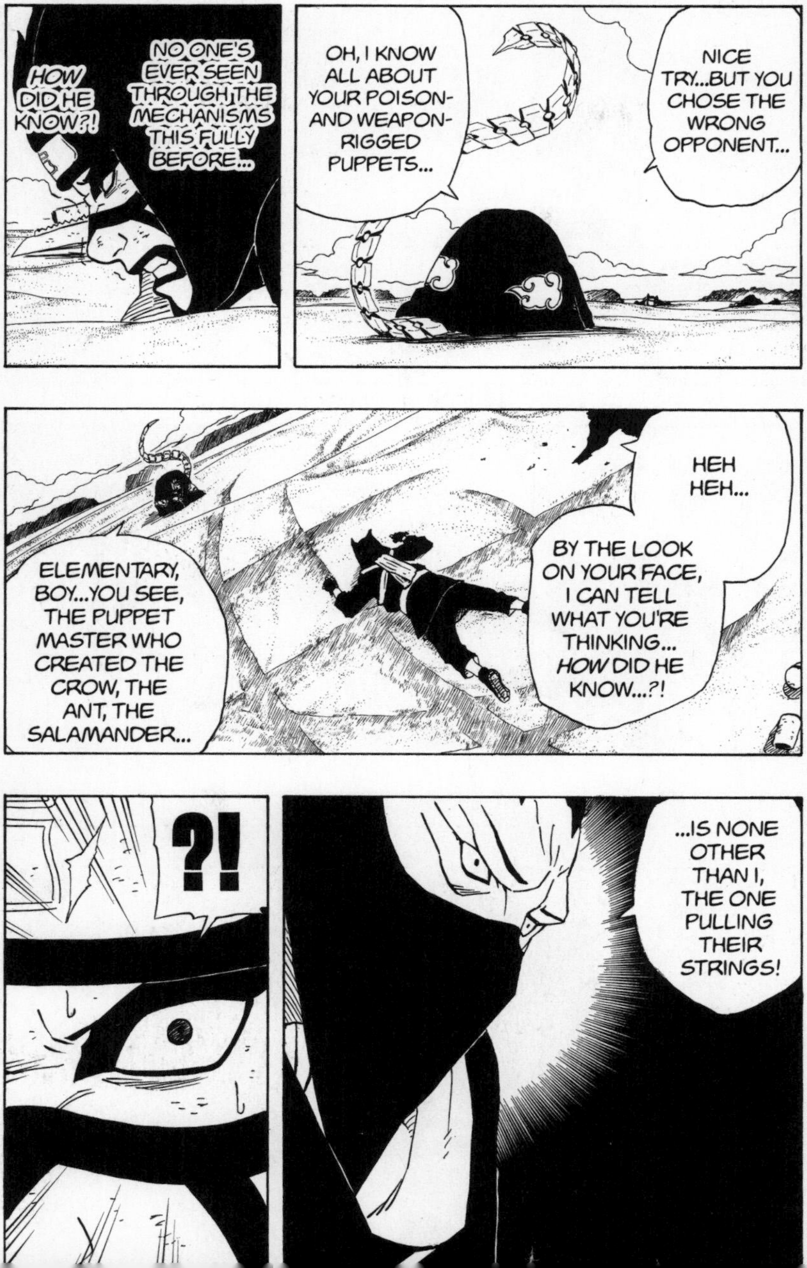
NICE TRY...BUT YOU CHOSE THE WRONG OPPONENT...
OH, I KNOW ALL ABOUT YOUR POISON- AND WEAPON-RIGGED PUPPETS...
NO ONE'S EVER SEEN THROUGH THE MECHANISMS THIS FULLY BEFORE...
HOW DID HE KNOW?!
HEH HEH...
BY THE LOOK ON YOUR FACE, I CAN TELL WHAT YOU'RE THINKING... HOW DID HE KNOW...?!
ELEMENTARY, BOY...YOU SEE, THE PUPPET MASTER WHO CREATED THE CROW, THE ANT, THE SALAMANDER...
...IS NONE OTHER THAN I, THE ONE PULLING THEIR STRINGS!
?!

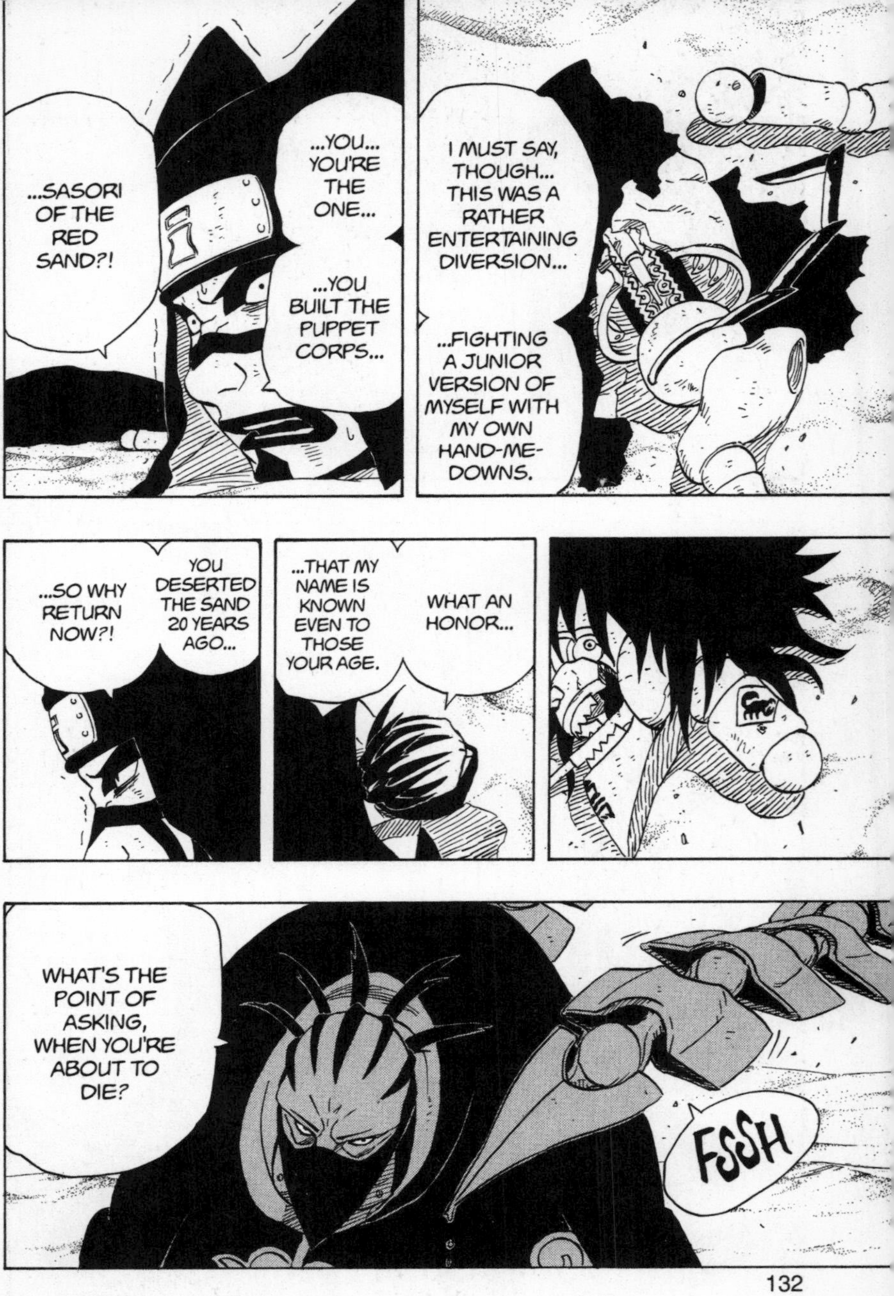
I MUST SAY, THOUGH... THIS WAS A RATHER ENTERTAINING DIVERSION...
...FIGHTING A JUNIOR VERSION OF MYSELF WITH MY OWN HAND-ME-DOWNS.
...YOU... YOU'RE THE ONE...
...YOU BUILT THE PUPPET CORPS...
...SASORI OF THE RED SAND?!
WHAT AN HONOR...
...THAT MY NAME IS KNOWN EVEN TO THOSE YOUR AGE.
YOU DESERTED THE SAND 20 YEARS AGO...
...SO WHY RETURN NOW?!
FSSH
WHAT'S THE POINT OF ASKING, WHEN YOU'RE ABOUT TO DIE?

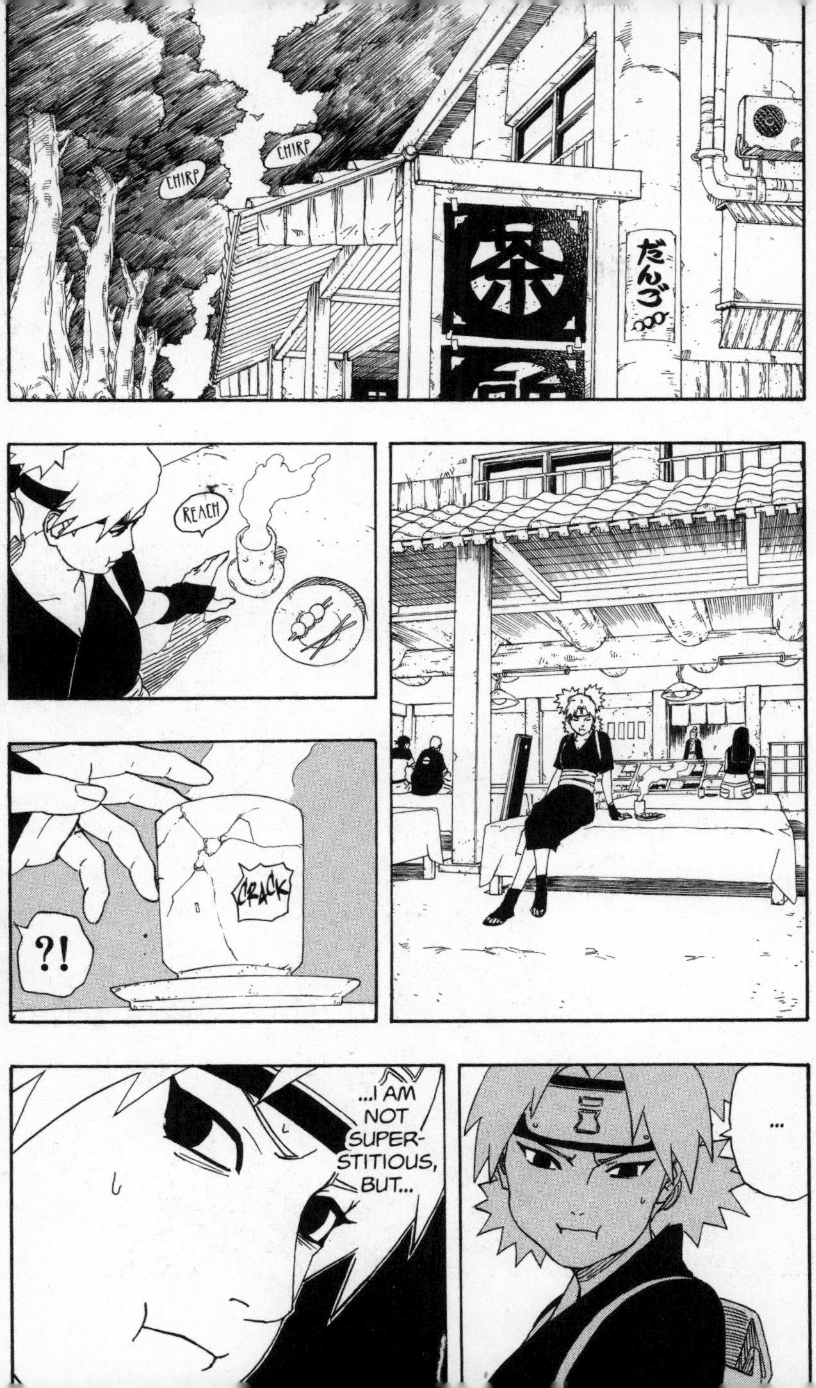
CHIRP
CHIRP
だんご
茶
REACH
CRACK
?!
...
...I AM NOT SUPER-STITIOUS, BUT...

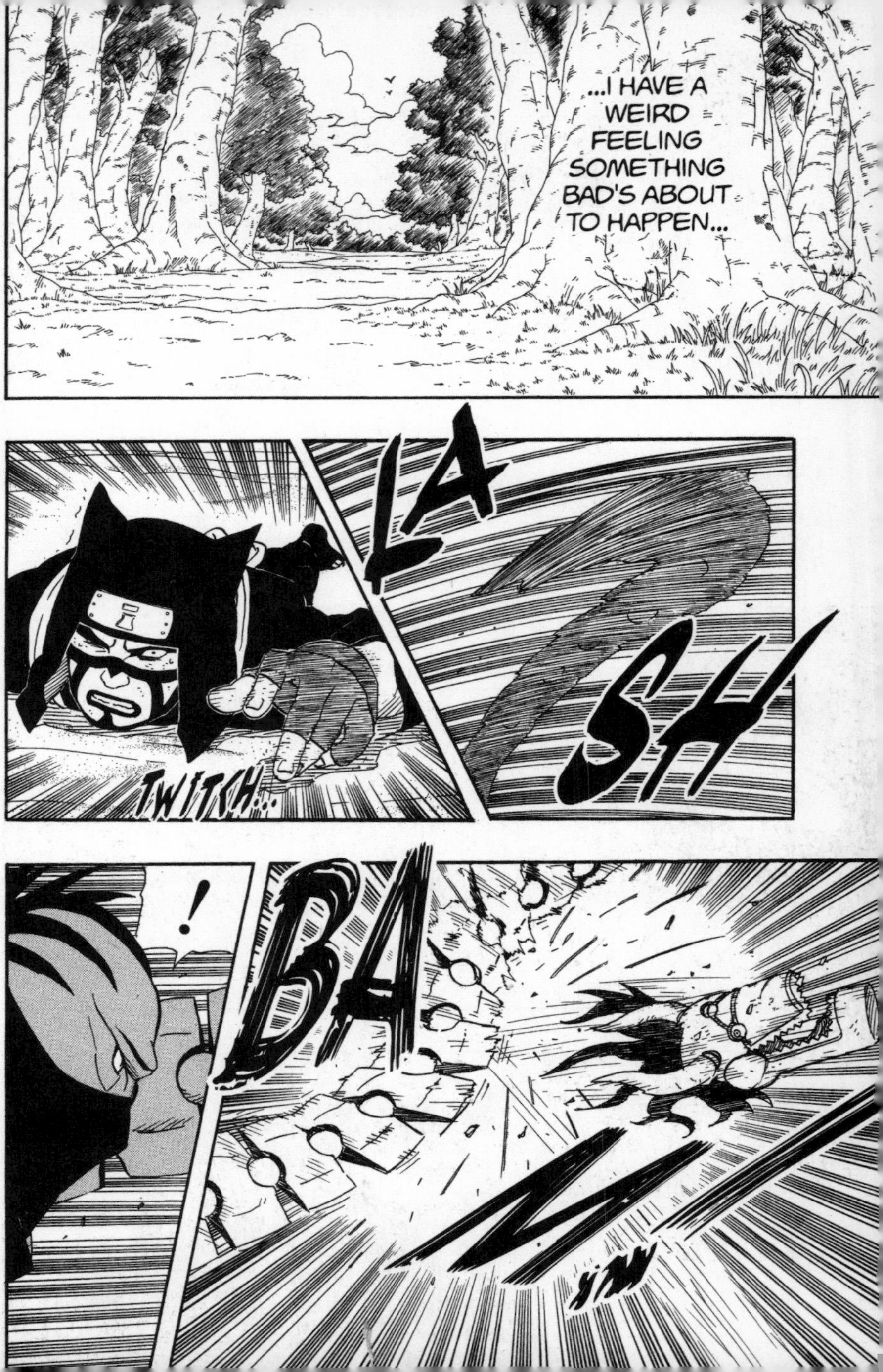

...I HAVE A WEIRD FEELING SOMETHING BAD'S ABOUT TO HAPPEN...
LASH
TWITCH...
!
BAN

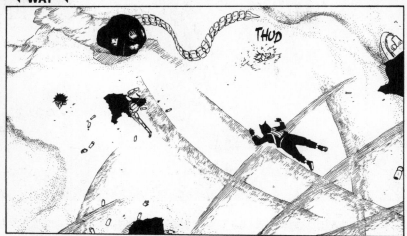

THUD

JERK

RIP

SLASH

KASHINK

WHIP

TAP

UGH...

ALMOST.

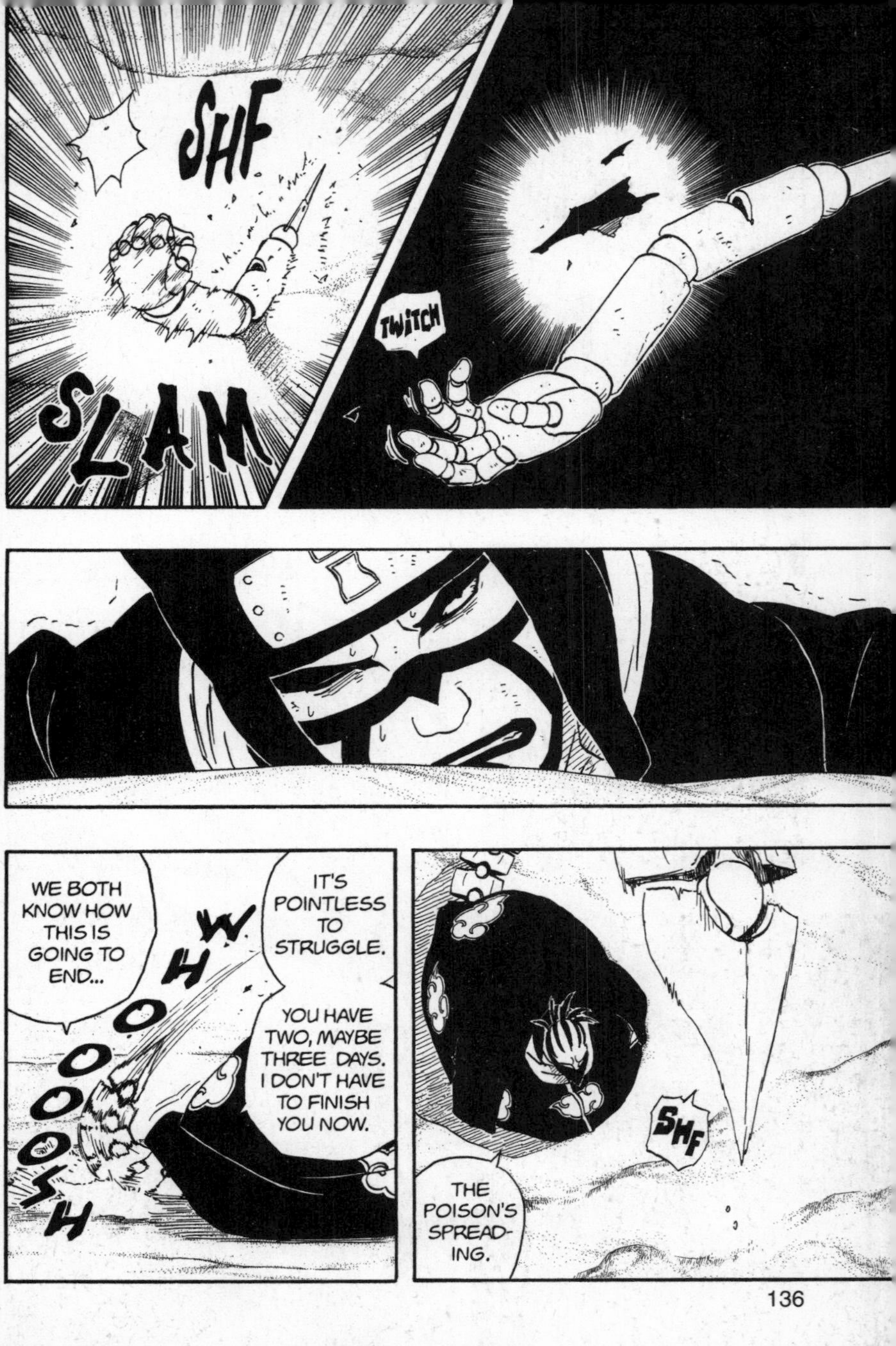
TWITCH
SHF
SLAM
SHF
THE POISON'S SPREAD-ING.
IT'S POINTLESS TO STRUGGLE.
YOU HAVE TWO, MAYBE THREE DAYS. I DON'T HAVE TO FINISH YOU NOW.
WE BOTH KNOW HOW THIS IS GOING TO END...
WHOOOOOSH

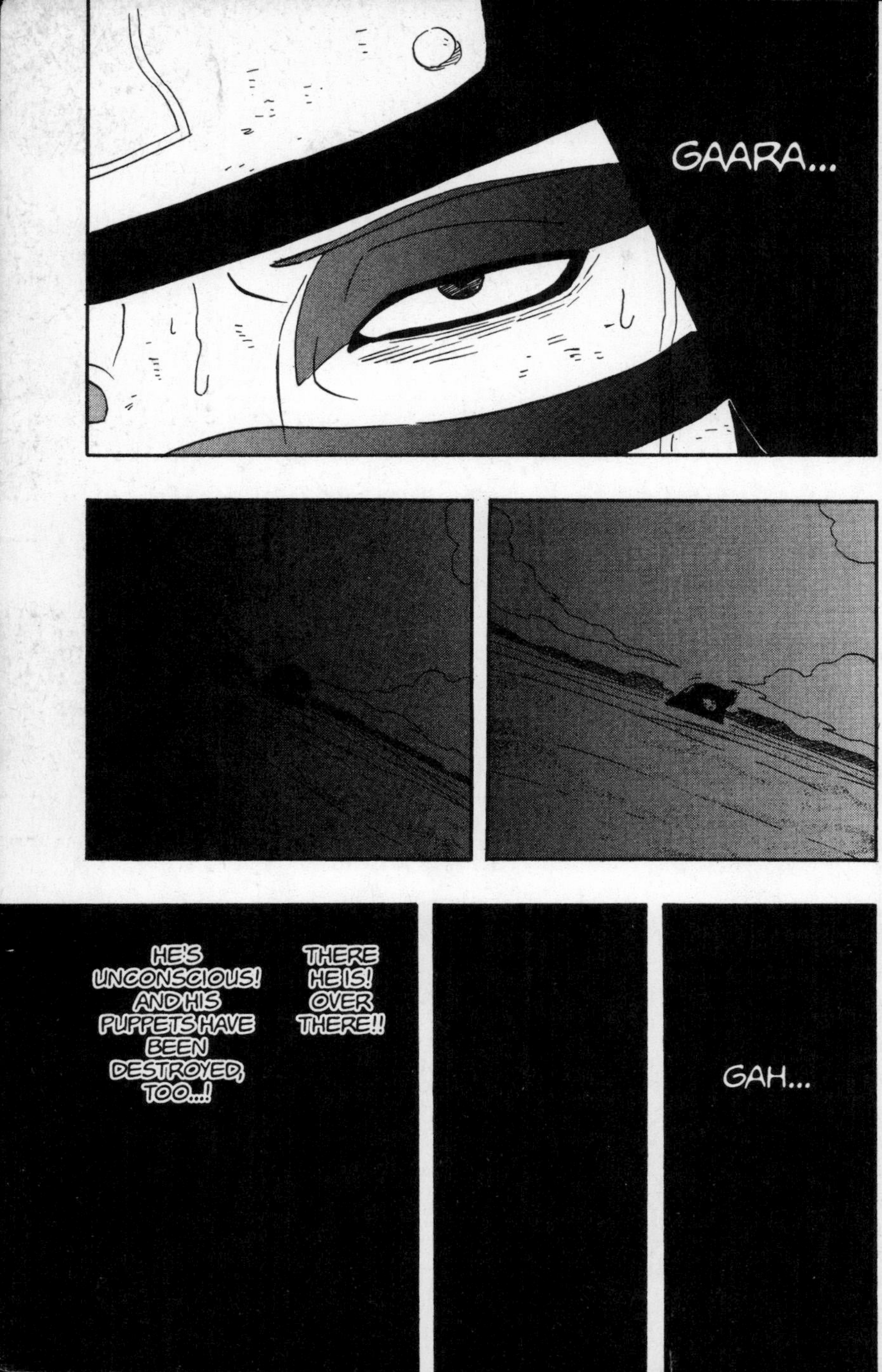
GAARA...
GAH...
THERE HE IS! OVER THERE!!
HE'S UNCONSCIOUS! AND HIS PUPPETS HAVE BEEN DESTROYED, TOO...!

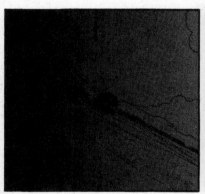

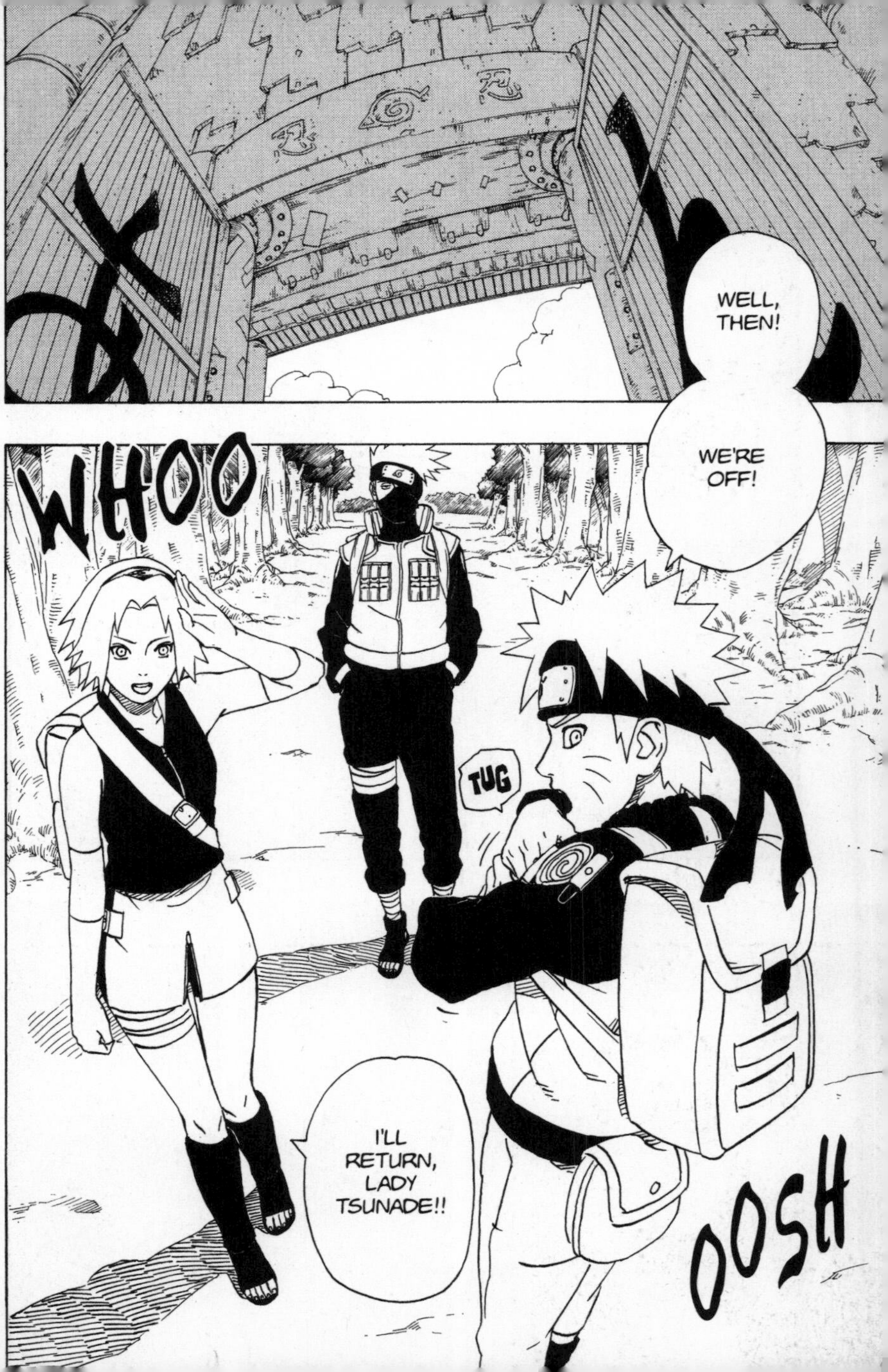
WELL, THEN!
WE'RE OFF!
TUG
WHOO
I'LL RETURN, LADY TSUNADE!!
OOSH

...

...

I HOPE SO.

THANK YOU!

GOOD LUCK!

!

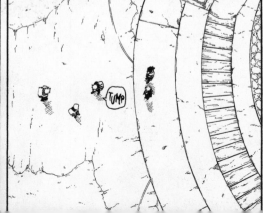

TUMP

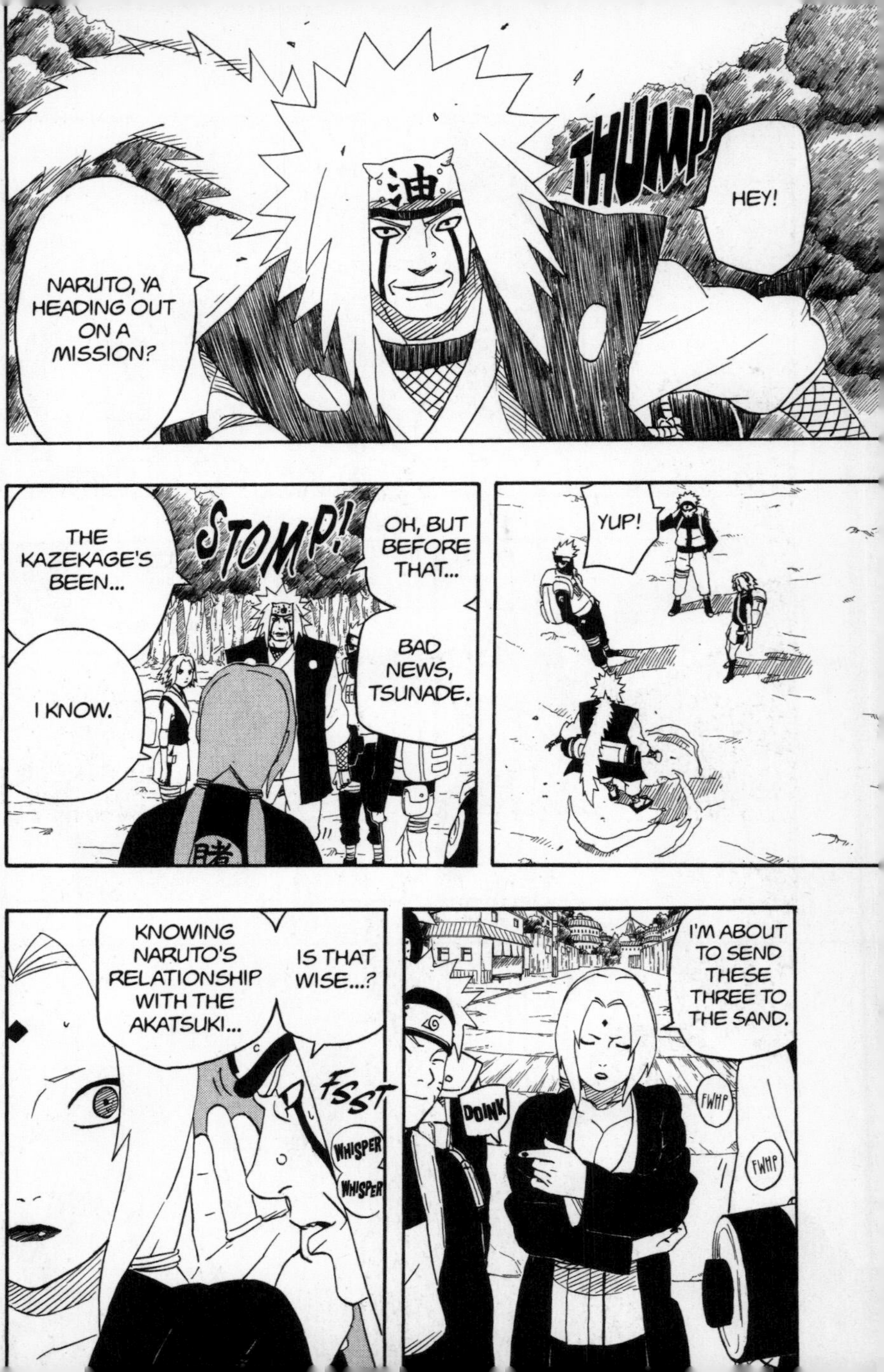

HEY!
THUMP
NARUTO, YA HEADING OUT ON A MISSION?
YUP!
OH, BUT BEFORE THAT...
BAD NEWS, TSUNADE.
STOMP!
THE KAZEKAGE'S BEEN...
I KNOW.
I'M ABOUT TO SEND THESE THREE TO THE SAND.
FWHP
FWHP
DOINK
KNOWING NARUTO'S RELATIONSHIP WITH THE AKATSUKI...
IS THAT WISE...?
FSST
WHISPER
WHISPER

READ THIS WAY

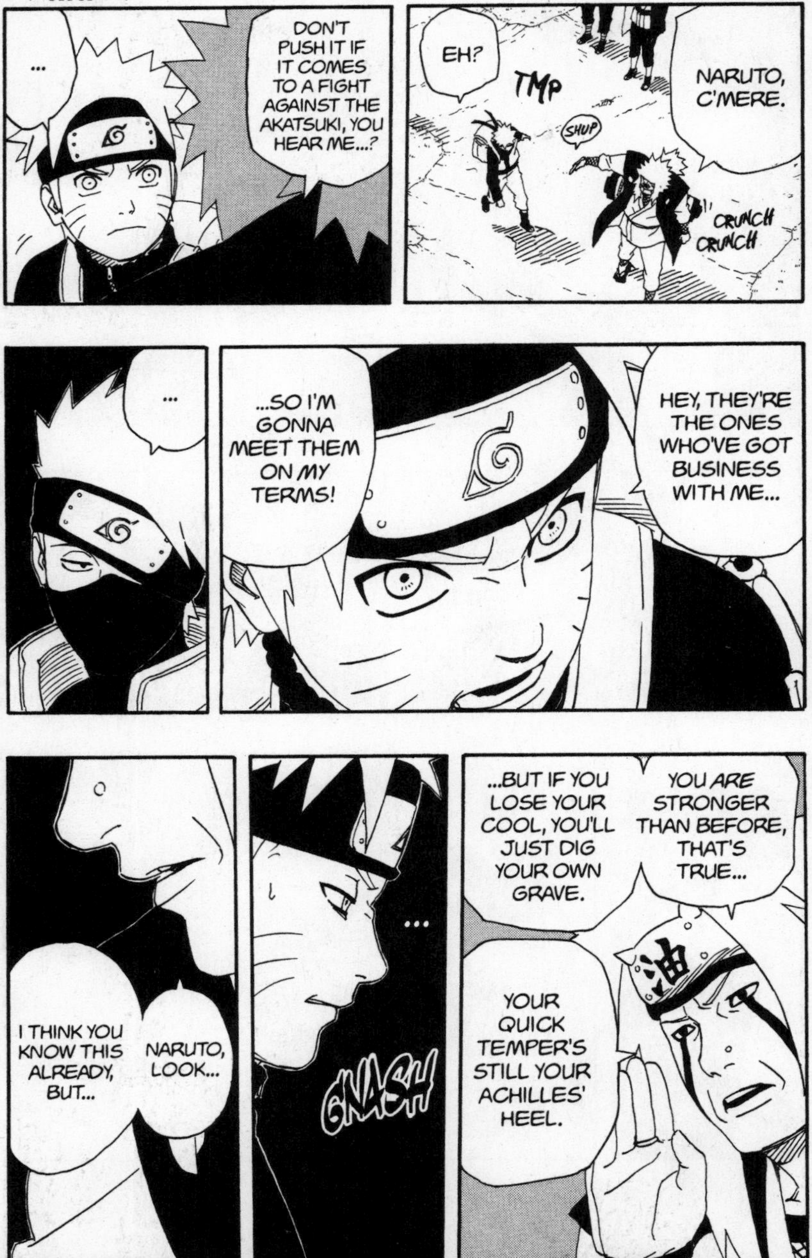
NARUTO, C'MERE.
EH?
TMP
SHUP
CRUNCH CRUNCH
DON'T PUSH IT IF IT COMES TO A FIGHT AGAINST THE AKATSUKI, YOU HEAR ME...?
...
HEY, THEY'RE THE ONES WHO'VE GOT BUSINESS WITH ME...
...SO I'M GONNA MEET THEM ON MY TERMS!
...
YOU ARE STRONGER THAN BEFORE, THAT'S TRUE...
...BUT IF YOU LOSE YOUR COOL, YOU'LL JUST DIG YOUR OWN GRAVE.
YOUR QUICK TEMPER'S STILL YOUR ACHILLES' HEEL.
...
GNASH
NARUTO, LOOK...
I THINK YOU KNOW THIS ALREADY, BUT...

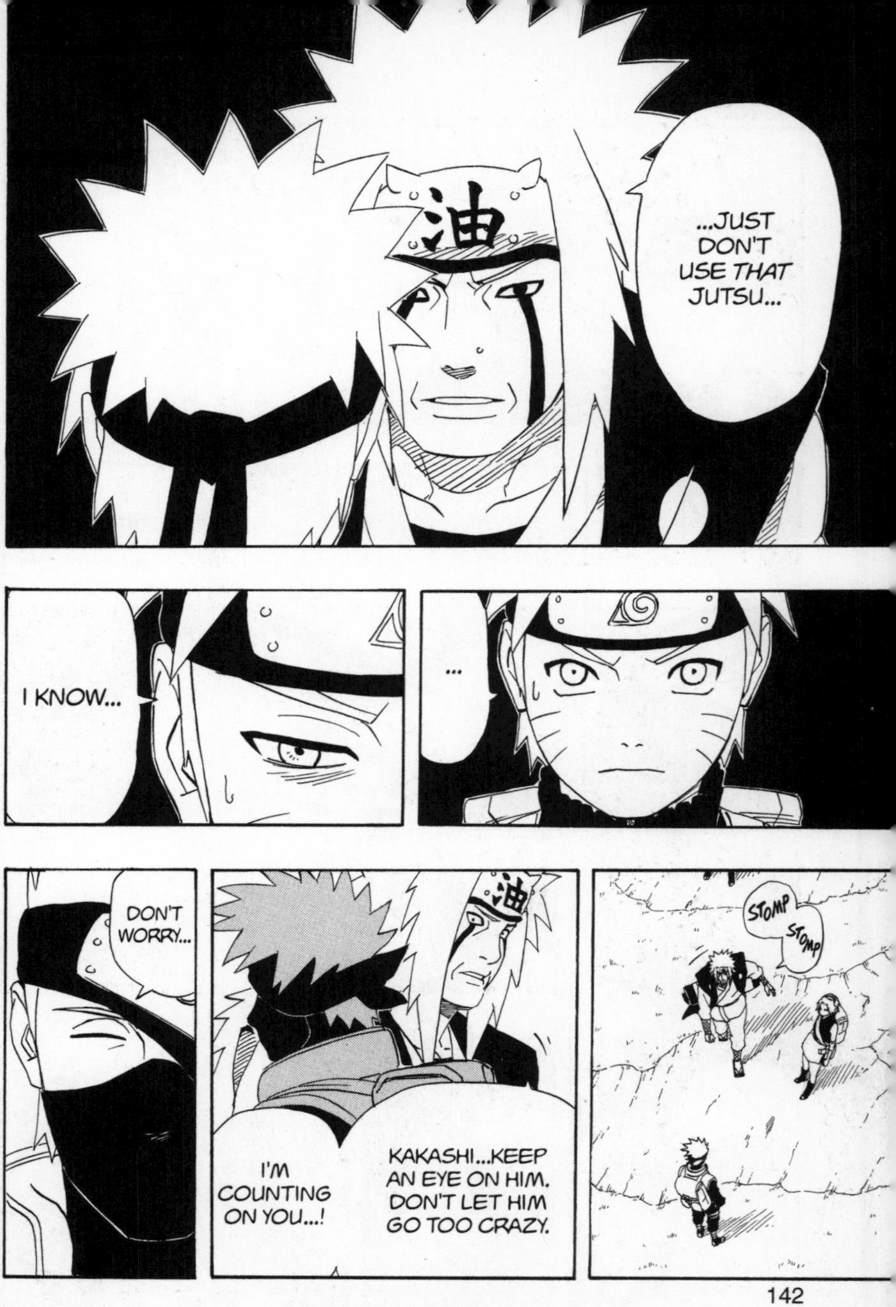
...JUST DON'T USE THAT JUTSU...
...
I KNOW...
STOMP
STOMP
KAKASHI...KEEP AN EYE ON HIM. DON'T LET HIM GO TOO CRAZY.
I'M COUNTING ON YOU...!
DON'T WORRY...

READ THIS WAY

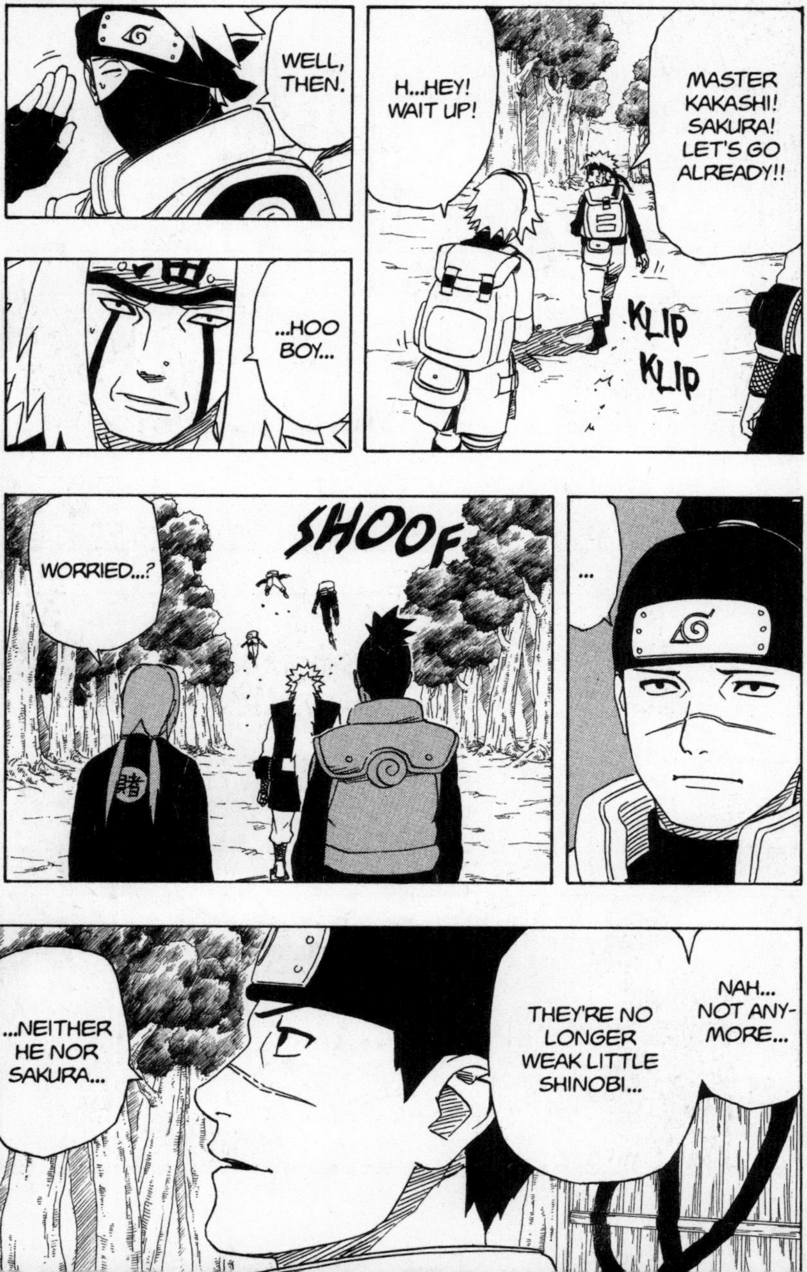
MASTER KAKASHI! SAKURA! LET'S GO ALREADY!!
H...HEY! WAIT UP!
KLIP KLIP
WELL, THEN.
...HOO BOY...
...
SHOOF
WORRIED...?
NAH... NOT ANY-MORE...
THEY'RE NO LONGER WEAK LITTLE SHINOBI...
...NEITHER HE NOR SAKURA...

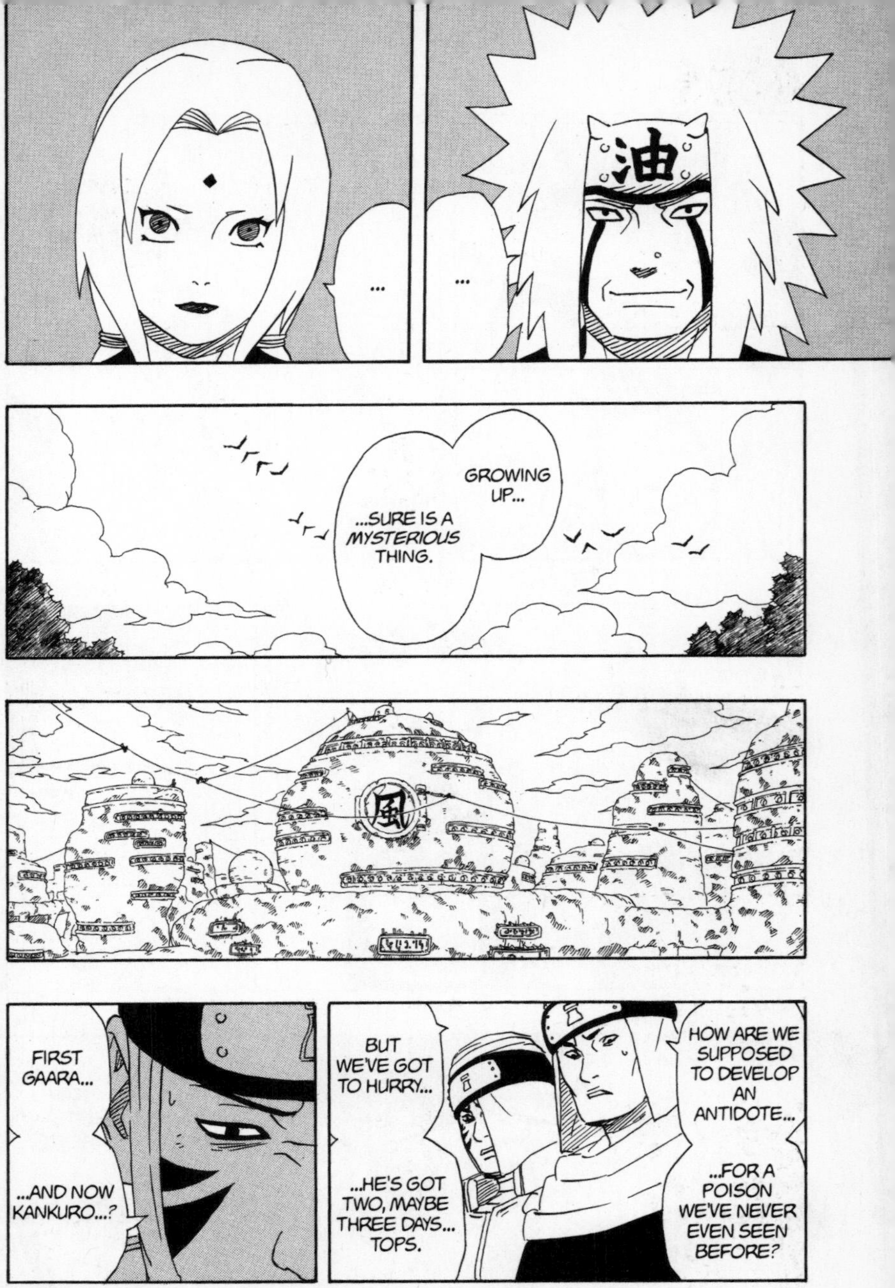
...
...
GROWING UP...
...SURE IS A MYSTERIOUS THING.
HOW ARE WE SUPPOSED TO DEVELOP AN ANTIDOTE...
...FOR A POISON WE'VE NEVER EVEN SEEN BEFORE?
BUT WE'VE GOT TO HURRY...
...HE'S GOT TWO, MAYBE THREE DAYS... TOPS.
FIRST GAARA...
...AND NOW KANKURO...?

READ THIS WAY

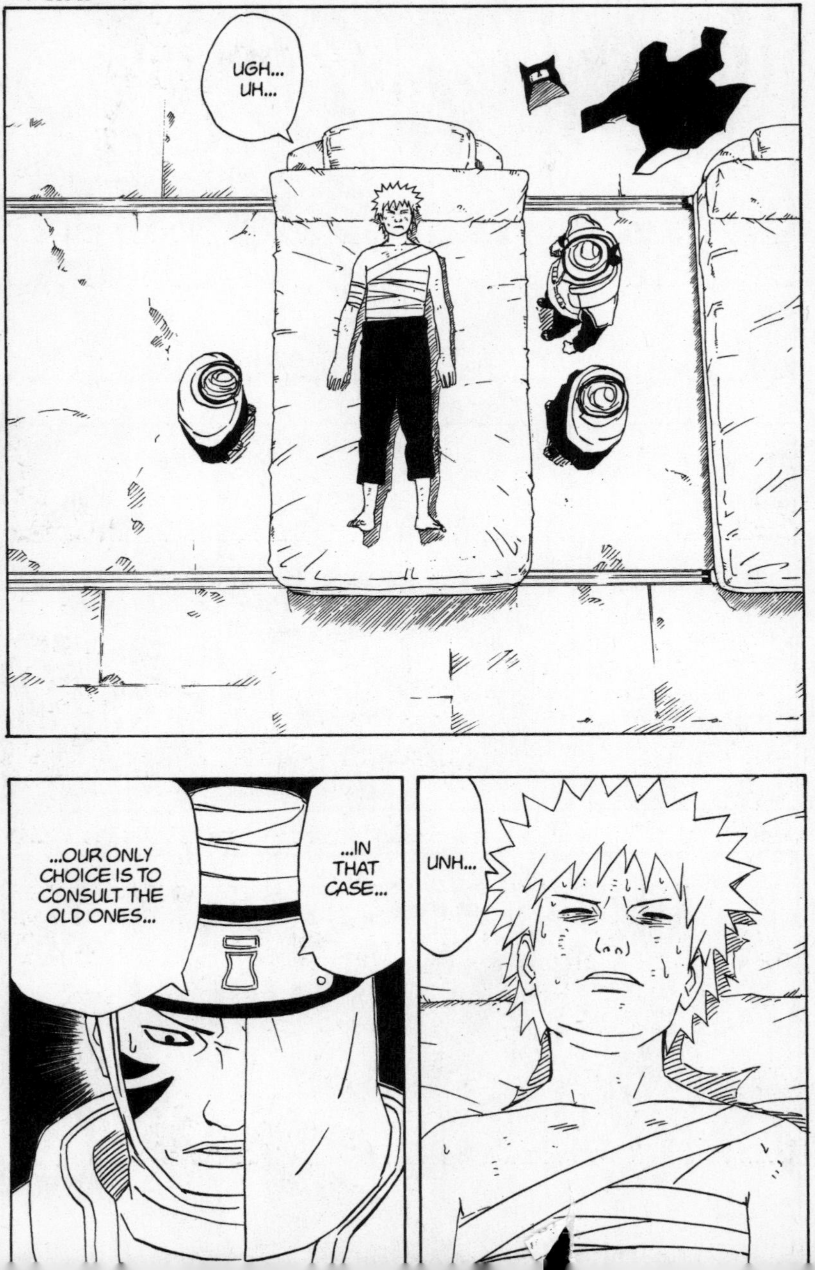

UGH... UH...
UNH...
...IN THAT CASE...
...OUR ONLY CHOICE IS TO CONSULT THE OLD ONES...

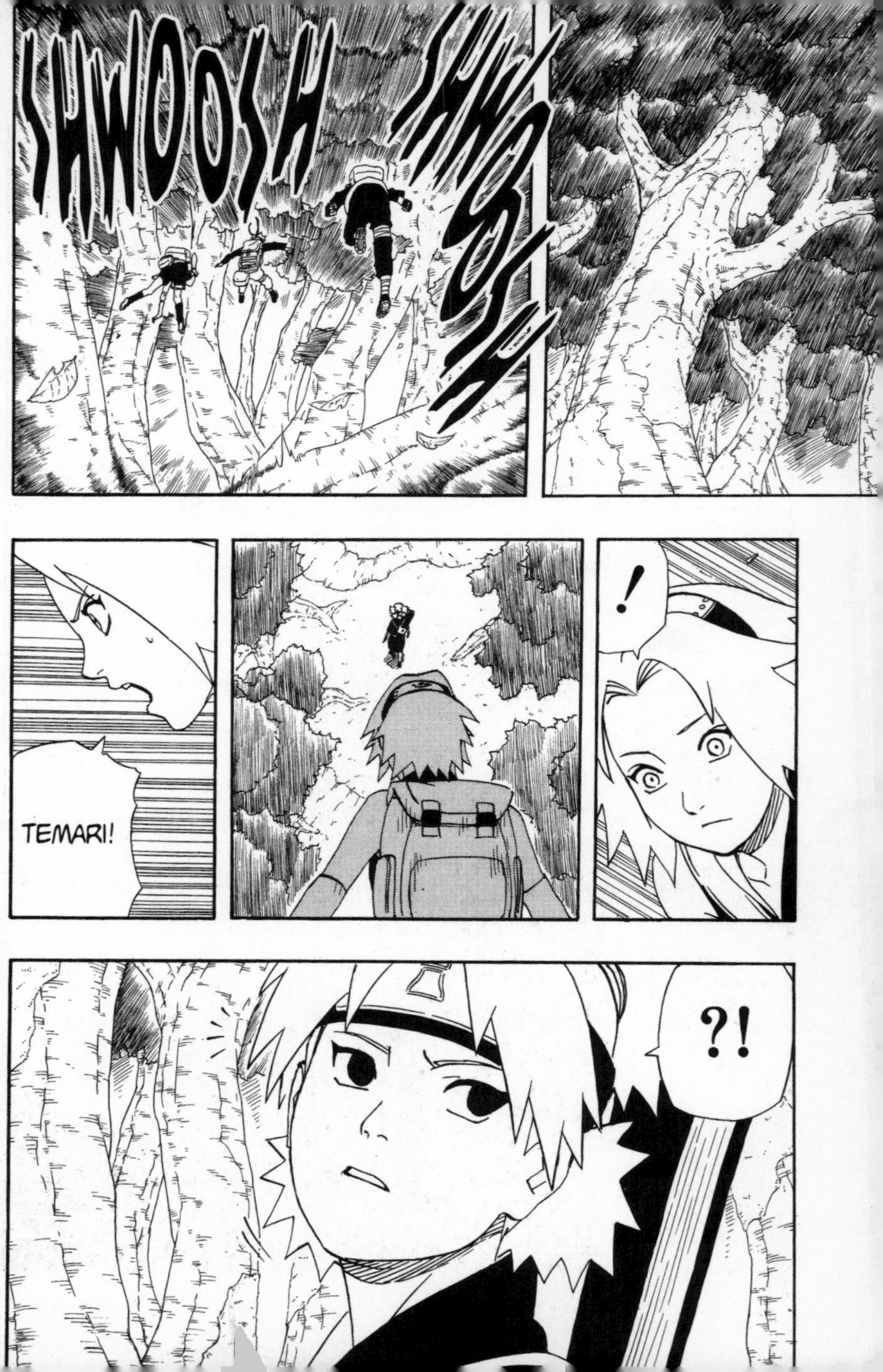
SHWOOSH
SHWOOSH
!
TEMARI!
?!

READ THIS WAY

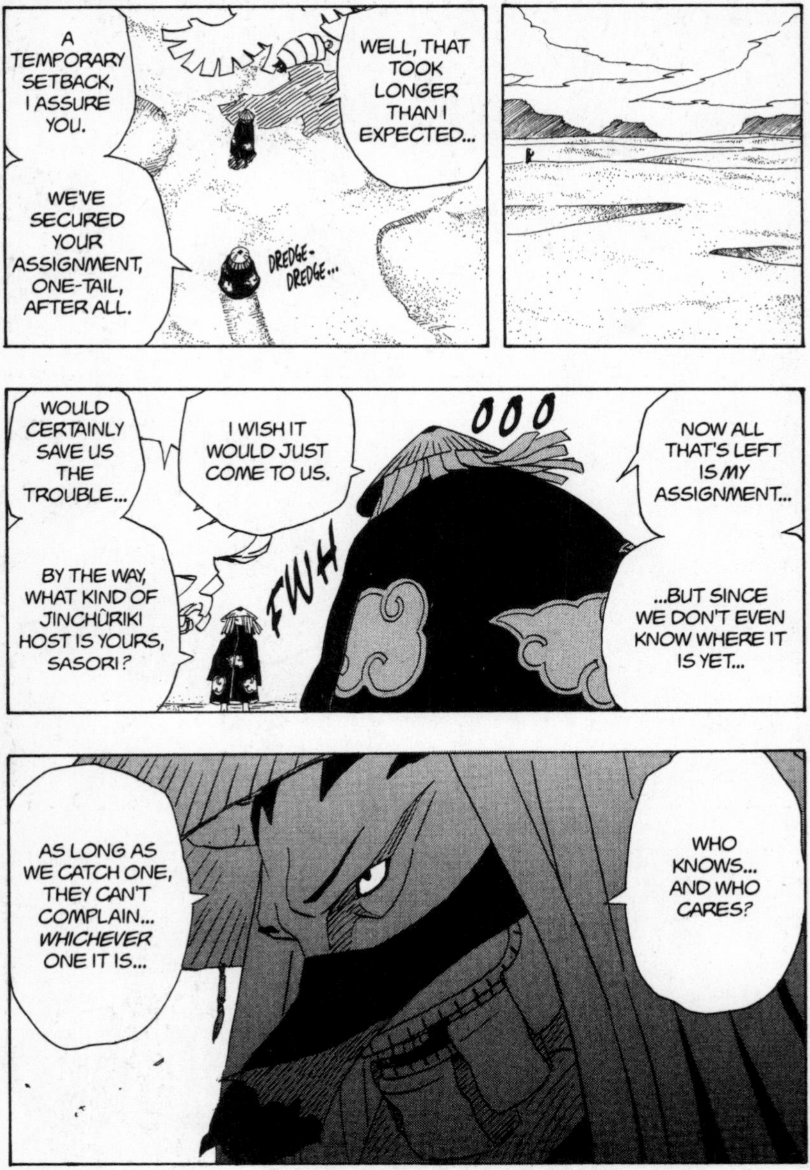

WELL, THAT TOOK LONGER THAN I EXPECTED...
A TEMPORARY SETBACK, I ASSURE YOU.
WE'VE SECURED YOUR ASSIGNMENT, ONE-TAIL, AFTER ALL.
DREDGE-DREDGE...
OOO
NOW ALL THAT'S LEFT IS *MY* ASSIGNMENT...
...BUT SINCE WE DON'T EVEN KNOW WHERE IT IS YET...
FWH
I WISH IT WOULD JUST COME TO US.
WOULD CERTAINLY SAVE US THE TROUBLE...
BY THE WAY, WHAT KIND OF JINCHÛRIKI HOST IS YOURS, SASORI?
WHO KNOWS... AND WHO CARES?
AS LONG AS WE CATCH ONE, THEY CAN'T COMPLAIN... *WHICHEVER* ONE IT IS...

NARUTO

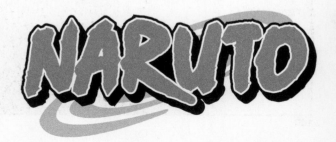

Number 252: Feelings Run Wild...!!

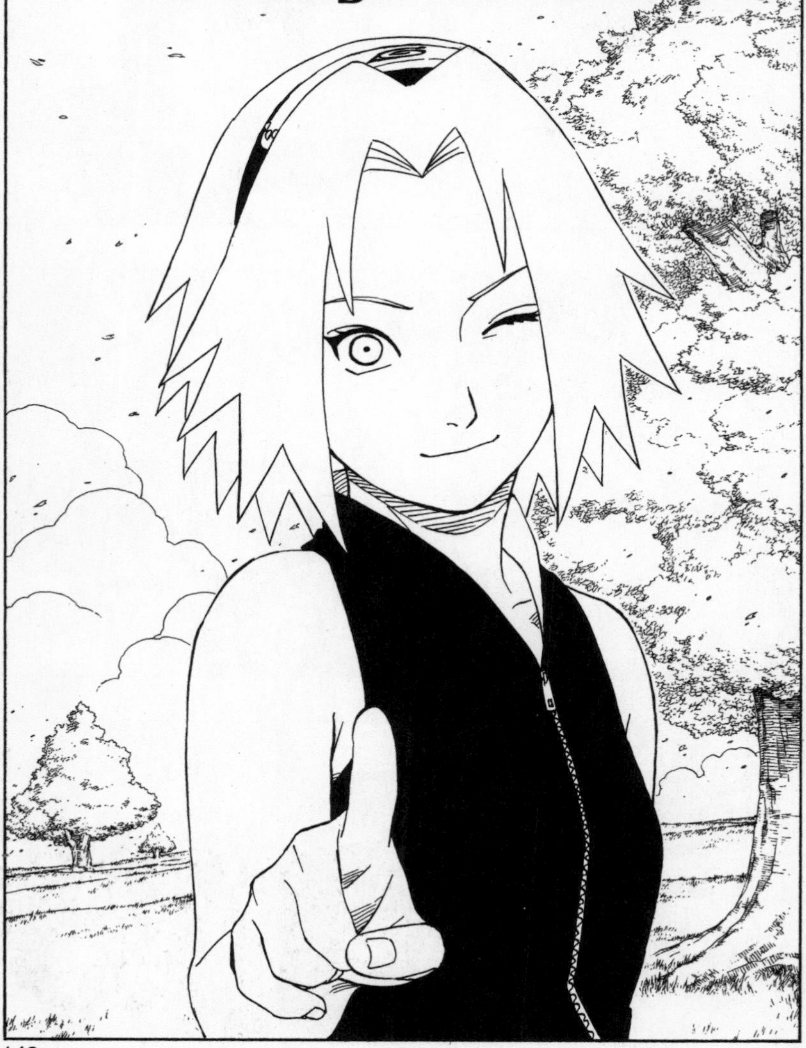

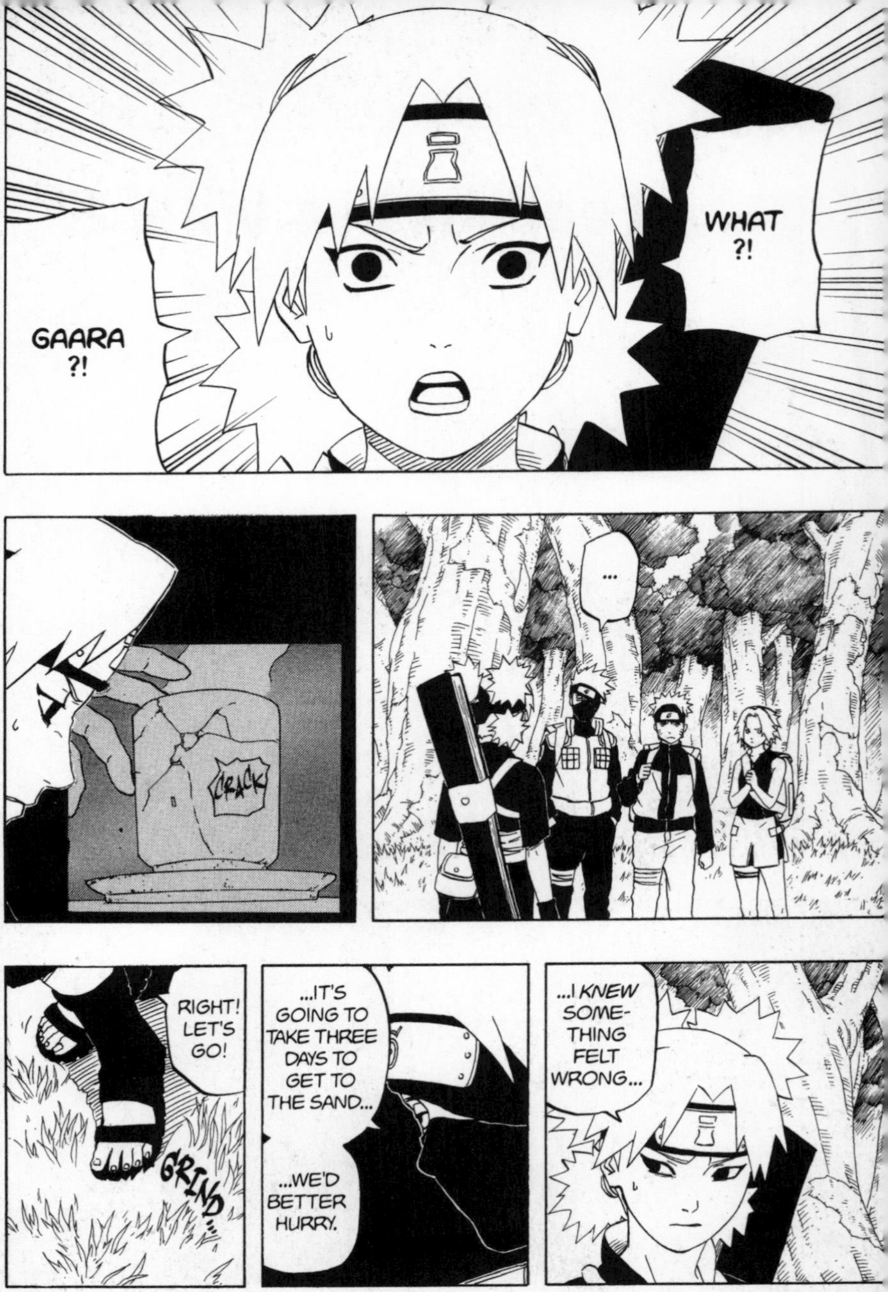
WHAT ?!
GAARA ?!
...
CRACK
...I KNEW SOME-THING FELT WRONG...
...IT'S GOING TO TAKE THREE DAYS TO GET TO THE SAND...
...WE'D BETTER HURRY.
RIGHT! LET'S GO!
GRIND...

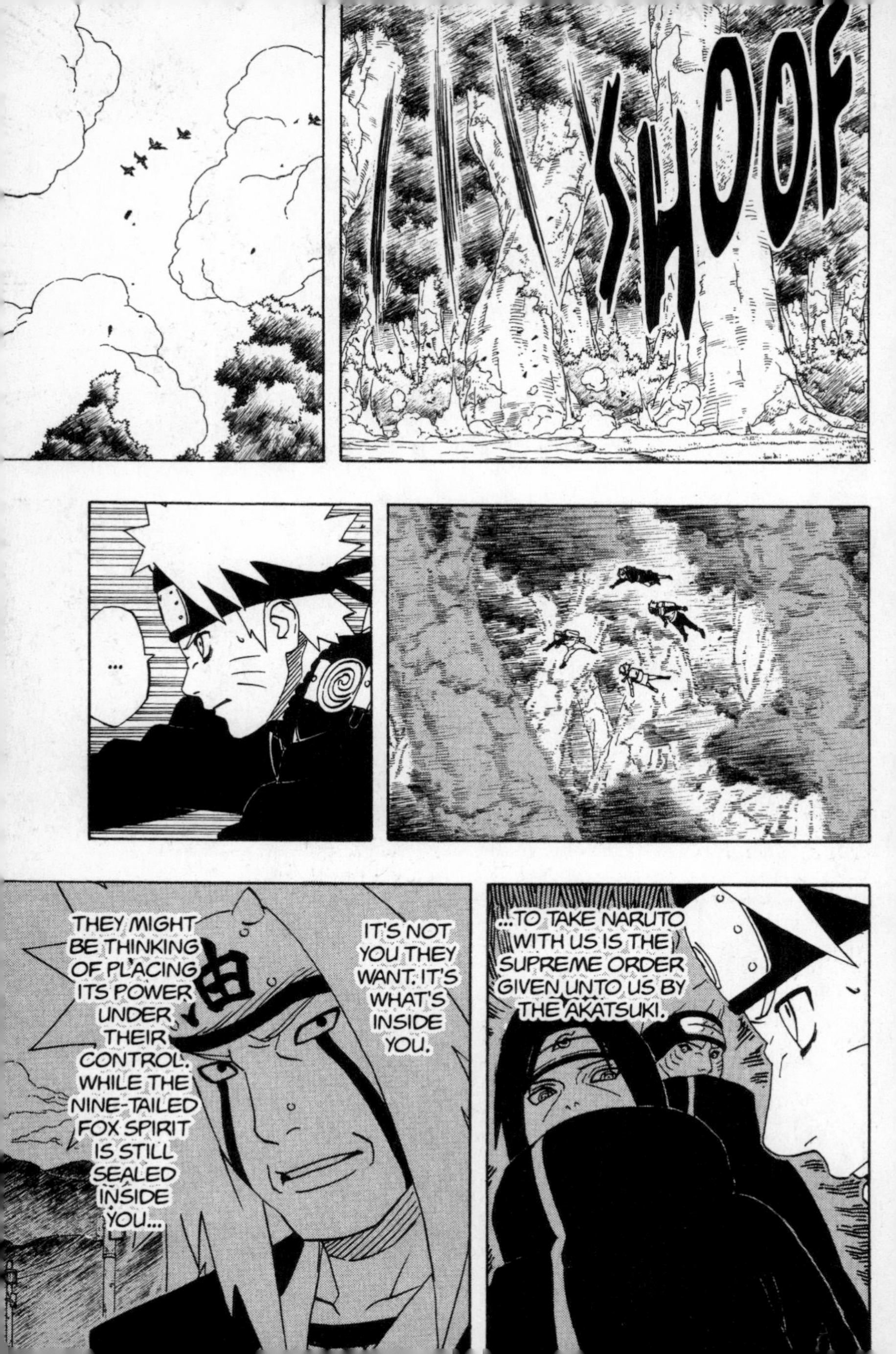
SHOOF
...
...TO TAKE NARUTO WITH US IS THE SUPREME ORDER GIVEN UNTO US BY THE AKATSUKI.
IT'S NOT YOU THEY WANT. IT'S WHAT'S INSIDE YOU.
THEY MIGHT BE THINKING OF PLACING ITS POWER UNDER THEIR CONTROL. WHILE THE NINE-TAILED FOX SPIRIT IS STILL SEALED INSIDE YOU...

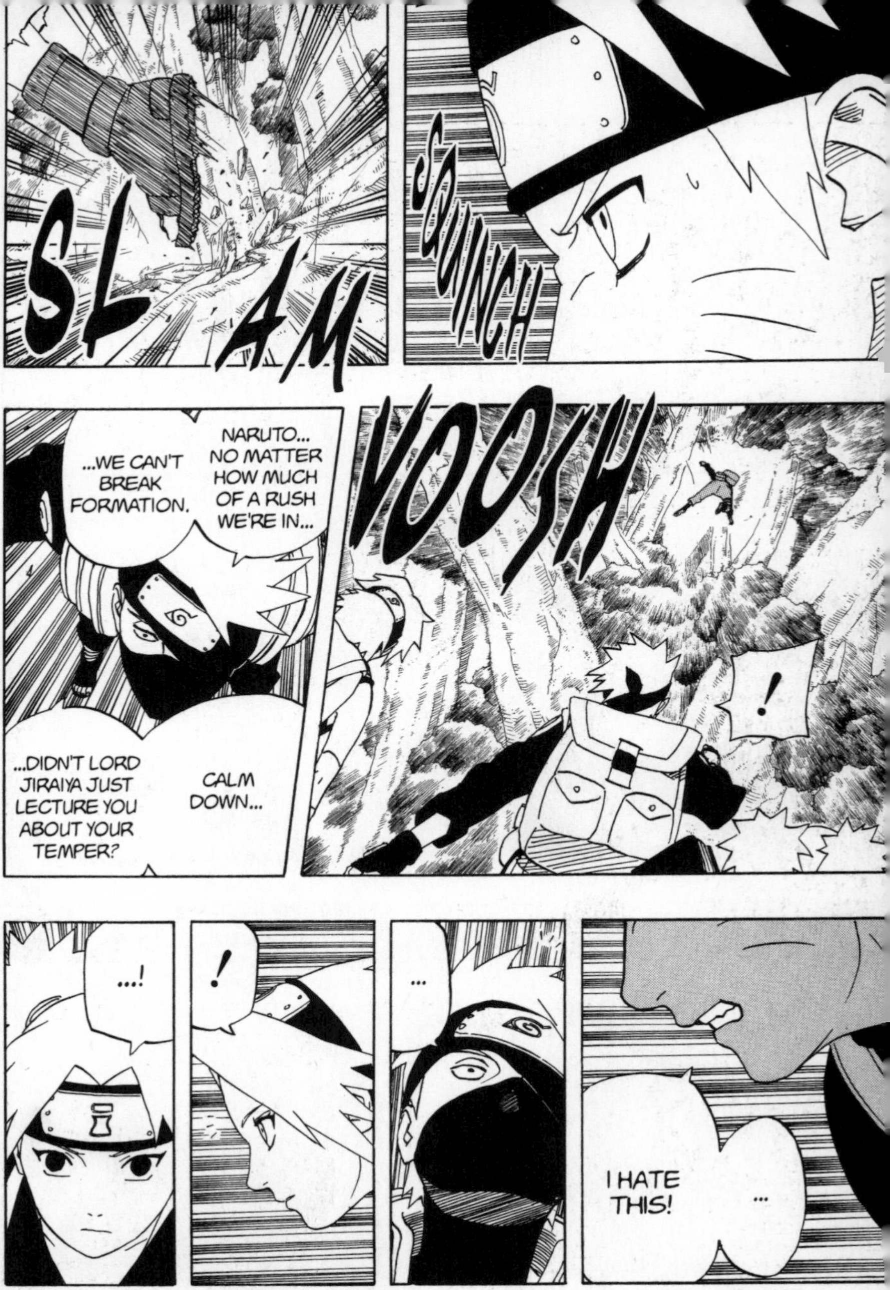
SQUINCH
SLAM
VOOSH
!
NARUTO... NO MATTER HOW MUCH OF A RUSH WE'RE IN...
...WE CAN'T BREAK FORMATION.
CALM DOWN...
...DIDN'T LORD JIRAIYA JUST LECTURE YOU ABOUT YOUR TEMPER?
...
I HATE THIS!
...
!
...!

READ THIS WAY

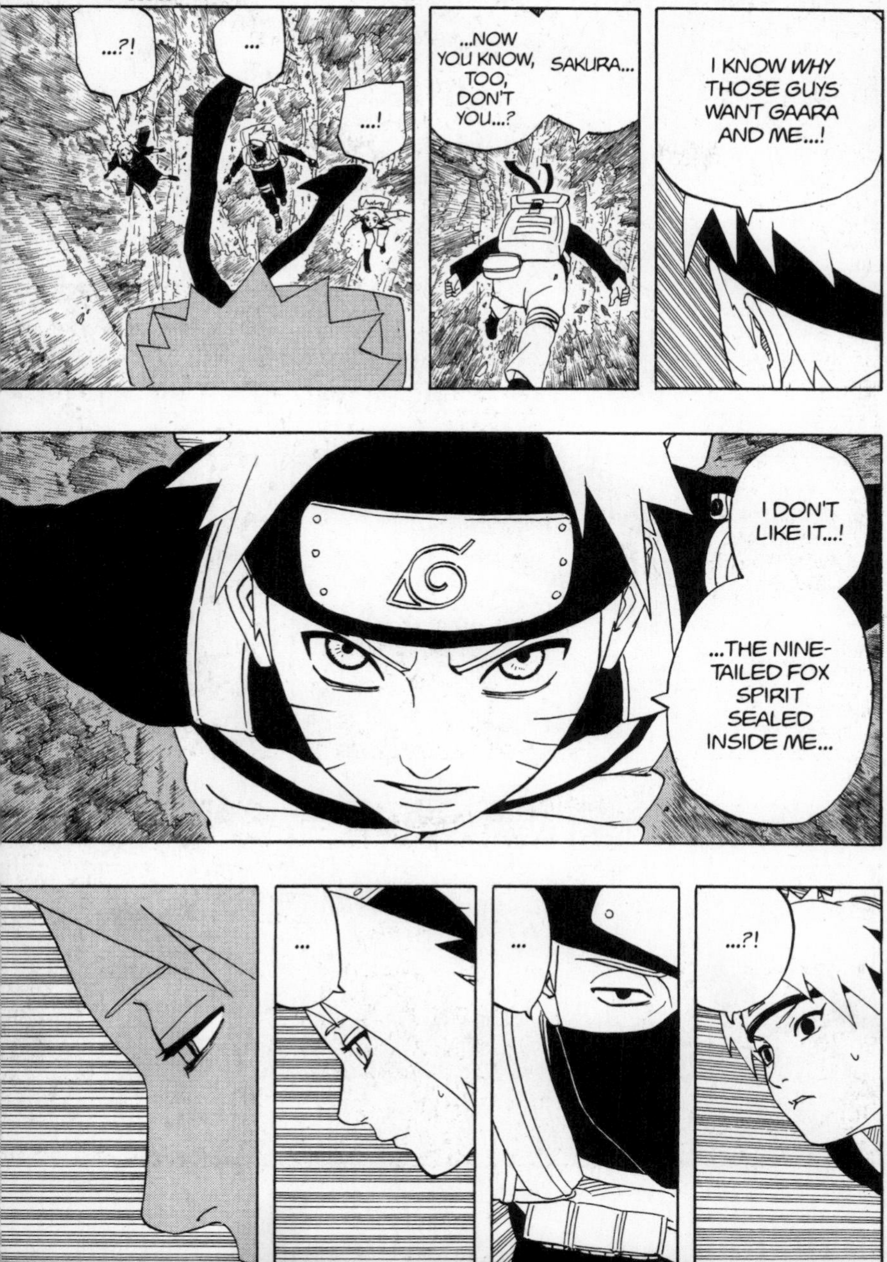
I KNOW WHY THOSE GUYS WANT GAARA AND ME...!
SAKURA...
...NOW YOU KNOW, TOO, DON'T YOU...?
...!
...
...?!
I DON'T LIKE IT...!
...THE NINE-TAILED FOX SPIRIT SEALED INSIDE ME...
...?!
...
...

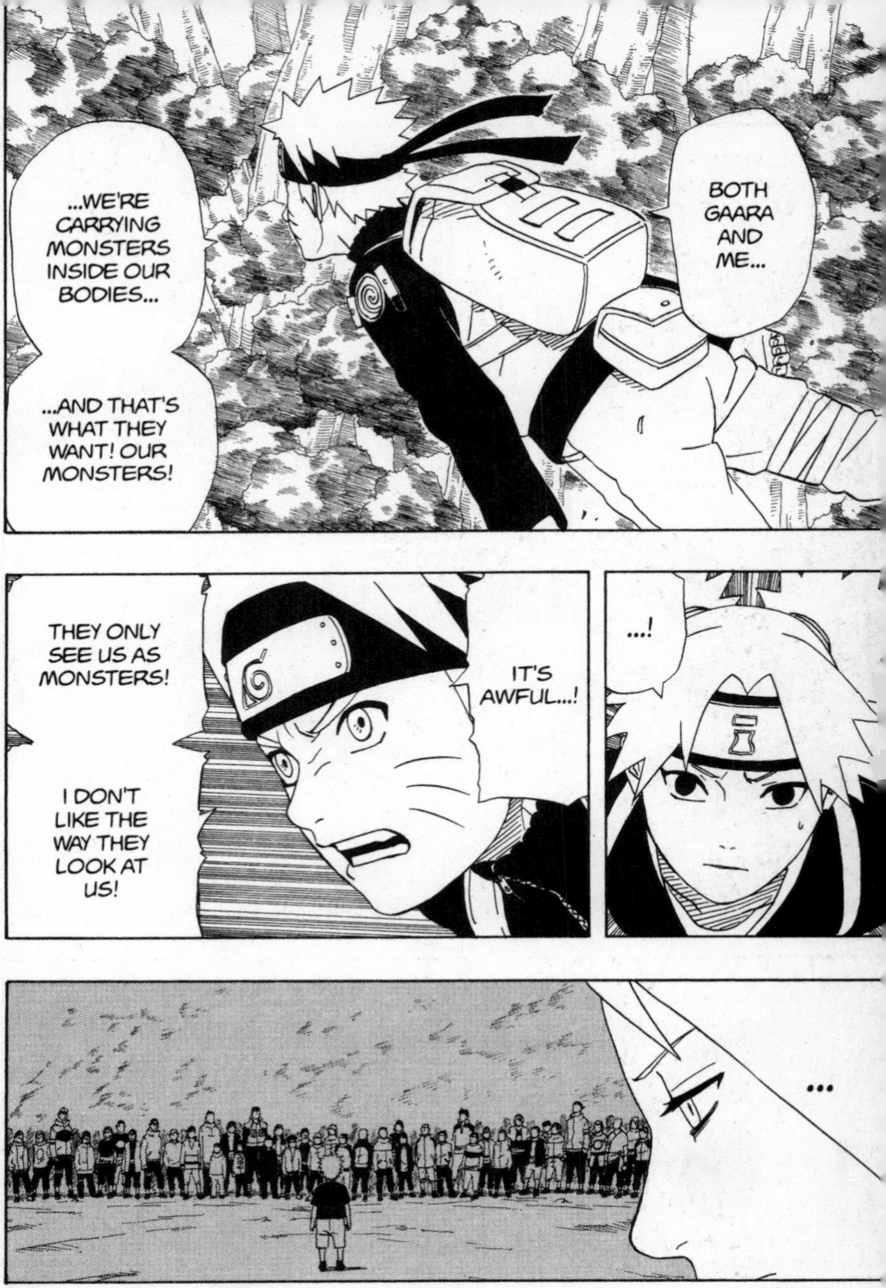
BOTH GAARA AND ME...
...WE'RE CARRYING MONSTERS INSIDE OUR BODIES...
...AND THAT'S WHAT THEY WANT! OUR MONSTERS!
...!
IT'S AWFUL...!
THEY ONLY SEE US AS MONSTERS!
I DON'T LIKE THE WAY THEY LOOK AT US!
...

READ THIS WAY

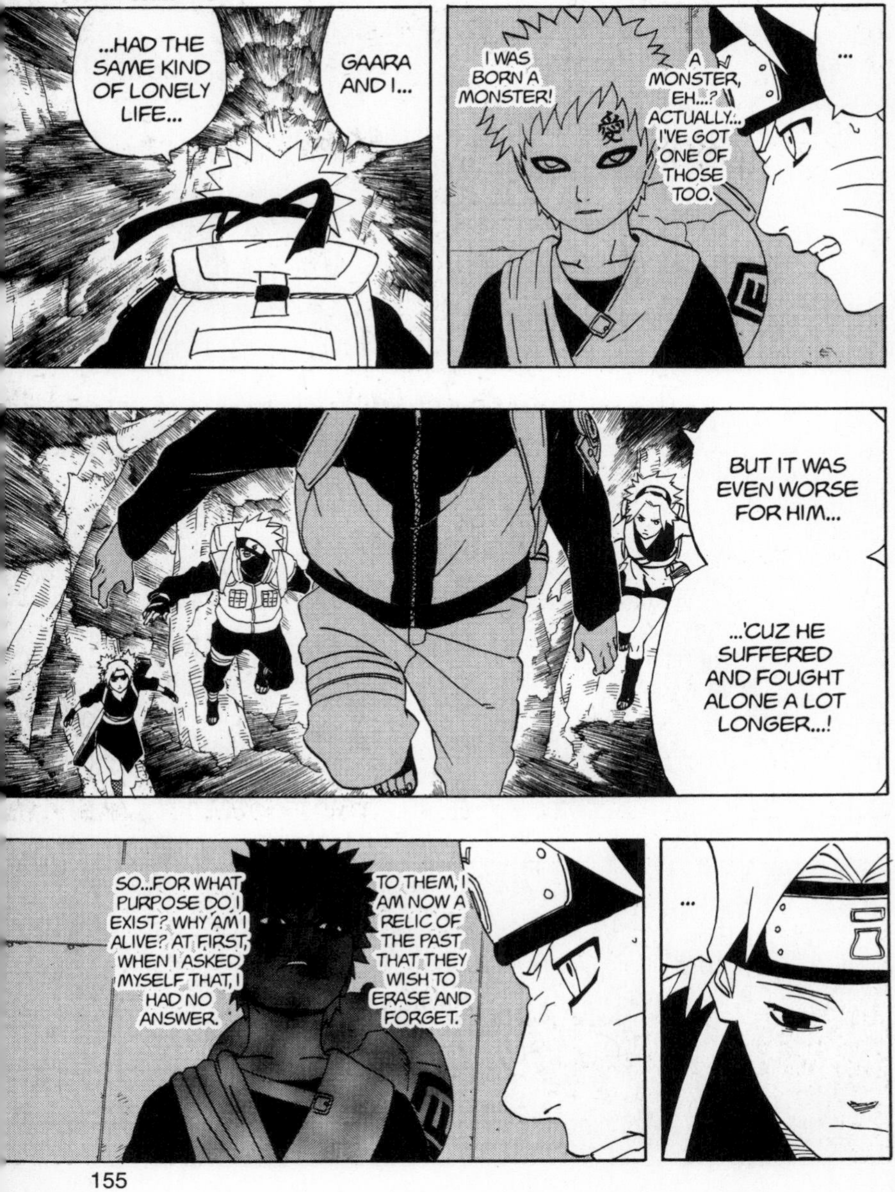
...
A MONSTER, EH...? ACTUALLY... I'VE GOT ONE OF THOSE TOO.
I WAS BORN A MONSTER!
GAARA AND I...
...HAD THE SAME KIND OF LONELY LIFE...
BUT IT WAS EVEN WORSE FOR HIM...
...'CUZ HE SUFFERED AND FOUGHT ALONE A LOT LONGER...!
...
TO THEM, I AM NOW A RELIC OF THE PAST THAT THEY WISH TO ERASE AND FORGET.
SO...FOR WHAT PURPOSE DO I EXIST? WHY AM I ALIVE? AT FIRST, WHEN I ASKED MYSELF THAT, I HAD NO ANSWER.

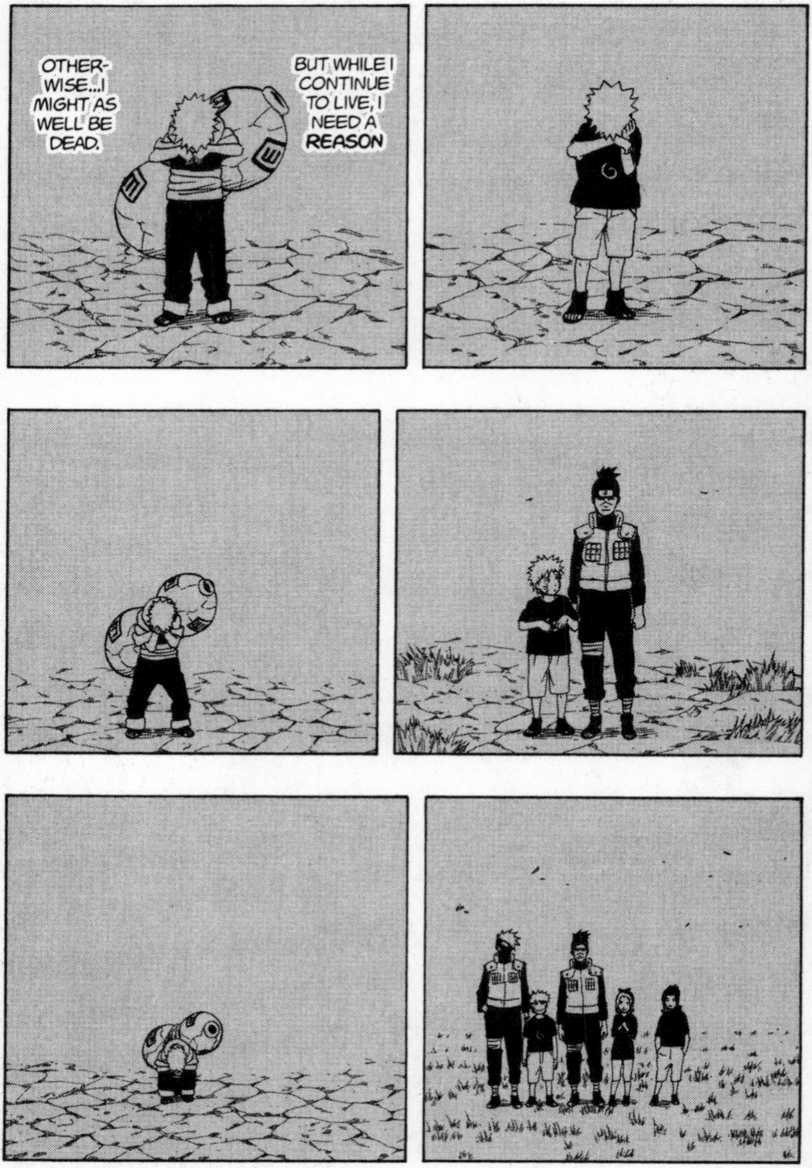
BUT WHILE I CONTINUE TO LIVE, I NEED A REASON
OTHER-WISE...I MIGHT AS WELL BE DEAD.

READ THIS WAY

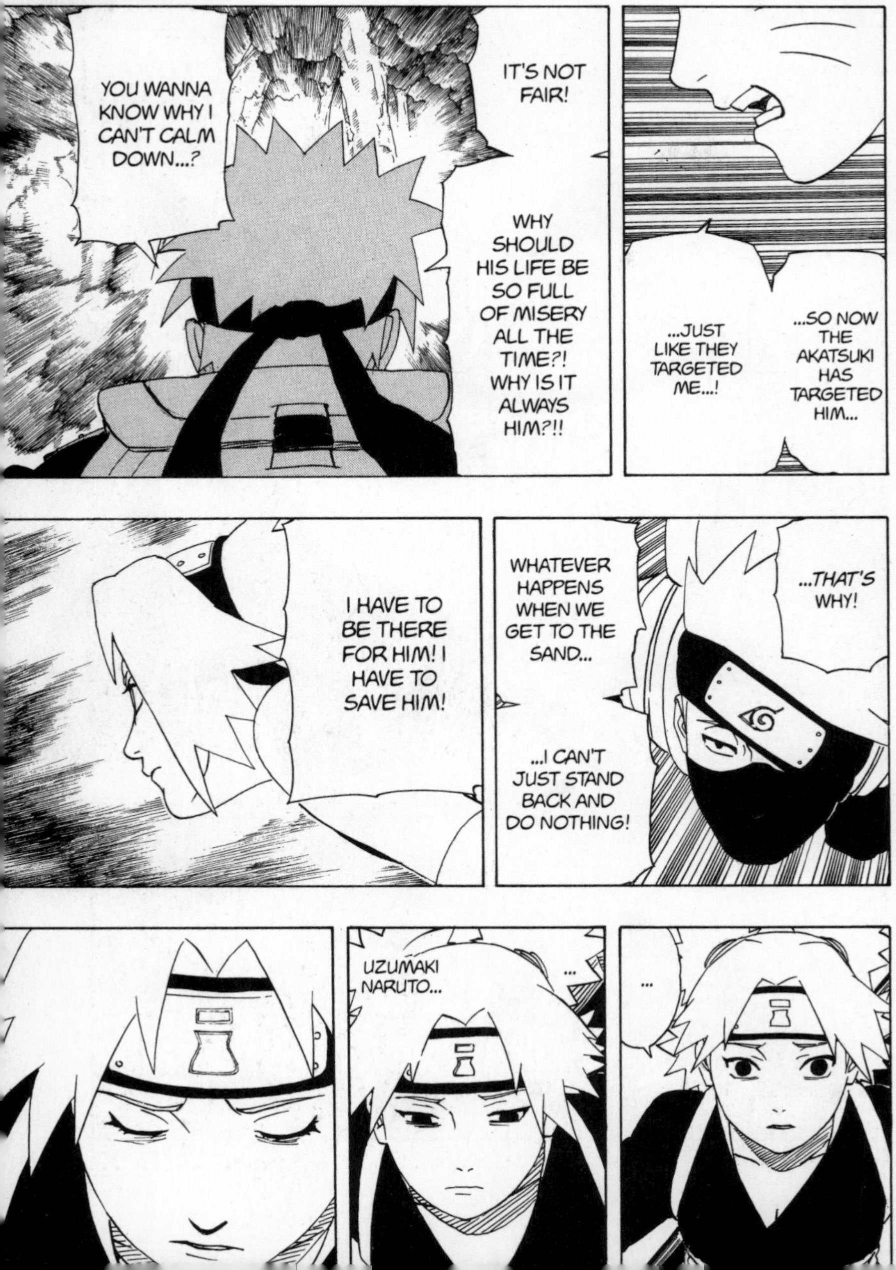

...SO NOW THE AKATSUKI HAS TARGETED HIM...
...JUST LIKE THEY TARGETED ME...!
YOU WANNA KNOW WHY I CAN'T CALM DOWN...?
IT'S NOT FAIR!
WHY SHOULD HIS LIFE BE SO FULL OF MISERY ALL THE TIME?! WHY IS IT ALWAYS HIM?!!
...THAT'S WHY!
WHATEVER HAPPENS WHEN WE GET TO THE SAND...
...I CAN'T JUST STAND BACK AND DO NOTHING!
I HAVE TO BE THERE FOR HIM! I HAVE TO SAVE HIM!
...
...
UZUMAKI NARUTO...

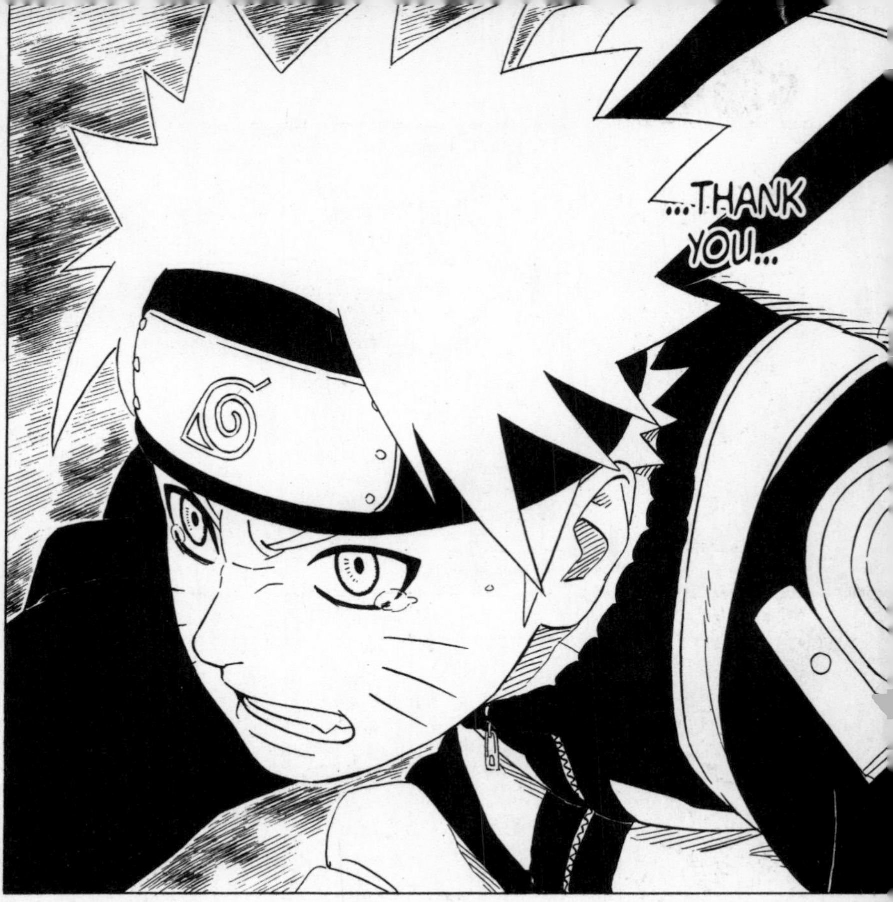
...THANK YOU...
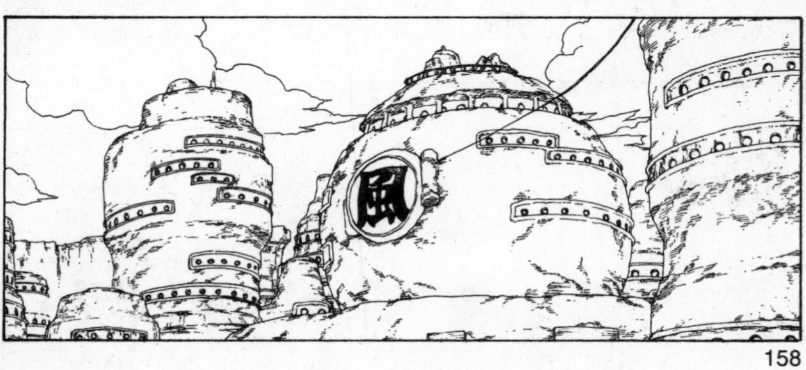
風

READ THIS WAY

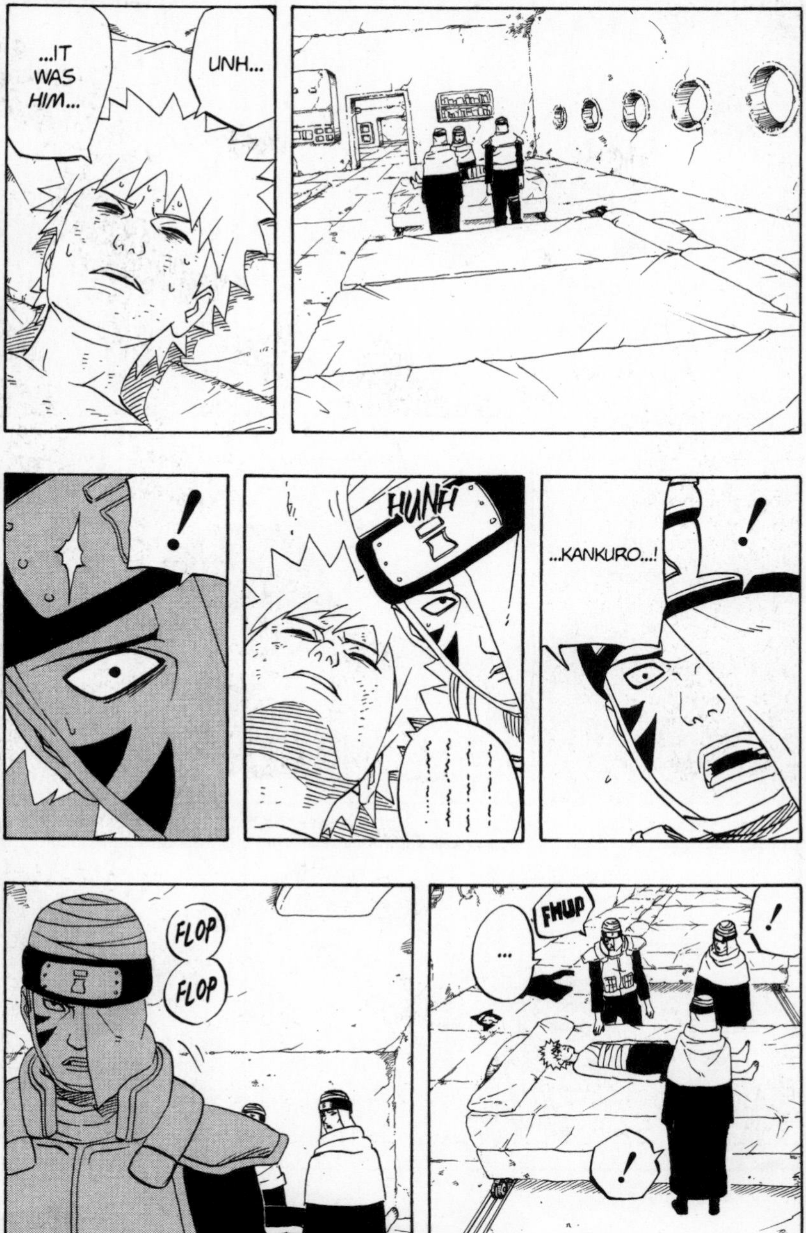
UNH...
...IT WAS HIM...
!
...KANKURO...!
HUNH
......
!
!
FHUP
...
!
FLOP
FLOP

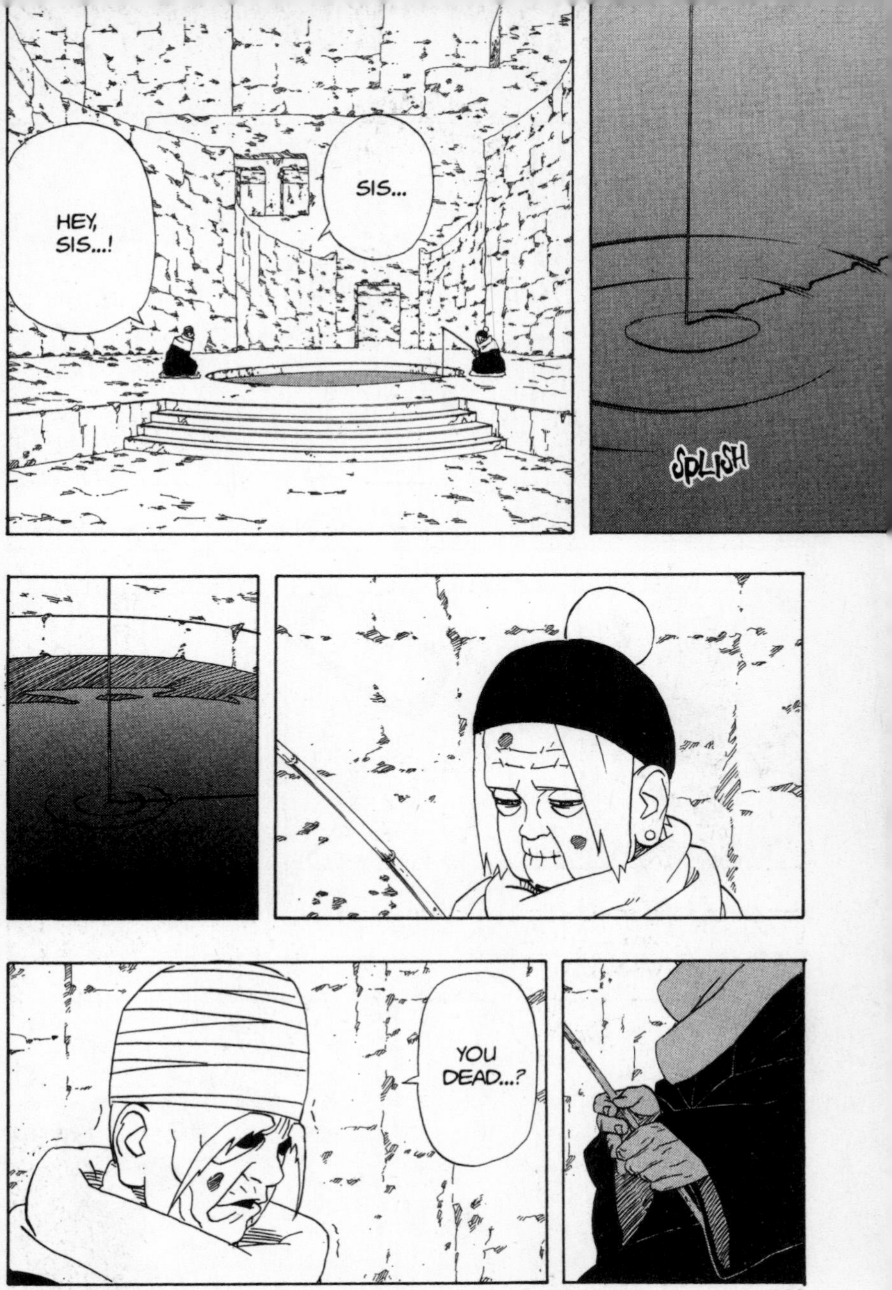
SPLISH
SIS...
HEY, SIS...!
YOU DEAD...?

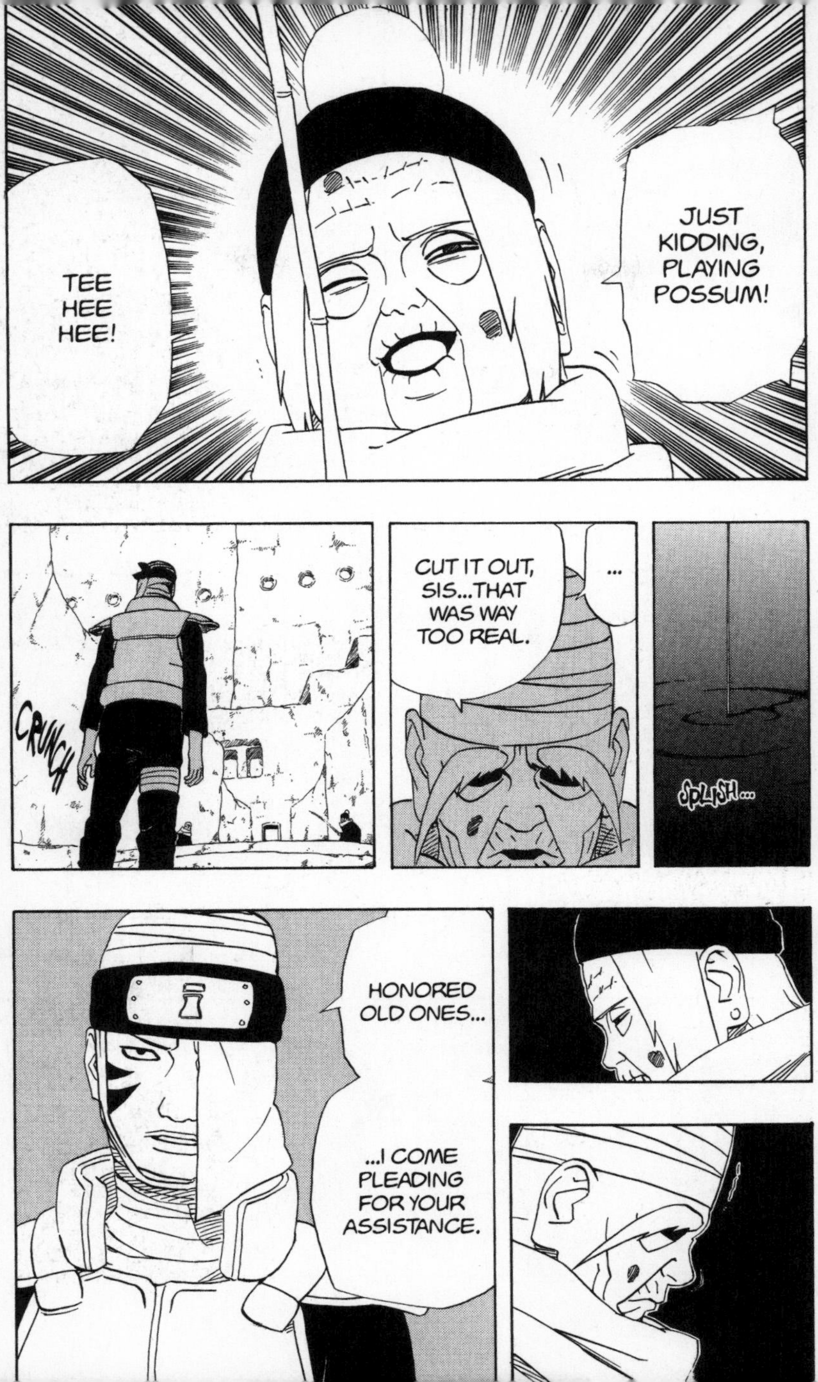

JUST KIDDING, PLAYING POSSUM!
TEE HEE HEE!
SPLISH...
...
CUT IT OUT, SIS...THAT WAS WAY TOO REAL.
CRUNCH
HONORED OLD ONES...
...I COME PLEADING FOR YOUR ASSISTANCE.

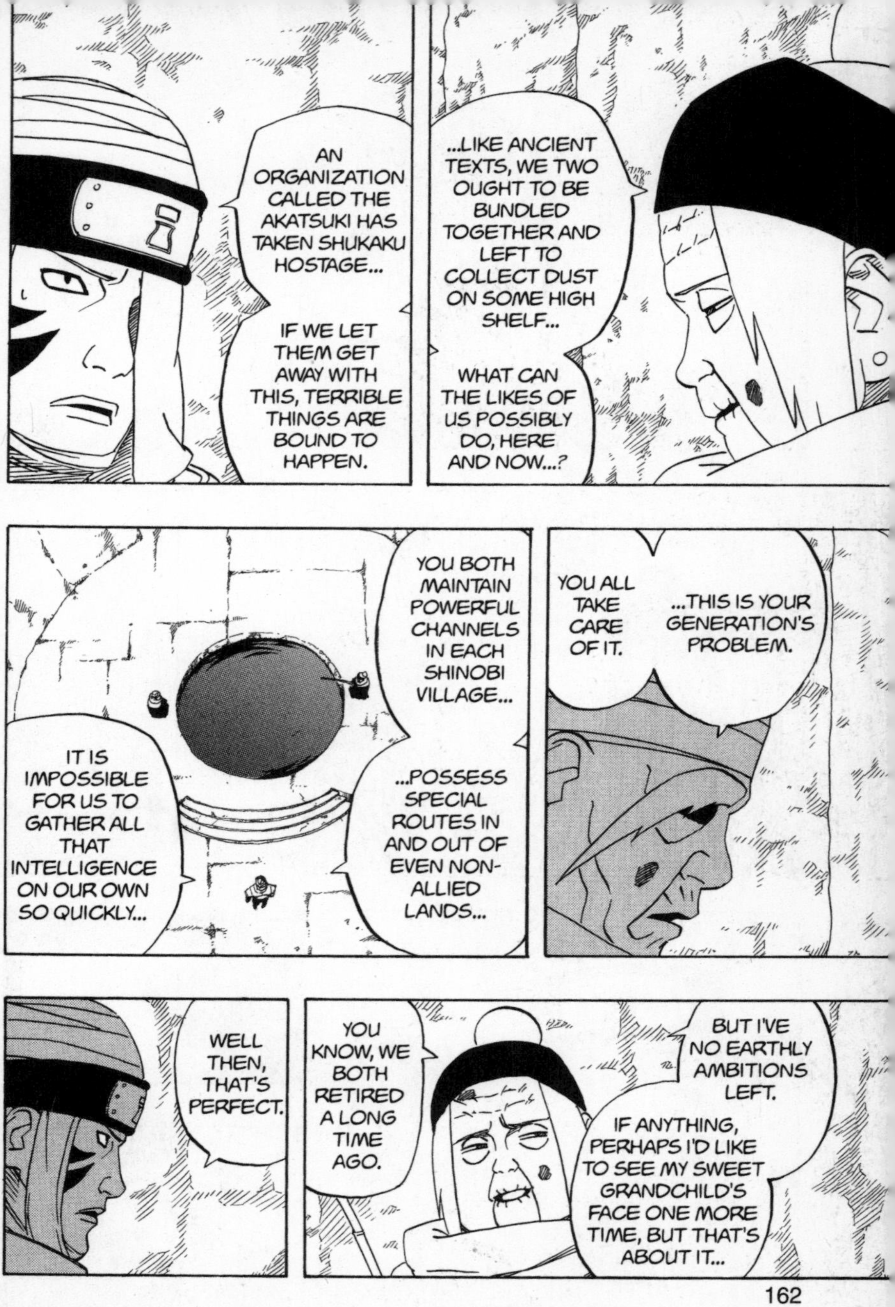

...LIKE ANCIENT TEXTS, WE TWO OUGHT TO BE BUNDLED TOGETHER AND LEFT TO COLLECT DUST ON SOME HIGH SHELF...
WHAT CAN THE LIKES OF US POSSIBLY DO, HERE AND NOW...?
AN ORGANIZATION CALLED THE AKATSUKI HAS TAKEN SHUKAKU HOSTAGE...
IF WE LET THEM GET AWAY WITH THIS, TERRIBLE THINGS ARE BOUND TO HAPPEN.
...THIS IS YOUR GENERATION'S PROBLEM.
YOU ALL TAKE CARE OF IT.
YOU BOTH MAINTAIN POWERFUL CHANNELS IN EACH SHINOBI VILLAGE...
...POSSESS SPECIAL ROUTES IN AND OUT OF EVEN NON-ALLIED LANDS...
IT IS IMPOSSIBLE FOR US TO GATHER ALL THAT INTELLIGENCE ON OUR OWN SO QUICKLY...
YOU KNOW, WE BOTH RETIRED A LONG TIME AGO.
BUT I'VE NO EARTHLY AMBITIONS LEFT.
IF ANYTHING, PERHAPS I'D LIKE TO SEE MY SWEET GRANDCHILD'S FACE ONE MORE TIME, BUT THAT'S ABOUT IT...
WELL THEN, THAT'S PERFECT.

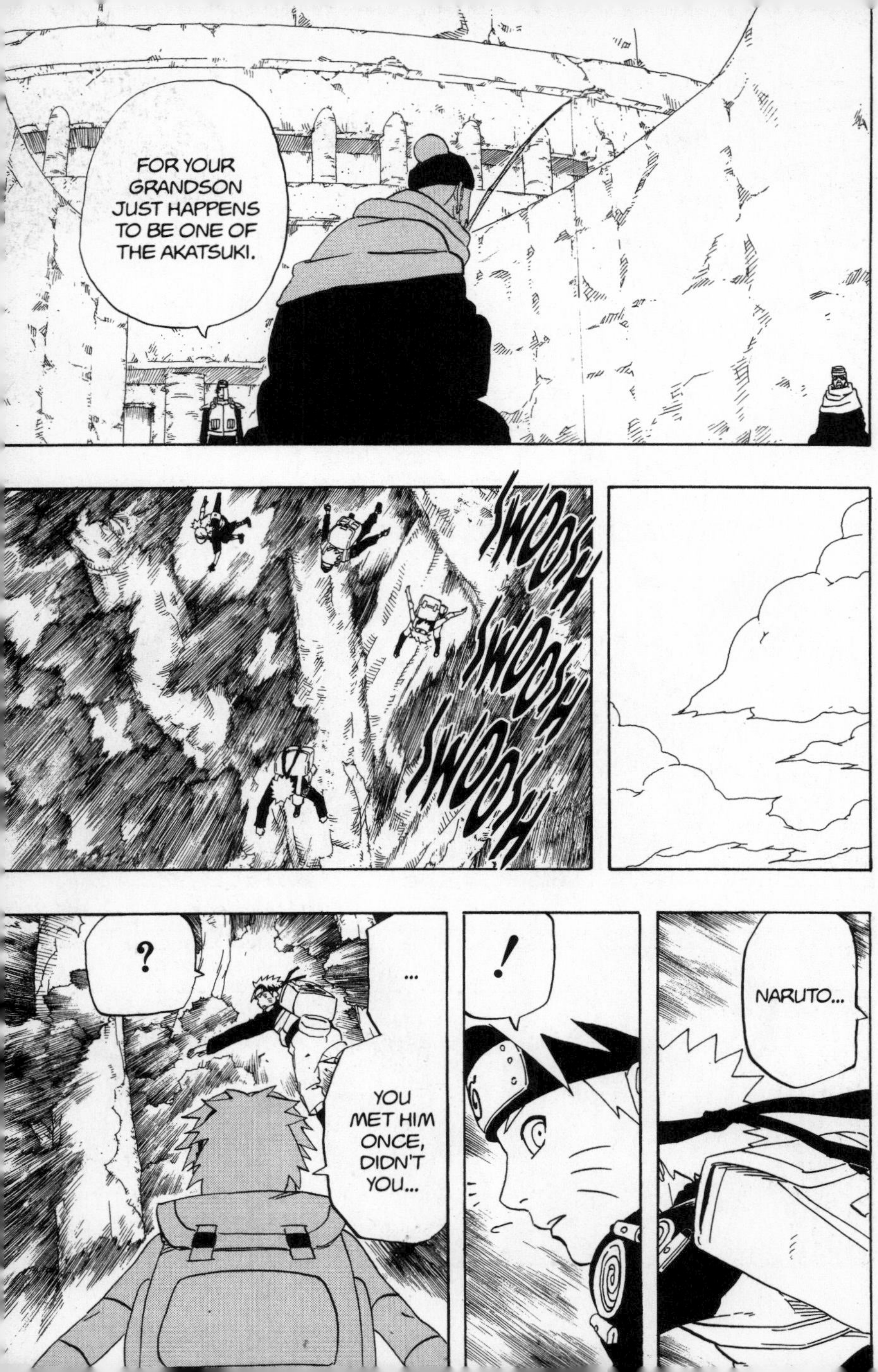
FOR YOUR GRANDSON JUST HAPPENS TO BE ONE OF THE AKATSUKI.
WHOOSH WHOOSH WHOOSH
NARUTO...
!
...
?
YOU MET HIM ONCE, DIDN'T YOU...

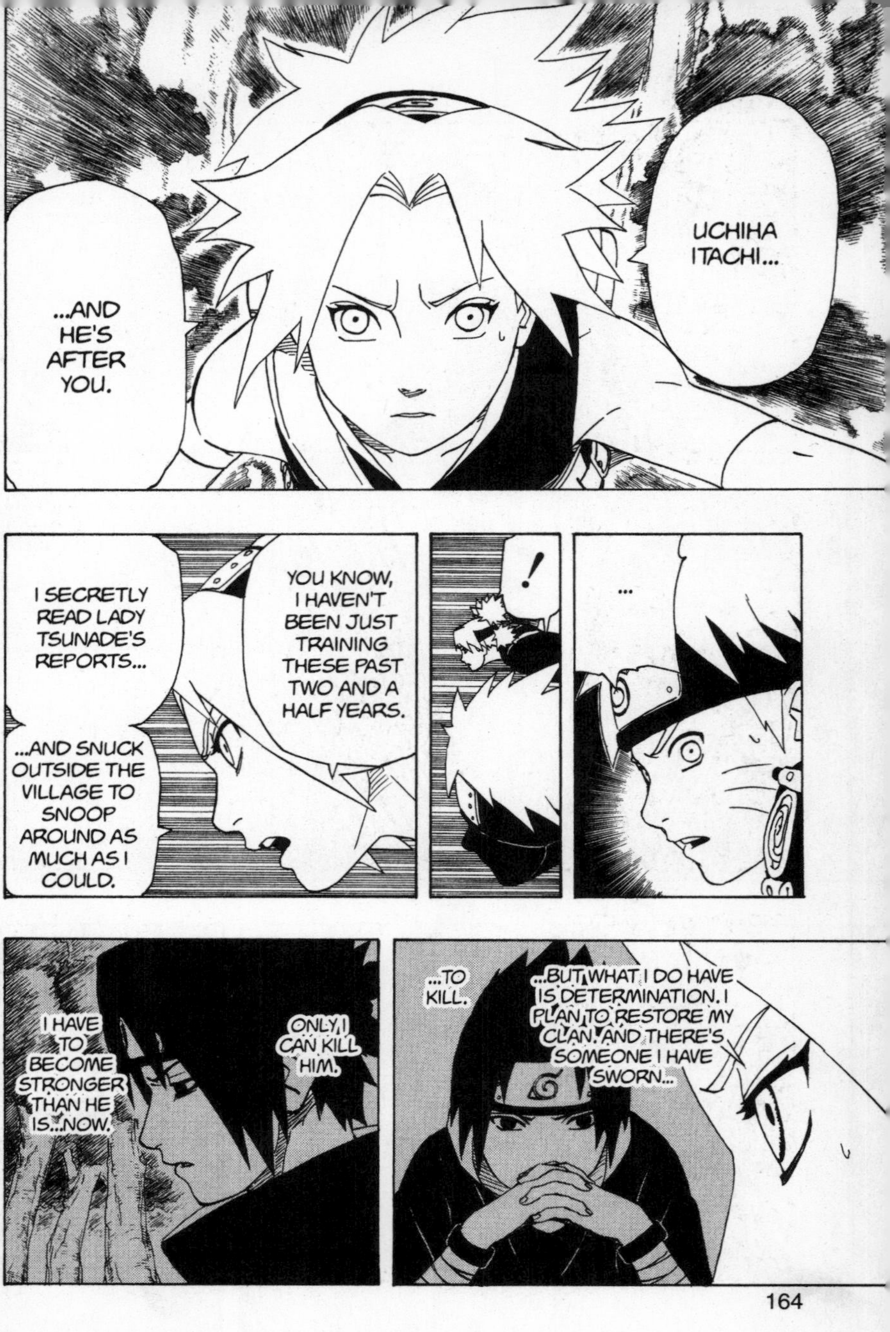
UCHIHA ITACHI...
...AND HE'S AFTER YOU.
...
!
YOU KNOW, I HAVEN'T BEEN JUST TRAINING THESE PAST TWO AND A HALF YEARS.
I SECRETLY READ LADY TSUNADE'S REPORTS...
...AND SNUCK OUTSIDE THE VILLAGE TO SNOOP AROUND AS MUCH AS I COULD.
...BUT WHAT I DO HAVE IS DETERMINATION. I PLAN TO RESTORE MY CLAN. AND THERE'S SOMEONE I HAVE SWORN...
...TO KILL.
ONLY I CAN KILL HIM.
I HAVE TO BECOME STRONGER THAN HE IS...NOW.

READ THIS WAY

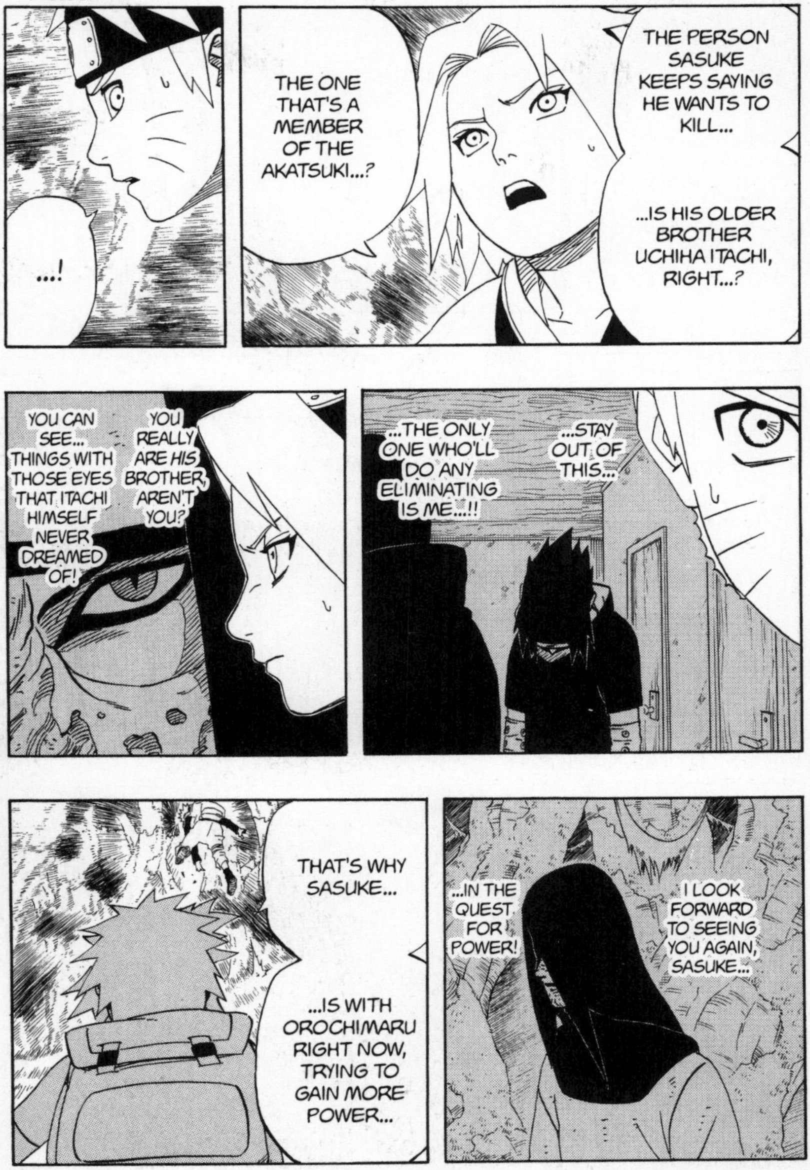
THE PERSON SASUKE KEEPS SAYING HE WANTS TO KILL...
...IS HIS OLDER BROTHER UCHIHA ITACHI, RIGHT...?
THE ONE THAT'S A MEMBER OF THE AKATSUKI...?
...!
...STAY OUT OF THIS...
...THE ONLY ONE WHO'LL DO ANY ELIMINATING IS ME...!!
YOU REALLY ARE HIS BROTHER, AREN'T YOU?
YOU CAN SEE... THINGS WITH THOSE EYES THAT ITACHI HIMSELF NEVER DREAMED OF!
I LOOK FORWARD TO SEEING YOU AGAIN, SASUKE...
...IN THE QUEST FOR POWER!
THAT'S WHY SASUKE...
...IS WITH OROCHIMARU RIGHT NOW, TRYING TO GAIN MORE POWER...

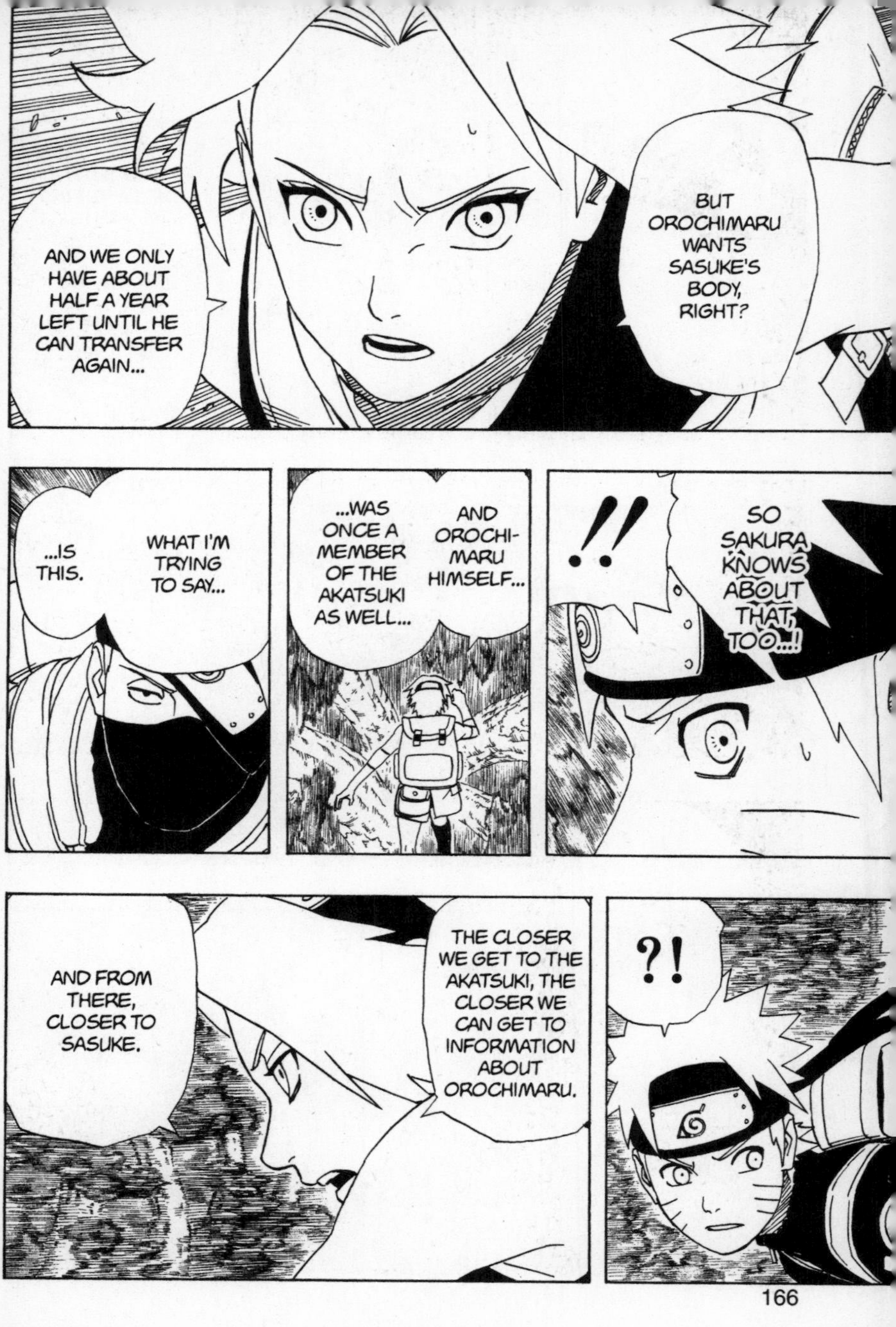
BUT OROCHIMARU WANTS SASUKE'S BODY, RIGHT?
AND WE ONLY HAVE ABOUT HALF A YEAR LEFT UNTIL HE CAN TRANSFER AGAIN...
!!
SO SAKURA KNOWS ABOUT THAT, TOO...!
AND OROCHIMARU HIMSELF...
...WAS ONCE A MEMBER OF THE AKATSUKI AS WELL...
WHAT I'M TRYING TO SAY...
...IS THIS.
?!
THE CLOSER WE GET TO THE AKATSUKI, THE CLOSER WE CAN GET TO INFORMATION ABOUT OROCHIMARU.
AND FROM THERE, CLOSER TO SASUKE.

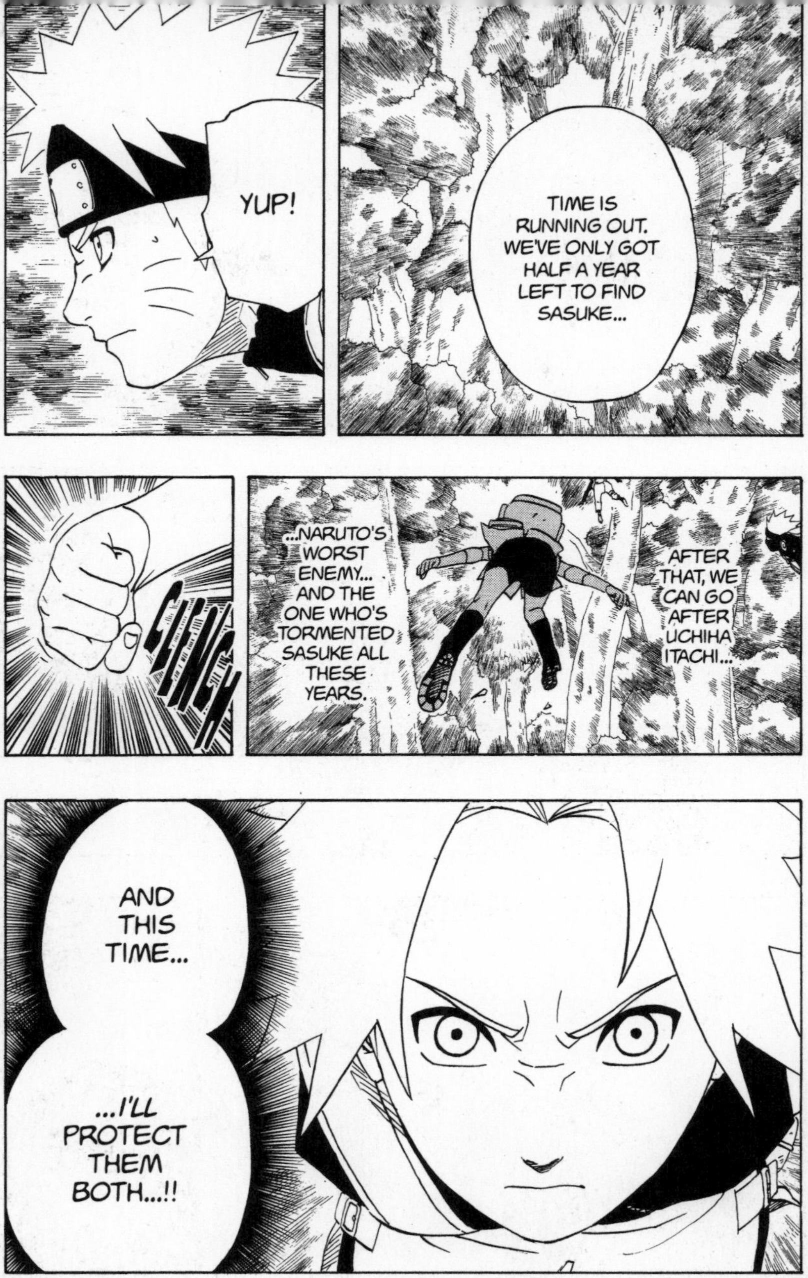
TIME IS RUNNING OUT. WE'VE ONLY GOT HALF A YEAR LEFT TO FIND SASUKE...
YUP!
AFTER THAT, WE CAN GO AFTER UCHIHA ITACHI...
...NARUTO'S WORST ENEMY... AND THE ONE WHO'S TORMENTED SASUKE ALL THESE YEARS.
CLENCH
AND THIS TIME...
...I'LL PROTECT THEM BOTH...!!

NARUTO

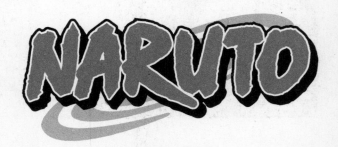

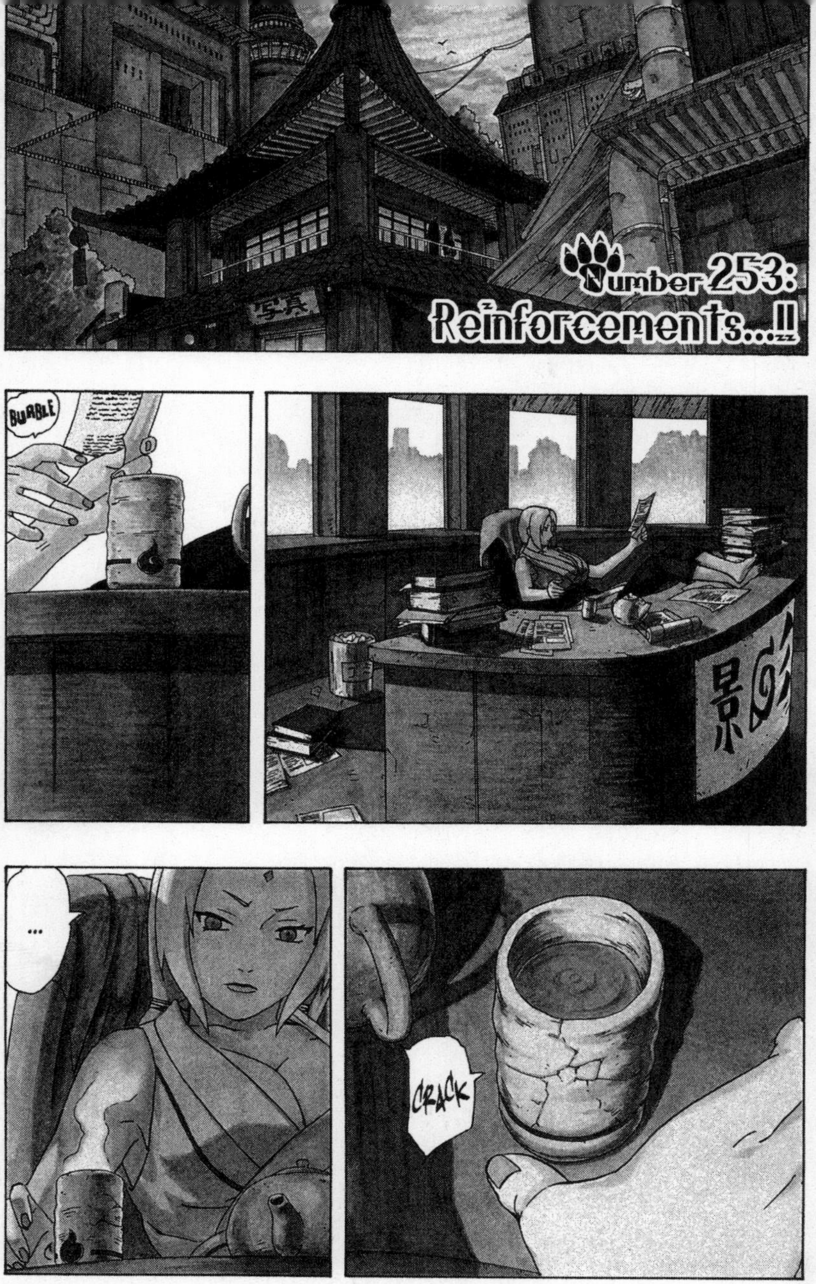
Number 253:
Reinforcements...!!
BURBLE
CRACK
...

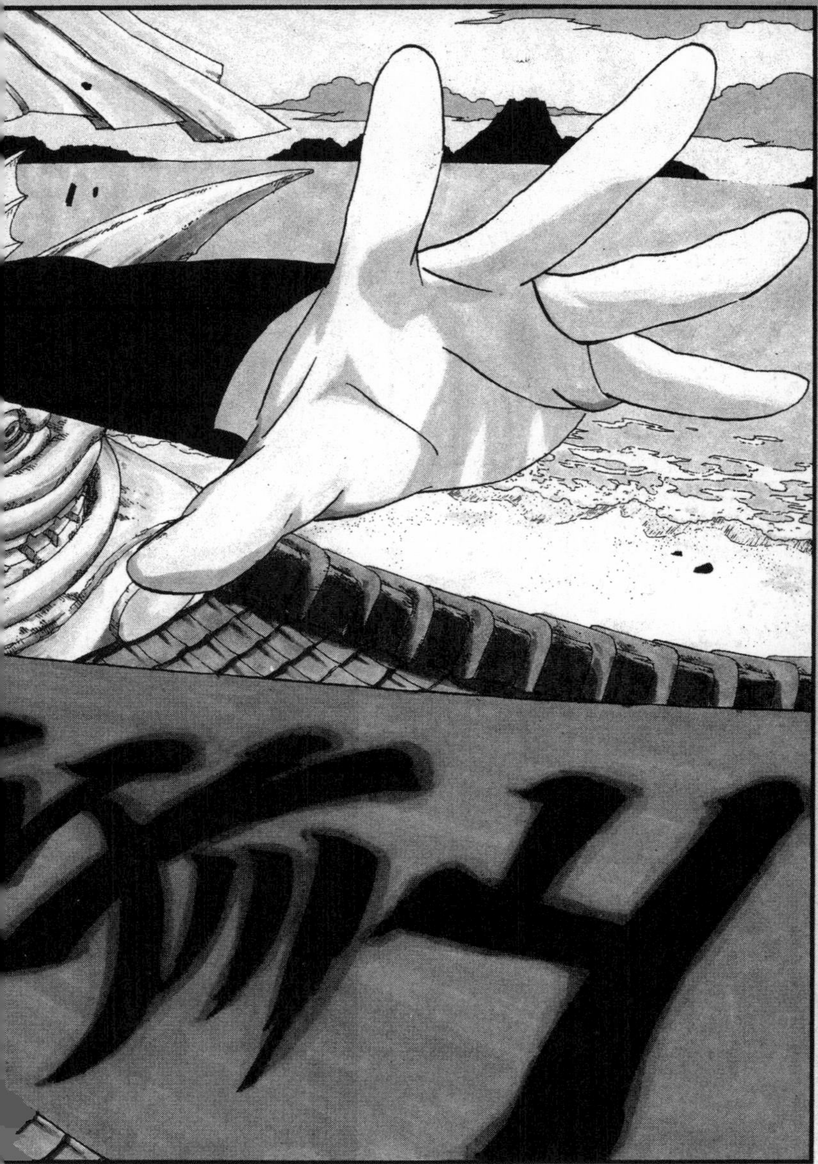

Number 253: Reinforcements...!!

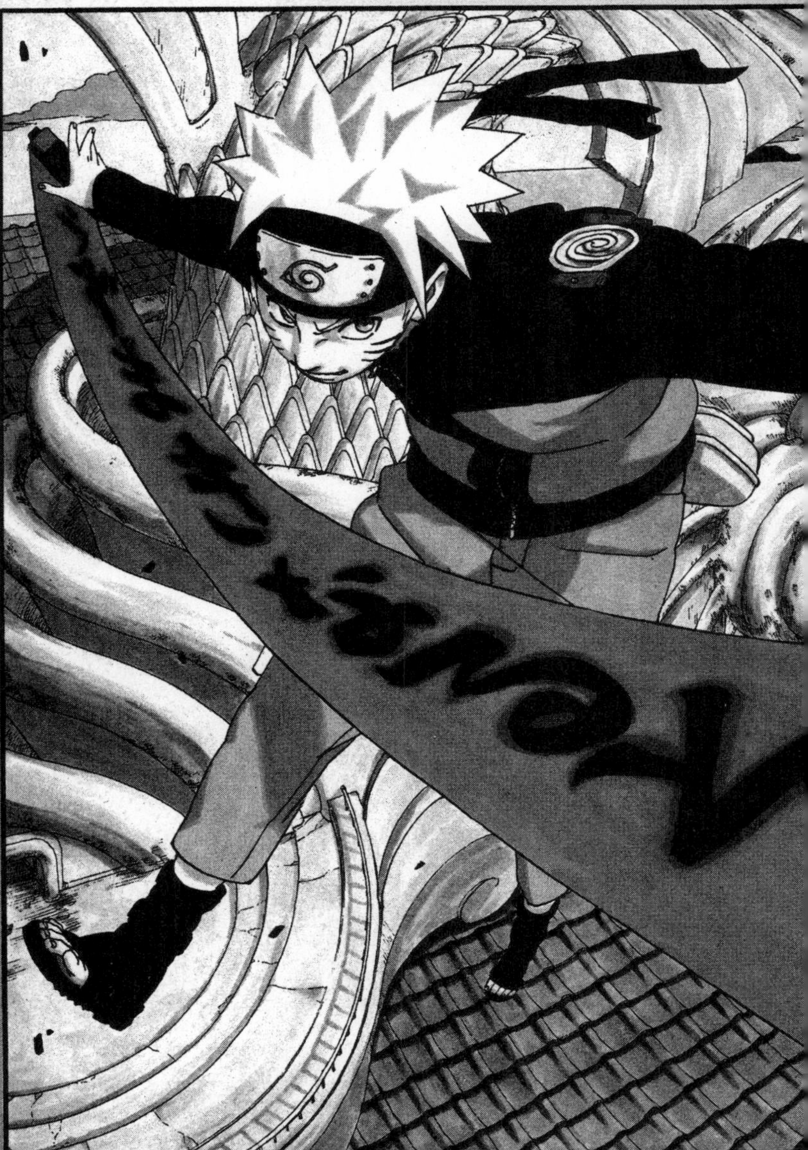

NARUTO
-ナルト-

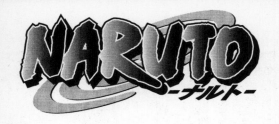

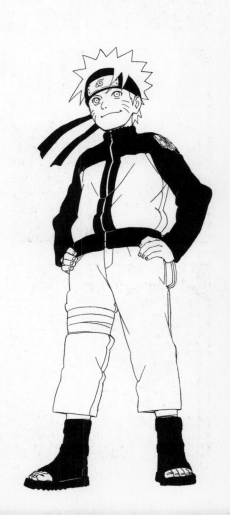

READ THIS WAY

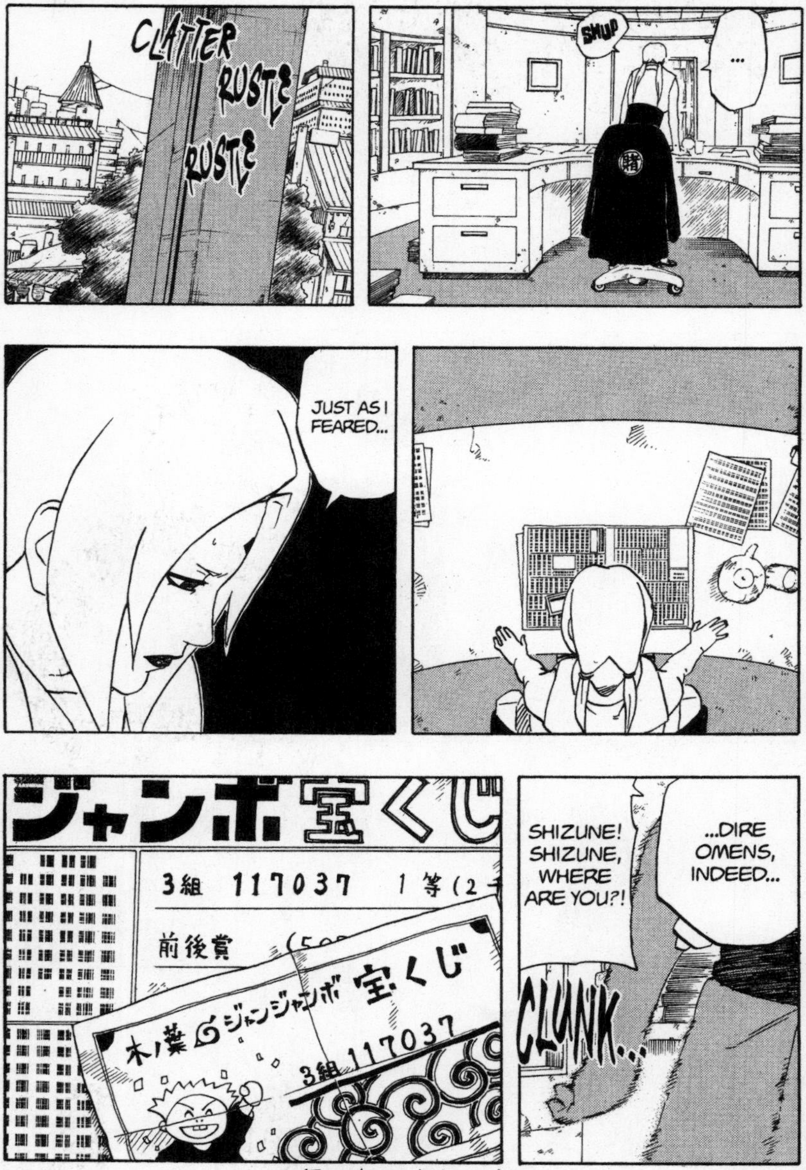
SHUP
...
CLATTER
RUSTLE
RUSTLE
JUST AS I FEARED...
...DIRE OMENS, INDEED...
SHIZUNE! SHIZUNE, WHERE ARE YOU?!
CLUNK...
ジャンボ宝くじ
3組 117037 1等
前後賞
木ノ葉ジャンジャンボ宝くじ
3組 117037

(Tsunade won the Lottery)

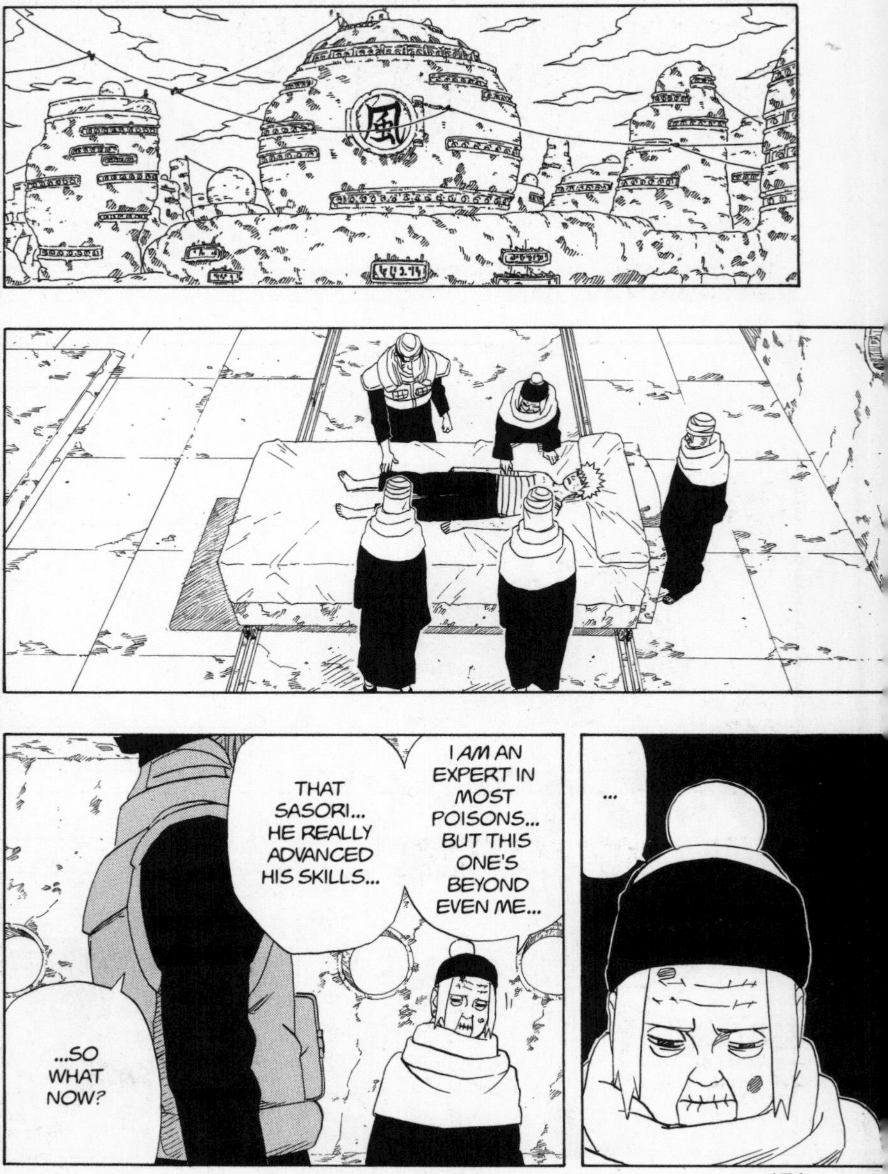
...
I AM AN EXPERT IN MOST POISONS... BUT THIS ONE'S BEYOND EVEN ME...
THAT SASORI... HE REALLY ADVANCED HIS SKILLS...
...SO WHAT NOW?

READ THIS WAY

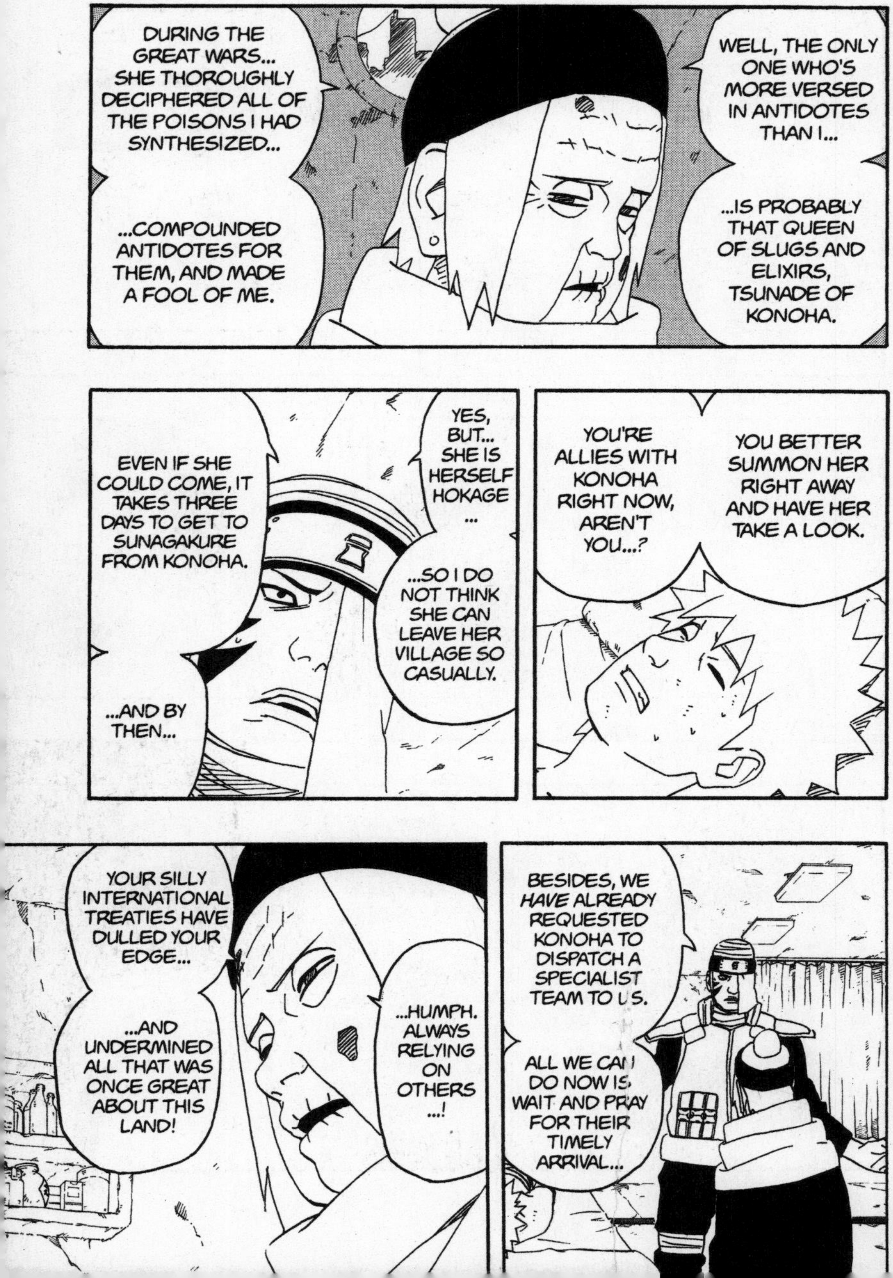
WELL, THE ONLY ONE WHO'S MORE VERSED IN ANTIDOTES THAN I...
...IS PROBABLY THAT QUEEN OF SLUGS AND ELIXIRS, TSUNADE OF KONOHA.
DURING THE GREAT WARS... SHE THOROUGHLY DECIPHERED ALL OF THE POISONS I HAD SYNTHESIZED...
...COMPOUNDED ANTIDOTES FOR THEM, AND MADE A FOOL OF ME.
YOU BETTER SUMMON HER RIGHT AWAY AND HAVE HER TAKE A LOOK.
YOU'RE ALLIES WITH KONOHA RIGHT NOW, AREN'T YOU...?
YES, BUT... SHE IS HERSELF HOKAGE...
...SO I DO NOT THINK SHE CAN LEAVE HER VILLAGE SO CASUALLY.
EVEN IF SHE COULD COME, IT TAKES THREE DAYS TO GET TO SUNAGAKURE FROM KONOHA.
...AND BY THEN...
BESIDES, WE *HAVE* ALREADY REQUESTED KONOHA TO DISPATCH A SPECIALIST TEAM TO US.
ALL WE CAN DO NOW IS WAIT AND PRAY FOR THEIR TIMELY ARRIVAL...
...HUMPH. ALWAYS RELYING ON OTHERS...!
YOUR SILLY INTERNATIONAL TREATIES HAVE DULLED YOUR EDGE...
...AND UNDERMINED ALL THAT WAS ONCE GREAT ABOUT THIS LAND!

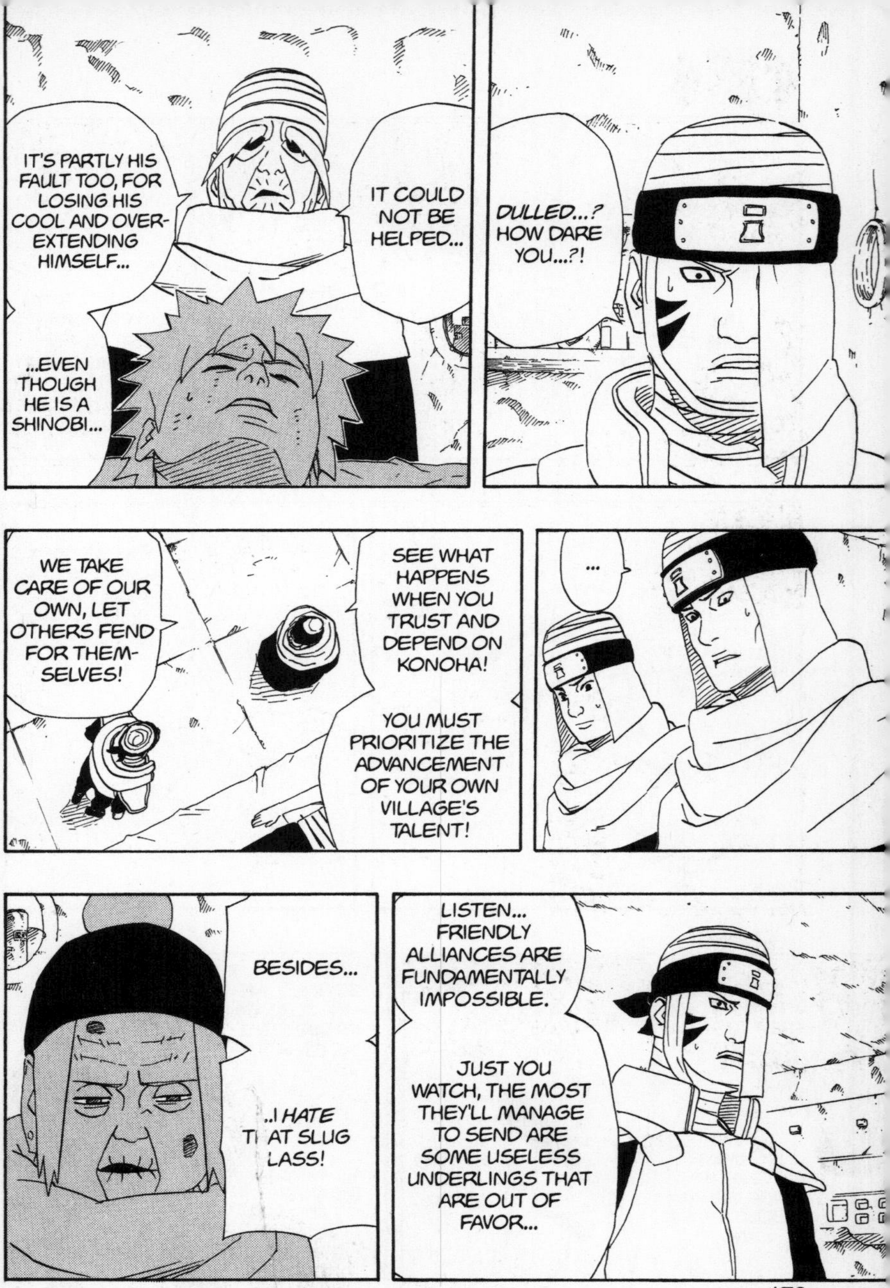
DULLED...? HOW DARE YOU...?!
IT COULD NOT BE HELPED...
IT'S PARTLY HIS FAULT TOO, FOR LOSING HIS COOL AND OVER-EXTENDING HIMSELF...
...EVEN THOUGH HE IS A SHINOBI...
...
SEE WHAT HAPPENS WHEN YOU TRUST AND DEPEND ON KONOHA!
YOU MUST PRIORITIZE THE ADVANCEMENT OF YOUR OWN VILLAGE'S TALENT!
WE TAKE CARE OF OUR OWN, LET OTHERS FEND FOR THEM-SELVES!
LISTEN... FRIENDLY ALLIANCES ARE FUNDAMENTALLY IMPOSSIBLE.
JUST YOU WATCH, THE MOST THEY'LL MANAGE TO SEND ARE SOME USELESS UNDERLINGS THAT ARE OUT OF FAVOR...
BESIDES...
..I HATE T AT SLUG LASS!

READ THIS WAY

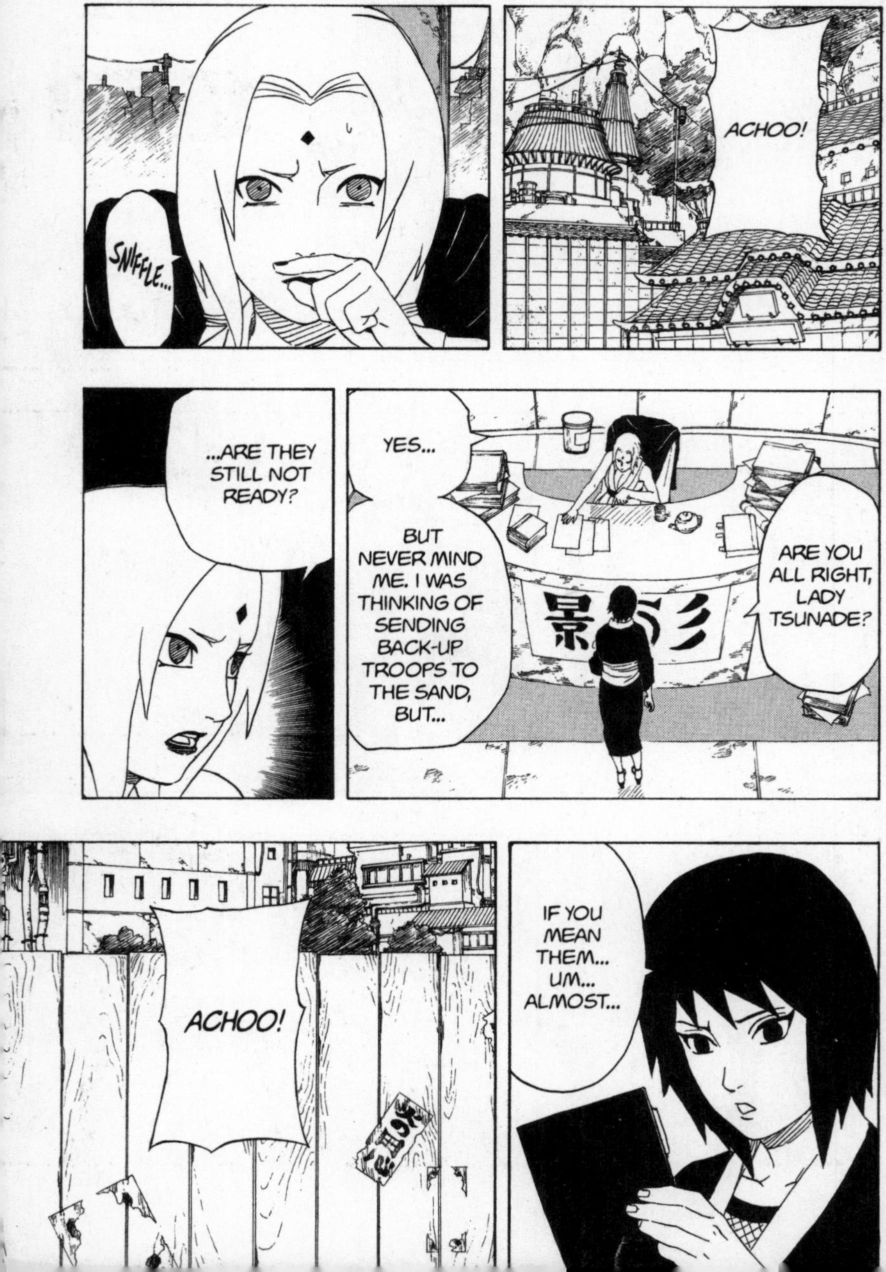
ACHOO!
SNIFFLE...
ARE YOU ALL RIGHT, LADY TSUNADE?
YES...
BUT NEVER MIND ME. I WAS THINKING OF SENDING BACK-UP TROOPS TO THE SAND, BUT...
...ARE THEY STILL NOT READY?
IF YOU MEAN THEM... UM... ALMOST...
ACHOO!

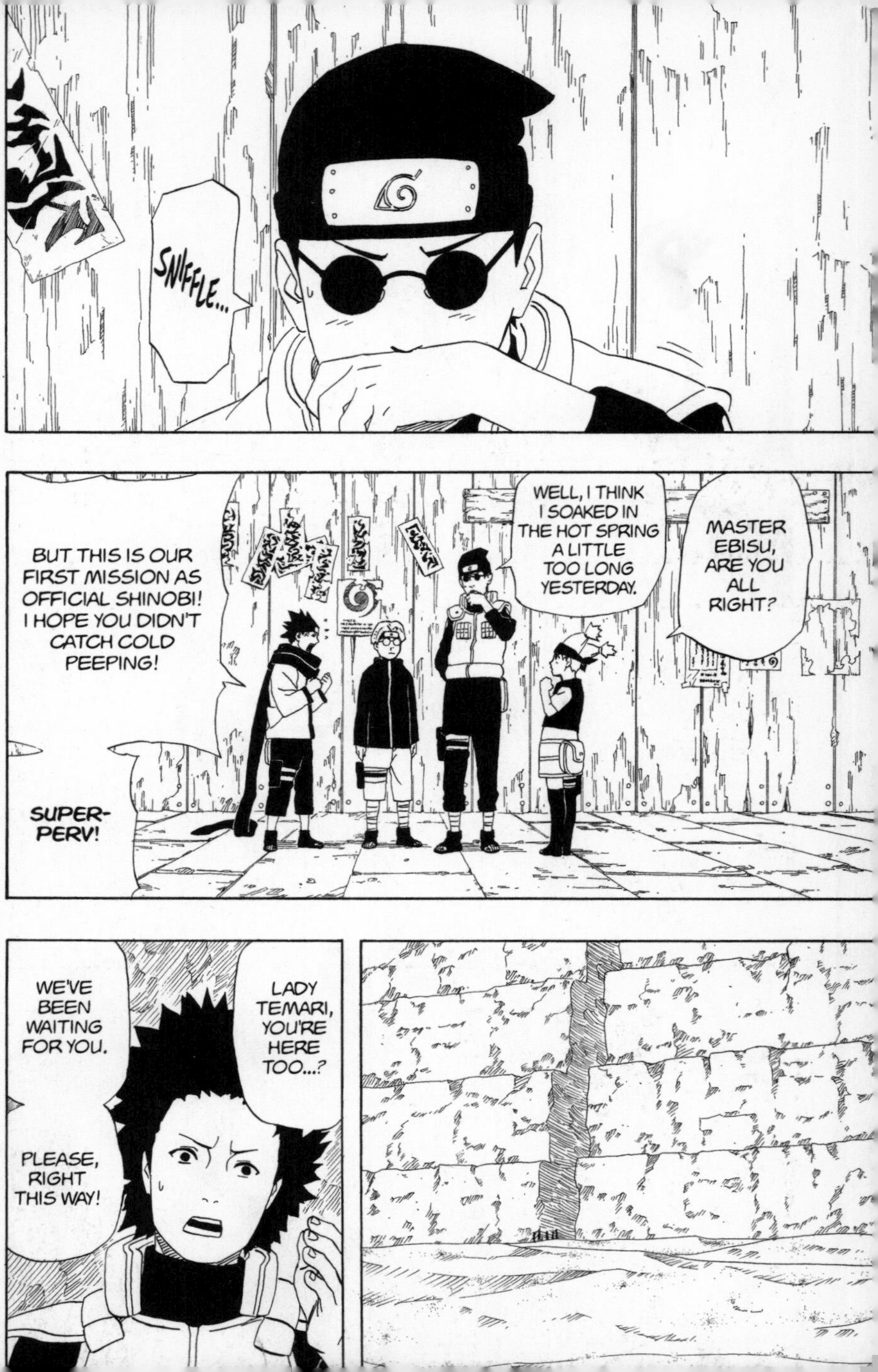
SNIFFLE...
MASTER EBISU, ARE YOU ALL RIGHT?
WELL, I THINK I SOAKED IN THE HOT SPRING A LITTLE TOO LONG YESTERDAY.
BUT THIS IS OUR FIRST MISSION AS OFFICIAL SHINOBI! I HOPE YOU DIDN'T CATCH COLD PEEPING!
SUPER-PERV!
LADY TEMARI, YOU'RE HERE TOO...?
WE'VE BEEN WAITING FOR YOU.
PLEASE, RIGHT THIS WAY!

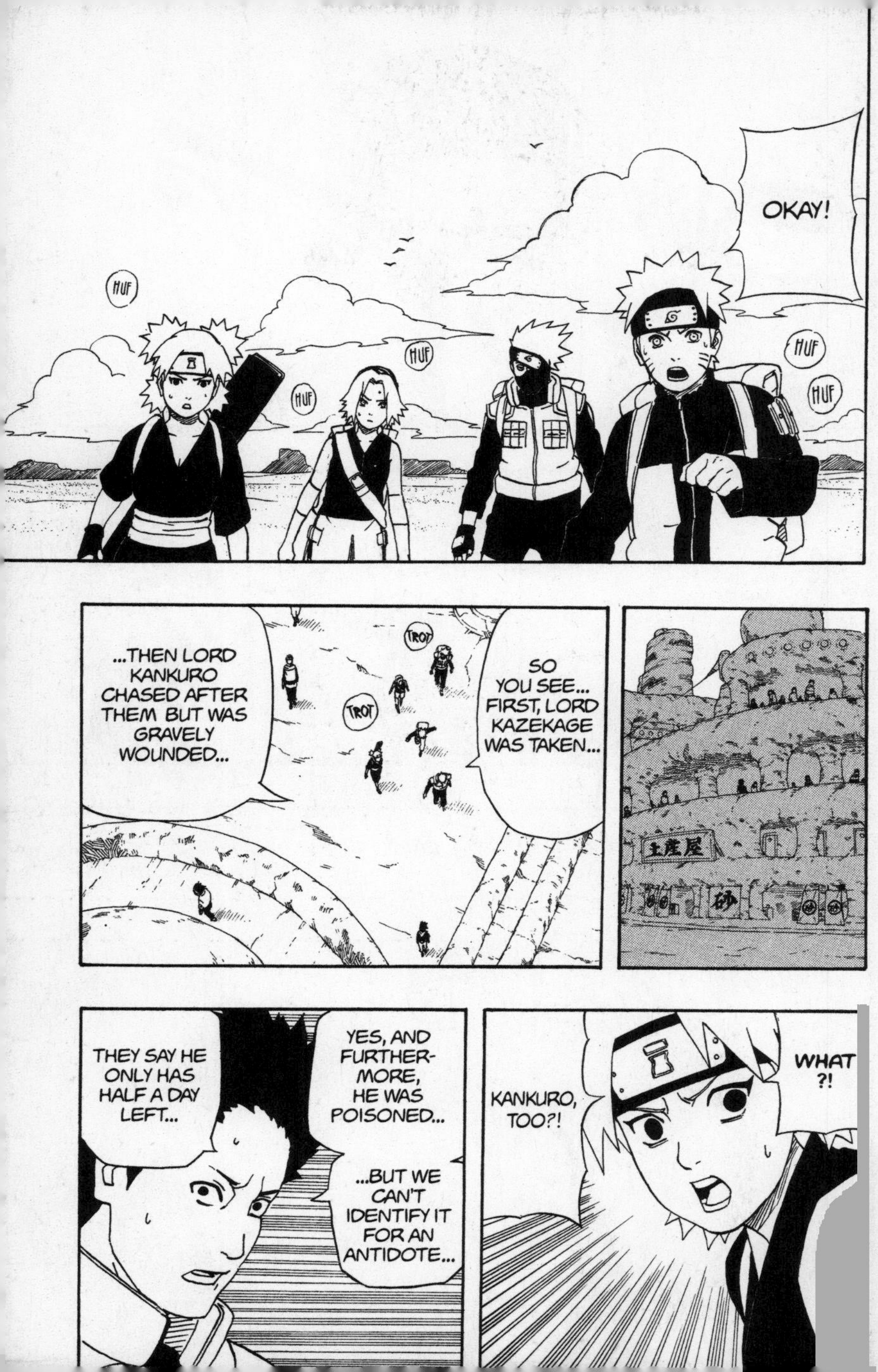
OKAY!
HUF
HUF
HUF
HUF
HUF
SO YOU SEE... FIRST, LORD KAZEKAGE WAS TAKEN...
TROT
TROT
...THEN LORD KANKURO CHASED AFTER THEM BUT WAS GRAVELY WOUNDED...
土産屋
砂
WHAT ?!
KANKURO, TOO?!
YES, AND FURTHER-MORE, HE WAS POISONED...
...BUT WE CAN'T IDENTIFY IT FOR AN ANTIDOTE...
THEY SAY HE ONLY HAS HALF A DAY LEFT...

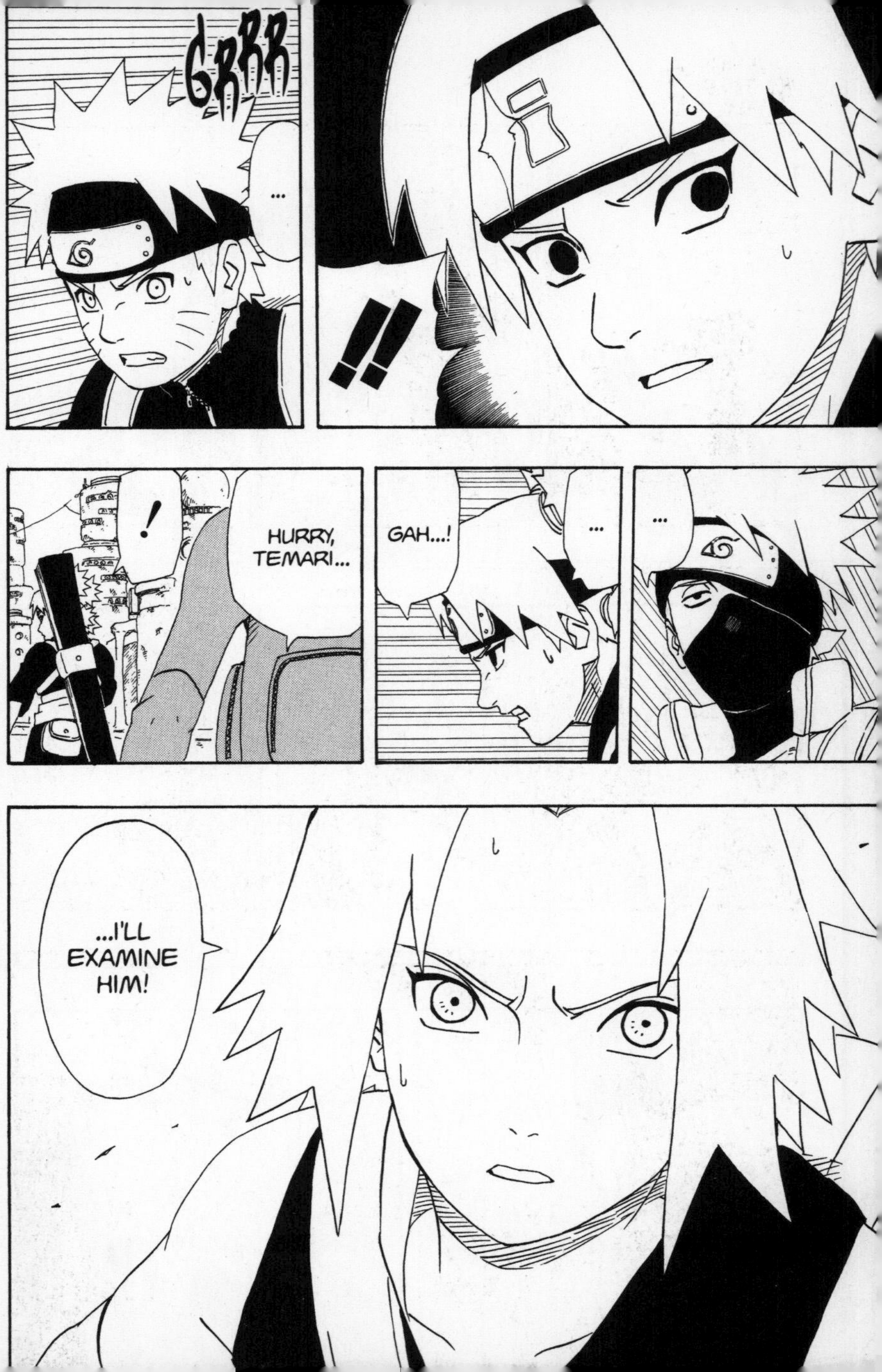
!!
GRRR
...
...
...
GAH...!
HURRY, TEMARI...
!
...I'LL EXAMINE HIM!

READ THIS WAY

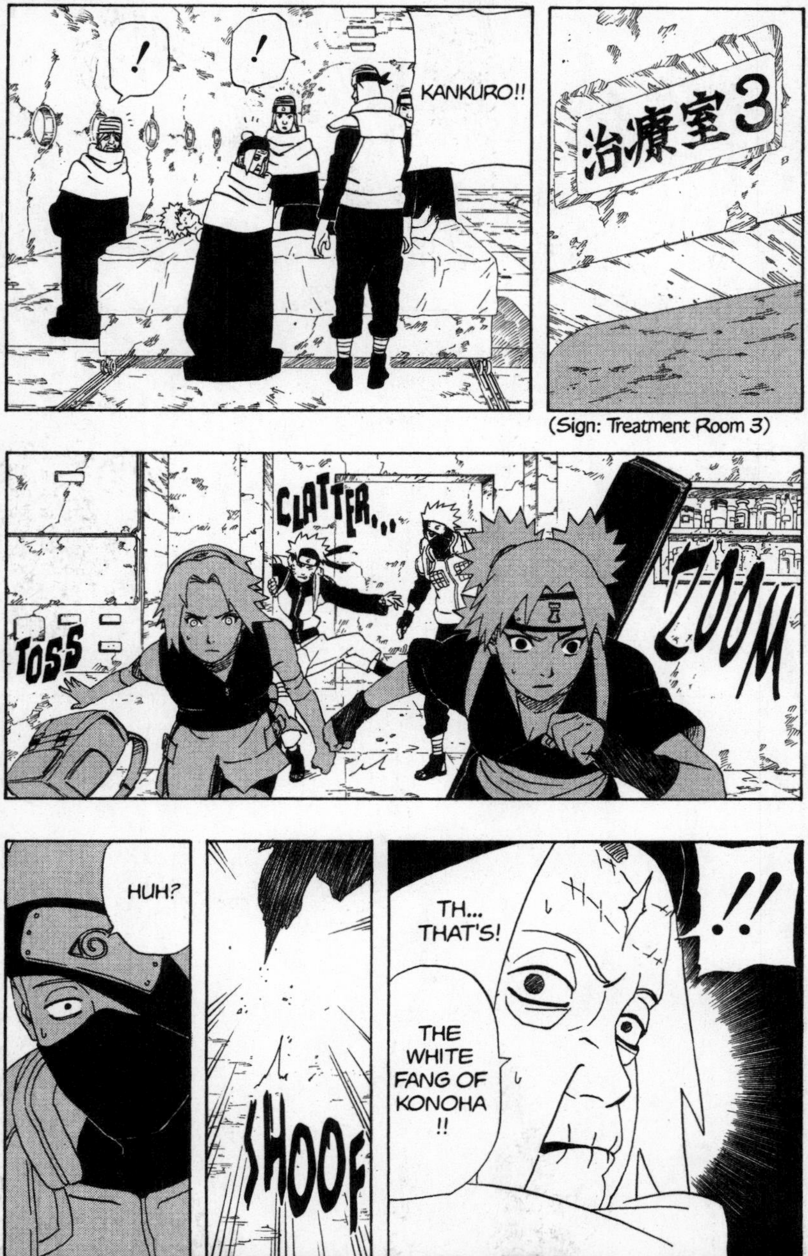
治療室3
!
!
KANKURO!!
ZOOM
CLATTER...
TOSS
!!
TH... THAT'S!
THE WHITE FANG OF KONOHA !!
SHOOF
HUH?

(Sign: Treatment Room 3)

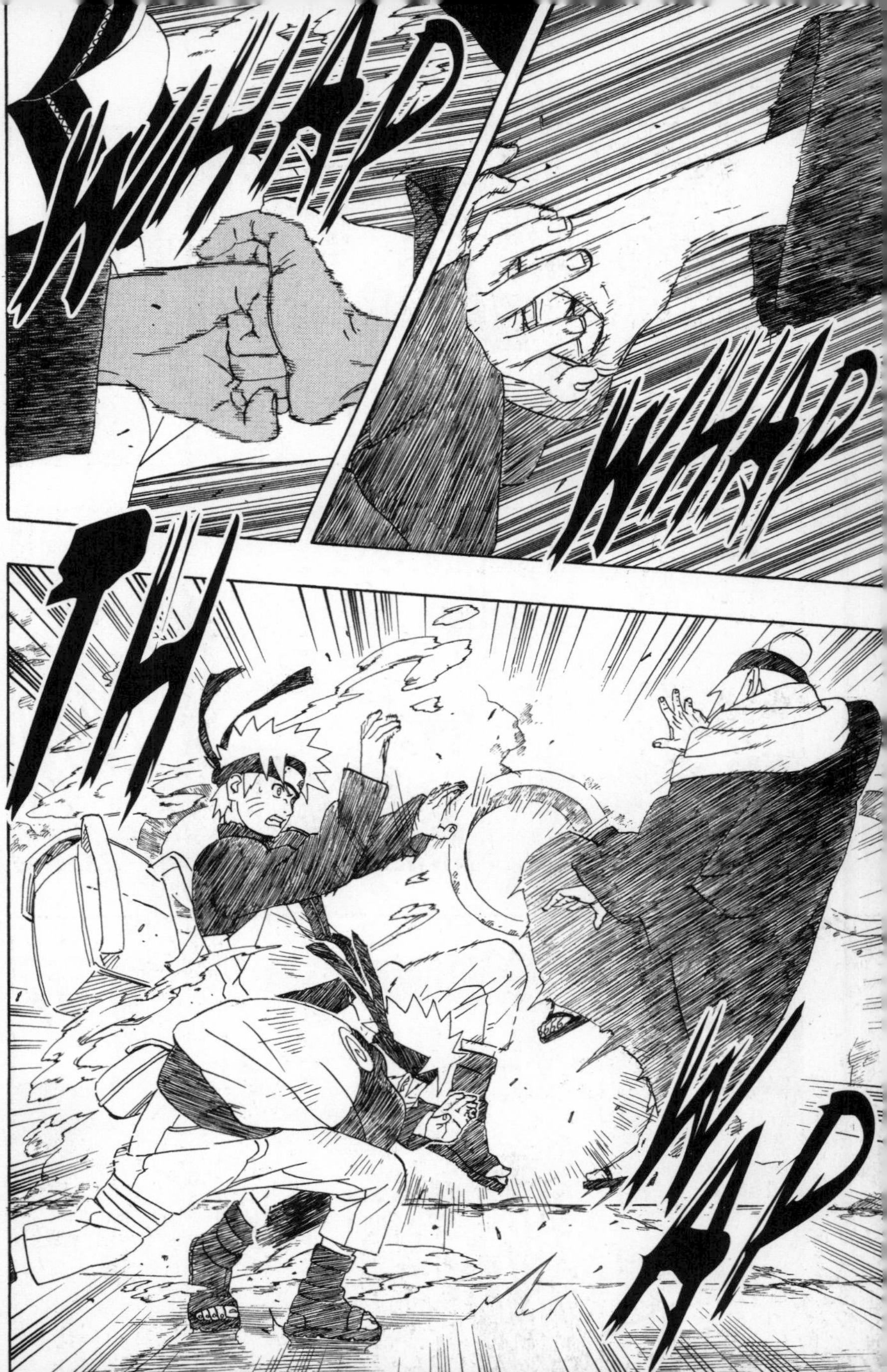
WHAP
SWHAP
TH
WHAP

READ THIS WAY

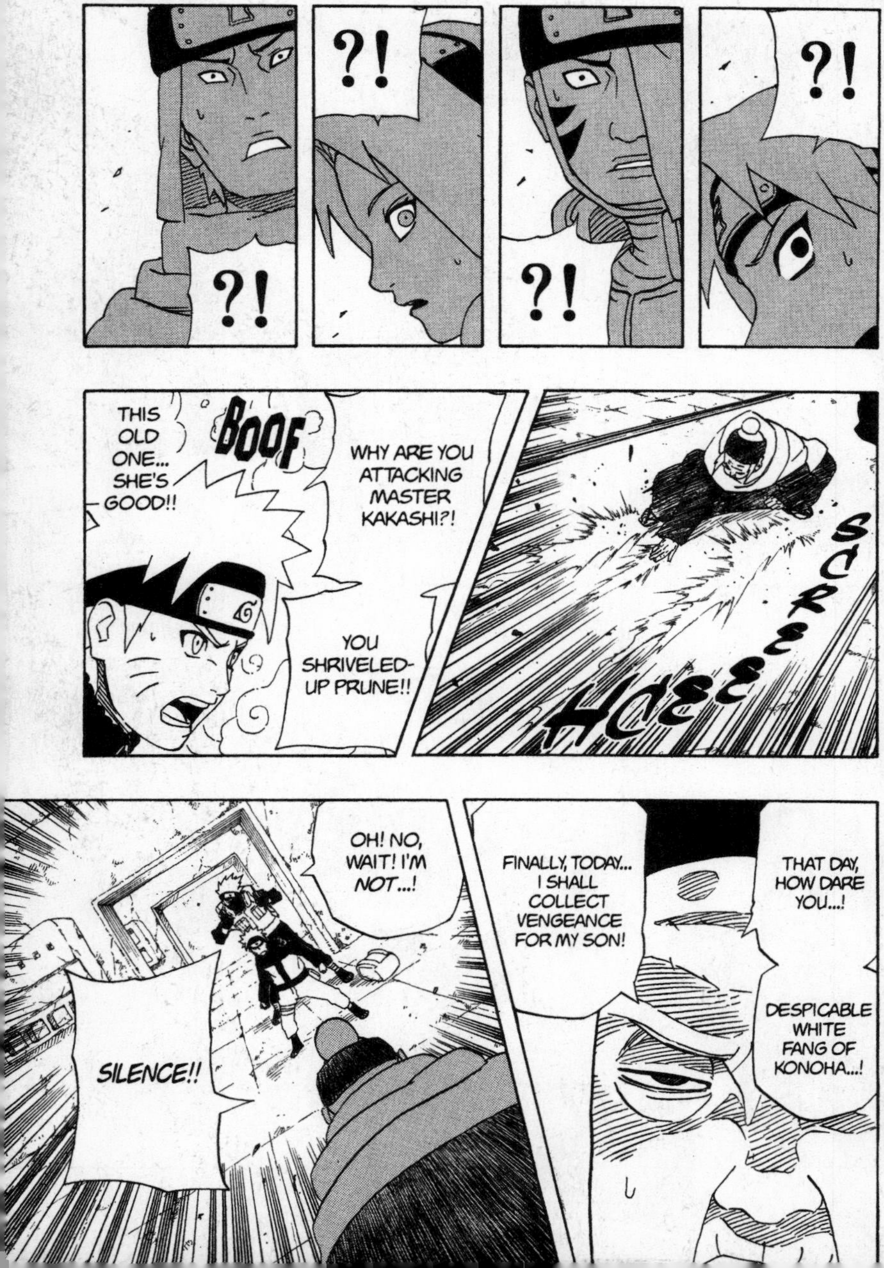
?!
?!
?!
?!
SCREEECH
WHY ARE YOU ATTACKING MASTER KAKASHI?!
YOU SHRIVELED-UP PRUNE!!
BOOF
THIS OLD ONE... SHE'S GOOD!!
THAT DAY, HOW DARE YOU...!
DESPICABLE WHITE FANG OF KONOHA...!
FINALLY, TODAY... I SHALL COLLECT VENGEANCE FOR MY SON!
OH! NO, WAIT! I'M *NOT*...!
SILENCE!!

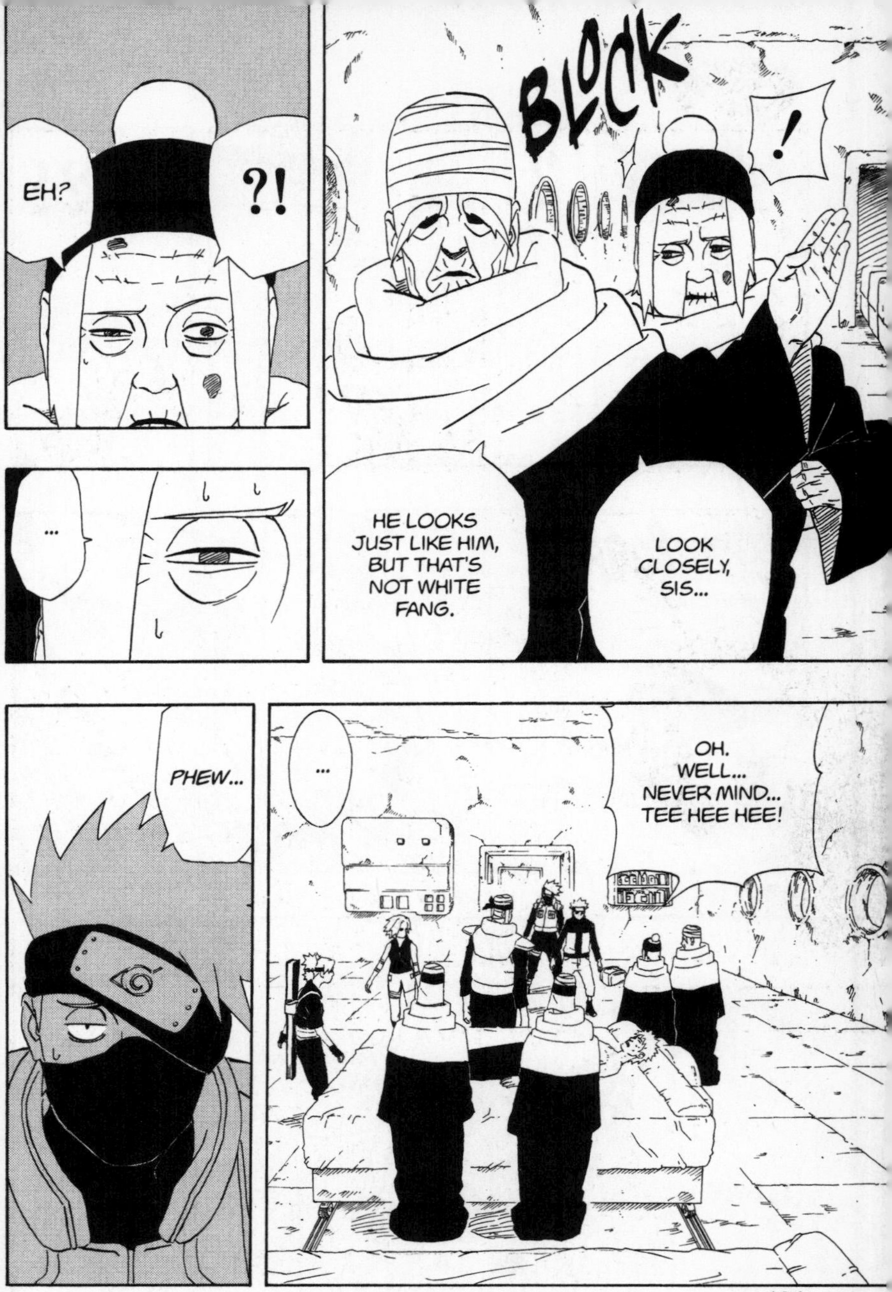

!
BLOCK
LOOK CLOSELY, SIS...
HE LOOKS JUST LIKE HIM, BUT THAT'S NOT WHITE FANG.
?!
EH?
...
OH. WELL... NEVER MIND... TEE HEE HEE!
...
PHEW...

PLEASE!

NOW, CAN WE
ALL JUST
FOCUS ON
KANKURO?

BLOOP...

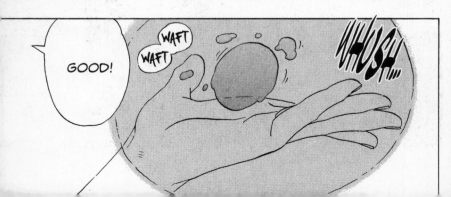

GOOD!

WAFT
WAFT

UHUSH...

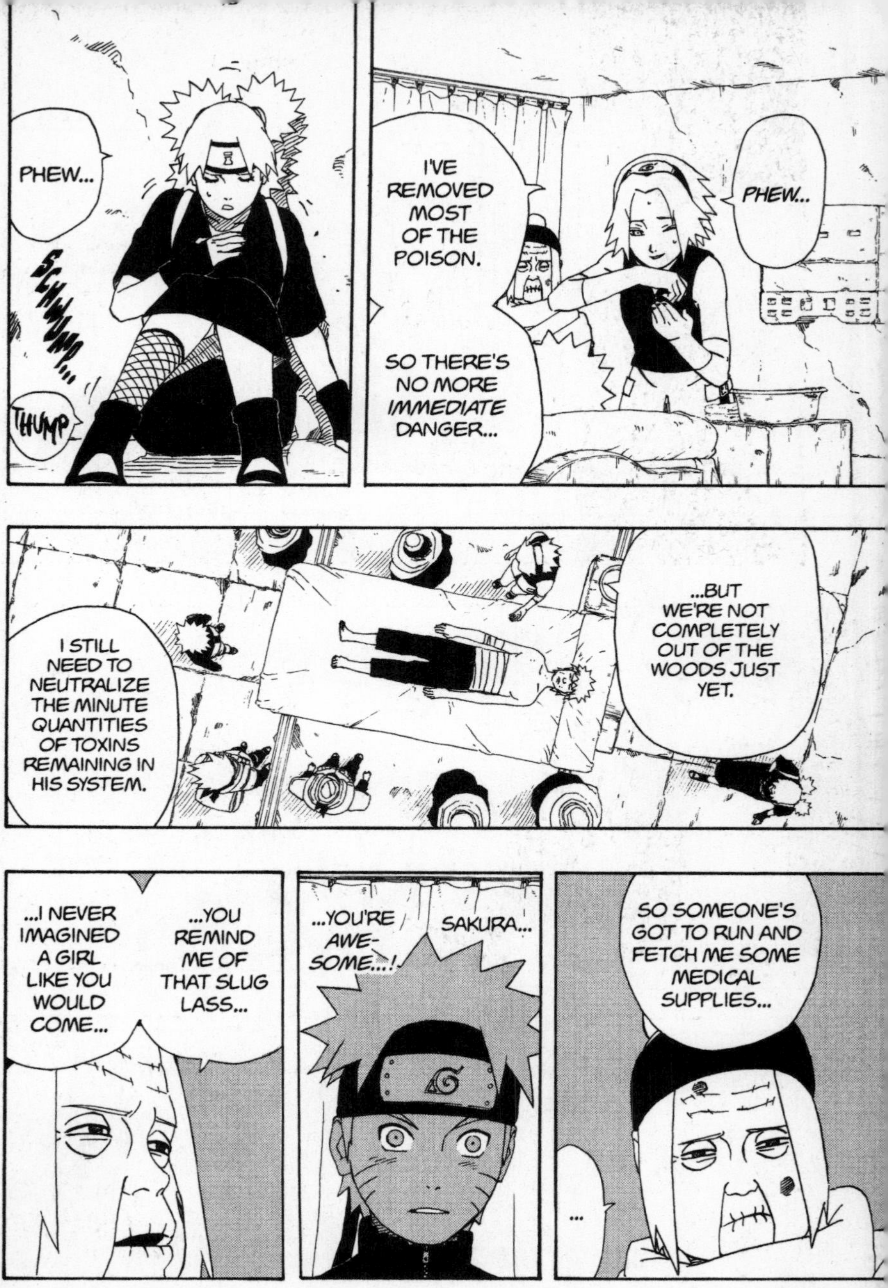
PHEW...
I'VE REMOVED MOST OF THE POISON.
SO THERE'S NO MORE IMMEDIATE DANGER...
PHEW...
SCHWUMP...
THUMP
...BUT WE'RE NOT COMPLETELY OUT OF THE WOODS JUST YET.
I STILL NEED TO NEUTRALIZE THE MINUTE QUANTITIES OF TOXINS REMAINING IN HIS SYSTEM.
SO SOMEONE'S GOT TO RUN AND FETCH ME SOME MEDICAL SUPPLIES...
...
SAKURA...
...YOU'RE AWE-SOME...!
...YOU REMIND ME OF THAT SLUG LASS...
...I NEVER IMAGINED A GIRL LIKE YOU WOULD COME...

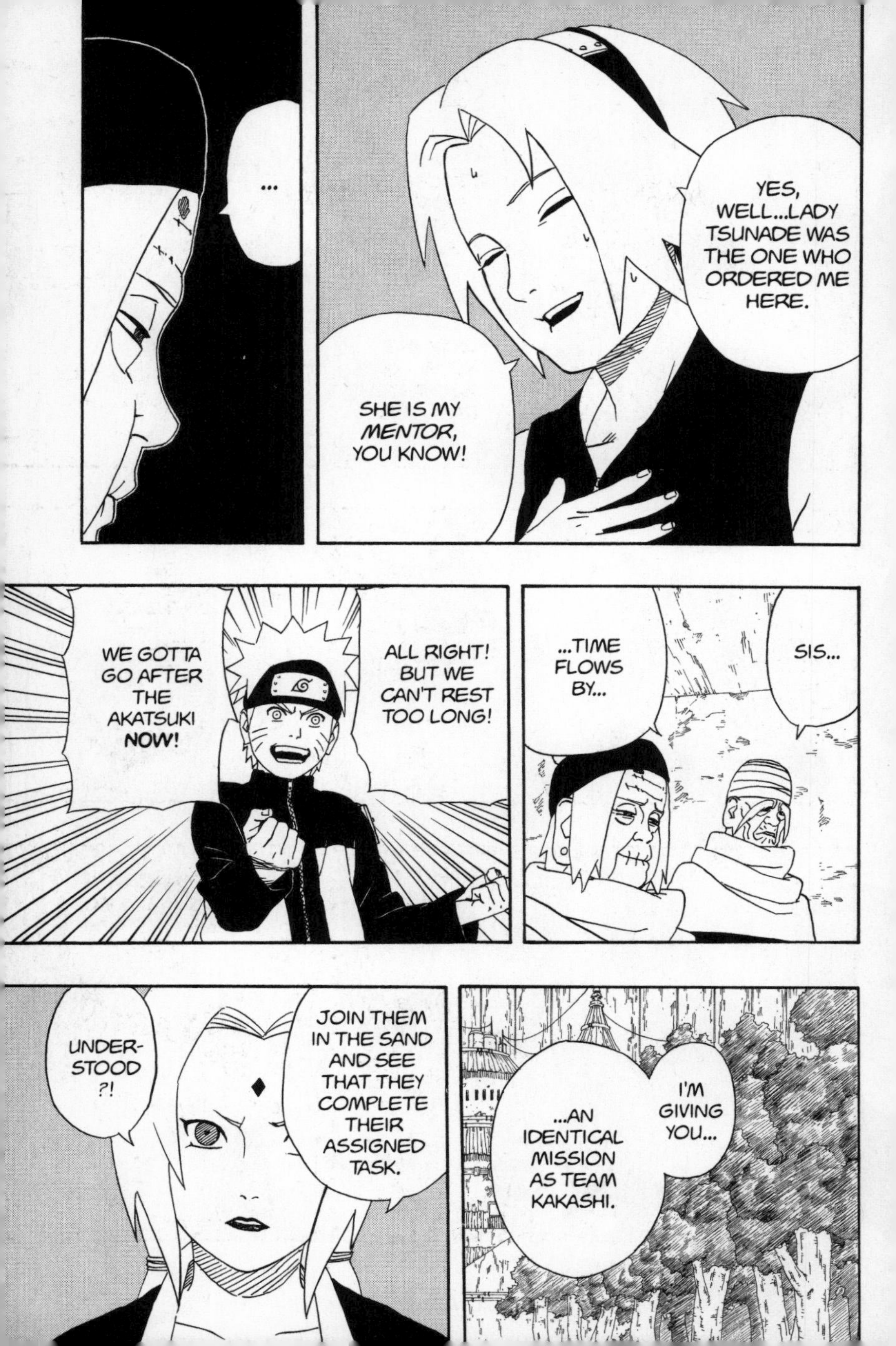
YES, WELL...LADY TSUNADE WAS THE ONE WHO ORDERED ME HERE.
SHE IS MY *MENTOR*, YOU KNOW!
...
SIS...
...TIME FLOWS BY...
ALL RIGHT! BUT WE CAN'T REST TOO LONG!
WE GOTTA GO AFTER THE AKATSUKI **NOW!**
I'M GIVING YOU...
...AN IDENTICAL MISSION AS TEAM KAKASHI.
JOIN THEM IN THE SAND AND SEE THAT THEY COMPLETE THEIR ASSIGNED TASK.
UNDER-STOOD?!

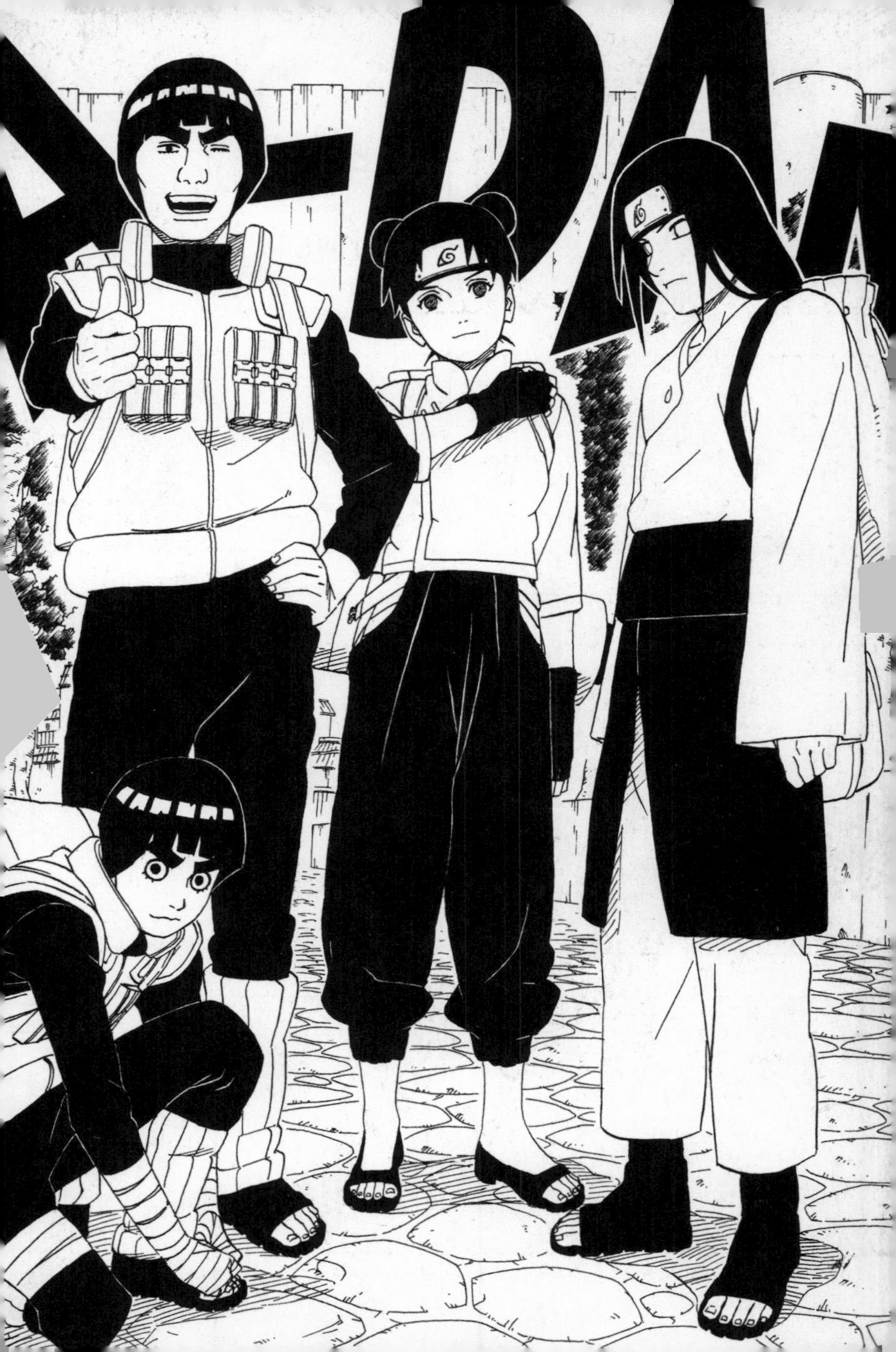

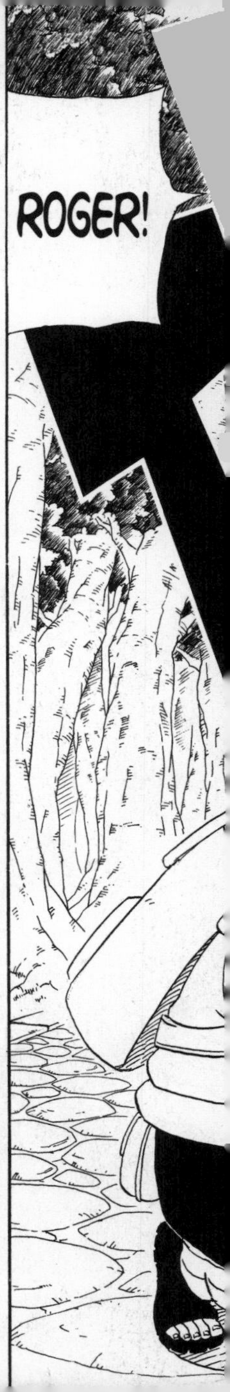
ROGER!

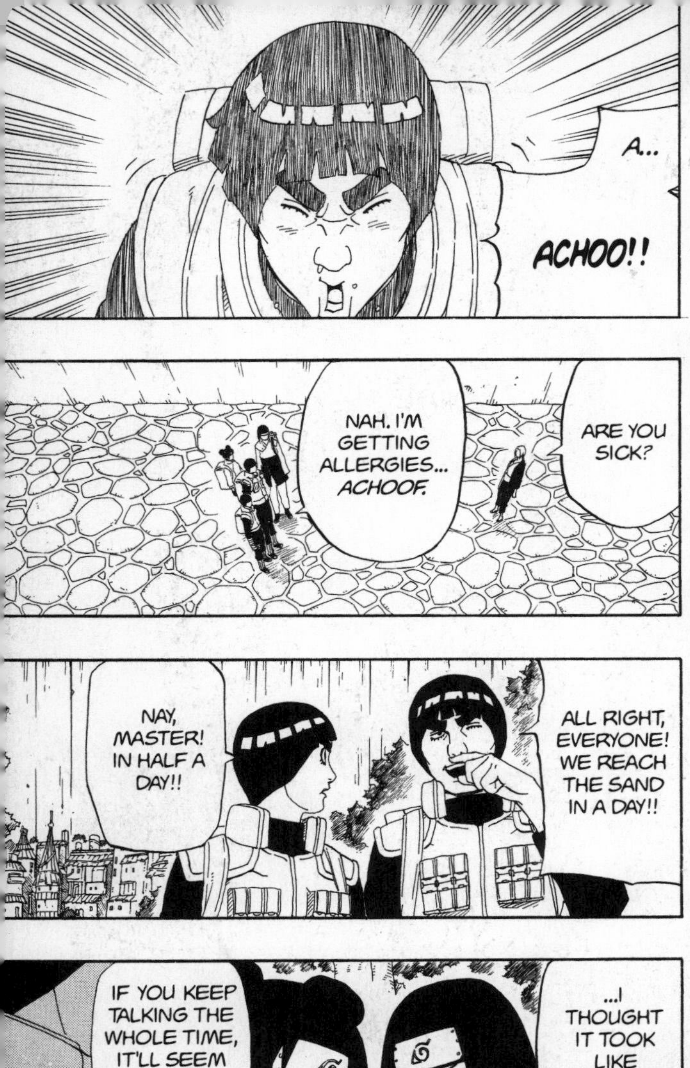
A...
ACHOO!!
ARE YOU SICK?
NAH. I'M GETTING ALLERGIES... ACHOOF.
ALL RIGHT, EVERYONE! WE REACH THE SAND IN A DAY!!
NAY, MASTER! IN HALF A DAY!!
...I THOUGHT IT TOOK LIKE THREE DAYS...
IF YOU KEEP TALKING THE WHOLE TIME, IT'LL SEEM LIKE FOR-EVER... CUT IT OUT!

TO BE CONTINUED IN *NARUTO* VOLUME 29!!

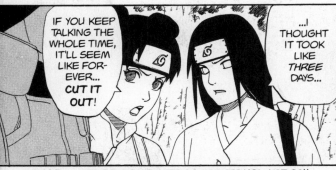

IN THE NEXT VOLUME...

KAKASHI VS. ITACHI

Sasuke's brother and teacher finally face each other down!
Plus, we learn what's happened to Gaara, and what might
also be in store for Naruto, as they both come face to face
with a devious common enemy...the Akatsuki!

AVAILABLE NOW!

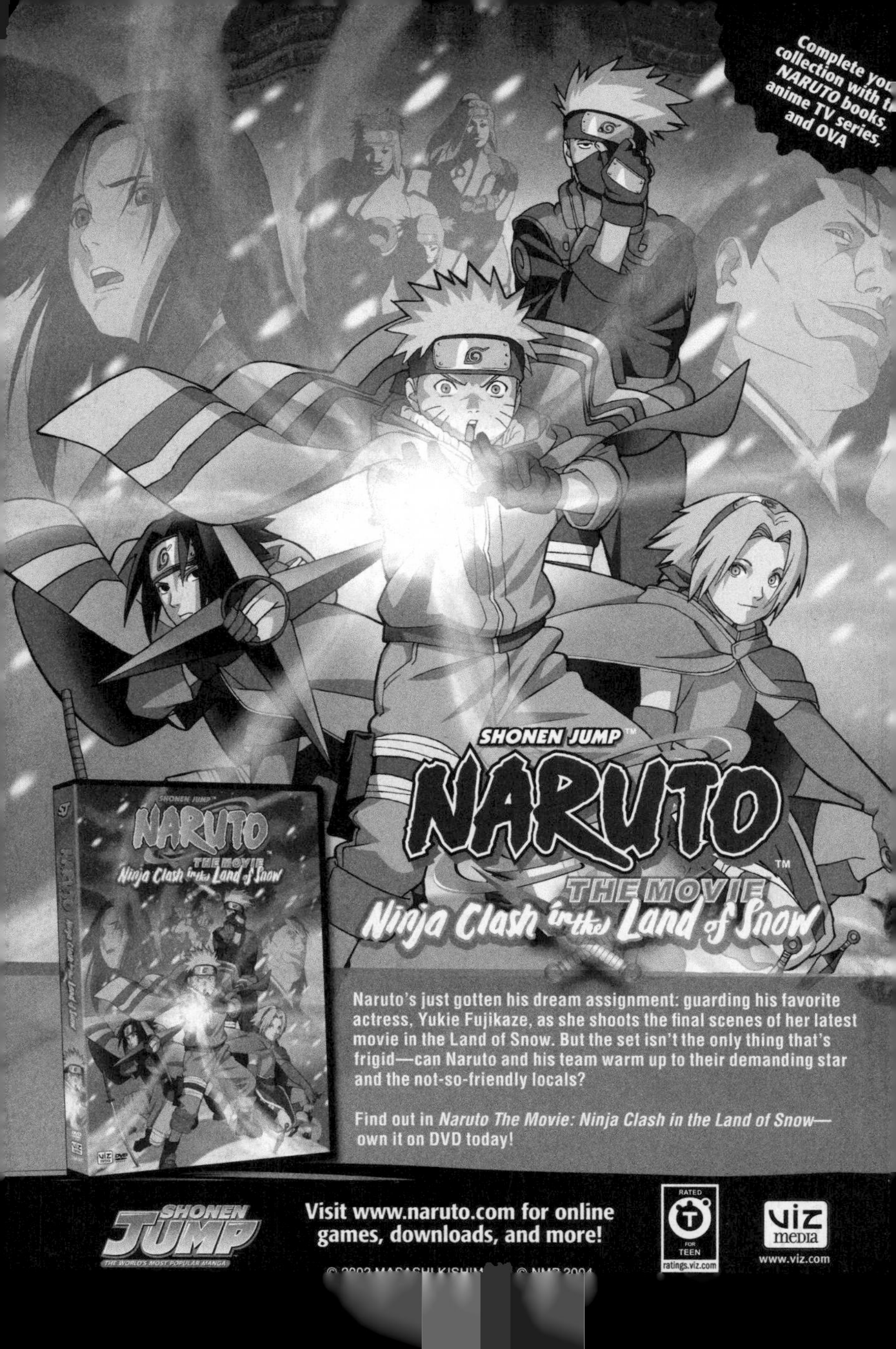
Complete your collection with the NARUTO books, anime TV series, and OVA
SHONEN JUMP
NARUTO
THE MOVIE
Ninja Clash in the Land of Snow
Naruto's just gotten his dream assignment: guarding his favorite actress, Yukie Fujikaze, as she shoots the final scenes of her latest movie in the Land of Snow. But the set isn't the only thing that's frigid—can Naruto and his team warm up to their demanding star and the not-so-friendly locals?
Find out in Naruto The Movie: Ninja Clash in the Land of Snow—own it on DVD today!
SHONEN JUMP
THE WORLD'S MOST POPULAR MANGA
Visit www.naruto.com for online games, downloads, and more!
RATED T FOR TEEN
ratings.viz.com
VIZ MEDIA
www.viz.com

Read where the ninja action began in the manga

Fiction based on your favorite characters' adventures

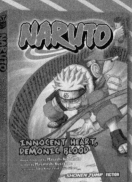

JOURNEY INTO THE WORLD OF NARUTO BOOKS!

Hardcover art book with full-color images, a Masashi Kishimoto interview and a double-sided poster

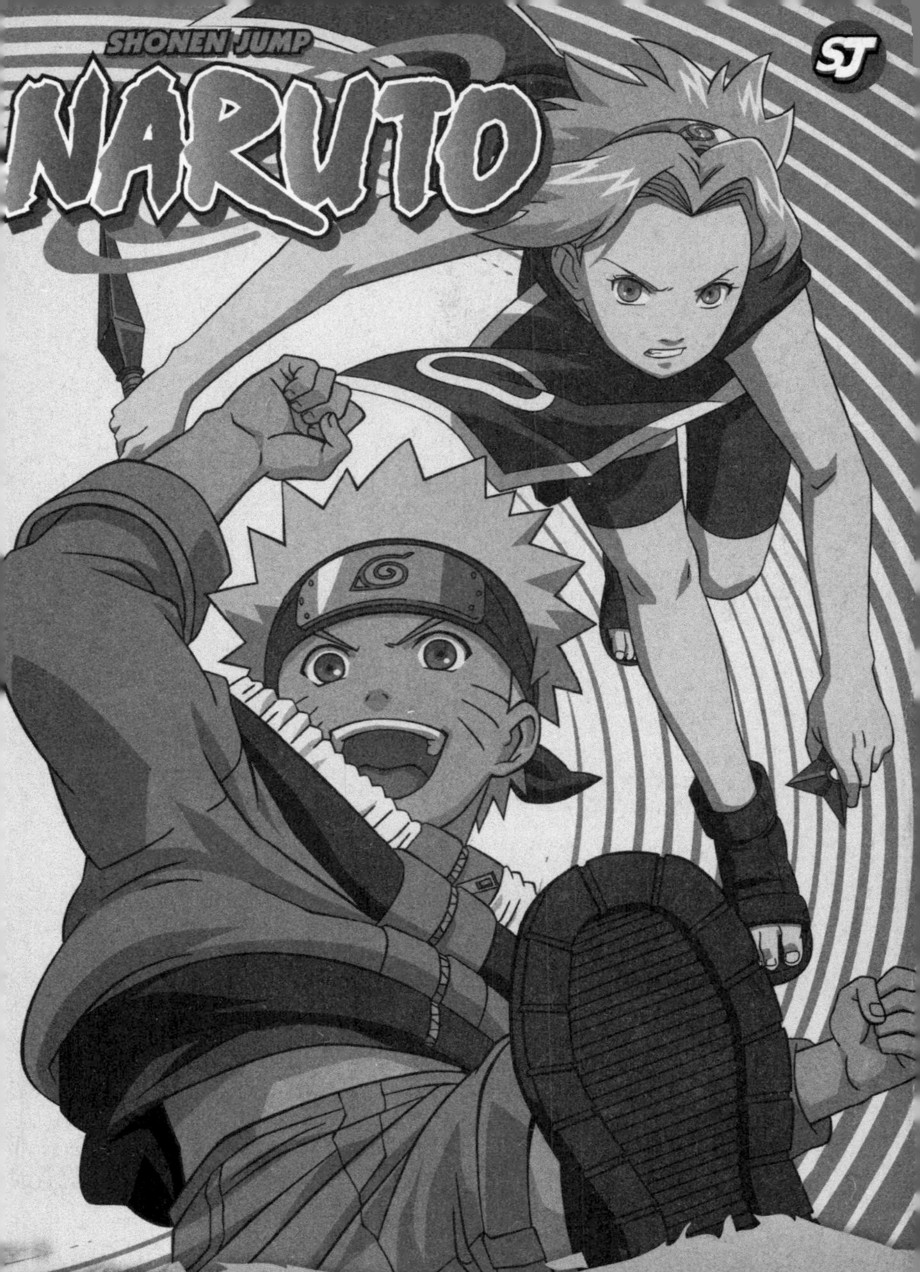
SHONEN JUMP
NARUTO
SJ

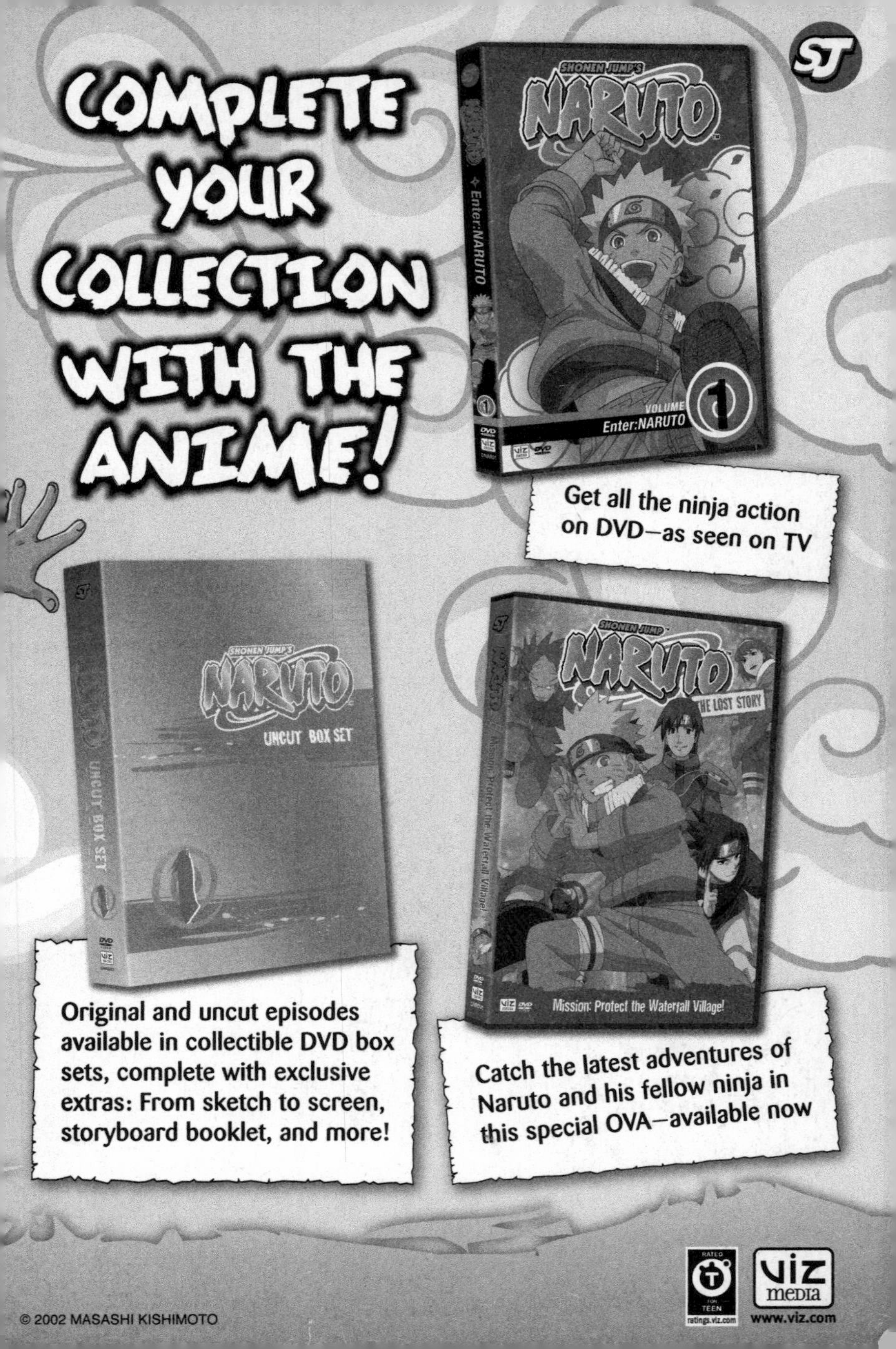
SJ
COMPLETE YOUR COLLECTION WITH THE ANIME!
SHONEN JUMP'S
NARUTO
VOLUME 1
Enter:NARUTO
Get all the ninja action on DVD—as seen on TV
SHONEN JUMP'S
NARUTO
UNCUT BOX SET
Original and uncut episodes available in collectible DVD box sets, complete with exclusive extras: From sketch to screen, storyboard booklet, and more!
SHONEN JUMP
NARUTO
THE LOST STORY
Mission: Protect the Waterfall Village!
Catch the latest adventures of Naruto and his fellow ninja in this special OVA—available now
RATED T FOR TEEN
ratings.viz.com
VIZ media
www.viz.com
© 2002 MASASHI KISHIMOTO

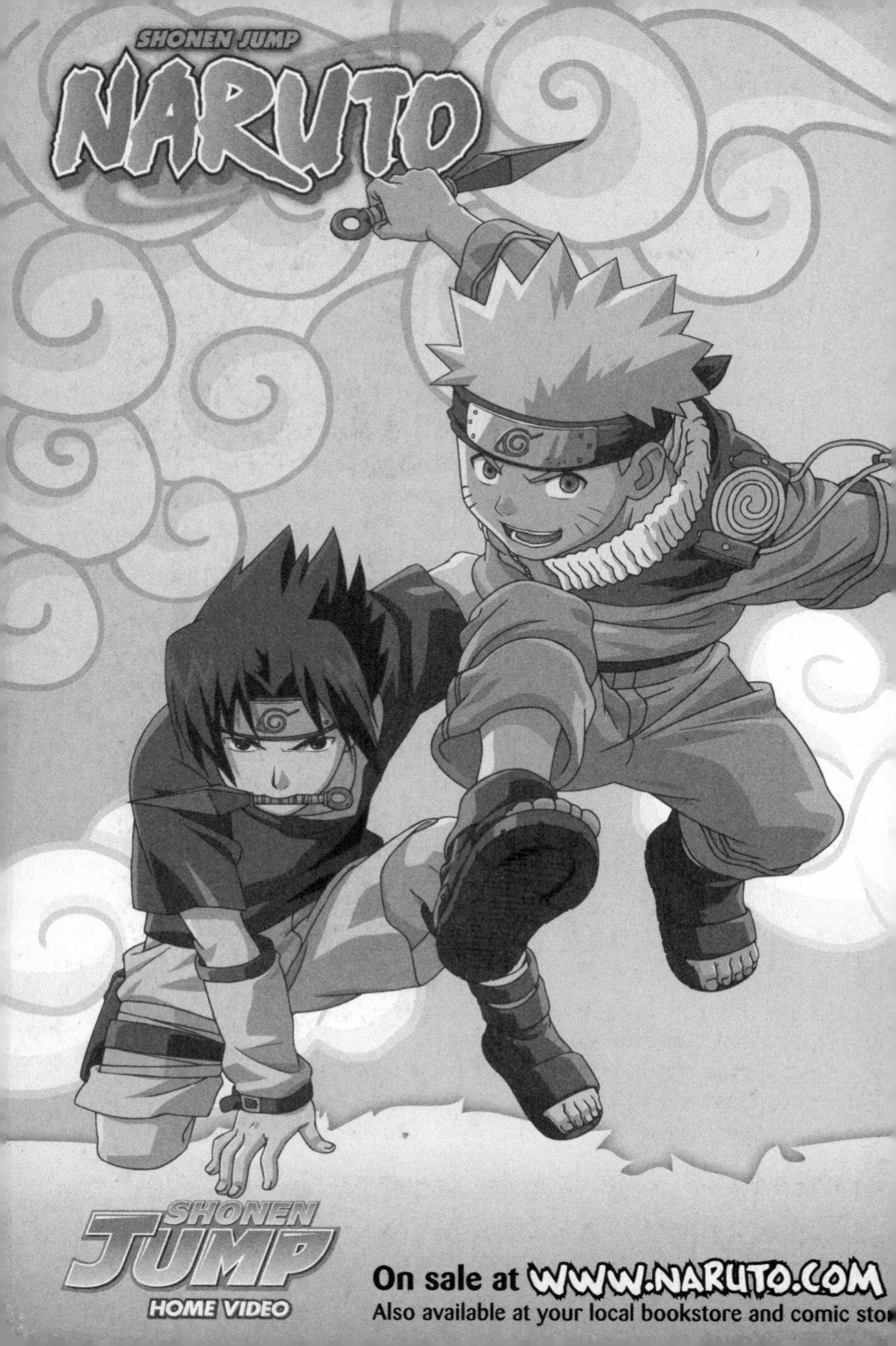
SHONEN JUMP
NARUTO
SHONEN JUMP
HOME VIDEO
On sale at WWW.NARUTO.COM
Also available at your local bookstore and comic sto

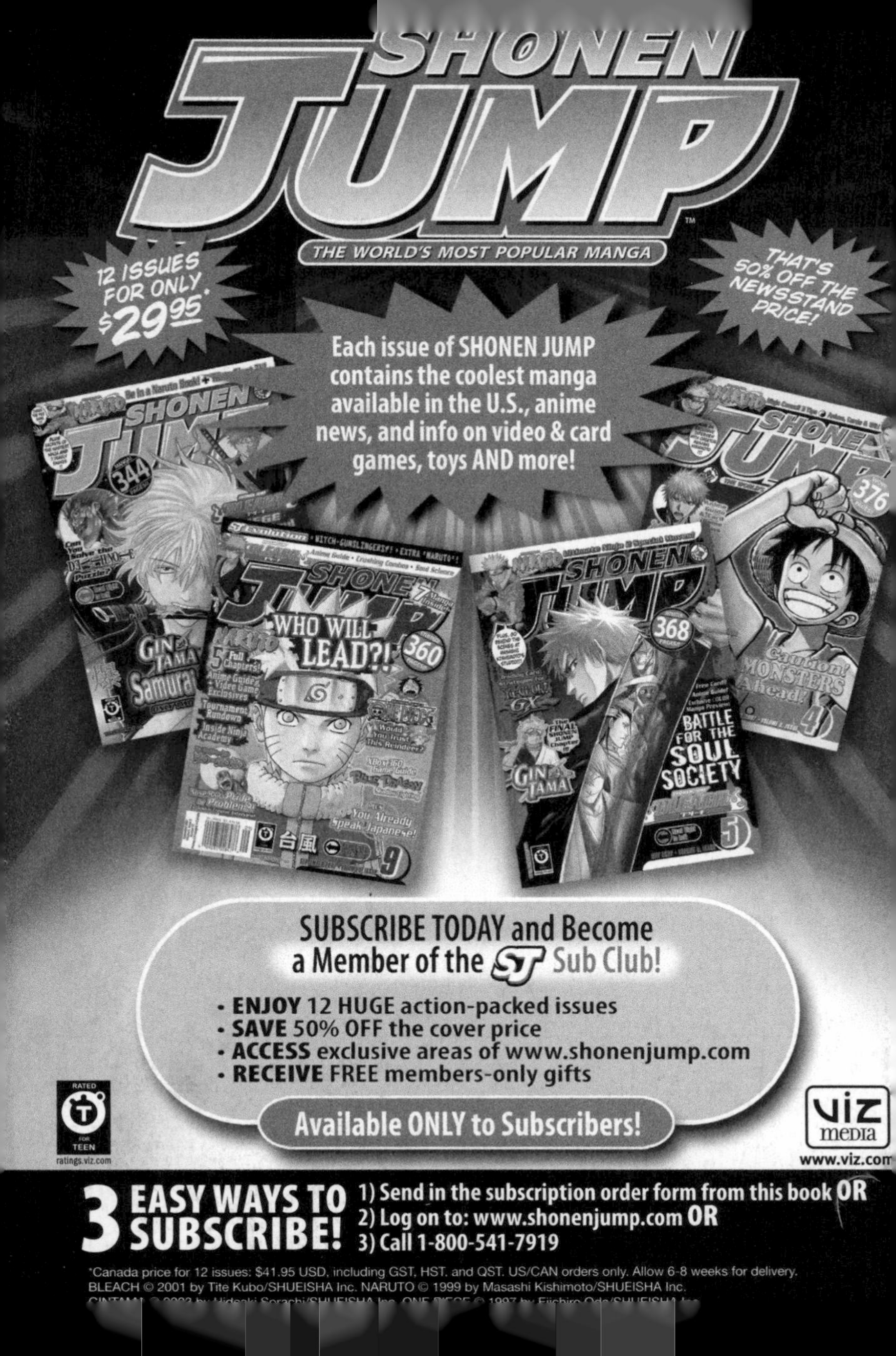
SHONEN JUMP™
THE WORLD'S MOST POPULAR MANGA
12 ISSUES FOR ONLY $29.95*
THAT'S 50% OFF THE NEWSSTAND PRICE!
Each issue of SHONEN JUMP contains the coolest manga available in the U.S., anime news, and info on video & card games, toys AND more!
SUBSCRIBE TODAY and Become a Member of the SJ Sub Club!
• ENJOY 12 HUGE action-packed issues
• SAVE 50% OFF the cover price
• ACCESS exclusive areas of www.shonenjump.com
• RECEIVE FREE members-only gifts
Available ONLY to Subscribers!
RATED T FOR TEEN
ratings.viz.com
viz media
www.viz.com
3 EASY WAYS TO SUBSCRIBE!
1) Send in the subscription order form from this book OR
2) Log on to: www.shonenjump.com OR
3) Call 1-800-541-7919
*Canada price for 12 issues: $41.95 USD, including GST, HST, and QST. US/CAN orders only. Allow 6-8 weeks for delivery.
BLEACH © 2001 by Tite Kubo/SHUEISHA Inc. NARUTO © 1999 by Masashi Kishimoto/SHUEISHA Inc.

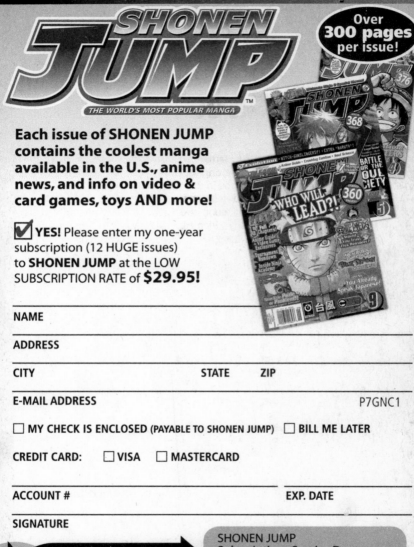